Demons,
the Devil, and
Fallen Angels

ABOUT THE AUTHORS

Marie D. Jones is the best-selling author of *Destiny vs. Choice: The Scientific and Spiritual Evidence behind Fate and Free Will*, *2013: End of Days or a New Beginning—Envisioning the World after the Events of 2012*, *PSIence: How New Discoveries in Quantum Physics and New Science May Explain the Existence of Paranormal Phenomena*, and *Looking for God in All the Wrong Places*. Jones co-authored with her father, geophysicist Dr. John Savino, *Supervolcano: The Catastrophic Event That Changed the Course of Human History*. She is also the author, with Larry Flaxman, of *11:11—The Time Prompt Phenomenon: The Meaning behind Mysterious Signs, Sequences, and Synchronicities*, *The Resonance Key: Exploring the Links between Vibration, Consciousness, and the Zero Point Grid*, *The Déjà Vu Enigma: A Journey through the Anomalies of Mind, Memory, and Time*, *The Trinity Secret: The Power of Three and the Code of Creation*, *This Book Is from the Future: A Journey through Portals, Relativity, Wormholes, and Other Adventures in Time Travel*, and *Viral Mythology: How the Truth of the Ancients Was Encoded and Passed Down through Legend, Art, and Architecture*.

Jones has an extensive background in metaphysics, cutting-edge science, and the paranormal; she has worked as a field investigator for MUFON (Mutual UFO Network) in Los Angeles and San Diego in the 1980s and 1990s.

Jones has been on television, most recently on the History Channel's *Nostradamus Effect* series and the *Ancient Aliens* series, and she served as a special UFO/abduction consultant for the 2009 Universal Pictures science-fiction movie, *The Fourth Kind*. She has been interviewed on hundreds of radio talk shows all over the world, including *Coast to Coast AM*, *NPR*, *KPBS Radio*, *Dreamland*, the *X-Zone*, *Kevin Smith Show*, *Paranormal Podcast*, *Cut to the Chase, Feet 2 The Fire, World of the Unexplained*, and *The Shirley MacLaine Show*. She has been featured in dozens of newspapers, magazines, and online publications. She is a former blogger for Jim Harold's *Paranormal Braintrust* and has written regularly for *Intrepid Magazine, Atlantis Rising, MindScape, Paranormal Underground, New Dawn Magazine*, and *Paranoia Magazine*. She has been a radio host for *Dreamland Radio* and *ParaFringe Radio*.

Jones has lectured on the subjects of cutting edge science, the paranormal, metaphysics, Noetics, and human potential at major metaphysical, paranormal, new science and self-empowerment events, including Through the Veil, Queen Mary Weekends, TAPS Academy Training, CPAK, Paradigm Symposium, Conscious Expo, and Darkness Radio Events. She is also a screenwriter and producer with several projects in development.

Her websites are www.mariedjones.com and www.whereslucyproductions.com.

In addition to the books he has written with Marie D. Jones (see above), **Larry Flaxman** has been actively involved in paranormal research and hands-on field investigation with a strong emphasis on attempting to apply the scientific method to unexplained phenomena. Flaxman is redefining the field of paranormal research with his focus on connecting quantum physics (specifically, entanglement and the observer effect) to human consciousness via the use of "real-time" EEG analysis of the experiencer. He is the president and senior researcher of the Arkansas Paranormal and Anomalous Studies Team (ARPAST), which has become one of the nation's most respected paranormal research organizations.

Widely respected for his advances in the field, Flaxman has appeared on the Discovery Channel's *Ghost Lab*, as well as the History Channel's popular show *Ancient Aliens*, and the History Channel special exposé *Time Beings: Extreme Time Travel Conspiracies*.

Flaxman has appeared on hundreds of radio shows worldwide, including *Coast to Coast AM, The Shirley MacLaine Show, The Jeff Rense Show, X-Zone Radio, TAPS Family Radio*, and *Paranormal Podcast*.

His websites are www.larryflaxman.com and www.arpast.org.

ALSO FROM VISIBLE INK PRESS

"REAL NIGHTMARES" E-BOOKS BY BRAD STEIGER

PLEASE VISIT US AT VISIBLEINKPRESS.COM

DEMONS,
THE DEVIL,
AND
FALLEN ANGELS

Visible Ink Press®
43311 Joy Rd., #414
Canton, MI 48187-2075
Visible Ink Press is a registered trademark of Visible Ink Press LLC.

Most Visible Ink Press books are available at special quantity discounts when purchased in bulk by corporations, organizations, or groups. Customized printings, special imprints, messages, and excerpts can be produced to meet your needs. For more information, contact Special Markets Director, Visible Ink Press, www.visbleink.com, or 734-667-3211.

Managing Editor: Kevin S. Hile
Art Director: Mary Claire Krzewinski
Typesetting: Marco Divita
Proofreaders: Brian Buchanan and Larry Baker
Indexer: Shoshana Hurwit

Front cover images: "St. Francis Borgia Helping a Dying Impenitent" and "The Sabbath of Witches," both by Francisco de Goya (public domain); illustration from The Devil in Britain and America, 1896 (public domain); illustration by Gustav Doré from Paradise Lost by John Milton (public domain).

Back cover images: Background (Shutterstock); "Lady Lilith" by Dante Gabriel Rossetti; bronze lion at Forbidden City (Shutterstock); Aleister Crowley (public domain); Annabelle doll (Felipe112233 at Wikicommons).

Library of Congress Cataloging-in-Publication Data
Names: Jones, Marie D., 1961- author.
Title: Demons, the devil, and fallen angels / by Marie D. Jones and Larry Flaxman.
Description: First Edition. | Detroit, MI : Visible Ink Press, 2017.
Identifiers: LCCN 2017022073| ISBN 9781578596133 (pbk. : alk. paper) | ISBN 9781578596669 (pdf)
Subjects: LCSH: Demonology. | Occultism.
Classification: LCC BF1531 .J66 2017 | DDC 133.4/2--dc23
LC record available at https://lccn.loc.gov/2017022073

Printed in the United States of America.

10 9 8 7 6 5 4 3 2 1

Demons,
the Devil, and
Fallen Angels

Marie D. Jones and Larry Flaxman

VISIBLE
INK
PRESS

PHOTO SOURCES

Stewart Adcock: p. 15.
Jacques Arago: p. 208.
Ashmolean Museum: p. 207.
BabelStone (Wikicommons): p. 174.
Tim Bertelink: p. 85.
Ivan Yakovlevich Bilibin: p. 52.
J. T. Blatty: p. 167.
Kim Dent-Brown: p. 278.
Gustav Doré: pp. 29, 275.
The Equinox, 1913: p. 187.
Felipe112233 (Wikicommons): p. 116.
GabboT (Wikicommons): p. 95.
Salvor Gissurardottir: p. 40.
Claire H. (Wikicommons): p. 57.
Hintha (Wikicommons): p. 55.
J. D. Horne: p. 116.
Huhsunqu (Wikicommons): p. 195.
Jjbowks (Wikicommons): p. 70.
LadyofHats (Wikicommons): p. 170.
Daniel Lange: p. 133.
Ephraim Moses Lilien, *Die Bücher der Bibel*:
    p. 122.
Megamoto85 (Wikicommons): p. 82.
MesserWoland (Wikicommons): p. 196.
National Gallery, London: p. 216.
National Portrait Gallery, London: p. 191.
Bill Nicholls, www.geograph.org.uk: p. 143.
NotFromUtrecht (Wikicommons): p. 163.
NsMn (Wikicommons): p. 192.

Ortsmuseum Zollikon: p. 260.
Esparta Palma: p. 115.
Peter Pelham: p. 233.
Michael Persinger: p. 150.
Prado Museum: p. 225.
RadioKirk (Wikicommons): p. 86.
Henry Meynell Rheam: p. 93.
Dante Gabriel Rossetti: p. 36.
Osmar Schindler: p. 80.
Seulatr (Wikicommons): p. 155.
Shutterstock: pp. 3, 6, 7, 9, 10, 12, 16, 17, 24,
    25, 27, 30, 34, 35, 42, 44, 47, 48, 50, 62,
    66, 72, 84, 89, 92, 98, 100, 104, 108,
    118, 124, 131, 142, 147, 149, 152, 153,
    159, 168, 169, 172, 182, 202, 203, 221,
    224, 226, 232, 236, 243, 254, 261, 264,
    270, 272, 273, 281.
Gage Skidmore: p. 141.
The Temptation of Christ, c. 1500: p. 33.
Tretyakov Gallery, Moscow: p. 175.
U.S. government: p. 79.
Wellcome Images: p. 235.
Chad White: p. 130.
www.robertthedoll.org: p. 128.
www.tedgunderson.net: p. 250.
Public domain: pp. 4, 13, 38, 46, 68, 76, 103,
    139, 176, 179, 185, 188, 189, 198, 200,
    211, 214, 219, 230, 245, 248, 253.

Contents

ACKNOWLEDGMENTS

Marie and Larry would like to thank Lisa Hagan, their wonderful agent, for securing this book deal. Lisa, you are the best! Thanks also to the entire team at Visible Ink Press, especially Roger Jänecke and Kevin Hile. Thank you, Roger, for allowing us the pleasure to work with Visible Ink Press, and thank you, Kevin, for your editing expertise and insights! We look forward to working with the entire staff to make this book a success!

Marie would also like to thank her family, including her mom, Milly, who is my biggest cheerleader and is always there for me; my dad, who is watching from the stars and galaxies above and hopefully proud of me; my sister, Angella, and brother, John, and my extended family; my friends and colleagues; and to all my readers, fans, and followers everywhere—thank you. I also must thank, of course, Larry Flaxman, for another great collaboration together. It has been a long journey over nine books together, with ups and downs, good times and bad, but it has all been worth it. Most of all, I would like to thank my son, Max, who makes it all worthwhile! He is my sun, my moon, and my stars, and everything I do is for him.

Larry would like to thank his mom and dad, who continue to be his biggest supporters even from the other side of the veil; his family, friends, fans, colleagues, followers, and even his critics. Thanks also to Marie D. Jones for putting up with me over the last nine books. The past few years have provided many, many challenges, opportunities, and new experiences. There have been many times when I doubted myself. Believe it or not, I even made a few mistakes that caused me to second guess myself. Not only did you help me to learn from my mistakes but you proved that I could succeed in the literary world and have pushed me in directions that I likely would not have explored without you. Finally (and most importantly), I would like to thank my sweet daughter, Mary Essa. You are truly my greatest creation. Through your eyes, I have seen the same spark that I held as a child. Your curious nature and wonder at our amazing world (and reality) drives me to be a better person. You have proven to me that true, unconditional love exists—and I will forever strive to not only be the best human being that I can be ... but also the best role model for you.

Introduction

When asked to write a book about the devil, demons, dark entities, fallen angels, and the like, your first reaction might be one of fear or even abject terror! Perhaps by writing about these scary and often misunderstood things, you might be inviting them into your experience, too, something other paranormal writers echoed when asked for advice. They claimed that electronics and computers would glitch. They did. They claimed sickness and sleep disturbances would occur. They did. But along with a number of other intriguing issues, were they really opening the door to looking deep into the heart of evil?

Yikes.

Devils and demons bring up frightening images and terrifying thoughts. We are trained to look upon them as objects of horror to be feared and avoided at all costs. But everything has an origin, and that means devils and demons do, too. Where did these concepts come from? Did they always exist? Are they only real to those who believe in them? Are they a part of our collective reality?

The quest to track an idea to its origin is what books like this are about. The best way to understand something is to know where it began and look at how it evolved over time. Sometimes, the origin—or zero point—of a concept can be completely different from the modern perspective or interpretation of it. Quite often, our attempts to interpret primitive and ancient ideas with our modern brains ruin the initial intentions behind these ideas. A demon may have originated one way, and now we experience it entirely differently because of the long road of changing perspectives (including those of the entertainment industry) that instantly make us think one particular thing when we hear the word.

Much of our modern perception of evil and the entities that represent it really do come from popular culture, but that is often rife with imagery, beliefs, and perceptions from far older times. Our history with such dark subjects is rich and deep, and like a snowball it gathers more mass as it rolls along. By reaching back into the past, we can better understand our present and possibly prepare for our future, and that includes our shifting concepts of bad, evil, death and destruction, and demonic entities that, as our religions tell us, may be responsible. It also might help us see the more than human origins of such ideas and how we ultimately need to take more responsibility for our own demons, devils, and evil behaviors.

Are demons real? Can the devil manifest into our world as human beings, a beastly entity, or even a nasty pet? Do fallen angels still walk the earth, or have they found their way back home? Or is this all simply the stuff of pure myth, paranormal speculation, and religious doctrine?

This book will serve as both an academic/objective and a speculative/subjective resource, as well as being just plain entertaining and enlightening. We will go way back in time to see from whence these dark beings emerged and how they got to be the way we see them today. It's a terrifying journey, no doubt, but it's been said that the more we know about something the less we fear it. In the immortal words of Eleanor Roosevelt, "You gain strength, courage, and confidence by every experience in which you really stop to look fear in the face. You are able to say to yourself 'I lived through this horror. I can take the next thing that comes along.'"

By reading this book, hopefully the reader won't be opening a doorway to the other side, allowing all kinds of evil things to enter your realm of experience. You just might learn enough about the dual nature of humanity and the world we live in to make you rethink many of your ingrained beliefs.

Throughout these pages you will find fact, history, speculation, and theory. There is solid information and astounding personal experiences. Looking at the devil, demons, and dark angels is not easy, not just because the sheer amount of information out there is mind-boggling, but because it becomes so easy to interpret that information based on our own religious or spiritual upbringing, our position in society, our own experiences with dark forces and darker people, and a host of other elements that create the illusion we call reality.

Let's go on a journey together as we take a much closer look at some shadowy beings and where they came from, how they evolved, and what they have to show us about our history, collectively and individually. From primitive concepts of light and dark, good and bad, and a crude relationship with the natural world; to ancient civilizations with a greater understanding, possibly even a secret one, of how the cosmos, and man, operate; to the Middle

Ages and dark times in history when humans turned against humans and slaughtered them in the name of God and the Devil; to the modern era and the rise of occult and paranormal interest and the influence of popular entertainment and culture in redefining the devil and his minions—this is a journey that does not end when the last page of this book is reached.

In the process, we face our greatest fears and see that they are there for a reason. We might also discover that reality has many doors leading to many levels of heaven and hell, with all sorts of occupants dwelling there that we hope will stay put and only enter our lives via myths, stories, and movies through which we can live vicariously. Many of the greatest philosophers who ever existed believed that what lies within is mirrored without. As above, so below. The evil that makes itself known in the form of demonic things and activities could be a reflection of the evil we harbor inside of us because we are human, and human behavior can be incredibly good and horrifically terrible. Maybe we ourselves help evil manifest in the world as physical beings that represent our own dark horrors, alive and crawling, flying and leaping, dancing to music that makes our ears bleed, yet they are creations of our own beliefs and collective unconscious.

Or maybe there really are ugly, scary things that exist entirely separate from us and without our help. Either option is quite frightening, don't you think? Perhaps the truth is a bit of both, something in between. We have demons within, and we deal with demons outside of us, and it's all a part of the human experience, and the territory of the soul to be treaded upon carefully. So, be careful as you read and explore and learn for there are foul beings afoot, and some say they don't like to be exposed to the light of day or have their names in print.

Fear not, dear reader. The authors of this book take full responsibility for that!

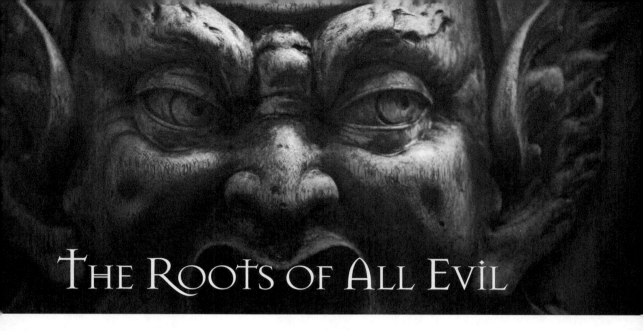

The Roots of All Evil

lways begin at the beginning. It sounds like dumb advice, but few
people take it. To understand a concept, it's best to start at the point
it began. Who first thought it up? Which group of humans first carried its flag? What segments of society first embraced or accepted it as dog-
matic truth? Evil is no different. Did it exist on its own before the birth of
humanity? Did we humans give birth to evil? Is it an integral and ingrained
part of us, separate from us, or perhaps a bit of both?

To know the representatives of evil, we first must come to realize that
we live in a world of duality. Darkness and light. Good and evil. Up and
down. In and out. Right and wrong. Heaven and Hell. But which came first,
or did these dual concepts evolve side by side as our primitive understanding
of the world around us became more sophisticated over time? Before we can
begin to understand the origins of demons and the devil and how they have
become such a strong presence in our religions, myths, philosophies and cultures, we must examine first where the need for their existence arose from,
and how the idea of evil and the demons that personify it transformed into
the beliefs we have held throughout history.

It makes sense to begin with the concept of evil, and how it has
evolved over time to encompass actual entities that are symbolic of something archetypal and universal to all human beings. Looking first at the etymology of the word "evil," we find that it has its roots in the English (Middle
English *evel, evil*; Old English *yfel*), German (Old High German *ubil, ubel*),
and Dutch (*evel*) languages. The first known use of the word "evil" dates to
the twelfth century and is used as an adjective (evil life), adverb (gone evil),
noun (evilness), and idiom (thy evil one, Satan).

The Etymology of Evil

According to Etymology.com, "In Old English and other older Germanic languages other than Scandinavian, Evil was the word the Anglo-Saxons used where we would use bad, cruel, unskillful, defective (adj.), or harm (n.), crime, misfortune, disease (n.). In Middle English, bad took the wider range of senses and evil began to focus on moral badness. Both words have good as their opposite."

The word "evil" as a noun comes from the Old English explanation for sin, wickedness, and anything that causes moral or physical injury. In Middle English, the word was "evilty," which was related to the Latin words for "evil eye," or "Evilly." (Source: Etymology.com.)

The general meaning of the word is "harmful, morally wrong, immoral, wicked, bad, sinful, mischievous," even "misfortune" (evil has befallen the poor soul!). Whether used as a noun or adverb, the word generally implies something to be feared, something awful, disastrous, nasty, primal, even murderous. It's just not a good word with any connotations of the positive. Most people use the term "evil" to describe another person's behaviors or actions, but the word has also become a symbol of a dark power that is the antithesis to goodness, purity, and light. If angels are good, demons are evil. Angels are typically depicted as being white (almost to show sterility and cleanliness), while demons are generally dark, black (portraying evil and uncleanliness). It is this association that gives rise to the evolution of the Devil himself, as well as the minions of death, Hell, and the Underworld. These can all be viewed as a representation of the dual nature of humans themselves, as well as the possibility of negative forces, energies, and entities. Where "evil" might have once simply described a terrible person, it soon became personified with supernatural entities that represented every opposite of good possible.

Interestingly, "evil" backwards is "live," implying perhaps that true evil is the opposite not of goodness, but of life itself. Death is not necessarily evil, but our obsession with the darkness of the unknown may have morphed its way into our psyche as the "anti-live," or evil. Switch the letters around, and you have "vile." Add a "D" and you have "devil." Interesting, huh? Words have incredible power to convey not just simple explanations or descriptions but deeper meanings that often are symbolic in nature and appealing to our subconscious as archetypal.

When did evil actually begin? Most likely the same time as the dawn of humanity. There is no proof that true evil existed before human beings were around to interpret darkness and bad behavior as such. Only light and dark forces and energies that gave rise to both creation and destruction in our natural world. The first humans needed a way to understand what was happening around them, which at the time, without scientific knowledge, must have appeared very frightening. The belief that everything had a "spirit," known as "animism," began our quest to gain some kind of control over our environment.

Religion and spirituality often look upon negative experiences as bad, giving them more power over us. It was, to our ancestors, a lot easier to believe in evil at first, because of its stark contrast to anything that was beneficial to survival. Why worship the good stuff? It was simply what was. But when something awful happened, something that caused great pain and death, it triggered fears that led to beliefs around those fears. Bad events were evil. The natural forces and entities and people behind bad events were evil, simply because they disrupted the flow of survival and being "OK." This concept will be explored further in the next chapter.

So as our primitive ancestors observed the world around them, they began noticing dualities, and categorizing them as good or bad, positive or negative, beneficial or dangerous to surviving and thriving. Those categorizations served as the basis for the oldest religions and belief systems on the planet and have followed us throughout history … even today!

Animism holds that everything that isn't human still possesses a spirit or essence, including inanimate objects such as rocks, thunder, and waterfalls. This idea that everything was supernatural, or connected to a spiritual whole,

The darkness of devils and demons, contrasted with the white purity of angels, highlights the dual nature of the good and evil within all of us.

is a fundamental concept to indigenous peoples today, but is considered the earliest inklings of religious belief in the history of humanity. To our earliest ancestors, everything possessed its own spirit, or soul, and no separation existed between the realm of the physical and that of the spiritual. That concept came later when duality was introduced into our mental awareness. To the animist, all was interconnected, and everything was alive.

Animists did not call themselves "animists." That term was later credited to nineteenth-century anthropologist Sir Edward Burnett Tylor, who called animism a "general doctrine of souls and other spiritual beings" in his extensively researched *Primitive Culture* (1871). Tylor saw this earliest form of what we now call religion as a basic concept of nature as something alive and purposeful, akin to fetishism, totemism, and even later shamanism, which imbued all of nature with an essence and connectedness. Although crude and scientifically illogical, it was inspired in part by dreams and visions, Tylor believed, and not scientific observations of natural phenomenon. His extensive research would lead to the creation of the field of anthropology as a new science, as a part of our understanding of primitive society.

The word "animism" came from a German scientist named Georg Ernst Stahl. In 1708, Stahl used the term *animismus* to describe the theory that the vital principle of everything in nature was the soul, and all phenomena, normal and abnormal, could be traced to the soul/spiritual, something today's followers of homeopathic medicine and wholeness-oriented health would understand, yet modern science stands against strongly. An intriguing side note: the argument over animism would even invade the world of child psychology, with warring camps debating whether children are born with an inherent animistic worldview (as per psychologist Jean Piaget [1896–1980]), or that children are not born with it, but accultured to it later as they become educated (as asserted by cultural anthropologist Margaret Mead [1901–1978]). Shamans might argue with Mead that education has not led to a better understanding of our world and our place in it, but a shallower one, and those shamans would be backed up by the research of quantum and theoretical physicists who suggest there is, indeed, a web of connectivity beneath the surface appearances of reality.

Psychologist Jean Piaget believed that children were born with an innate animistic worldview.

Other theories on the origin of religious belief during the nineteenth century suggested that early humans gave a symbolic or mythological explanation of natural phenomena, called "naturalism"; some theories point to "hedonism" as the precursor to what would become monotheism. These theories have been debated and often given limited credibility, although mythology does lend credence, as we shall explore later, to a symbolic origin for religious concepts embedded in stories that science deems outlandish, yet that contain hidden truths.

If everything had a soul, or spiritual essence, then how did some go rogue and become interpreted as bad, evil, and dangerous? Observation told early humans that some things were creative and generative, and some were utterly destructive and terrifying. Assigning a spirit to each—say, to thunder and to rain, to lightning and to earthquakes, to animals and to plants—gave humans a way of categorizing and interpreting objects as either beneficial or something to be avoided, something that could be detrimental to their survival. Watching the moon at night gave a sense of awe and wonder, much different than the fear inspired by a lightning strike that caused a fire in dry brush; thus the lightning spirit would be more negative, possibly even one to be feared. The moon, on the other hand, would be given a spirit that evoked awe and wonder, and later one that was associated with the menses of women once a pattern was discerned.

Good spirits and bad spirits embodied the natural world, creating some order out of chaos and some wisdom out of fear. We began, in a sense, to take sides, putting some phenomena in the positive category, and others in the negative, entirely on the basis of how each influenced our ability to survive. Thus arose the need to give spirits themselves a good or bad name, dividing the unified world into dual camps.

This duality, though, coupled with our own evolution and increased knowledge of science and nature, actually led to a demand for a new belief that could, once again, unify everything. If there were indeed good and bad spirits, and good and bad events, then there must be an overseer behind the curtain, giving birth to the "one God" concept of monotheism that led to the Abrahamic "Western" traditions. In his book *The History of the Devil and the Idea of Evil*, scholar Paul Carus writes that although animism was the first stage in the development of religious thought, the principle of unity would dominate its later development. "Man tries to unify his conceptions in a consistent and harmonious monism. Accordingly, while the belief in good spirits tended towards the formation of the doctrine of Monotheism, the belief in evil spirits led naturally to the acceptance of a single supreme evil deity, conceived as embodying all that is bad, destructive and immoral." This mental evolution towards monotheism, he suggests, along with "monodiabolism," constitute a dualism that is still held today as the most widely accepted world conception in our traditions of Judaism, Christianity, Islam, and Zoroastrianism.

A dancer dresses as a leopard in a re-creation of Maya animism beliefs.

Other regions of the world adopted belief systems that organized lower deities under main or superior deities, such as the panentheism of Sikhs; polytheism; the prevailing religions of ancient Rome and Greece; the Germanic and Norse forms of paganism; and Mesoamerican cultures such as the Maya, Inca, and Aztec. Eastern traditions such as Buddhism, Jainism, and Hinduism would adopt a monistic worldview. Gnostics preferred dualism.

But whether one believes in no deities at all, such as in atheism, and that man alone was responsible for the good and evil in the world, or one believed deities were everywhere, and there were those on the side of the light, and those on the side of darkness, everyone has a concept of evil. As our primitive ancestors grouped things into the good and bad columns, and gave each names and symbols, creating what would one day be the cosmogenesis stories and mythologies of world cultures we study in school, they also sought to unify those columns back into a singular whole. Yet, in doing so, they realized that each column might have its own unifier, or main deity.

As the concept of religion developed, creating offshoot belief systems all over the world, so, too, did the concept of evil. Along with those concepts grew a surrounding idea of a particular place where evil reigned supreme, under the directive of the darkest of souls, the opposers of the light and of goodness. Most of us came to know of this place as "Hell," having grown up with a Western religious background.

The *Dictionary of Philosophy* (Penguin, 1999) states, "There is evil in the world; bad things happen to people, and people do bad things," personifying evil as exemplified "when the wicked prosper and good people meet a grim fate." This definition brings up the question of whether or not the presence of evil negates the existence of an opposing force, deity, God … or one might even go so far as to attempt to accommodate the possibility of both existing alongside each other, like the scales of Libra, meant to keep balance and order.

What if evil were a totally manmade expression? No doubt many believe that men such as Adolf Hitler, Josef Stalin, or Saddam Hussein were and continue to be the personification of evil, or Pol Pot, or any mass murderer or serial killer. But this kind of evil just seems so extreme to us. We all have the capacity for being "bad," even violent, but is there something deeper behind extreme, radical evil? Religion would have us believe there is a demonic aspect to this, that men like Hitler were working for the Devil, as opposed to a Mother Teresa, working for God. Yet extremely good people are often called "angels," even as those on the other side are called "demonic."

ORIGINAL SIN

In the Old Testament book of Genesis, the first evil comes to Adam and Eve in the form of a serpent bringing temptation into their innocent worldview. First Eve, and then Adam, disobey God's orders and eat of the Tree of Life, and suddenly everything changes and they are given the knowledge normally reserved for God—the knowledge of good and evil. They are exposed to the nature of duality. Eventually, this serpent morphs into other Judeo-Christian personifications of "bad to the bone," namely Lucifer, who is the Devil himself, and an entire echelon of demons and fallen angels, not to mention hundreds of humans capable of the most horrific behaviors and actions toward their fellows. Now, knowing good and evil, we had a choice. A tempting decision that would forever divide us with ourselves, and each other.

Throughout the rest of the Old and New Testaments, humans are asked to make choices between good and evil, between doing as they are told by God or his angels, or being tempted away from God's will by his demons. One choice leads to life, the other to a sure and torturous death. Authors Paul O. Ingram and Frederick John Streng state in *Buddhist–Christian Dialogue: Mutual Renewal*

Evil comes to Adam and Eve in the form of a snake in the Book of Genesis.

and Transformation that evil in the Abrahamic traditions is "usually perceived as the dualistic antagonistic opposite of good, in which good should prevail and evil should be defeated." In Buddhist cultures, both good and evil are a part of an antagonistic duality that must be overcome through the process of *Sūnyatā,* which is the emptying of the recognition of good and evil as two opposing principles, and instead perceiving the oneness, the void of the duality. This openness or emptiness is a sort of zero state, before ideas of duality can separate us into warring philosophical factions within our own bodies, minds, and spirits.

Islam does not adhere to a concept of absolute evil, instead believing that it is essential to believe all is of Allah, whether perceived as good or evil by humans. Things perceived as evil in Islam are either of a natural origin, such as a natural disaster that kills thousands, or come from the use of free will by humans to disobey the will of Allah. Evil itself does not exist, except in the concept of its being a lack of good.

It is certainly interesting that evil became tag-team associated with death, and good with life, and yet nature tells us quite directly that both are a part of the cycle of life and the duality we deal with on a daily basis as our human experience. The fear of death may have been highly influential in adding to the association with darkness, fear, rage, and extermination of the life force. We fear death more than anything. To us, who long for life eternal, it is evil.

Many religions include a list of behaviors and actions that, if adhered to, keep followers pure and good. If broken, all hell breaks loose, no pun intended. Judeo-Christians have their Ten Commandments and the Golden Rule of "do unto others."

The Ten Commandments, introduced in the Book of Exodus as the ten laws given to Moses by God on Mount Sinai in the form of two stone tablets, are:

1. Believe in God alone.

2. Do not worship anyone or anything except God; do not make, bow to, or worship an image or statue that is supposed to be God.

3. Do not take God's name in vain.

4. Observe Sabbath, rest, and do not work on the seventh day.

5. Honor your parents.

6. Do not murder.

7. Do not commit adultery.

8. Do not steal.

9. Do not testify as a false witness.

10. Do not be jealous of anything someone else has.

The 10 Commandments that Moses brought to his people as a gift from God established basic ethical principles to society (stained glass window at St. James's Church, Stockholm, Sweden).

These basic laws, also known as the Decalogue, or Ten Statements, were meant to guide the people of Israel, and have become the foundation of ethics in our judicial system, despite being broken over and over again by most humans at some point in time, including upon Moses' descent from the mountain, when he discovered the people had made gold calves honoring pagan deities. Moses smashed the tablets into the ground (thus himself breaking one of the seven deadly sins by expressing wrath!).

Sikhs have a list of vices that cause suffering they call "The Five Thieves," and include Attachment, Greed, Wrath, Lust, and Egotism. Buddhism looks upon killing, lying, abuse, slandering, hatred, and clinging to false beliefs as evil and holds that illusion itself is the root of all evil. Modern humans often say money is the root of all evil, or at least the love of money.

SIN AND HELL

There are seven deadly sins, also known as cardinal sins, of the Christian ethical teachings, introduced around the fourth century C.E. These are: Gluttony, Lust (including fornication), Greed, Sloth, Pride, Envy, and

Wrath. They were also called "capital" sins because from these seven, all other ideas of sin originate, and because they were considered mortal or venial. A mortal sin is described as a thought, deed, or action that goes against eternal law and deprives a person's soul of grace, charity, and goodness. Mortal sins cannot be repaired. Venial sins are a little less harsh and are reparable through actions and deeds.

Additional sins, later added by the Greeks, were *acedia*, which means dejection or despair; and *vanagloria*, or vainglory, sometimes grouped in with sorrow, pride, and depression.

In addition, the Book of Proverbs 6:16–19 tells us of six specific things the Lord hates: a proud look/vanity; a lying tongue; hands that shed the blood of the innocent; a wicked heart; feet that swiftly run toward mischief; bearing false witness; and sowing discord among others. Many of these made the cut into the Ten Commandments, as well.

If religions evolve to distort the true origin of evil, being the opposite of good and pure and kind, based upon their own perceptions and beliefs, then it also adds into the mix additional ideas of how evil is punished. Hell is a place, the opposite of Heaven, where those who break the laws of God are meant to spend eternity burning for their sins. In the triadic worldview of Abrahamic religions, Heaven was in the sky, Purgatory was more earthbound, and Hell was below the Earth, somewhere in the depths, the "Underworld" filled with fire and molten lava flows and cries of despair.

Traditionally, Hell is a place where sinners get punished for the rest of eternity, but in recent years some church leaders have said that Hell is just a fabrication.

In August 2006, retired Episcopal bishop and author John Shelby Spong did an interview with journalist Keith Morrison of *Dateline NBC*. The subject was the use of Hell as a punishment tool by the Church to control its followers by playing on their deepest fear—what happens to bad people after they die. "I don't think Hell exists. I happen to believe in life after death, but I don't think it's got a thing to do with reward or punishment." Spong went on to explain that even as he was raised in the Church, he saw the use of Hell as a control method for producing guilt, as opposed to the promise of Heaven as being a place where one was rewarded for good. This fear-based control kept the population in check, Spong said, by "scaring the hell out of people" throughout Christian history.

Spong, who is no stranger to controversy, having written numerous scholarly books that challenge all sorts of accepted Christian beliefs, was met with incredulity by Morrison. But Spong insisted that the Church didn't like people to grow up and accept responsibility for their actions, wanting them instead to be controlled by fear and the promise of torment and hellfire for their actions.

The idea of Hell as a sort of jail for sinners is present in most religious traditions, cultures, myths, and even in folklore, and continues to be a big part of our modern cultural beliefs. Perhaps not surprisingly, it's even a popular subject for movies, novels, and television shows. It's always helpful to look at the etymology of the word for clues to its origin. "Hell" in modern English terms can be traced back to around 725 C.E. with the Old English *hel, helle,* which mean "netherworld, abode of the dead, place of torment for the wicked after death, infernal regions." In turn, this word comes from the earlier Proto-Germanic *haljo* for "the Underworld," the Old Saxon *hellia,* and the Old Norse *hel* and *hellir,* which meant "cave, cavern." Hel is known in Old Norse mythology as the ruler of the underworld of Hel.

The pagan concept of an underworld as a hidden place that is also the lowest of worlds comes from Old Norse mythology and no doubt was incorporated into the later Christian version of Hell as the abode of the Devil. Referred to in the Old Testament as "Sheol," and later in the New Testament Greek as "Hades," and "Gehenna," Hell was a place of misery, a place of horror and fear and torment and despair. Hell was definitely not a place you would want to vacation in for eternity.

In most religious traditions and myths, Hell was all about life after death for those banished there. Many religions believe that geographically, Hell is hidden somewhere beneath the surface of the planet, with special entrances guarded by monsters and demons. Other cultures did not view Hell as a place of punishment, but simply where the dead went, either ruled over by a demon or some other entity designated for the role (Hades, Hel, Enma …). Hell might be broken up into rooms, with each room depicting a particular sin to be punished, and often the suffering was doled out according to a particular sin, one at a time.

Christianity and Islam both depict a fiery, agonizing Hell that is all about guilt and suffering, but sometimes Hell is a place of ice-cold barrenness—think Dante's "Inferno" and the ninth level of Hell as a frozen lake of blood. Tibetan Buddhists describe Hell as either hot or cold, but the word "inferno" is most often associated with Hell.

According to the *Catholic Encyclopedia*, there are four theological meanings of Hell:

1. Hell is, in the strictest sense, a place of punishment for damned men and demons.

2. Hell is the "limbus parvulorum," or limbo of infants, where those who die in original sin alone, without personal mortal sin, are confined and punished.

3. Hell is the "limbus partum," or limbo of the fathers, where the souls of the just who died before Christ awaited their admission to heaven, for in the meantime heaven was closed against them in punishment for the sin of Adam.

4. Hell is a purgatory, where the just who die in venial sin or who owe a debt of temporal punishment for their sins are cleansed by suffering before they can be admitted to heaven.

In the Old Testament, the term Gehenna is most often used to describe Hell, even more so than Hades. The New Testament favors Hell, although many names are used, including "lower hell," "place of torments," "abyss," "everlasting darkness," "eternal fire," "unquenchable fire," "perdition," "second death," and many more. Early beliefs suggested Hell could be everywhere, with the eternally damned wandering around at liberty, but the idea of Hell being a fixed location won favor, and again, that location was often relegated to an underworld, deep within the bowels of Earth, where those who were estranged from God would be as far away from the divine light as possible.

A couple centuries ago, it was suggested that Hell might be located on Mars.

During the eighteenth century, Englishmen suggested that Hell might be on the moon, or even Mars, or possibly outside the confines of the known universe. Before then, Hell was thought to exist on some deserted island, out at sea, or at either of the Earth's poles, before humans ventured there and discovered it wasn't there!

Even as cultures debated the physical or geographic location of Hell, the duration a soul would spend there was also open for debate. Was Hell an eternal destination, with no chance of redemption or salvation beyond? Was it a truck stop along a soul's journey where the sins of the previous incarnation were somehow cleansed and the soul itself purified? Or was it just the blackness and utter emptiness and finality of death itself? Conditionalists hold fast to the idea that the soul is immortal, but suggest after a certain amount of punishment, the souls of the wicked are annihilated. Universalists teach that the damned will attain beatitude. Some Catholics have even gone on record as stating that sinners can achieve grace after death if they are not too wicked.

But the Bible of the Abrahamic religions focuses on the eternal nature of Hell, and that the torments of the damned, as stated in Revelation 14:11, 19:3, and 20:10, will last forever. The fire of Hell, therefore, is eternal and these souls shall not abide in the Kingdom of God (1 Corinthians 6:10, Galatians 5:21). No getting a do-over, then, for the worst of souls.

The finality and sheer terror of the promise of Hell, though, has in no way stopped humans from engaging in a wide variety of sins against nature and one another, showing that even though used as a tool of fear-based control by the Church, it still may not override the desire to sin. The original idea was to provide a social and moral code to live by, one that would result in some semblance of order into the world, but it hasn't quite worked out that way. People still don't really know what happens after death, and without scientific proof, it would appear faith isn't quite enough to wipe them clean of the drive to break the cardinal rules.

Within the Catholic Church alone, a debate rages over whether the "fires" of Hell are literal or metaphorical. Does the fire denote an actual physical fire, as in a huge fire pit with bodies writhing in a pain that never ends? Or is it a metaphor for a fire that cleanses the wickedness and sin from the spirit and from the soul? Is the nature of the fires of Hell the same as or different from fire in the real world of the living? Does the fire vary according to the venial or mortal sin/s committed by each soul? Is there one big fire or a fire for each person, fitted specifically to his or her situation?

In ancient Egyptian polytheism, sinful souls of the dead were either welcomed into the Two Fields, approved for good behavior by the goddess Maat, or sent to a "devourer" and thrown into a lake of fire if they didn't meet Maat's approval. The devourer took the poor soul and punished it before annihilating it altogether. But there was also a level of purification for sinners

The Egyptian goddess Maat (here shown wearing the Feather of Truth) served as judge to determine who was to be thrown into a lake of fire after death.

who didn't break the worst rules, allowing them to be reborn after overcoming evil and not be forced into a total state of nothingness, or "nonbeing."

The Greek Tartarus was a pit or abyss, a dungeon-like place of torture and torment somewhere within the confines of Hades. This was where souls judged as deserving of punishment were sent. Mesoamerican cultures such as the Aztec had "Mictlan," a place far north that was neutral and took four years to get to. Along the way, souls overcame challenges and, aided by Axolotl, ended in a nine-level underworld. The Mayans also had a nine-level underworld called "Mental" that could be accessed only via a dangerous, thorny, steep road.

Judaic teachings perceive Hell rather as deep shame instead of an actual destination of souls after death. Sins and misdeeds cause great shame, and that suffering atones for the sins themselves. Being outside the will of God, or being in Gehinnom, corresponds with the more metaphorical concept of Hell as a state of being, such as, "I'm in hell right now with this job," rather than a geographical location. There are a number of references in both the Torah and mystical Kabbalah that talk of the Underworld of Sheol, the doom and perdition of Abbadon and the purgatory of Gehenna, which obviously helped shape the later Christian/New Testament beliefs. Gehenna also refers to an actual place called the "Valley of Hinnom" outside of the city of Jerusalem where garbage was burned, as well as the bodies of sinners and those who committed suicide. This fire never went out—thus, the eternal fire.

Similar to the Gehenna of Judaism is the Jahannam of Islam, which is also said to be a fiery place with boiling water and wicked tortures galore for those who do not accept God. After the Day of Judgment, unbelievers and sinners alike enter this hellish place when they die, passing over a bridge so narrow that most fall into the hellfire. This is the opposite of Jannah, or Paradise, the equivalent of Christianity's Heaven, and is located below. In Islam, the suffering endured in Jahannam is physical and symbolic, with seven different levels designated depending on the actions of the sinner; one level is made of ice and cold. The guardian of Hell is Maalik, an angel who oversees the Zabaaniyah, or guards of Hell.

Interestingly, in Islam, being a hypocrite or worshipping more than one God are believed to be the biggest offenses, immediately sending a soul directly to the lowest pit, called Hawiyah. Not all Islamic scholars agree on whether being in Hell is permanent or temporary, though.

Yet, in the most literal sense, the Catholic Church states that Hell is really the absolute and definitive exclusion of the self from Communion with God. If you asked for forgiveness or mended your ways before death, accepting God's grace and love, asking for mercy, and accepting the ways of the Lord, then Hell could indeed be avoided. The key was to ask for it before death, not after. Hell is considered in Greek Orthodox churches as that final place for those who were not found worthy of redemption after the Resurrection and Last Judgment. It seems a lot of religious traditions give humans a bit of choice and leeway in avoiding the fires of Hell, but they have to do it within a certain construct of time.

The Soul

Some more modern religious scholars suggest conditional immortality of the soul, which dies along with physical death and doesn't live again until post-resurrection. Protestantism of the early Reformation period rejected the immortality of the soul as well, and Seventh-day Adventists support the idea of total annihilation of the soul, denying the concept of purgatory, where souls wait their fate in a middle world between Heaven and Hell.

Unitarians and Universal Reconciliationists believe that the souls of the wicked will once again reconcile with God and be allowed into Heaven. This seems to be the most compassionate of many hellish beliefs in punishment that never ceases, with no chance at all after death for a renewed soul that begs for forgiveness and learns its lessons. The Church of Jesus Christ of Latter-day

The Mormons view Hell as a place that repentant souls can escape.

Hell on Earth?

There are places on Earth that some cultures believe are the literal gateways to Hell. These entrances to the Underworld happen to be found all over the globe, often in remote and hard-to-access places, and are often linked to the mythology of the region.

Located in the Tapir Mountain Nature Reserve in Belize, this network of caves was once used by the Mayans as an entrance to their underworld, Xibalba. It was a vast maze of passageways with rivers of blood and scorpions crawling everywhere, ruled over by the Lord of Xibalba and his minions. The caves contain stalactites and bits of pottery and bones, suggesting human sacrifices were performed here, possibly to the rain god, Chac. The cave system was discovered in 1989 and is now a popular tourist destination.

The entrance to Actun Tunichil Muknal Cave leads to Xibalba, the Mayan underworld.

Cape Matapan Caves

Located in Greece, along the southernmost tip of the mainland, are the caves of Cape Matapan, on the Mani peninsula. These caves may depict the actual gateways to the underworld of classical Greek myth. Located at sea level, the caves are suggested as the entrances to Hades itself, also known as the Kingdom of the Shades; Hercules may have used these same caves to enter the Underworld.

Cave of the Sibyl

In Naples, Italy, there is an alleged gateway to Hell that lays claim to being possibly the oldest in the world ... or close to it. This portal to Hell was first written about over 2,000 years ago. In *The Aeneid*, Virgil wrote of the hundred entrances deep beneath the earth, stretching all the way to the Underworld. In ancient Rome, it was thought to be the portal to the Devil's abode.

Lacus Curtius

Also in Italy, this time in Rome, is the landmark known as the Roman Forum, a hot tourist spot. At the center of the Forum is a small standing stone believed by ancient Romans to be the entrance to the Underworld. The modern stone replica is said to represent the place where Marcus Curtius sacrificed his own life after hearing about the fall of Rome from an oracle. Other legends suggest it as the resting place of other Roman soldiers or centurions, but whoever died there was said to have been swallowed up by a chasm that opened, then closed again.

Pluto's Gate

In the Denzili Province of Turkey, an ancient ruin was discovered, during an archeological expedition, that was believed to be the gateway to Hell. Set upon a thermal spring, the ruins of the ancient Temple of Pluto mark a large cave from which toxic fumes escape.

These fumes were said to put priests of Pluto into altered states of consciousness during rituals and even today are alleged to be the cause of bird and small-animal deaths near the cave opening. A popular tourist attraction, the temple supports itself by selling birds and small animals so that the lethal properties of the carbon dioxide gases can be tested.

St. Patrick's Purgatory

Ireland's Lough Dreg is the home to a gateway to Hell mentioned in Scripture. St. Patrick's Purgatory is a small monastery on Station Island, where St. Patrick himself is alleged to have received visions of Hell from Jesus that confirmed he was on the spot where the entrance to Satan's pit was located, although archeologists and historians suggest that this was a place used for prayer and contemplation. The area was filled in and sealed up and has been since 1962, but even today people travel there to hold pilgrimages and meditate upon Hell and evil.

Fengdu City of Ghosts, China

China's own Hell gate is a two-thousand-year-old settlement in the heart of the nation, located on Ming Hill near the northern Yangtze River. The ruins of this city depict the location of Naraka, the Hell of Chinese myth, and the streets of the long-abandoned city are filled with statues of demons and ghosts, with a huge carved face looking down upon the ruins known as "The Ghost King." It is, in fact, the largest rock sculpture in the world, measuring 452 feet tall and 712 feet wide. This particular Hell gate is where two officials came to get

Fengdu City in China is a historic, abandoned town located where Chinese Hell (Naraka) is

(Continued from previous page)

away from the emperor. Their names were Yin and Yang.

HEKLA VOLKANO, ICELAND

The Hekla Stratovolcano, located in southern Iceland, was believed to be the pit of Hell. Medieval Christians referred to it as "Hekla Fell," and it has also been called "the eternal prison of Judas" and thought to be massive in comparison with other volcanoes such as Pompeii. Since 847 C.E. there have been over twenty major eruptions at Hekla, and no doubt our ancient and primitive ancestors looked up at this fiery inferno as the place where the Devil made his abode, especially during an eruption. One local superstition held that witches would gather around Hekla every Easter.

Saints looks at Hell as an in-between state after death, but before resurrection, where souls can either repent and move on or not repent and suffer.

Obviously, the belief in Hell, and in evil, is directly tied into beliefs about what happens after we die. The belief drives whether we are reincarnated or given a new life, or even reborn at the side of the Lord (or whichever deity is worshipped). Not knowing what happens after death usually leads to all kinds of assumptions, positive and negative, good and bad, joyful and downright horrific. From Buddhism, we have five levels of rebirth that are divided into differing sublevels of agony and misery, or of pleasure. Suffering of souls can go on for a long time but is not permanent, as souls are reborn. The teachings of Buddhism emphasize the desire to escape the wheel of reincarnation and rebirth (really the entire cycle of the soul) and to achieve a state of Nirvana, or being off the wheel completely.

Hinduisms' roots have no concept of Hell but rather a tri-level world of different realms: the sky, the Earth, and the air/atmosphere, although later Hindu texts mention a fourth realm not unlike Hell called the Naraka. As in other traditions, sinners go to this hellish realm and must accept the prescribed punishment in accordance with their individual sins, facing the Yamaraja, the god associated with death, before getting their punishment orders from the record keeper, Chitragupta. If a soul completes its doled-out punishment, then it is reborn depending on its "karmic balance," kind of like a spiritual bank balance. Jainism has a seven-level Hell that also holds souls accountable with karma either carried over from a previous life or taken with them into a new life. Once karma has been used up, a higher level of rebirth can be achieved.

The Eastern traditions allow for those who commit sins to redeem their souls, but the Abrahamic religions are not so generous, which is why today's pop culture and religious "big three" are more influential in how we perceive evil in general. Taoism, for example, does not contain a concept of Hell, because of its belief that morality is totally a human choice, and there is no such thing as an immaterial soul. But Taoism does have a karmic system of punishment, especially after later religious influences became a part of the original, ancient beliefs. Which also brings up the concept that evil, like beauty, is in the eye of the beholder.

Most of the world can agree that the actions of dictators like Hitler, Stalin, Pol Pot, et al., are sins of the most extreme, resulting in the deaths of millions and the untold suffering of millions more. Yet, to the dictators, are they not fulfilling some destiny or plan they feel is the correct or righteous one? Do they not believe they are doing "good" in the world and that they are often "divinely inspired" or "chosen" as many cult leaders state? What is one man's evil can be another man's good, even if the evil man's actions are because of psychopathic tendencies. Serial killers, however horrific, probably believe they are doing what they are doing for a reason in their own mentally tortured minds. The same goes for the concept of "good." While one person might think it good that all guns and weapons be banished, another might see it as a terrifying threat to personal liberty and the ability to self-protect.

Thus, when evil is defined by a religious body or institution in a fixed sense, with a Hell as the threat lorded over the heads of the populace, those definitions become accepted as the norms for society as a whole, making it incredibly difficult to trace, really, where they originated, and why. Evil is about duality, as is Hell, as is sin, and only those spiritual belief systems that deny duality for a more unifying explanation seem somewhat free of the need to distort the true origins of these concepts for a specific agenda based upon their tradition's doctrines of belief.

Though many people believe, as writer Jean-Paul Sartre conveyed in his 1944 play, *No Exit*, that "Hell is other people," one need only turn on the news at night for ample proof that the association of Hell with deities and angels and guardians that are not human prevails today. It's impossible to talk about evil, and even Hell, without mentioning the one entity most associated with fire and brimstone, torture and damnation, eternal anguish and punishment, no matter what religious or geographic or cultural upbringing one might have—and that would be the Devil.

The Devil
and His Counterparts

Just as God came over the course of religious evolution to represent good, the Devil came to represent the polar opposite. Evil, darkness, death, pain, suffering, sin, and all points in between needed a representative of their own in the hierarchy of deities. Just as the concept of an overseeing, all-knowing force for love existed, there must also be one for hate, for we are a world of dualities.

The Devil

The word "devil" means "of evil." It comes from the Greek word *diabolos* for "slanderer or accuser," and the later Middle English *devel*, from the Old English *deofol*. He is diabolical, to be sure. He is the King of Death, the Prince of Darkness, and the Overlord of the Underworld, among other names. His realm is all that we fear. His presence is all that we hope to avoid. Yet, the Devil is as much a necessity to a concept of God, or a dualistic understanding of the world, as up is a necessity to the understanding of down. Even monotheistic religious systems believe in a devil, although he may not be on equal footing with God. It depends on which religion we are talking about. In fact, his names are Legion.

But, who, or what, really, is the Devil? Some say he is the counterpart of God, of goodness, the opposing dual nature of God. Others say he is the king of fallen angels, once loved and beautiful in the eyes of God, now reigning over Hell with his demonic hordes. Often he is referred to as "the adversary," "the deceiver" and "the liar and tempter and accuser," as if he represents the darkest sides of our own humanity. Some refer to him as Old Nick, which is an appellation that may derive from the Dutch word *Nikken*, meaning "devil."

We mostly know of the Devil from the Old and New Testaments, which are rife with various monikers for the Devil. Some of these are:

- Abbadon/Apollyon—"And they had as king over them the angel of the bottomless pit, whose name in Hebrew is Abbadon, but in Greek, he has the name Apollyon." (Revelation 9:11)

- Accuser of Our Brethren—"And I heard a loud voice saying in heaven, now is come salvation, and strength, and the kingdom of our God, and the power of his Church; for the accuser of our brethren is cast down...." (Revelation 12:10)

- Adversary—"Be sober, be vigilant, because your adversary the devil walks about like a roaring lion, seeking whom he may devour." (1 Peter 5:8)

- Anointed Cherub—"You were the anointed cherub who covers; I established you; You were on the holy mountain of God; You walked back and forth in the midst of fiery stones." (Ezekiel 28:14)

- Antichrist—"And every spirit that does not confess that Jesus Christ has come in the flesh is not of God. And this is the spirit of the Antichrist, which you have heard was coming, and is now already in the world." (1 John 4:3)

- The Beast—"Then a third angel followed them saying with a loud voice, 'If anyone worships the beast and his image, and receives his mark on his forehead or his hand, he himself shall also drink of the wine of the wrath of God....'" (Revelation 14:9–10)

- Beelzebub, Ruler of Demons—"Now when the Pharisees heard it they said, 'This fellow does not cast out demons except by Beelzebub, the ruler of the demons.'" (Matthew 12:24)

- Belial—"And what concord hath Christ with Belial? or what part hath he that believeth with an infidel?" (2 Corinthians 6:15)

- Devil—"He who sins is of the devil...." (1 John 3:8)

- Dragon—"And he laid hold on the dragon, that old serpent, which is the Devil, and Satan, and bound him a thousand years...." (Revelation 20:2)

- Father of Lies—"Ye are of your father the devil, and the lusts of your father ye will do. He was a murderer from the beginning, and abode not in the truth, because there is no truth in him. When he speaketh a lie, he speaketh of his own: for he is a liar, and the father of it." (John 8:44)

- God of This Age—"Whose minds the god of this age has blinded, who do not believe, lest the light of the gospel of the glory of Christ, who is the image of God, should shine on them." (2 Corinthians 4:4)

- The God of This World—"In whom the god of this world hath blinded the minds of them which believe not, lest the light of the glorious gospel of Christ, who is the image of God, should shine unto them." (2 Corinthians 4:4)

- King of Babylon—"That you will take up this proverb against the king of Babylon, and say, 'How the oppressor has ceased, the golden city ceased!'" (Isaiah 14:4)

- Lawless One—"And then the lawless one will be revealed, whom the Lord will consume with the breath of His mouth and destroy with the brightness of His coming." (2 Thessalonians 2:8)

- Leviathan—"In that day the Lord with His severe sword, great and strong, will punish Leviathan the fleeing serpent, Leviathan that twisted serpent; And He will slay the reptile that is in the sea." (Isaiah 27:1)

- Lucifer—"How you are fallen from heaven, O, Lucifer, son of morning!" (Isaiah 14:12)

- Power of Darkness—"Who hath delivered us from the power of darkness, and hath translated us into the kingdom of his dear Son.…" (Colossians 1:13)

- Prince of the Power of the Air—"Wherein in time past ye walked according to the course of this world, according to the prince of the power of the air, the spirit that now worketh in the children of disobedience.…" (Ephesians 2:2)

- Prince of This World—"Hereafter I will not talk much with you: for the prince of this world cometh, and hath nothing in me." (John 14:30)

- Satan—"And Satan stood up against Israel, and provoked David to number Israel." (1 Chronicles 21:1)

- The Serpent—"And the serpent said unto the woman, Ye shall not surely die.…" (Genesis 3:4)

- Son of Perdition—"Let no one deceive you by any means, for that Day will not come unless the falling away comes first, and the man of sin is revealed, the son of perdition, who opposes and exalts himself about all that is called God or that is worshipped.…" (2 Thessalonians 2:3–4)

- Star/Fallen Star—"Then the fifth angel sounded: And I saw a star fallen from heaven to the earth. To him was given the key to the bottomless pit." (Revelation 9:1)

- Tempter—"And when the tempter came to him, he said, 'If thou be the Son of God, command that these stones be made bread.'" (Matthew 4:3)

- The Thief—"The thief does not come except to steal, and to kill, and to destroy. I have come that they may have life, and that they may have it more abundantly." (John 10:10)

- Wicked One—"When any one heareth the word of the kingdom, and understandeth it not, then cometh the wicked one, and catcheth away that which was sown in his heart. This is he which received seed by the way side." (Matthew 13:19)

The Abrahamic religious traditions have had the most say in the evolution of the devil, which represents the archenemy of God, the divine. The ongoing battle between the Devil and God for the souls of humanity is the stuff not only of religious traditions and texts, but also of myths, fairy tales, folklore, and modern fiction, film, and television shows. Judaism doesn't have a strong concept of a devil, although the Old Testament looks upon him as the adversary to God and a fallen angel, so we look to Christianity and Islam for more detail on who or what he is, and that runs the gamut again from a fallen angel (Lucifer) to the Middle Eastern dark entities known as *djinn* or *jinn*, and all things in between.

Demons and dark angels are the minions of the Devil. We will get to those later. The Devil is a supernatural being and is often depicted as governing over Hell, in direct opposition to God in Heaven. If there is one thing the Devil is not, it's human, although more-modern fictional tales seem to enjoy portraying him as such. In the Old Testament, the Devil is responsible for death and possesses the sacred knowledge of good and evil, something humans were not supposed to catch on to. He is sometimes depicted in angelic form, as in the Watcher of the Book of Enoch, other times as an "evil spirit," and still other times as the ruler over angels who goes by the name Satan, Sataniel, and Satan'el. Some scholars suggest he may have been a fallen archangel, alongside his "good" fellow archangels Michael, Gabriel, Uriel, and Raphael.

Sometimes he is referred to as the Serpent that tempted Eve in the Garden of Eden, and other times he is called "Lucifer," a once-beautiful fallen angel that is now not only the torturer of souls in Hell but also himself tortured.

There are many names in the Bible for Satan.

Lucifer is the ruler over Hell, the fallen angels who serve him, and all who are unlucky enough to be sent there. But he himself is also a tortured prisoner there.

Satan is the devil that we know best. Though there is mention of Satan in the Old Testament (Chronicles and Job), most of our associations come from the New Testament of Christianity. The Devil goes by many faces even in just one religion: Christian beliefs vary from a personification of human evil and sin, to the Serpent of the Old Testament, to the head fallen/dark angel that oversees an army of lesser fallen angels. He may be the "dragon" of the Book of Revelation, or the "prince of the world" in John's Gospel, as opposed to the "prince of heaven," who is Christ. He is sometimes Lucifer, the Son of Morning referenced in Isaiah, and even Beelzebub, a god of the Philistines. There are even those who suggest that the God of the Old Testament was the Devil himself, due to his proclivity for violence, incest, bloodshed, rape, and warfare. Perhaps the idea of a devil as the opposite side of God makes sense in a dualistic belief system. Humans are capable of both good and evil. Why not our deity?

Early Christians, according to Paul Carus in *The History of the Devil and the Idea of Evil*, believed Satan to be the Prince of This World, and that idea dominated in the Church during the time pagan authorities remained in power. "As soon as they were replaced by Christian rulers, and when Christianity became the state religion of the Roman Empire, Satan was gradually dethroned and God reinstated in the government of the world." Carus also equates the idea of the *need* for a view of atonement of sin and the redemption from the terrors of hell, as he calls it, with the reason for the fear of evil that drove the organization of religious institutions during ancient Greek and

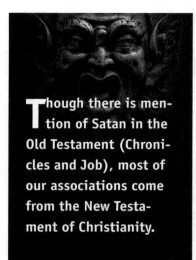

Though there is mention of Satan in the Old Testament (Chronicles and Job), most of our associations come from the New Testament of Christianity.

Roman times. "The ideas of evil sin, hell, salvation and immortal life were familiar to the Greek mind even before the days of Plato, but were still mixed up with traditional mythology." Carus goes on to say that when philosophers began waging war against the idolatry of Greek polytheism, "a fermentation set in which prepared the Greek nation for the reception of Christianity."

In an interview for *Live Science* in October 2016, Rabbi Abner Weiss, who is also a psychologist, said, "The ancient world struggled with the coexistence of good and evil…. They hypothesized a kind of demonic, divine force that was responsible for all evil, arising out of the notion that a good god could not be responsible for bad things." Though Satan was not a prominent figure in Judaism, he did appear as the tempter, the adversary, and one who challenges those who wonder how God could allow bad things to happen and not do anything about them.

The fear of punishment of evil, then, led to the formation of the Christian Church during ancient times as the institution responsible for delivering humanity from the clutches of evil, including Satan and his devilish ways. Interestingly, this same time period saw the rise of human sacrifices to serve as atonement for sins, a barbaric practice later abandoned or replaced with animal sacrifices.

SATAN

During the early years of Christianity and the rise of the Church, there are few reports of Church leaders rewarding good behavior, but plenty of rewarding bad, even with torture. Going over to "the dark side" had its price, which resulted in pagans going deeper "underground" to practice anything that might even hint of nature worship, as it might mistakenly be associated with Satan worship and love of the Devil and his ways. In the Bible, Satan appears in the Gospels as the tempter of Christ, with little background as to who he was and how he got into that position. Christian theologists then filled in the blanks by suggesting that if God created everything in the universe, and God was good, then Satan/the Devil was a good thing that went bad!

Going back to the Old Testament story of Adam and Eve, it was Satan who deceived and lied to Eve, tempting her with the fruit of forbidden knowledge that would set humanity's destiny in stone. Satan even tells Eve she will not die if she eats the forbidden fruit, and that her eyes will be "opened" to the knowledge of good and evil. She will become "godlike." Who could resist such a temptation?

Author and religious scholar Elaine Pagels wrote in her 1995 book, *The Origin of Satan*, that the concept of Satan often emerged when communities in the past split, with radical groups wanting a break from their enemies, their opposers. Thus, they would describe their enemies as Satan or devils that would face God's judgment one day. "Turning an enemy into Satan is useful because it suggests our opponents are not just people we disagree with—they're bad. You can't negotiate with them. You can't do anything with them, because they are essentially evil." This same tactic is used today in religion and politics to vilify the "others" as terrorists and extremists. The idea that "they" are evil, but "we" are not, is a hallmark of terrorism and extremism; pointing out the other's sins while denying one's own.

In fact, when human beings have major challenges, often their first instinct is to blame the Devil, even as the Devil himself is saying that if God truly loved his children, he would not bring such suffering down upon them. This perception of the Devil attempting to control behavior is where the power of faith arose from and is spoken of so much in the New Testament. If one believes in God, then it goes without saying that he or she will experi-

Are these soldiers brave heroes or devils? Calling your enemies evil or describing them as satanic is a tactic used to vilify your enemy. It is a matter of perspective.

ence the temptations of the Devil, which in turn will challenge the faith the person has in one deity over the other. Throughout the writings of Christianity, this battle, between the will of God and our own free will, which includes the ability to choose to act against God, continues to this day.

Islam's Satan

Islam has its own version of Satan in "Shaytan," or "Shaitan," an Arabic name that refers to demons that were under the command of Iblis, a fallen angel. Iblis is the original name for Satan, possibly derived from the Greek *diablos*, and meaning "desperate for God's mercy." Before his fall from divine grace, he went by "Azazel," a name that also shows up in the Book of Enoch and the Talmud as the head fallen angel who fornicated with earthly women and taught humans how to use magic and weapons. Islam states Satan was a creation of God, along with demons known as djinn, or jinn, which were made of smokeless fire. Satan was proud and bold and made humans think and do evil, but he held no power against God.

According to Islamic belief, after God made Adam, he commanded all to bow before his human creation, but one did not. That one was Satan, and God condemned Satan forever after that act of disobedience, even though Satan had a decent argument that humans were made of lowly clay and not fire. Then for some reason, Satan asked God's permission to cause evil in the world and lead people astray, which God accepted. Therefore, Satan and his jinn were not cast out or rejected in the formal sense but instead were punished for questioning the authority of humans and for disobeying a divine order.

Muslims worship the creator God, Allah, and not the material world of creation that is represented as evil and the realm of Satan. However, Satan also represents truth-seeking and intelligence, which were believed to be against God because for humans and demons to have that truth and knowledge meant they were tasting of the same Tree of Knowledge that caused Adam and Eve to be cast out from the Garden of Eden.

One of the angels of Islam is Maalik, whose job is to guard the gates of Hell and watch over sinners who rejected the teachings of Muhammad the Prophet. Along with his nineteen guard angels, Maalik tortures the poor souls of Hell as punishment for their sins. But one can escape the wrath of Maalik by reciting the words, "Allah, the Compassionate, the Merciful," which are the opening words of the Koran, known as "bismillah." Those lucky enough to say these words will then be relieved of torture. The rest are doomed to all eternity in Hell.

WHERE DID SATAN COME FROM?

Allegedly, he began as a beautiful light, an angel in heaven alongside God, until he sinned in ways that got him expelled, cast down upon the earth and into the Hell he became lord over. In Ezekiel 28:15–16, it says, "You were perfect in your ways from the day you were created, till iniquity was found in you.… By the abundance of your trading you became filled with violence within and you sinned; therefore I cast you as a profane thing out of the mountain of God." In Isaiah 14:12, we read, "How you are fallen from heaven, O Lucifer, son of the morning! How you are cut down to the ground, you who weakened the nations." The Devil/Satan/Lucifer came from the very place the angels and God himself did. Ephesians 2:2 refers to him as "the prince of the power of the air, the spirit who now works in the sons of disobedience." Angel of Light. Prince of the Air. Proud beautiful angel. Satan's origins show that at one time, he was revered for reasons other than sin and disorder. His ultimate purpose? To challenge faith, attempt to sway believers, and to provide a duality to the good of God and his son, the Christ. His field is the world, as stated in

An illustration by Gustave Doré (for John Milton's *Paradise Lost*) depicting Lucifer being expelled from Heaven by the Archangel Gabriel.

Matthew 13:37–39, upon which he operates with the same deceptions that got him cast out from the heavens and turned into God's arch enemy.

From the time Adam and Eve were cast out of the Garden because of the deception of the serpent, representing Satan, the Devil has been at work on a mission to counter good with evil, long after his rebellion in Heaven got him a black mark on his record. In the story of Job, we see the Devil constantly asking for access to the protected man and his family, as a challenge to his servitude toward God. Poor Job was subjected to the tests of Satan to see whether his faith in God would stand up, and his health was used as a pawn between God and Satan to see whom the human would remain faithful to. Job holds fast to his faith in God, even through the worst physical pain, even after his wife begs for mercy to stop the pain.

This pattern of the Devil, going by the name of Satan, choosing to test humans and challenge their faith and devotion to God is seen throughout the stories of the Old and New Testaments. In 1 Chronicles 21:1, we see Satan attempting to influence events, not just people. "Now Satan stood up against Israel, and moved David to number Israel." Satan strove to be a powerful influence not just on those who were considered leaders but on the actual events they were involved in, as well.

Lucifer or Venus?

Historians and scholars have long debated who Lucifer really was. Maybe he wasn't a person at all. There is some argument that the original Lucifer was the "son of dawn" referred to in the Old Testament's Book of Isaiah (14:12), which references the king of Babylon as the "day star." The passage in question reads: "How are you fallen from heaven, day star, son of the dawn!"

In astronomical terms, the day star, or star of dawn, is the planet Venus, whose brightness so early in the morning would inspire such reverence. In Latin, Venus was "the light bringer"—*lucem ferre,* or "bringer of light." Could the king of Babylon have been given the name "day star" because he shone so brightly, but not at night with the other stars?

Because "Lucifer" is not a Hebrew name, and only makes its appearance in the Old Testament Book of Isaiah, a Hebrew manuscript

The planet Venus is also called the Day Star, which in the Bible has also been used to refer to the king of Babylon and to Lucifer, or Satan.

written *before* there was a Roman language, confusion reigns. But the close parallels found in the Book of Isaiah (14:12–14) between Lucifer and the king of Babylon are actually more frequent than those attaching the name Lucifer to the Devil, which seems to have occurred much later when Christianity merged Lucifer with its version of Satan, the Devil.

In Roman astronomy, Lucifer was Venus, the morning star before it was renamed Venus after the goddess. It heralded the rising of the sun each dawn. In the passage in Isaiah, the word is used to describe the King of Babylon before his death with the Hebrew word *Helal,* which is "Son of Shahar," which is then translated to "Day star, son of the Dawn." Possibly, scholars writing the King James translation using translations made in the fourth century by St. Jerome simply mistranslated the actual appearance of the morning star as a metaphor, and the morning star, the day star that appears at dawn, became the fallen angel cast from Heaven to Hell below.

Adding even more confusion are early references to Christ as the morning star, such as the passage in Revelation 22:16 in which he says, "I am the root and the offspring of David, and the bright and morning star." Add to that other phrases in the Hebrew texts that spoke of a shining star, son of dawn, shining one, all of which at the time referred to Venus.

The Theosophical University Press writes that "Lucifer" meant "light-bringer" and reiterates that the name is found only once in the Bible, in Isaiah 14:12, but only in the King James and later versions. "How are thou fallen from heaven, O Lucifer, son of the morning!" "O shining star of the Dawn!" "O morning star, son of the dawn!" All are found in various translations of the Hebrew text. "The King James version is based on the Vulgate, the Latin translation of Jerome. Jerome translated the Hebrew 'Helel' (bright or brilliant one) as 'Lucifer' which was a reasonable Latin equivalent."

Other references suggest that because Venus was associated with pagan, solar cults and the "feminine," the name was given a negative connotation when the Roman church did away with the link to the planet altogether. This same possible association may even go back to the Zoroastrian myth of the sun god Mithra conquering the divine feminine Venus, which may equate to the archangel Michael conquering Lucifer in the biblical story. Solar cults that focused on the power of the female/matriarch were eventually replaced, often violently, with masculine monotheistic belief systems that cast out the feminine from the seats of power—just as Lucifer was cast out of his heavenly place with God.

So the Latin *Lucifer,* which means Venus, morphed into the king of Babylon, a bright and powerful light who then faded (just as Venus does when morning breaks) into the name given the beautiful angel that turned against God and fell from the heavens. St. Jerome's translations may have been the originating point of Lucifer's association with Satan and the Devil. This is but one example of how so much of our history, religious or otherwise, has been structured around the interpretation, and later misinterpretation, of words, phrases, metaphors, and concepts that had pagan and natural origins, especially those labeled or categorized as evil or negative to promote a specific ideology.

Later Jesus himself is tempted by the Devil, after announcing he will retreat to the desert for a test of his flesh and spirit. Matthew 4:8 begins a passage about the Devil showing Jesus all the kingdoms of the world and the glory he could have if he would but rebuke his Father, God. "Again, the devil took him upon an exceedingly high mountain and showed him all the kingdoms of the world and their glory. And he said to him, 'All these things I will give you if you will fall down and worship me.'" Jesus rebuked Satan instead, saying, "Away with you, Satan! For it is written, 'You shall worship the Lord your God, and him only shall you serve.'" Satan leaves, defeated in trying to sway Jesus with the pleasures of materialism, power, and greed. Jesus would tell his Apostles to resist the temptations of the Devil, who would then flee.

We do see in both Christianity and Islam the expulsion of Satan from heaven, which must have left his massive ego quite bruised, thus leading to a vengeful, evil personality. However, Islam's version of Satan states he was not really an angel at all, but perhaps a jinn. Angels do not have the free will to determine choosing evil over good. But the nasty jinn did and as a result were kicked out of paradise. The eminent seventh-century Muslim theologian Hasan of Basra even wrote, "Iblis was not an angel even for the time of an eye wink. He is the origin of Jinn as Adam is of Mankind." This would place the devil of the Koran more on the level of humans than of a major deity. In fact, being considered equal to humans made the Devil mad because he believed himself to be better than lowly humans who were made of clay, when he himself was created of fire.

DEMONS, THE DEVIL, AND FALLEN ANGELS

Knowing where Satan came from brings up the question: What happens to the Devil in Christianity in the end of time? His destiny is one that causes both joy and grief for Christians. The Book of Revelation tells of the capture of Satan, who will be bound up for a thousand years, during which time the judgment of the righteous will take place. In Revelation 20:3 we see that after he is bound for this period, though, he will be unleashed upon the world again. In Revelation 20:7–10 we are told that when the thousand years of bondage have expired, "Satan will be released from his prison and will go out to deceive the nations which are the four corners of the earth, Gog and Magog, to gather them together to battle, whose number is as the sand of the sea." This battle will result in the Last Judgment after Christ reigns for a thousand years, shattering peace with all-out earthly and heavenly war until God finally casts Satan into a lake of fire to writhe in eternal damnation and torment.

So while evil is said to have its time, it is always submissive in the end to the forces of good.

WHAT DID SATAN LOOK LIKE?

So, what did Satan physically look like? It has been said that he had the appearance of everything from a beautiful angel to a serpent to a human-like entity with a goat or ram's head and horns, reminiscent of the pagan roots of Christianity and the "Horned God" called Pan. Because all religions have paganism at their roots, it helps to look further back to the concept of a deity in mythology and folklore that represented sexual reproduction and fertility, our more natural roots and beliefs, decadence and hedonism, and the trickster spirit … all of which were at odds with the desired behaviors of the good guys! Pagans were thought to worship nature, and thus were inferior in the view of religions that looked upon nature as crude, primal, and undesirable—something to be controlled and overcome rather than something to be revered and cherished.

Folklore tends to look at the Devil as more playful and mischievous than pure evil, although his playfulness is indeed destructive and sometimes even malevolent. He went by names like Old Nick, Scratch, Old Hob, the Stranger, and even Trickster and had many nasty characteristics mixed in with a little seductive charm and humor. Because folklore has more pagan roots intact, the Devil in the lore was closer to the entities found in pagan beliefs and caused more trouble than outright harm or appealed to the baser instincts of humans, including their sexual desires and lusts. In fact, during the Middle and Dark ages, witches accused of consorting with the Devil were burned at the stake and tortured, mainly for practicing the pagan arts of using herbs and potions, medicine, and healing. Often they would be persecuted simply for having their menstrual cycles, which all women had, thus making them all possible targets for accusations of witchcraft and being considered dirty and evil. True witches don't believe in Satan, and never did, because the Devil was a concept of religious traditions foreign to nature worship. Thus, the Horned God of witchcraft and paganism was hijacked into a devil when Christianity became the accepted state-sponsored religion across the world, and those who worshipped the Horned God fought, and still fight, misrepresentations and misinterpretations of their naturalistic beliefs. The Goddess traditions suffered as well from the death of matriarchal societies around the rise of the age of agriculture and the more widespread development of written language, which allowed false information and outright propaganda to be spread more freely.

There was a time when simply being looked at with lust by a man on the path to the local goods provider meant that a young woman would meet her awful death at the hands of those who thought her to be in cahoots with the Devil. Interesting how the lustful men were never put to death!

A c. 1500 drawing of Satan has him appear as an ugly monster.

Eastern traditions have entirely different ideas about gods and devils and even good and evil. The Gautama Buddha was tempted with visions of gorgeous women while seeking enlightenment by a dark distractor named Mara, who may just be a figurative interpretation of the death of the ego for the sake of spiritual growth. Temptation again played a key role in the Garden of Eden, where Eve ruined everything by taking the apple from the serpent and she and Adam ate from the Tree of Knowledge. Temptation and the Devil go hand-in-hand.

Hinduism has more than one deity, so it has no real dualistic, evil opposer to a God. Instead, Hindus have different entities that cause suffering and evil in the world. There are asuras, or negative beings, that can incarnate and cause chaos, such as Rahu, but in turn there will be a counter-incarnation of Vishnu, an avatar sent to defeat that evil presence. Avatars such as Krishna and Rama are incarnated to battle evil and its forces in the world.

THE NUMBER OF THE BEAST

The Devil of the Christian Bible, especially the Book of Revelation, or the Apocalypse of John as it's known in the Greek version, even had a number. That number is recorded as 666, "the number of the Beast," in Revelation 13:15–18, and it will be found on the body of the one deemed the Antichrist. "Here is wisdom. Let him that hath understanding count the number of the beast," the passage states. However, some theologians believe the correct number is actually 616 and has been misinterpreted by scholars. Regardless, the beast has a number or marker by which his identity is to be known.

In the New International Version (NIV), Revelation 13:15–18 reads:

15 The second beast was given power to give breath to the image of the first beast, so that the image could speak and cause all who refused to worship the image to be killed. 16 It also forced all people, great and small, rich and poor, free and slave, to receive a mark on their right hands or on their foreheads, 17 so that they could not buy or sell unless they had the mark, which is the name of the beast or the number of its name. 18 This calls for wisdom. Let the person who has insight calculate the number of the beast, for it is the number of a man. That number is 666.

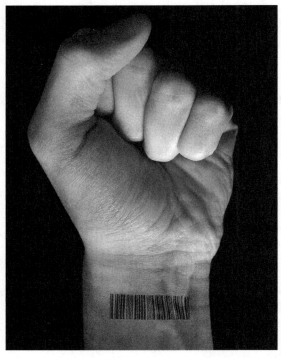

Some conspiracy theorists think one day people will be forced to have some kind of implant or tattoo for identification that will actually be the mark of the Beast.

Conspiracy theorists suggest the mark of the Beast is a mark that all humans will one day receive and that will determine who will be able to purchase goods. Some say the chipped debit and credit cards we use globally might actually be that Beast, determining who can buy and sell and who can't. The number 666 has become a feared number because of this association, although in Chinese belief, it is considered a lucky or beneficial number!

Some suggest 666, which adds up to the master number of 9 (adds to 18, then add the 1 and the 8 to get the master number of 9), is a poke at the Holy Trinity in triplicate. The Trinity of the Father, Son, and the Holy Spirit is a triad describing the personage of God himself and is considered a powerful and sacred use of the perfect number, 3. Three sixes add up to 18, which adds to 9, as if the Antichrist's identifying mark were a tripled blasphemy of the "face" of God. Numerologists will point to the importance of number symbolism; our ancient ancestors were steeped in the traditions of both numerology and astrology, both involving numbers, number sequences, and symbolisms assigned to each number.

Even today, scholars still do not fully understand the meaning or symbolism of the 666 sequence. The only person who would know for sure would be John of Patmos, the author of the wildly imaginative, apocalyptic Revelation text, and he isn't talking. John's actual identity is itself up for debate, with scholars agreeing only that he must have been a Christian prophet. The entire Book of Revelation is filled with powerful and dreamlike symbolism, suggesting that John may have written down a dream or series of dreams, which may be more allegorical than historical in content.

The Serpent

Another interesting association with the Devil comes in the origin story of Adam and Eve. In Genesis 3:14–15, we are told of the Devil's introductory appearance in the Old Testament in the form of a snake or serpent that tempts Adam and Eve in the Garden of Eden into eating the forbidden fruit of the Tree of Knowledge of Good and Evil. This decadent act, which Eve initiates, gets both Adam and Eve booted from the Garden with a strong admonition for allowing sin to come into being. It also gave humans, lowly as they were, the knowledge of life and death and the duality of existence, which included good and evil. Up to that point, only God was a known entity. The Serpent came along with an apple and the Devil made them do it, eat of the knowledge once available only to the "gods."

Interestingly, in Revelation 12:9, there is a reference again to an "ancient serpent called the devil, or Satan, the one deceiving the whole world" that "was thrown down to the earth with all his angels," suggesting that the Devil is also a fallen angel.

It's easy to see why the Devil would have been portrayed as a serpent. The snake played important roles in ancient Greek, Mesopotamian, and Egyptian traditions and was thought to be a symbol of power, evil, greed, and the world of the dead. Perhaps because many snakes have a poisonous bite, that toxic quality was attached symbolically

St. George slays the dragon (a version of the serpent) in this sculpture seen at the Church of the Nativity in Bethlehem.

Lilith: Queen of She-Demons

Most demons appear to be male, but there are female demons that are just as notorious and dangerous as their manly counterparts. These demons devour children, tear apart grown men, and appear either as horrific and ugly beasts or hags, or as beautiful and mesmerizing creatures that men cannot resist.

Among the she-demons, Lilith reigns supreme. Her name is from the Sumerian *lilitu,* or female wind-and-storm spirit/demon, as well as *lilith* or *lilit* in Hebrew for "night demon/spirit," and she is the most notorious of demons in Hebrew tradition, even referenced as a hag. She is one of the most ancient of demonic entities, mentioned both in the Bible and the Talmud, and even in the *Epic of Gilgamesh,* dating back as far as 2100 B.C.E. Today she has an all-female rock festival in her name. She may have originated in the Mesopotamian region, as mention of her is found in cuneiform texts of Sumer, Akkad, Assyria, and Babylonia.

Lilith appeared around the same time in a number of early Jewish sources. In the Talmud of ancient Babylonia, she is a dark and dangerously sexual spirit that makes demons out of sperm she fertilizes herself, thus giving her the name "Mother of Demons." But she is best known as Adam's first wife, thanks to Jewish folklore and a book of satire called *Alphabet of Ben Sira,* written approximately 700–1000 C.E., in which she was described as being created along with Adam out of the same dirt in Genesis 1:27, rather than from his rib, as Eve was in Genesis 2:22. Rabbinical writings often suggest Lilith was the first feminist, as she wanted her independence from Adam in the Garden! This biblical reference is most associated with Lilith today by people suggesting she was the first woman, and not Eve, for, as Genesis 1:27 states, "So God created man in his own image, in the image of God created he him, male and female created he them."

The legends surrounding Lilith grew over time, with stories of her defying Adam and, instead of lying beneath him, leaving the Garden of Eden, to return later after having sex with Archangel Samael. In earlier Mesopotamian writings, she is often associated with a tree and represents the branches of a tree along with other demons. Throughout Mesopotamian mythology and early Jewish folklore, she was considered the representation of sexual temptation, disease, death, sickness, storms, and even terrorizing young children, as written in Jewish mystical writings.

Babylonian texts depict her as a prostitute for the goddess Ishtar. Sumerian accounts reference her as a handmaiden to the goddess Inanna, but that she was also a beautiful prostitute that Inanna would send into the fields and streets to lead men astray.

There have been many artistic renditions of Lilith over the centuries, including this painting by Pre-Raphaelite Brotherhood artist Dante Gabriel Rosetti, who depicts her as a femme fatale.

Continued...

(continued from previous page)

An ancient Hebrew tradition holds that a boy must wait three years before his hair is cut so that Lilith will think the child is a girl and spare his life. In the *Gilgamesh* epic poem, she is mentioned as having wings and dark hair, but many art depictions show her as either a dark and ugly demon or a beautiful woman worthy of the title of the first independent, sexually aware mother of humanity.

Lilith is revered in modern ceremonial magic, where she is described as being lusty and dark with black wings and lips as red as roses, and especially in Luciferianism and neo-paganism. She is considered a consort of Lucifer and called the Queen of the Succubi. Her mating with Samael, the fallen angel, produced an offspring known as the "Goat of Mendes," or "Baphomet," as it is better known, and she, Samael, and Cain form the Luciferian trinity.

Pagans look to Lilith as a revered example of a Dianic priestess or a chief among witches, along with Isis, Inanna, Asherah, and Ishtar.

as well, giving the snake a bad rap in the religious rituals and texts that originated in those regions.

However, the snake/serpent also represented fertility, nature, and even healing in a more-pagan worldview and very easily could have gotten its negative spin from the later absconding of pagan beliefs into Christianity. Many pagan symbols went from being positive and natural to negative and evil, once the state religion was established. Rabbinical tradition looks at the snake or serpent as a symbol of sexual desire, once again equating the baser parts of natural existence, including fornication, with something bad or evil or sinful. In the story of Adam and Eve, once they knew of the ways of the gods, they also knew of sex and probably began having more of it! Sexuality has often been associated with the darker side of human nature, even though it is, like many pagan fertility-driven beliefs, perfectly natural. "Then your eyes shall be opened and ye shall be as gods, knowing good and evil" states Genesis 3:5. The Devil made them do it!

Serpents have also been associated with monsters, beasts (as in Revelation) and dragons, and in addition to the Satanic association, they were also identified with the female demon, Lilith, who was thought to be Adam's first wife.

A serpent called Ouroboros represents infinity, seen in a circle with its tail in its mouth. This symbolic serpent harkens back to the pagan cycle of birth, life, death, and rebirth, and also the concept of immortality. Ouroboros may have challenged God's superpower, thus giving the serpent a bad reputation in the animal kingdom. Any animal that suggested it could live beyond death was making a vain attempt to usurp the ultimate power of God. Serpent-cult objects and statues dating back thousands of years suggest that the creature was a conveyor of life and death, a god or deity in and of itself. Later Christians labeled it a somewhat blasphemous pagan-influenced challenge to the power of the One True God.

The circular Ouroborus grasping onto its own tail represents infinity.

Another noted biblical mention of the serpent as devil comes from Psalm 91:11–13, in which the Lord is tempted by the Devil and defeats and triumphs over the "dragon." In fact, the Lord tramples the dragon under foot, along with a lion, asp, and basilisk, all of which are symbolic interpretations of the Devil, seen in iconography of the Late Antique and Early Medieval periods. Luke 10:19 refers to the serpent as a "deadly, subtle, malicious enemy." This description may have led to the modern interpretation of someone who is malicious as a "snake in the grass."

However, as much as the Devil in serpent form was hated and reviled, he was also viewed as a symbol of wisdom in Hebrew tradition and a necessary piece of the puzzle that would become the mythology of Christianity and the coming of Christ. Without the Devil as an adversary, Christ would not have been able to become the iconic religious hero. Every protagonist needs an antagonist.

Though most of our concepts and beliefs about the Devil come to us from Christianity, Elaine Pagels says in *The Origin of Satan* that belonging to a particular religious tradition no longer necessarily requires a "Devil" on which to blame the evils of the world. "Many religious people who no longer believe in Satan, along with countless others who do not identify with any religious tradition, nevertheless are influenced by his cultural legacy whenever they perceive social and political conflict in terms of the forces of good contending against the forces of evil in the world." We look at modern warfare, poverty, violence, rape, mass shootings, child murders, and other aberrations of humanity as being evil, and the works of something dark and "against the light," even if we don't ascribe responsibility for them to Satan himself. In fact, much of what is evil today might instead be an entirely human endeavor.

DEMONS

When it comes to the Devil's underlings, things get even more complicated. Demons are the battlebots of the Devil, the minions and ground troops. There are dozens, if not hundreds, of names of demons associated with different religions, myths, and geographical regions. A list is below, but it is in no way exhaustive, for demons can manifest in a variety of ways and means, each with its own purpose or destructive characteristic. From the Greek word *daimon,* demons are believed to be unclean spirits, unknown entities that can possess human souls, and fallen angels. Basically, any dark entity that is not the Devil himself is a demon, a malevolent and supernatural creature that once had more pagan roots and fewer evil inclinations.

Pagans often created statues and figurines around the deities that they worshipped, and later Roman Catholics looked upon these *daimones,* the Greek plural for demons, as something negative, simply because they did not fit into the new Christian dogma. Once again, a pagan object of worship was turned into a Christian object of evil and disdain, showing that the root histories of many demons are not as frightening as they evolved to be later when pagan traditions were all but wiped off the map. What was once an object of reverence and even beauty to the pagans was reinterpreted as a representation of evil by those who conquered them. Again, we saw that with the Horned God and Pan, morphed into Satan and Baphomet, who sports a ram's head and is associated with Satanic practices.

There are demonologists who say that it is dangerous to speak aloud the name of a demon for it might provoke an appearance or possession. This, they say, will happen whether or not you actually believe in devils and demons and their ability to manifest so easily. By speaking a name of something you give it power. This primitive belief is also found in aboriginal traditions that call an object into being by singing its name. And recall that the entirety of creation in the Book of Genesis began with the Logos, the Word of God. The sound of creation itself.

> There are demonologists who say that it is dangerous to speak aloud the name of a demon for it might provoke an appearance or possession.

But also keep in mind, according to the website "Gods and Monsters": "Most of the ancient gods of myth were considered 'daemons' at some point. It wasn't until Catholicism came into power that we get the same interpretation that we have today." So, whatever power the name of a demon may have might be suggestive indeed and based upon your own beliefs. Be warned!

HOLIDAY DEMONS

Today, we might encounter demons of technology and social networking, which threaten to swallow up our time, attention, and energy! Not to mention demons associated with certain holidays, such as Halloween and Christmas. Christmas, you say? Imagine a demonic "anti-Santa" that punishes children at the holiday season by swatting naughty children with a bundle of birch sticks … or worse. Early pagan traditions often incorporated both an entity that rewarded children for being good, and his or her counterpart, which punished them for being bad. The duality of good and evil spawned legends of such sinister beings, some of whom actually accompanied the good St. Nicholas, going door to door to check up on children and gauge their behavior.

The legend of Krampus (see sidebar) comes to us from Norse mythology. From the German word *krampen*, meaning "claw," Krampus was thought to be the son of Hel in Norse myth. German folklore turned Krampus into a full-fledged counterpart of St. Nicholas, constructing the story of how he turns up on Krampusnacht, December 6, to reward good children with sweets and punish bad children with beatings and terror after kidnapping them and taking them to his lair. Austrian legend tells of Krampus Night on December 5, when both Krampus and St. Nick would walk the cobblestone streets together and bring blessings or curses.

The Germanic and Norse peoples celebrated Christmas starting early in December several hundred years ago, encouraging children to behave even before Christmas Eve and Day. Krampus shares characteristics with both demons and pagan deities such as Pan, as well as various fauns and satyrs, and gave the story of St. Nicholas the good a dualistic counterpart, just as God has his devil and Satan his Christ.

Other versions of the anti-Santa include Jólakötturinn, the Christmas Cat. This Icelandic tradition centers on a wicked cat that encouraged children to work hard by rewarding those who did with new clothes. But if you were lazy, you would be sacrificed to the Yule Cat. Germany and Austria had their Frau Perchta, an ugly, demonic witch who rewarded and punished children accordingly during the twelve days before Christmas. Her punishment included tearing out the inner organs of children and replacing them with garbage. She may have had more pagan roots originating with a legendary Alpine goddess of nature, as most Christian holiday traditions borrowed greatly from nature beliefs and lore.

Another Icelandic tradition involves Grýla, the mother of the Yule Lads. The Yule Lads were thirteen trolls that stole things and created chaos at Christmas, scaring children into behaving well. Their mother, Grýla, was said to be an ogress who kidnapped, cooked, and ate bad children who disobeyed their parents. She apparently had three different husbands and a total of seventy-two children, all of whom had their own special brand of mayhem. And the Yule Cat was her pet.

Grýla is an Icelandic troll who scares children straight and causes a certain amount of chaos during the Christmas season.

France had its own traditions, including Père Fouettard, "Father Whipper," who was an evil butcher. He loved to eat children and lured three boys to his shop, where he brutally chopped them up and salted them. St. Nicholas came to their rescue, resurrecting the boys (note the Christ reference here) before making Pere his servant.

In the Netherlands during the Middle Ages, St. Nicholas wore crimson episcopal vestments and rode into town on a white horse carrying a gold miter. He was followed by a black-faced horned being called "Black Peter." He often looked like a Moor, which at the time was a personification of the Devil. St. Nicholas would reward good children, and Black Peter would whip bad children with a switch and tell them they were going to Hell. Interestingly, during the Spanish occupation in the sixteenth century, Black Peter stopped threatening to take bad children to Hell and instead told them he would take them to Spain!

Similar to this is the Cert, a black-dressed demon carrying a whip and chains that terrorized bad children in Czechoslovakia. Cert rode with St. Nicholas and a good angel from Heaven to distribute rewards and punishments. Sometimes the demon that accompanied St. Nick was female, as in the legends of Bercheel, Perchte, Pudelmutter, and Buzebergt.

In all of these rather disturbing traditions, we see the dual nature of good and evil played out with two beings that parallel God and Satan, even Christ and the Antichrist. The job of anti-Santas was to use ugly, terrifying, and demonic beasts to scare children into behaving, because fear was, and still is, a strong motivator. Yet one has to wonder how many children remained scarred for life from these harrowing tales, even if they did grow up to discover they were not true.

In Greece, a Christmas lamp called the sharkantalos was kept lit for the twelve days before Christmas to protect the home from demons such as the Kallikantzaroi, half-human trolls that chopped away all year at the roots of trees that bore up the earth. On Christmas, the tree roots would be renewed by the rebirth of Christ, releasing spiteful Kallikantzaroi to search for people who had overeaten and fallen asleep. The Kallikantzaroi would then beat the sleeping people senseless and even ride on people's backs or force them to dance until they dropped with exhaustion. The lamp was symbolic for the light that dispelled darkness and for the Christ, or light of the world, that drove away demons.

Holiday demons such as the above are rooted in older myths and pagan stories and folklore, and yet often have stood the test of time to continue to be celebrated today, and even become the subject of pop-culture movies, such as *Krampus*. Today, however, we no longer punish children who are bad at Christmas with stories of potential torture, dismemberment, and abuse. We just put coal in their stockings.

Krampus the Christmas Devil

BY DAVID WEATHERLY

He arrives in December after preparing all year. Trudging through the snow with a bag slung over his shoulder, he visits children around the world. He's all-knowing, all-seeing, and as the saying goes, "He knows if you've been bad or good, so be good for goodness' sake."

After all, misbehaving children get pitched into his basket and taken away. You see, it's not jolly old Saint Nick we're talking about, it's Krampus.

Yes, Virginia, there is a Christmas devil!

The Krampus is a counterpart to Saint Nick and is charged with punishing bad kids on Krampus Night a few weeks before Christmas.

The legend of Krampus originates in Europe's Alpine countries, many of which still celebrate him to this day. In early depictions, Krampus stood seven feet tall, had cloven feet, long horns, and was covered in black or brown fur. His name was derived from the term "Krampen," meaning claw, and he was likely derived from the pagan god of the hunt, a primal nature spirit, wild and untamed.

Krampus was used to frighten children into being good. If they were mean or naughty, if they didn't go to sleep when they were told, then Krampus might come and take them away in his bag.

With the spread of Christianity, the image of Krampus began to change. From a wild, shaggy beast, the holiday demon took on an image more akin to modern views of the Devil. Once he made his way to the United States, he became less sinister and more of a mischievous devil. Decked out in a suit instead of fur, a long red tongue, devilish horns, and red skin, he became the new form of the Christmas figure.

German businessmen began importing Krampus holiday cards to the United States and the Devil became a popular naughty symbol of the holidays. With this change, Krampus came to represent the Devil, who had been captured and forced to work for the powers of good. Now, in servitude to the benevolent St. Nicholas, Krampus became the antithesis to Santa Claus, responsible for punishing children who had misbehaved.

While Santa passed out candy and toys, Krampus was given the power to punish the bad children, a task he enjoyed very much. He could take away presents left by St. Nick and leave the child nothing but a lump of coal. He could dole out other punishments too, such as beating children with switches from a birch tree. In some places, if children were especially bad, Krampus would stuff them into his bag and carry them off to Hell.

Over the years, as the lore of Santa Claus evolved, elements of the Krampus legend were woven into St. Nick's story. In modern times, it is Santa who has the naughty list, checking it twice before leaving gifts.

There's been a resurgence of interest in the Krampus legend all over the world, reflected in pop culture and a slew of horror movies. Once again, people are celebrating "Krampusnacht" or "Krampus Night" on December 5. Men dressed as Krampus wander through the streets for Krampus parades, rattling rusty chains and ringing cowbells. With a branch from a birch tree, they take swats at anyone in their path. The festivals are dedicated to warding off evil spirits and bringing fortune and prosperity to the community.

Ironically, the Christmas devil's popularity continues to grow, and perhaps, with time, his story will again stand separate from St. Nick's. Imagine how children will feel once it's known again that a holiday demon is watching to see whether they're good or bad.

(David Weatherly is the author of *Strange Intruders* and *The Black-Eyed Children*. His website is http://twocrowsparanormal.blog spot.com/.)

Another Germanic anti-Santa is Belsnickel, who is still celebrated in Pennsylvania Dutch country in the United States. This hobo in rags was known to travel around with candy for good children and a tree branch to whip bad children with.

Demons can be actual entities, with names and histories, but they can also represent dark energies or forces that work through human beings, as we will see in a later chapter. Can energy; itself be evil? Physicists tell us energy is not good or evil, but just energy, therefore we must assume that it's the forces behind the use of that energy, or the intention behind it, that can be judged good or evil. So a demon might have no form at all, but manifest in a black, ugly, dreadful energetic imprint or influence on a person, in a home or building, or within society as a force operating en masse in the world in such things as hatred, intolerance, violence, abuse, greed, and warfare between populations, nations, religions, and races.

It may very well be that the demons we can see, feel, hear, and interact with are far less deadly than those we cannot.

WORLD MYTHS AND FOLKLORE

Africa

Southern African Bush tribes believe that Guana is the ruler of the Underworld. Guana is the enemy of Cagn, or the god that created the world. Guana comes to Earth to cause trouble with humanity and take people against their will to the realm of the dead. He might also make the spirits of the dead haunt their own families!

Abiku was a ravenous demon of the Yoruba tribe of Nigeria and Benin. He was thought to eat humans and especially liked children, but incredibly, he was easily driven away by the sound of bells. Adro was an African god of evil to the people of Zaire and Uganda. Once the nasty opposing deity to the Creator God, Adroa, Adro lived in the world's rivers among the snakes and produced an evil son, Adroanzi, from a slit in his side. Gaunab was a God of misfortune, evil, death, and disease. He is called an unspeakable evil force in the mythology of the Xhosa of South Africa and Namibia, even though he is also the force behind rainbows!

Asia

Nian is known as a beast with the body of a bull and the head of a lion in Chinese folklore. On Chinese New Year, Nian was said to come down from its mountain lair to the villages below and eat the crops, livestock, and even people until its hunger abated. Eventually, villagers left food out for Nian on their front stoops so that Nian would spare their lives. The villagers also used the color red and loud noises to keep Nian at bay, hanging red lanterns above doorways and windows and setting off firecrackers nearby.

Nian statues are often seen in Chinese architecture, such as this one outside the Forbidden City. The creature has the head of a lion and body of a bull.

Another Chinese legend involves the souls of the dead that either choose to become good spirits, known as shen, or malevolent ones, known as gui. The gui are demons who wander around the earth as evil ghostly entities, because their families did not provide them with a proper funeral or burial.

Japan brings us the legend of the Agi Bridge demon, which lurked under the bridge and attacked an egotistical, boisterous man who refused to believe in it. When the man crossed over the bridge as a way of proving to his friends there was no demon, the demon shape-shifted into an old woman who needed help. As the man went to help her, the demon turned into a nine-foot beast with green skin who chased the man off the bridge. But the man got away and ran home. Then one night the demon appeared at the man's door in the form of his own brother. The man let him in, and the demon bit off the man's head, then held it up for the family to see before vanishing.

Japanese mythology tells of the Oni, demons as big and strong as giants, but with square horned heads, sharp teeth, claws, and three eyes. They are cruel and cause great chaos for anyone who encounters them, but legend has it they are also capable of becoming good, and some have even gone on to become Buddhist monks! The Kappas were water demons in Japanese mythology that looked like monkeys with heads shaped like saucers. Their skin was yellow-green. Their heads were filled with water, but if the water spilled out in any way, the Kappas would lose their superpowers and be easily defeated.

Throughout India, there are many demonic beings, most of which we will cover under the Hindu religion, which is rife with stories, legends, and myths. One of the most terrifying were the Vetala of India. The beings were believed to be terrifying vampire creatures that were said to be dead, but not at rest, for they did not have a normal funeral. They would occupy corpses and live in cemeteries, venturing out to kill children and livestock to feed upon. Their hands and feet were said to be turned backwards.

Australia and New Zealand

The Aborigines of Australia have a rich pantheon of deities that are responsible for creating the natural world. Like other more nature-based cultures, they often represent a particular aspect of the natural world, or a part of human nature. The Gurumukas are a bizarre vampire demon with long, spindly limbs and sharp teeth. Though they are vampiric, they were said to be cowards and would often have to sneak up on their prey.

Another vampire demon is Yara-Ma-Yha-Who. He appears as a short red man with no teeth, which can be a problem for a vampire! When a human would stop under a tree to rest, this demon would jump down upon the person to suck his or her blood via suckers on its hand and feet, much like an octopus.

The Bunyip is a spirit monster that sleeps in rivers, swamps, and waterways and prowls the land at night, looking for human and animal prey. It has

The Bunyip is a demon from Australian folklore that inhabits swamps and rivers and preys on people and animals.

an awful scream and can take the appearance of a snakelike human, which could represent a now-extinct predator from Australia's past, similar to the Muldjewangk of Southern Australia. This water monster has been blamed for boat accidents and attacks on people who get too close to the Murray River. Many of the myths of the region involve creatures that could easily fall into the category of cryptozoology—strange lake and land beasts that could have been wild creatures the Aborigines mistook for something demonic and sinister.

British Isles

In Ireland, there is a legend that speaks of a dark man who comes to foretell death. This legendary figure is known as the Dullahan, and he rides a black horse with fiery eyes, while carrying his head under his arm, much like the legend of the Headless Horseman from the American Northeast as told in Washington Irving's "The Legend of Sleepy Hollow." The Dullahan has the power to speak your name, much like the Grim Reaper himself, and once this is done you will die soon thereafter. Also, the Dullahan is tasked with punishing sinners by making them go blind or covering them in blood as he rides by.

The Scottish kelpie is a water devil that lives in lakes and rivers, often appearing as serpent-like or even in the shape of a horse. The kelpie would appear as a horse to weary travelers who stopped by the waters, and when a traveler would mount the horse, the kelpie would slip into the waters and drown the poor rider.

Welsh mythology features demonic dogs known as hellhounds, the Cwn Annwn, that are the hunting dogs of the Lord of the Underworld himself, Arawn. The leader of the pack, Flyddmyr, is black, and the three other wolfen members of the pack are white with red-tipped ears. They are capable of extreme speed and immense strength. The Fomori are Celtic demons that live in the darkness of the ocean's depths and in lakes and dark pools of the Upper World. These demons were once the minions of the great Balor, who fed them human victims. Upon Balor's death, they turned to the waters in the form of sea monsters and bizarre water creatures.

Egypt

Egyptian mythology has its own devil in Set, the god of thunder, storms, and war, who once ruled the Kingdom of the Blessed Dead; however, all of that changed when Set murdered his brother, Osiris. Isis, the wife of Osiris, reassembled the body of her dead husband and conceived a son, Horus, with the resurrected body. The followers of Horus, the supreme deity, then turned on Set, and the priests made Set the enemy of all the other gods and the source of all evil. Interestingly, as we'll explore in more depth later, one of the largest modern Satanic organizations is called the Temple of Set.

The Egyptian mythology surrounding Apep and Ma'at also speaks to the duality of good and evil, Devil and God forces. Apep was the ancient Egyptian deity of chaos, often called the Lord of Chaos. Apep was an opposer of Ma'at, the goddess of truth, morality, law, order, harmony, and justice. She was responsible for the actions of the stars and the order of the universe, as well as the actions of mortals and deities involved in bringing order out of chaos. Though the true opposite deity of Ma'at was Isfet, Apep was also considered to have represented this role.

The Egyptian god Set has the head of a jackal and body of a human and was the god of thunder, storms, and war.

Apep was a male deity that also served as the great enemy of Ra, the solar deity and light-bringer. Apep was really the personification of evil, just as the Christian Satan was, and often took the form of a serpent or giant snake, just as Satan did.

Germanic and Norse Mythology

German mythology tells of a dragon that lives at the base of the Cosmic Tree, Yggdrasil. The dragon, Nidhogg, lives at one of the three roots of the tree, in the lowest of nine worlds called the Nifiheim, a land of mist and cold. The dragon fed off corpses and often gnawed at the root of the Cosmic Tree itself, the roots of which were crawling with snakes. The dragon/snake symbolism is something we also see in the Christian depictions of the Devil as a dragon or serpent.

Another entity in Norse mythology, Ymir, is said to be the first living creature, who appears as a frost giant that comes from the ice itself. Ymir is evil and the mother and father of all frost giants. It is said his flesh became the Earth itself.

Hawaii

The Hawaiian myth of Hiiaka is both beautiful and frightening. The young sister of the goddess of fire, Pele, Hiiaka was often sent on adventures and is a big part of Hawaiian mythology. She once battled demons, when her sister Pele sent her to find Pele's lover, Lohiau. Hiiaka climbed out of the volcano they lived in, Kilauea, and ventured forth to the lava plateaus, urged on by her angry and impatient sister.

Hiiaka wore a beautiful skirt of ferns made for her by the goddess Pau-o-palae, and soon Hiiaka was on a quest filled with danger around every corner, encountering a variety of creatures, such as eepas, kupuas, and mo-os. The eepas were deformed, deranged, gnomelike creatures, and the kupuas were supernatural gnomes and elves. The mo-os were dragons. Hiiaka had several tests of endurance, including battles with such entities, before she reached the forest dwelling of the reptile-man, Pana-ewa, who could shape-shift and often robbed and even ate passing strangers. He was the ruler of all darkness and dark things. Hiiaka fought Pana-ewa until she dropped with weariness, when Pele came to her aid, and they drove the demon god down into the deep forest and into a river bed where he was eaten by sharks.

The land then became a place of great peace. What is notable about this story is the battle between light and dark and the banishment of the demon to the depths of a hell where, this time, he was consumed by sharks,

resulting in the coming of a peaceful time to the land and its inhabitants. In the Book of Revelation, we see a similar story play out in the banishment of Satan to a prison of a thousand years, followed by a golden reign of peace. The common themes, motifs, and symbols of myths around the world mirror the religious texts and stories of the duality and the battle between what is good and what is evil.

Inuit

The Inuit Eskimos believed in a sky god named Torngasuk, a mischievous demon worshipped throughout Greenland and northeastern Canada. Though he was the master of whales and seals, he was also a supernatural demon that often appeared as a bear or a one-armed human, invisible to all but the shamans of the communities. He was often called upon by fishermen to help

Torngasuk is an Inuit sky god and mischievous demon who often appears as a bear.

Demons, the Devil, and Fallen Angels

stop an illness or disease, echoing the dualistic good/evil nature of so many of the more pagan demonic entities in global myths.

Another Inuit demon was Irdlirvirisissong, a sky demon that was a cousin of the moon god, Aningan. This demon would leap to earth and dance about like a clown, and if you were unlucky enough to look at him, your intestines would freeze and be removed as his next meal!

Malaysia and Indonesia

The Pontianak are female vampires/ghosts that are the spirits of women who died during pregnancy. They also go by the names Mataniak and Kuntilanak. The Pontianak were said to intervene on behalf of women who were harmed or killed by taking vengeance on the abusers who caused their deaths. They sometimes did this by crushing the man's genitals. In the Philippines, a similar demon called the Tiyanak is a part of folklore, but this demon is the spirit of the dead children and not the mothers. Another Philippine demon is the Tikbalang, which was a demon horse with long limbs, the head and hooves of a horse, and the body of a human. It would roam forestlands, raping women and impregnating them.

The Philippines was also home to the mythological Manananggal, an old woman vampire that preyed upon pregnant women and sucked the blood of their unborn babies with her tongue. Any child who was born with a facial deformity was thought to be the offspring of Manananggal, who could only be destroyed by being exposed to copious amounts of salt, garlic, and ashes.

Mesoamerica

To the central and south American nations, demons often appeared in their mythology as supernatural deities that were both creative as well as destructive. Because of their lack of scientific understanding of nature, often their demons were simply personifications of natural disasters such as hurricanes, volcanic eruptions, and earthquakes, just as in other cultures that ascribed deities to natural events.

The Mayan myths included Vucub Caquix, a large bird, arrogant and vain, that proclaimed himself the Lord of the World after the great flood. He also went by the name Seven Macaw and represented vanity at its worst, pretending to be both the sun and the moon! This bird demon was written about in an eighteenth-century document that was part of the Popol Vuh, known as the creation stories of the Mayan peoples. Seven Macaw was defeated by the Hero Twins, the true heroes of the sun and moon, who took away the bird demon's eyes, teeth, and worldly riches and power.

Hurakan was a one-legged Mayan creator god who lived in the mist and represented the wind and storms. He called the Earth into existence by

Tezcatlipoca was an Aztec god of darkness, night, and sorcery. He was also associated with the leopard, a very important spiritual animal.

repeating the word "Earth" over and over again until it manifested. But when the solid land appeared, the chief gods became angry with the first humans who emerged, so Hurakan unleashed a deluge that destroyed them all (possibly the same Great Flood as that of the Noah story). Perhaps not surprisingly, the word "hurricane" is derived from this demon/god's name.

Aztec mythology is rich with various deities that took on aspects of both good and evil, god/goddess and demon, such as Tzitzimime, which translates to "monsters descending from above." Like the fallen angels of the Book of Enoch we will read about in the next chapter, these demons were a threat to the world and represented the stars that battled the sun and moon every twilight and dawn. Though some representations show them as male deities of destruction, most depict them as female skeletal figures wearing skirts and headdresses with skull and crossbones. They were thought to be the reason for solar eclipses, which portrayed them as attacking the sun and then coming to Earth to devour her inhabitants. Surprisingly, these demons were also sometimes depicted as the protectors of feminine power and procreation.

Other deities that had dual good/evil natures were Tlazolteotl, the goddess of both purification and filth, as well as vice and sexual misdeeds, which she had the power to forgive; Tezcatlipoca, Lord of the Night, Darkness, and Sorcery, who also represented change and conflict, both positive and negative; Mictlantecuhtli, the God of the Underworld who took on a skeletal appearance and ruled the Mictlan, the Underworld, along with his wife, Mictlancihuatl; and Tlaltecuhtli, the Earth goddess that took on a monstrous, terrifying appearance despite being an important part of the actual creation of the Earth itself.

Native Americans

The rich myths and creation stories of the various Native American tribes of the North American continent speak of spirits and tricksters, forces of nature and the rise of humanity, both the tribal peoples and the white men who came into their world. Though they did not believe in demons in the religious sense of the word, they had many spirits that were creators of chaos, trouble, and subterfuge.

The Shoshone people of North America told of the Dzoavits, an earthquake demon that chased the sacred dove to steal her eggs. The demon was trapped by the allies of the dove, who tricked him into jumping into a hole where, they told him, the dove was hiding from him. He did, and was pummeled from above by a badger and other animal and bird allies with hot rocks, burying him alive. The Malisseet of the Northeast had their own vampire, and he was a hairy one. The demon Apotamkin sported long fangs and had a special taste for children (recall the prevalence of vampire demons in aboriginal culture).

The Navajo had a group of monster gods known as the Anaye, which were said to be the offspring of lesbians! These demons could be female or male, and included Theelgeth, the Great Hairy Beast with no head, and Binaye-Ahani, who had no arms and legs, but could stare you to death.

The Iroquois feared the Flying-Head that had flaming eyes and huge fangs. This demon would feed upon livestock, and because it didn't have a body, its hunger was never satisfied. Flying-Head was said to be destroyed when he devoured what he thought were piping-hot chestnuts, only to discover they were hearthstones. His head imploded and he was never seen again. The Cherokee had their owl demons known as Skili, said to be witches that roamed during the night in search of victims to eat.

Persia (Iran)

In Persian mythology, there is a battle between the forces of good and evil. Ahura Mazda is the god that represents order and goodness in the world. His twin brother, Ahriman, is the opposing force of evil and disorder. The world, according to regional beliefs, is rampant with the tension of these opposing forces represented by God and the Devil, light and dark, good and evil, representing the same duality found in Christianity. Ahriman even rules a legion of demons called daevas that are similar to those ruled by Satan in the Underworld.

Romania

In Romanian folklore, God created Earth with the help of animals, while Satan tried to sabotage God's plans. Both God and the Devil lived in a boundless ocean called Apa Sâmbetei in the roles of master and servant. The Devil was called Nefartatul and was often considered the foolish brother of God. These stories appear in Slavic Macedonian and Bulgarian folklore. God wanted to create the Earth and sent the Devil for a handful of clay from the floor of the World Ocean. This task was to be done in God's holy name. The Devil tried to bring it to the surface in his name instead, but could not do it until he said the name of God. The clay grew into the Earth and God rested.

The Devil tried to push him over the side, but the ever-expanding Earth stopped God from falling, so the Devil tried the same thing in the other three cardinal directions, creating the shape of a cross that disempowered the Devil in his tracks.

Slavic Nations

Slavic folklore tells of the Rusalka, demon/water nymphs that always appear as females. They are believed to live at the bottom of rivers and lakes, but are not mermaids, despite a similar appearance. They are instead the spirits of dead women who have killed themselves over bad love affairs and now want to take revenge. They seduce attractive men to their watery graves at night by singing, dancing, and charming them, much like the Sirens of Greek mythology. It is believed that the charm the Rusalka have is so powerful that men cannot resist following them into the water's depths.

Another creepy Slavic demon is Lady Midday, who appears as a terrifying ghost. Her role is to bring heatstroke to the poor men who labor in the hot sun all day. Field workers claim she approaches on a cloud of dust, carrying a scythe.

Most of the Slavic nations worshipped a range of deities, with an overall acceptance of Perun as the supreme deity. Most historical records point to folkloric stories of Perun, but also of his opposer, Veles. Perun was the god of thunder and lightning and all things heavenly. Veles was the lord of the waters, and the Underworld, who ruled the realm of the dead in the roots of the World Tree or Cosmic Tree. Both deities had positive qualities and benefits to the people of the times but were locked in battle as storm god and dragon. Perun threw bolts of lightning at Veles, who took on a serpentine nature (Satan) and slithered over the Earth trying to escape. Perun could shape-shift into animals and people, as could Veles, and when Perun befriended Veles as a dog, he picked him up and threw him into a lake, drowning his counterpart. Thus, Veles was returned to the watery world of the dead. Throughout Slavic myth and folklore, the concept of a god using thunder and lightning from the skies to battle his earthly counterpart has been a prevalent part of the beliefs that would one day morph into the iconology of the Christian concept of God and the Devil.

Sometimes translated as "mermaid" the Rusalka is a female demon of Slavic orgins.

Ukraine

Ukrainian mythology has a female demon similar to the Rusalka, known as the Mavka. Mavkas are beautiful young girls who entice men into the woods and proceed to tickle them to death. Mavkas have no reflection on water, no shadows, and no backs, so that you can see their innards. They live in groups in forests and mountain caves and wear flowers in their hair. The Mavka hold festivals where they are accompanied on the flute by a demon much like the pagan Pan.

THE DEVIL AND DEMONS IN OTHER WORLD RELIGIONS

Though most of our understanding of the Devil and his ilk comes to us from the Big Three traditions of Judaism, Christianity, and Islam, other religious traditions also had a concept of an opposing force of evil to their vision of a creator god or goddess. Traditions such as Hinduism even have their own pantheon of demons, but with an Eastern influence.

No matter where we are in the world, or who we are, the concept of good and evil does not and cannot escape us. The only differences are in how we interpret that concept, and whom or what we choose to represent it in our mythology, creation stories, and spiritual/religious beliefs. The Devil is ever-present as the enemy of the supreme power and the challenger of spiritual power. He is worldly power, though not always an evil thing, because materialism itself is not evil. It becomes evil when it becomes out of balance, with the material overtaking the spiritual, the humane. The role of Satan in all world religions, in all forms, has been to glorify the opposite of that which was glorified by the Creator.

But in many religions, even pagan traditions, the concept of Satan or a deity like him represents the darker aspects of nature itself, including death. In the essay "Who Is Satan? The Accuser and Scapegoat," Vexen Crabtree writes, "Satan is the dark force in nature representing the carnal nature and death of all living things" and that "Satan is good and evil, love and hate. It is the gray; the totality of reality undivided into arbitrary dichotomies." How Satan or the Devil may be synonymous with the harsher aspects of reality and life is to be interpreted by each tradition in a way that makes sense to its cosmic understanding and its place in it.

Bahá'i Faith

The Bahá'i Faith originated in the 1800s as a type of Abrahamic religion that believes there is a present-day messiah and more messiahs to come. The founder was an Iranian man who went by the name Baha'u'llah and was believed to be a messenger of God much like Moses, Jesus, Muhammad, and other religious leaders of that ilk.

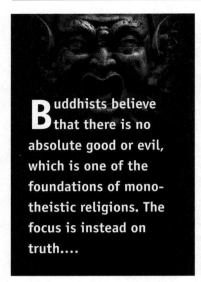

Bahá'i states that God is unknowable, that he is the One God, but has many different names. They also believe that all the great religions have the same source and that all humans are equal in the eyes of God, men and women alike. They also look well upon science as one side of a coin, with religion as the other side, but complementary.

Their concept of evil and the idea of humans being born with "original sin" does not exist in the same way as in the other Abrahamic traditions. No devils or demons are involved. Evil is simply a choice someone might make, with his or her own God-given free will to be imperfect, to turn away from the source, which is God. That imperfection is the evil itself. The Bahá'i deny the existence of the Devil or Satan, because evil does not exist independently but is the absence of good, just as darkness is the absence of light. The prophet Baha'u'llah taught that the Satan of other religious scriptures was symbolic and represented the lower nature of humans, capable of destroying people if they did not see their sinful ways and turn to the good.

Buddhists believe that there is no absolute good or evil, which is one of the foundations of monotheistic religions. The focus is instead on truth....

Buddhism

Buddhists believe that there is no absolute good or evil, which is one of the foundations of monotheistic religions. The focus is instead on truth, the impermanance of everything, and the interdependence of all living things. Buddhism is more of a practice than a religion, but believe it or not, demons are a part of the Buddhist tradition, mainly as powerful spirits that represent different parts of nature. These deities are not demons in the traditional sense that we understand, coming from Satan or the "side" of evil, but instead speak more to the law of karma and the position of a person or entity in the lower realms of karmic expression.

Using compassion, ritual actions, appeasement, and detachment, one may lose the more demonic aspect of his or her nature and rise up the ladder of karma, especially by working on one's dharma, or actions and behaviors. Because Buddhists believe in the continuing cycles of birth and rebirth, which is called *samsara*, the suffering and pain of that cycle must be overcome in order to reach Nirvana. Nirvana is a complete escape from the wheel of suffering and the end to experiencing the cycles. The desires and wants of the world are in a sense the demonic, as they distract us from the path to enlightenment and keep us from Nirvana and "getting off the wheel."

The main demon deity is Mara, Sanskrit for "killer" or "death," and often called "the evil one," a male deity that appears in early Sanskrit writings about the Buddha. Mara's daughters are named Lust, Discontent, and Craving, and their job is to try to distract the bodhisattva, Siddhartha Guatama, during his final meditation under the Bodhi Tree before he is enlightened and becomes the "Buddha." This is similar to the last tempation of Christ in the desert, when the Devil tried to offer him worldly powers and fortunes.

Obviously, those efforts fail, and the bodhisattva becomes the Buddha, overcoming the temptations of the daughters of Mara, the king of the realm of desire and death (the lower realm). Mara also sends legions of demons to stop the Buddha's transformation, unsuccessfully, and even resorts to revealing himself in a vision. After trying to tempt the Buddha, it is written that Mara continued to tempt humanity with sexual and sensual pleasures via his army of female temptresses from his stronghold in the Realm of Desire, one of the six heavens in Buddhist thought. Mara may have failed to stop Buddha from becoming enlightened, but his goal of distracting humanity has certainly proven quite successful!

Demons in the various forms of Buddhism are seen more as malignancies or types of spiritual illness; there are such things as exorcisms in Vajrayana Buddhism, and demon expulsion is a part of Tibetan medicine and healing. These exorcisms have been credited with ending diseases, physical and mental, including leprosy, and they take on an almost shamanic nature. Tibetan Buddhism also includes the concept of corpse-animating demons associated with death and dying.

Like the Christian Satan, Mara is more of a representative of many things that bring suffering and death than an outright anti-good/Antichrist figure. In *Buddhism and the Mythology of Evil*, author Trevor Ling writes, "Enumerated in detail in the Suttanipata, Mara's forces consist of passion, aver-

The demon Mara tries to temp the Buddha with evil desires in this Burmese-style artwork.

sion, hunger and thirst, craving, sloth and torpor, fear, doubt, self-will, cant and various forms of self-exaltation. Prominent among these, and specially closely connected with Mara, is the first, passion." Thus evil could be stated as the darker aspects of humanity coming to light, and demons our passions and lustful cravings for the carnal and material things in life. Buddhists pacify and/or overcome their demons by standing against and resisting the forces of greed, avarice, lust, and the like. And ultimately, even demons, though on the lowest karmic level of existence, could potentially improve their lot and rise in the ranks via good deeds and compassionate acts!

One such example of this is a female demon named Hariti, a cannibal who, legend has it, ate all the childrein in Rajagrha, but then converted to Buddhism and, at the Buddha's personal request, gave up her demonic ways. Other demon spirits in Buddhism mythology include the snake-like nagas, demons associated with water that have both a good and evil side. Their good side promoted fertility and the bounty of nature, but they could also be horrible when subverted.

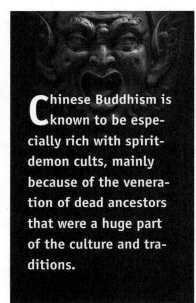

Chinese Buddhism is known to be especially rich with spirit-demon cults, mainly because of the veneration of dead ancestors that were a huge part of the culture and traditions.

The Yakshas, Karsasas, and Pisacas are all demon spirits of ancient Buddhist legend and lore, but among them, only the nagas were tamed and even converted to Buddhism, again by the Buddha himself.

Sri Lanka had its own spirit-demon cults that used sorcery for healing and believed in Yakkas, and Burma was also home to spirit cults that believed illnesses and even economic failures in the villages were the byproducts of malevolent demons, spirits, and ghosts called nat. The word "asuras" was denoted to mean demonic entities in Southeast Asian cultures, although in Thailand they were called Phi.

The Tibetan Himalayas, because of strong and enduring shamanic influences, have a rich history of demons, possibly because of the remote and harsh landscape. The Srin were demons found only in Tibet, and they were very resistant to Buddha's attempts to convert them to the ways of good. A myth of the region tells the story of an Indian Buddhist missionary named Guru Rinpoche, who was visiting the area. He was in an epic war with a demoness named Balmo, who was the head of the resistance against Buddha's conversion attempts. In a way, this myth is similar to stories of Christian missionaries entering pagan regions and trying to convert them, only to be met with forceful resistance. These demons were territorial in nature and only fell to violent subjugation from protector deities or "guardian deities."

Chinese Buddhism is known to be especially rich with spirit-demon cults, mainly because of the veneration of dead ancestors that were a huge part of the culture and traditions. In medieval China, families would perform mortuary rituals designed to assist a deceased relative on his or her journey through the Underworld. The Chinese had their own child-devouring demon goddess, Guizumu, "Mother of Demons," and a part of the Chinese Buddhist text the *Mahayana sutra* contains many references to the demonic and to possession.

Hinduism

The Buddhist demon Mara is said to be a more-recent offshoot of the Hindu Namuchi, showing the influence the more-ancient tradition had in the East. Hindu traditions are rife with demons and deities that personify evil, including the Daitya, giant evil spirits that are the offspring of the Goddesses Diti and Kasyapa. The Daityas' leader is a giant dragon/serpent that, during the dawn of existence, the Krita Yuga, battled with the gods and defeated them. Hindu is a polytheistic religion, so there is no comparison per se to the Christian concept of Satan, but there are many deities that display both a good and an evil aspect. The oldest Hindu beliefs did include the idea of a singular god of good and one of evil, as written about in the Rig Vedas, the Hindu sacred texts. Those roles were attributed to the gods Indra and Vritra, respectively.

But they morphed into the more widely known and acceptable concepts of polytheism, of many gods that could be good, and many that could be equally in opposition. These gods, called originally the Asuras, eventually became demons who went to war agains the gods. Another early Hindu demonic group, the Rakshasas, were in service to a king of demons called Ravana. This evil king battled with the hero, Rama. Demons in early texts and imagery often took on the form of a snake with wings, or a dragon/serpent. Rakshasas could shape-shift, had magical abilities, and were said to be the children of the Vedic goddess of death, Nirriti. But some point to the Ramayana, an ancient text that says they were created from the foot of Brahma and tasked with protecting the primeval waters.

The demon Hayagriva, a huge and ugly enemy of the gods whose name means "having the neck of a horse," was later to be found in Japanese and Tibetan Buddhist thought as an important deity associated

A statue of Ravana at the British Museum. Ravana had ten heads, which indicated that he was the master of the six *shastras* and four *Vedas*.

with demons, the wrathful, the dead, and ghosts (although it was elevated in Tibet and could cure diseases, showing its dualistic nature).

The Hindu concept of evil lent itself to this duality of gods and deities as both good and evil. The creator God, Brahma, created both good and evil, seeing evil as a necessity, a part of the universal dynamic, and a part of the development of karma. Interestingly, the *Mahabharata* tells that Brahma created women to delude men because he was jealous that they were initially created as virtuous, like the gods. Women would lead men into temptation and a fall from virtue. When the women became wicked, Brahma filled them with passion and desire, which in turn inspired those same things in men. As a result, Brahma created anger, and from that point on all creatures were born with both anger and desire. The *Vishnu Purana* states that the reason mankind is evil is that "His fourth creation produced creatures in whom darkness and passion predominated, afflicted by mistery; these were mankind." Yet the humans were simply mirroring the bad examples of many of the gods themselves, who constantly battled with their own "inner demons!"

Taoism

Taoism is over 2,500 years old. Its main text is the *Tao-te-Ching*, or "the Book of the Way and Its Power," by Lao Tzu, as well as the writings of Chuang Tzu in *Inner Chapters*. Lao Tzu is the main force behind Tao, a spiritual practice that is as popular today as ever, thanks in part to the works of metaphysical writers such as Wayne Dyer, who was a proponent of Taoist philosophy and thought.

Taoism embraces the Ultimate Reality as the entirety of existence, and the supreme being is considered an abstract that cannot be reduced to words. The Tao, or the Way, is the understanding of the supreme being and reality itself, from the cosmos to man. Evil in Taoism is simply the other side of a duality that is part of the interdependence of everything else; one cannot have good without automatically creating evil.

The reality of the Tao holds that good and evil are an aspect of each other, shown in the popular and well-known yin/yang symbol. Any action has both a positive and negative aspect, and nature is constantly striving to balance the two sides. There is no concept of salvation in Taoism because there is no belief that anything needs to be saved. Thus, there are no devils or demons in Taoism, as there is no need for them in a belief system that posits good and evil as conceptual abstractions and not concrete and permanent manifestations.

The *Tao-te-Ching* states, "When beauty is abstracted, then ugliness has been implied; when good is abstracted, then evil has been implied." This suggests that anything positive also involves an opposing negative factor, and what is called evil corresponds to a larger lack of balance between the two principles of yin and yang striving for balance. Yin, the negative, never manifests alone but is always accompanied by Yang, the positive. Evil is a part of the nature of the world, and humans are called upon to find the harmony of the two aspects and respect the equilibrium of the polarities of Yin and Yang, female and male, dark and light.

> The *Tao-te-Ching* states, "When beauty is abstracted, then ugliness has been implied; when good is abstracted, then evil has been implied."

The Tao is influenced by earlier Buddhist and Chinese beliefs, and Taoism has different sects with differing ideals. The ancient Chinese text "Zhuangzi" looks at nature as being amoral because it doesn't care for individuals. Death is natural as part of the grand cycle, and illnesses and misfortunes are simply aspects of a normal human life. They are not punishments for sins or misdeeds, and they are not evil in any way. However, some Taoists do believe that illness is a result of misdeeds and impurities, and that it requires a sort of "exorcism" of the misdeed involving a special talisman to banish the disease from the sufferer. Others believe that sins will be punished in a hell-like place in the afterlife and that good behavior will be rewarded in a heavenly place. One is also responsible for the sins and misdeeds of ancestors up to ten generations! Talk about the ultimate guilt trip!

Zoroastrianism

One of the most ancient of all religions, Zoroastianism is over three thousand years old and arose around the region of Iran before the rise of Islam. The religion was founded by Zarathustra or Zoroaster, an Iranian prophet who lived from approximately 628 to 551 B.C.E. Like the later Christ, Zoroaster was tempted by Satan and performed miracles and healings. He had followers who believed he was of a supernatural nature. He is credited with introducing to the world the first monotheistic religion.

Combining elements of both dualism and monotheism, the supreme being of Zoroastrianism is the Ahura Mazda, a male god, lawmaker, and master of day and night. Ahura Mazda was the creator of heaven and earth. He had a twin brother, Ahriman, the god of evil, creator of snakes and *daevas* (demons) and the evils of the world. The two brothers were the personifications of good and evil. These dual forces of the truth, *asha,* and the lie, *druj,* battled constantly, and possibly were the precursors to the later God and Satan of more well-known religions. They would battle each other throughout time until the God of Evil was defeated, leading to the resurrection of the dead and a last judgment that would divide the good, bound for heaven, and the bad, doomed to hell—again, concepts we would see thousands of years later in the Western traditions of Judaism, Christianity, and Islam.

In the *Gathas*, hymns of Zoroastrian teachings, two religious parties are described: the worshippers of nature gods later turned into demons, or daevas; and those who followed Ahura the Lord. The daevas were the followers of Ahriman, which means "the evil spirit" and of Druj, "falsehood." There were three classifications of daevas, all of which were agents of chaos and disorder: Aka Manah, which was Evil Mind, created to oppose Good Mind, and was second in command to Ahriman; Druj, the lie or falsehood created to oppose truth, a female wickedness and chief rival of Asha, or truth (Druj can also represent a class of female demons); and Aeshma, the "fiend of the wounding spirit" written of in the Yasna of the *Gathas*. A fourth pseudo-demon was Azi Dahaka, which was also human and may have taken snake form. Interestingly, Azi Dahaka's destiny is to be chained and bound on Mount Demavand, but eventually he breaks loose to return to disturb the order of creation, much like Satan's return after a thousand years of peace in Revelation.

Ahura Mazda was the creator of heaven and earth. He had a twin brother, Ahriman, the God of Evil, creator of snakes and *daevas* (demons) and the evils of the world.

Interestingly, the teachings claim that Ahriman was not created by Lord Ahura but came into being independently and was not considered equal in power or worth and dignity to Ahura. Another interesting concept that shows the interplay between the two is the belief in the Law in Nature, which was wisdom represented by Ahura, and the War in Nature, represented by Ahriman and his intrusion into the creation of Ahura as a force of evil. This last concept is a central tenet of Indo-Iranian religious thought.

In the 13th Yasna of the Gathas, we read, "Well known are the two primeval spirits correlated but independent; one is the better and the other is the worse as to thought, as to word, as to deed, and between these two let the wise choose the light." Despite the presence of Ahriman, though, the true God and Lord Supreme was Ahura and all who chose to do good would be rewarded justly, with sinners punished accordingly. In the Yasna 43.5 it states, "As divine and sacred I recognized Thee, O Mazda Ahura, when I realized Thee as the First and eternal when life began: and when Thou ordained rewards for good thoughts, words and deeds: and when Thou specified through Thy wisdom that evil shall be the lot of wicked persons and that good persons shall reap the fruit of their goodness. Thus it will continue up to the end of creation."

So followers had a choice: be tempted by the darker force to commit sins that would remove their just rewards or follow the supreme teachings and hold fast to the law of Ahura. There are still over two million followers of this ancient religion today, which, along with pagan concepts already in existence, laid the foundation and blueprint for the greater religions that followed.

There are so many striking similarities in all the religious traditions when it comes to evil, the Devil, and demons. The symbolism of the snake and dragon, the serpent as great deceiver and tempter, the battle between dual forces of dark and light, the temptation by the great devil/demon to try to sway the messianic hero away from enlightenment; the punishment of sins and reward of good as promises of damnation and salvation; and the dual nature of Gods are archetypal aspects of creation itself that are found in all corners of the world, albeit with some regional differences.

There are so many striking similarities in all the religious traditions when it comes to evil, the Devil, and demons.

Human evolution included the evolution of beliefs, ideals, and awareness of our place in the greater scheme of things. By simply observing the natural world around us, we figured out a long time ago that what was born would die. That night followed day followed night again. That crops vanished, then grew strong again in the next seasonal cycle. That stars appearing overhead disappeared, to return again in a year's time. And that we had within us the ability to be good and kind, and to be evil and harmful. The observations of those dualities led to the development of hierarchies of spirits and angels and gods and demons responsible for what we humans could not yet put into words, understand with our limited scientific acumen, or take responsibility for ourselves.

ATHEISM AND EVIL

Atheism is not a religion, but it must be included in the discussion of evil. Obviously, atheists do not believe in any god and therefore do not believe in the counterpart of God, or the Devil. Agnostics believe in some kind of universal force, but not a personal God that is apparent in more traditional religious doctrines. So, if the concept of a personified deity such as God is missing, can evil still be a part of a person's philosophy?

Why not? It is entirely possible for atheists to put the blame for evil on the humans either committing it or interpreting it. Long ago, natural disasters that destroyed towns and villages and killed children and adults alike were thought to be caused by the wrath of the gods, or demons, and labeled as evil. But these events were not inherently good or evil in and of themselves. They were natural, and neutral. The interpretation of them as evil stayed with humanity throughout our development, such that we still pray to God when a tornado takes out a town, or a hurricane strikes a coast.

Even with no God, evils certainly can exist. Humans have suffered for thousands of years from one affliction or another that were viewed as evil in intent and source. Michael Novak writes in *Atheism and Evil*, "The atheist view of the world is actually rather bleaker than that of Jews and Christians:

There is no doubt that there is evil in the world. Police officers deal with it every day. People seek out religion as one way to explain it, even empower themselves to fight against it.

suffering under the weight of evil is meaningless, and so is any struggle against evil. Everything in the atheist's world begins and ends in randomness and chance." This implies that humans have a need to believe there is a greater, grander plan at work and that their struggle against suffering is not for nought. But such a plan isn't a necessity for existence itself, just a way to make it more meaningful and tolerable.

While this book is not about arguing pro or con for any belief, evil can exist apart from a deified force behind it. Men can be evil to other men. Nature can be evil to humans and animals. Perhaps it is not necessary to believe in gods and demons to understand that the capacity for evil exists—or at least what we interpret evil to be. Many atheists argue that God cannot exist because of all the evil, pain, and suffering in the world, that a good and loving Father God would not allow it. Therefore, because there IS evil, there can be no God.

Yet, an atheist might believe in the existence of demons were they to be interpreted differently, not as religious entities of evil, but some type of paranormal creature from another dimension or parallel universe! Still, if we are referring to traditional demons, they cannot exist in a world where their counterparts, angels, do not exist, just as the Devil has no purpose without a God to oppose him.

In modern times, Satan has become less and less influential and important. This is because of a few factors, one of which is the proliferation of atheism, humanism, and pagan/Earth-based belief systems that are on the rise, the result of our own philosophical and intellectual evolution. Another factor is the modern Satanic worship groups that look upon Satan as more metaphor than actual entity. More people are choosing to think of evil as something entirely human, or as the misinterpretation of natural causes that are neutral in intent and meaning.

Because of this, the stronghold of Satan is not what it used to be, having been relegated to the more-conservative religious traditions, and demons have taken on a more "paranormal" bent, thanks to pop culture and recent reality shows where ghost hunters claim to confront demonic energy and put it back in its place with Bibles and holy objects. Except for the more-devout followers of traditional religions, most people look at Satan not as an actual being, but as a part of our own dark nature, pointing to the violence and horrific actions we commit by our own choice.

Satan may not be all he used to be, but he still lurks in the darkest hearts of humanity, and perhaps in the bowels of Hell waiting to make his move.

Fallen Angels

In some ancient Near Eastern traditions, demons were often inter-changed with fallen angels, as well as spirits that could actually possess someone (or something, as we will see when we cover demonic objects!). Demons in general were thought to come from an underworld, or netherworld—Hell—become earthly beings once they possessed a human being, making them vulnerable to exorcism by human priests trained as exorcists. Demons ruled the powers of the underworld, while fallen angels ruled the forces of evil from a more heavenly realm, or even on Earth or in Hell if they were ordered to do so by the god who cast them out in the first place.

One of the more widely known categories of demons comes not from down below but from up on high. These powerful entities have a decidedly Judeo-Christian bent and do not, as many demons do, possess human bodies or souls. They have their own bodies, with wings, of course, and appear to be the upper echelon of the hierarchy of demons.

The greatest fallen angel of all is Lucifer, which many associate with Satan. Lucifer has origins in the Old Testament references to a "Light Bringer" (Isaiah 14:12), a name later interpreted as the "Morning Star" of Babylonian royalty, specifically a king who had Bel and Ishtar as his divine parents. Over time, Lucifer became associated with Satan because he was called Lucifer until he was cast from Heaven, when he then became known as Satan.

Some demonologists believe that Satan, Lucifer, and Beelzebub are the evil holy trinity! Beelzebub was once an actual cherubim, a good angel in Heaven, who then engaged in two of the seven deadly sins, pride and glut-tony, and was cast out of the pearly gates.

Dark angels are those that rebelled against God and that now, in their anger and bitterness, attempt to drag human beings away from the light as well.

What makes a dark angel dark is some act of disobedience of God that results in an expulsion from heaven. Dark angels are not associated with the Angel of Death, who is sent from God to aid those who are approaching their time of death. Instead, dark angels are often rebellious, angry, bitter, and violent entities that have misused their divinely given free will. These are not loving angels that want to guard, heal, or protect humans, as they do not care for human beings at all. In fact, they make attempts to lure humans into sin whenever they can. Just as the Devil is known for tricking and beguiling people to sin and commit acts of evil, the dark angels have the same power. They are wicked, rebellious, and often depicted with dark wings and dark hair, whereas the good angels wear white as a symbolic representation of purity and innocence.

Gustav Davidson, in his *A Dictionary of Angels*, points out that all angels share one common denominator. "It is well to bear in mind that all angels, whatever their state of grace—indeed, no matter how christologically corrupt and defiant—are under God, even when, to all intents and purposes, they are performing under the direct orders of the Devil." He goes on to say that evil is itself an instrument of the Creator, who will use evil for His own divine agenda, and that because angels were created with free will, but gave up that free will upon their formation, they had to make at that moment the choice between working on behalf of God or turning away from Him. Once that choice was made, it was fixed and irrevocable.

WATCHERS AND NEPHILIM

Some of the oldest references to fallen angels are the "Watchers," which have their origins in the Old Testament, in the Book of Daniel. Watchers are holy angels that are also mentioned in the Book of Enoch of Judaic tradition. In Enoch, Watchers were corrupted when they came down from Heaven and had sexual intercourse with human women, thus creating a new lineage called the Nephilim. Also referred to as "Grigori," these Watchers committed the ultimate sin of lusting after human women and giving in to sexual desires.

The "sons of God/Elohim" in Genesis 6:1–6 are said to have seen "that the daughters of men were beautiful: and they took wives for themselves, whomever they chose."

The Nephilim were giants on Earth—the offspring of the mating between sons of God and daughters of men before the Great Deluge. Although there is still controversy over the exact identity of the Nephilim, the word itself is related to the Hebrew verb series "to fall," which some biblical scholars suggest means they were fallen angels themselves, while others defend the angel/human offspring theory. But most agree they were indeed giants among humans, at least in physical size. Genesis 6:4 states, "There were giants in the earth in those days: and also after that, when the sons of God came in unto the daughters of men, and they bore children to them, the same became mighty men which were of old, men of renown."

So these "sons of God" were the fallen angels whose offspring brought about the Great Flood, and these giants, the Nephilim, remained on Earth as demons. The Book of Enoch spends the most time mulling over the Nephilim and their relationship to the fallen ones, stating in 1 Enoch 15:8–10:

> But now the giants who are born from the union of spirits and the flesh shall be called evil spirits upon the earth, because their dwelling shall be upon the earth and inside the earth. Evil spirits have come out of their bodies. Because from the day that they were created from the sons of God they became Watchers; their first origin is the spiritual foundation. They will become evil upon the earth and shall be called evil spirits. The dwelling of the spiritual beings of heaven is heaven, but the dwelling of the spirits of the earth, which are born upon the earth, is earth.

What the passage tells us is that the entities that fornicated with human women automatically became evil and were forced to dwell in the realm of evil, Earth. This harkens back to the idea of original sin in the Garden of Eden, with Eve being the temptress who causes Adam, the son of God, in a sense, to eat of the forbidden apple, thus giving him and herself the knowledge of good and evil. The concept of Earth being a place rampant with evil, and Heaven being where the good spirits dwell, leaves out mention of Hell, unless Hell is really Earth itself.

Yet in the Book of Daniel, Watchers are equated as being "holy ones." It also suggests the sons of God came to Earth on their own accord and were not "cast out" but did have sexual relations with human women to create the giant race of Nephilim.

This kind of confusion is rampant in efforts to find original sources for demons and angels and evil itself. Every religion and every region of the planet has its own spin that shifts and changes according to beliefs and traditions.

Nephilim: Angels or Demons?

BY SCOTT ALAN ROBERTS

While not necessarily a household word, the Nephilim have gained a lot of recognition and reputation in the world of alternative history. They have been identified in cross-cultural references as everything from the mythical descendents of the Anunnaki (ancient Mesopotamian giants/genies) to the Faerie Folk of ancient Celtic lore, but their origins are found squarely in the realm of Israelite/Hebrew religious mythology. They are mentioned for the first time in the pages of the Book of Genesis, the first book of the Old Testament, attributed to the authorship of Moses.

The scant few verses state explicitly, "When human beings began to increase in number on the earth and daughters were born to them, the sons of God saw that the daughters of humans were beautiful, and they married any of them they chose.... The Nephilim were on the earth in those days—and also afterward—when the sons of God went to the daughters of humans and had children by them. They were the heroes of old, men of renown."

There has arisen much controversy over precisely who these beings were. Biblical scholars have linked them with the "Fallen Angels," who descended to Earth after the great war in Heaven, when Lucifer declared himself equal to God. Others have claimed they were the offspring of those fallen angels, whom the scripture defines as "the Sons of God." And still others have made an extraterrestrial connection, believing them to be part of an ancient alienist agenda.

To be sure, the Nephilim were indeed linked to celestial beings, but perhaps not in the way the accepted nomenclature would identify them. One thing that becomes ultimately apparent is that they are anything but fallen angels or the offspring of such—and it is necessary to take a brief jaunt through some of the linguistics of the Genesis text to reach that conclusion.

Another important point to take note of in the Genesis text is that the Nephilim seem to be completely differentiated from the "the Sons of God" and their offspring that were the result of procreation with the "daughters of humans." Read more closely the text of Genesis 6:4: "The Nephilim were on the earth *in those days—and also afterward—when the*

The Fall of the Rebel Angels by Hieronymous Bosch. Some biblical scholars have said that the Nephilim were actually these angels.

sons of God went to the daughters of humans and had children by them. They were the heroes of old, men of renown."

Who were the "Sons of God"?

The beings mentioned in Genesis 6:1 are called "the Sons of God" in the English translation. These are the beings who came down from the heavens and interbred with human women—the "daughters of men." The passage states that these Sons of God saw that they were beautiful and married any of them that they chose. In the Book of Enoch—which also refers to these Sons of God as the "Watchers"—it goes so far as to state that they "loved" them. This was no hostile invasion from some group of extraterrestrial beings, but an act of love. They went to the human women, wooed them, married them, and had children with them. It also states in Enoch that they dwelt with them, taught them skills and even the "forbidden knowledge" of the gods.

In Hebrew, the term "Sons of God" is *bene ha'Elohim*, or, "sons of/those of the Elohim." When these beings are referenced as "fallen angels," a huge linguistic error is being made. In the Hebrew, the word for angel is *melakh*, and in the plural, *melakhim*, the "im" being the suffix that denotes a plurality. But the term *melakh* does not appear in the Genesis text concerning these Sons of God. They were not angelic beings at all. What does appear is the term *Elohim*. So, the literal reading for Sons of God is "those who are of the Elohim." The word Elohim is one of the many names used for God in the Old Testament, and it appears nearly 2,800 times in the pages of those Hebrew scriptures. Its literal rendering when used in the context of the name of God is "God of many gods." Note the "-im" suffix at the end of the name, denoting plurality. It is a name for God that can be used to signify both the singular and the plural, much like the English word "deer."

So, the Sons of God in the Book of Genesis—"those who are of the Elohim"—can lit-erally be rendered, "Those who are of the God of many gods." In a very real interpretation of the language, those beings are part of a cast of minor gods whose chief was the God of the Old Testament. It was they who descended to the Earth in both the Genesis 6 passage and in the Book of Enoch, and intermingled with human women, having children with them.

Cross-reference the term Elohim with Psalm 82, in which God is standing in the midst of the gods, referring to them all as "gods," or "Elohim," the "bright, shining princes of heaven," equating them to himself, yet having dominion over them.

The Sons of God in the Genesis 6 passage are not angels. They are members of what the scripture refers to as "the Divine Council," the cast of minor gods. One of the members of this council can also be found in Genesis 3, in the serpent character who beguiles Eve to eat of the forbidden fruit. In that passage the serpent is called Nachash, whose name is defined as "the bringer of knowledge and chaos; illuminator; bright shining one." Could it be that this serpent character is also one of the Elohim, the "bright shining princes of heaven"?

Note that in Genesis the names Satan, Devil, and Lucifer never actually appear in the text. The biblical references to those names were first made over a thousand years after the writing of the Book of Genesis.

As noted, Enoch also refers to these beings as the Watchers. These celestial beings were sent to Earth to watch over humanity. They, as the story goes, broke the rules and intermingled with the human women, loving them, teaching them, and eventually impregnating them.

So far, we see that the Sons of God who supposedly fathered the Nephilim are not fallen angels but rather members of the Divine Council, the gods of the ancient Hebrews. They are never called malakhim, but are precisely called Elohim. That is a huge difference and should settle forever whether or not they were part of the cast of fallen angels.

Continued...

So, what of their offspring, the Nephilim?

Then who are the Nephilim?

According to the Genesis 6 text, the Nephilim were already present on the Earth when the Elohim descended to mate with human women. They are referred to in the text as "the heroes of old; the men of renown."

One of the most famous identifications of the Nephilim in "ancient alienist" theory was Zechariah Sitchin, who referred to these beings as "those who came down from above" or "those who descended to earth" or "people of the fiery rockets" (see *The Twelfth Planet,* pp. vii, 128ff.) The problem is that Sitchin mistranslated the term and forced his definition. He assumed that the word Nephilim comes from the Hebrew root word *naphal,* which means "to fall." But using that

word would render a completely different spelling, with a completely other meaning than the word used in Genesis 6.

Digging into the etymology of the linguistics of the word Nephilim can be a long, tedious, drawn-out process, and Hebrew scholar Michael S. Heiser does an amazing job of it. But for the sake of simplicity, let's cut to the chase: when the Book of Genesis was reconstructed during the Babylonian captivity of Israel, in the post-Israelite monarchy period, the Israelites adopted Aramaic in their writings. The Aramaic word for Nephilim is *Nephiyla,* which translates to the word "giant." The plural of the word is *Nephilyim,* accommodating the Hebrew "-im" suffix.

So, there we have it. The Nephilim in the Book of Genesis are rightly called giants. And they existed on the Earth before and after the descent of the Sons of God—the Elohim, the Watchers—to the Earth.

The only evil or demonic link made to the Nephilim is when Enoch refers to them as the beings who were killed as a result of Noah's Flood. It says in Enoch 15:8–12:

> And now, the giants, who are produced from the spirits and flesh, shall be called evil spirits upon the earth, and on the earth shall be their dwelling. Evil spirits have proceeded from their bodies; because they are born from men, and from the holy Watchers is their beginning and primal origin; they shall be evil spirits on earth, and evil spirits shall they be called. As for the spirits of heaven, in heaven shall be their dwelling, but as for the spirits of the earth which were born upon the earth, on the earth shall be their dwelling. And the spirits of the giants afflict, oppress, destroy, attack, do battle, and work destruction on the earth, and cause trouble: they take no food, but nevertheless hunger and thirst, and cause offences. And these spirits

Russian-American author Zechariah Sitchin believed that human civilization had extraterrestrial origins.

men and against the women, because they have proceeded from them.

Enoch refers to these Nephilim as the children of the Watchers, which seems to contradict the Genesis passage stating that they were already on the Earth when the Sons of God/Elohim/Watchers intermingled with humans. But one thing is made clear in the Enochian text: the spirits of the Nephilim giants who met their end in the judgmental waters of the Great Deluge would be bound to the Earth in spirit form and would become the demonic cast that would forever, in spirit form, plague the humans of the Earth.

The next time you read or hear the account of Noah and the Ark, a story that has been relegated to the annals of biblical fairy tales, remember that it is also the story of the Watchers who left their first duty, as well as the story of the Elohim, who impregnated human women, thus filling the Earth with the mixed offspring of celestial beings and human women. It is also the story of how the demonic entered the world. All, of course, according to Hebrew religious mythology.

(Scott Alan Roberts is an author, explorer, radio host of *Intrepid Radio*, researcher and public speaker. His books include *The Rise and Fall of the Nephilim, The Last Exodus, The Secret History of the Reptilians,* and more. His website is www.scottalanroberts.com.)

Still, the fallen angels are often interpreted as being bad, evil, and even demonic because of the punishment they incurred in being cast out from the holiest of realms. Yet, they might also be angels who "fell" only in the sense of coming down to Earth on their own, with Satan as their oft-suspected leader, at least in Christian belief.

In the Book of Revelation, we get references to Satan, the Great Dragon symbol of evil, the serpent symbol of evil, and fallen angels all in one. In Revelation 12:3–14, we read of the great red dragon whose tail sweeps a third of the stars of heaven and casts them down to Earth. There is a great War in Heaven, during which this Great Dragon and his angel army fight the Archangel Michael and his good angels. "The great dragon was thrown down, that ancient serpent, who is called the devil and Satan, the deceiver of the whole world, he was thrown down to earth and his angels were thrown down with him."

Judaism also has a connection with Satan and Azazel, the fallen angels, but only during the era of the Second Temple. After the Middle Ages, Jewish scholars saw the concept of evil differently, as the absence of good, and therefore did not have a belief in fallen angels or rebellious angels that fall from heaven. Modern Orthodox rabbis believe angels don't have free will but have specific functions and duties to perform, and once they do, they cease to exist.

In Islamic tradition, Satan was more of a jinn than an angel, as angels cannot disobey God. Satan had the free will either to obey or disobey God and be rebellious and evil, which is why he was banished to Earth. But the Koran states angels did not have free will.

Referred to as the Great Dragon in the Book of Revelation, Satan is the symbol of all that is evil, including all the fallen angels.

An intriguing Dead Sea Scrolls fragment called "Curses of Belial" gives a glimpse into the beliefs of the Second Temple Qumran community. Belial was their Satan, a powerful evil entity that promoted sin among humans, angels, and demons alike. Belial was believed to be able to poison the thoughts of those who were not sinners with wickedness and inclinations towards evil. His forces of darkness were intended to drive people away from God and to cause sin, and to "ensnare you from every path of righteousness" (Jubilees 1:19). Another reference, in the War Scrolls, Col. 1, Verse 1, states: "The first attack of the Sons of Light shall be undertaken against the forces of the Sons of Darkness, the army of Belial" (IQ33–1:1). Thus, God and the good angels made up the Sons of Light, and Belial led the bad angels and demons in his Sons of Darkness.

However, Belial also controlled armies of demons that were given him by God for purposes of doing evil and is, despite his nasty proclivity for sin, still an angel himself.

The interchangeability of demons, devils, and dark angels is frustrating for scholars, although many of these beings obviously are the same entities operating under different regional names. But might aliens and fallen angels somehow be the same thing? Although it sounds crazy, the world's religious texts are filled with imagery and stories of entities from the sky that came down in ships or chariots, and beings that came "from the heavens," which to some suggest other parts of our universe. Some reports of alien abductions include impregnations of human women by aliens and the resulting hybrid children. Could this be yet another offshoot of the Sons of God story coming to Earth to procreate with our women and create the giant Nephilim? Might this type of activity still be going on today, except that we call the entities visitors from another world and not angels that fell from grace?

There are hundreds of names of fallen angels, mostly because many are variations of one name and they often have a specific job or assignation. Satan himself went by many different names. There are, according to the tabulation of the fifteenth-century Cardinal Bishop of Tusculum, 133,306,668 fallen angels, making up a third of all of angels in existence. In the Book of Revelation, it is said their fall from Heaven took nine days. This idea is not found in

Greek mythology, however, which holds that Hell and Heaven are the same place, just different "regions" or "levels." In *A Dictionary of Angels*, Gustav Davidson writes of the Elysian fields of paradise, which were in the immediate vicinity of Hades. "This is close to what one finds in a commentary on Psalm 90 (Midrash Tehillim) where it is stated that there were seven things that preceded the creation of the world, and that among the seven things were Paradise and Hell, and that 'Paradise was on the right side of God, Hell on the left.'" He also points to later commentary on Ecclesiastes by Yalkut Koheleth who says the two realms are "only a hand-breadth apart." Thus, the fall from heaven for these angels may not have been such a long trip down.

Many fallen angels may be adversaries of God and good, but in some cases, they are also acting as avengers of holy justice. The New Testament is most responsible for dividing existence into the established two kingdoms of Heaven and Hell we have today in modern Christianity. Thus, angels may have once inhabited the Kingdom of Heaven and either sinned, fornicated with human women, or exercised free will, all of which were punishable by banishment to the other kingdom, the one of hellfire and damnation. Other traditions say fallen angels are meant to roam the Earth until Judgment Day, when they will be banished into Hell.

Spirits, Elves, Cryptids, IDEs, and Other Nasty Entities

Cryptids and Demons

Like aliens, it might be possible that various cryptids are some type of demon. A cryptid is an animal or entity not recognized by science, thought to be extinct, or mythological in nature. Cryptids often inspire legends and can actually be a part of the evolutionary chain that has yet to be discovered and categorized. The field of cryptozoology is devoted to seeking, identifying, and studying cryptids. Some of these creatures do sound as if they could be interchangeable with demons. The more-prominent cryptids (Bigfoot, Nessie, and Yeti) are not usually associated with demonic activity, but the following are:

- Aswang—A shape-shifting vampire or cannibal human-like entity that is prominent in the Philippines.

- Beast of Bray Road—A carnivorous wolfman found in the state of Wisconsin, US.

- Big Cats—Huge, often black, wild cats that are said to be interdimensional (coming from another spatial dimension) and have red or yellow glowing eyes. Also known as phantom cats, mystery cats, and alien big cats. Include the Beast of Bodmin and Beast of Exmoor. Reported often in the UK.

- Black Shuck—A large carnivorous doglike creature, found in England, with red or yellow glowing eyes. Fierce. Interdimensional in nature.

- Boggy Creek Monster—Also known as the Fouke Monster, and Jonesville Monster, a Bigfoot-like hominid found in Fouke, Arkansas, US.

- Cardiff Giant—A giant hominid said to be made from minerals and found in the area of Cardiff, New York, US.

- Chupacabra—A creature said to be goat-like that sucks the blood out of goats and other domestic animals. The name comes from the Spanish word for "goatsucker." Reported in Puerto Rico, South America, Central America, and now in the southern part of the United States, including Texas.

- Dover Demon—an allegedly extraterrestrial bipedal creature found in Dover, Massachusetts, US.

- Flatwoods Monster—An extraterrestrial monster with a spade-shaped head found in western Virginia, US.

- Goat Man—A bipedal half-goat, half-human creature that looks like a satyr and has been reported in several states in the US, including Maryland, Georgia, and Texas.

This rather famous illustration from a 1909 Philadelphia newspaper shows an artist's rendition of the Jersey Devil.

- Hellhounds—Large, black, spectral creatures, like the Black Shuck, with red, glowing eyes. Said to be interdimensional and associated with the Devil and the gates of Hell.

- Jersey Devil—A legendary cryptid reported in the Pine Barrens of southern New Jersey that is described as a kangaroo-like creature with the head of a goat, bat-like wings, horns, small arms with clawed hands, cloven hooves, and a forked tail. It has been said to emit a blood-curdling scream.

- Mothman—A giant, winged, human-like entity, said to be interdimensional and appearing around major natural and manmade disasters. Appeared mainly around the Point Pleasant area of West Virginia in the early 1960s.

- Wendigo—A mythical creature of the Algonquian people. It is a malevolent, cannibalistic spirit into which humans could transform, or which could possess humans. Native to the northern forests of the Atlantic Coast and Great Lakes Region of both the United States and Canada.

INTERDIMENSIONAL ENTITIES (IDEs)

There are dozens, if not hundreds, of other types of cryptids that represent a mysterious menagerie of creatures not known to ordinary science. Many are the stuff of lore and legend and may not be real. Others might be misidentified animals or perhaps even new species of animals rarely seen in the light of day. Others still might fall into the category of IDEs, or interdimensional entities, which potentially come to us from other realities, universes, and dimensions.

The world of quantum physics has taught us that there are possibly infinite numbers of alternate dimensions to what we call reality. Though these dimensions may be either very tiny or unimaginably massive in size, it is certainly fun to speculate that perhaps some of them operate from the right laws of physics that allow for life. That life might be quite different from what we experience here on Earth, and thus might account for numerous inexplicable reports of everything from ghosts and apparitions to aliens, cryptids, and entities like angels, demons, and humanoids.

In addition to the possibility of other dimensions, we also have the possibility of parallel universes that exist beside our own, or even parallel timelines, that may be rife with life forms that are somehow able to cross over into our world. The often projection-like quality reported by many witnesses of entities and creatures could be fluctuations in the physical manifestation of something moving between worlds, so to speak. The often erratic, static nature of some of these entities sounds much like a physical or semi-physical form making a quick and often inconsistent appearance in our physical world. Witnesses will report things like "flickering object that came into and out of view," "it shimmered, almost like heat on the pavement," "it appeared like an image from a movie projector onto the sky, then vanished instantaneously," or "it appeared in and out of view like an image coming through static on a television screen."

These bizarre descriptions have all been associated with cryptids, aliens, ghosts, and entities that don't have constant physical form or seem to live in our world but are able to take on a physicality while they are here making an appearance. Because they might be following a whole different set of physical laws where they come from, they may not be able to maintain full physicality while they are here. But they have found a way to walk between worlds that we humans have yet to discover.

IDEs are also referred to as multidimensional entities, and reports go back thousands of years to the ancient jinn of the Middle East, demons of Christianity, the asuras of Hinduism, the shayatin of Islam, the alu of the Babylonians, and the shedim of Judaism. Though not all IDEs are evil, many seem to have a darker agenda, and, in fact, some might be the very same entities reli-

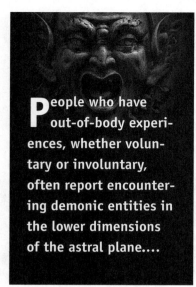

People who have out-of-body experiences, whether voluntary or involuntary, often report encountering demonic entities in the lower dimensions of the astral plane....

gions have given their own specific labels to. Described as non-physical beings from lower dimensions, these entities are often associated with out-of-body experiences, near-death experiences, sleep paralysis, nightmares, and even altered states of consciousness, although they can certainly appear to witnesses at any time in any state of mind.

Some of the lower dimensions that they might origi-nate from include Hell, Sheol, the Underworld, the Netherworld, the abyss, Xibalba, Narakka, and a host of other names assigned to darker worlds filled with suffering, fear, pain, and violence. People who have out-of-body experiences, whether voluntary or involuntary, often report encountering demonic entities in the lower dimen-sions of the astral plane, where these entities move about and can influence the minds and bodies of astral travelers who are not protected and careful. These IDEs can be human in form, or once were humans; they can be animal-istic, or so different from us that we cannot even give them a name. Often they are described as bestial, and shape-shifting, maybe more human one minute, more horrific creature the next. Firsthand experiencers of demonic interaction report that they often try to tempt the astral travelers to "the dark side." At least this implies that we have free will even on the astral plane!

There has been a long battle of debate in the paranormal world over whether or not IDEs are extraterrestrial or not. They are not. Something that is extraterrestrial is still a part of this terrestrial world or part of this universe. IDEs come from a different world, a different universe entirely, and do not just exist in another galaxy or solar system outside of our own. Sometimes these demonic IDEs may give warnings to those they encounter of coming disasters and events. Sometimes they can be thwarted by certain spells or practices such as casting a circle or bringing protective amulets during astral travel. There are no reports of anyone ever actually being killed by an IDE either in our world or another … although there are thousands of missing-person cases all over the globe that have yet to be closed. Food for thought.

ALIENS OR DEMONS?

When it comes to aliens, there have been people throughout history who have likened these entities from space, or another dimension, with demons, suggesting that they are all the same beings, with different names for different times. Some famous quotes are telling:

"An impressive parallel can be made between UFO occupants and the popular conception of demons."—Jacques Vallée, astronomer, researcher and author.

"Many UFO reports seem to pertain more to accounts of poltergeists and ... psychic manifestations.... I cannot accept the 'obvious' explanation of UFOs as visitors from space."—Dr. J. Allen Hynek, scientific advisor to the US Air Force and Project Blue Book

"Many of the UFO reports now being published in the popular press recount alleged incidents strikingly similar to demonic possession and psychic phenomenon that have long been known to theologians and parapyschologists."—Lynn E. Catoe, Library of Congress senior bibliographer

"We are part of a symbiotic relationship with something which disguises itself as an extra-terrestrial invasion so as not to alarm us."—Terrence McKenna, author and visionary

"Today they call them angels and demons. Tomorrow they will call them something else."—Aleister Crowley, occultist

The idea that UFOs may be piloted by something other than men (or women!) from Mars has taken hold not just in the UFO research community, as we can see. Perhaps these beings have been around since the dawn of humanity, and as we evolve, our labeling and conception of them evolves as well, often mirrored by our advances in science and technology. Could aliens in fact be fallen angels or demons in disguise in the modern space age? As our understanding of the cosmos, and our ability to travel to the moon and send probes beyond, increased, the idea of "men from Mars" became the new "other thing" to be feared and wondered about.

In our modern times, do we still believe in demons and fallen angels? Science began to question religious claims, suggesting they were nothing more than the myths of the times, and as we found ways to reach out into our own solar system, angels and demons evolved into what we imagined we might find there. Aliens. Little Green Men. From the 1960s on, reports of alien abductions of human beings hit the news, increasing throughout the next few decades. Often those reports involved aliens having intercourse with Earth women and bizarre breeding programs producing human-alien hybrid babies. This harkens directly back to the Nephilim, the offspring of fallen angels mating with human women, and even the abduction and impregnation of women in folklore by fairies and elves, resulting in hybrid children.

Astronomer Dr. J. Allen Hynek (left) with ufologist Jacques Vallée have both suggested that alien visitors have been mistaken in the past for demons, poltergeists, and other such paranormal beings.

Were the fallen angels of old aliens coming to Earth from other worlds? Surely it can work both ways. Imagine having no understanding of science, astronomy, or physics, or any idea that worlds beyond our own existed (possibly in other dimensions, too!). With that level of perception, to ancient peoples the entities coming down from the skies would appear to be angels falling from heaven, perhaps coming on their own accord to mate with women, or perhaps being kicked out of their heavenly abode by an angry and vengeful God. Mythology and folklore are often nothing more than the expression of scientific understanding regarding real events and circumstances, told in the language of the times. Today, we think of a UFO as a metallic craft skipping through space beyond light speed. In the past, it appeared as a chariot from heaven carrying angels down to Earth to do God's bidding.

The giants known as the offspring of the fallen angels of Enoch, who mated with women, are the hybrids of Genesis and the Old Testament. The fallen angels were the aliens, able to shape-shift into humans to have sex with human females, and having six fingers and six toes, as some accounts suggest. These aliens and their hybrid offspring may have then "vanished" or evolved into the concept we have today of the grey aliens, with their big almond-shaped eyes and slits for noses, and the large foreheads, oversized heads, and sparse hair of the hybrid babies. The "sons of God" that were fallen angels may have indeed been men from Mars, or some planet or universe far beyond our own. Recall that the Bible itself states that Satan does not reside in Hell but rather in the first and second heavens, thus in space and not underground.

The giant Goliath, whom David slew in the Bible, may have been a descendant of the Nephilim.

Many religious scholars believe the giant Nephilim were destroyed in the great flood God sent to punish them and man, but David later fought a giant named Goliath, suggesting the "hybrid" race continued on. One interesting theory comes from biblical scholar I. D. E. Thomas (note the name—IDE!) who suggested that the race of Nephilim discussed in both Genesis and Numbers resembles the Pleiadian "Nordic" aliens often reported by UFO contactees in the 1960s–1990s. The Nordics were blonde, pale-skinned, and tall, up to nine feet. Were these the "new Nephilim" of the twentieth century? According to Christian beliefs,

God made all living things, so would that not include aliens, as well? Unless they were one and the same with fallen angels and demons, even good angels. Not all reports of aliens and UFO abductions involve horrific beings that harm the subject. Many are said to be wise and filled with extensive knowledge of physics, science, and the laws of the universe that far exceed our human limitations. Perhaps demons represent spiritual aliens, and aliens represent physical demons. The occupants of UFO reports are said to be actual physical beings, not invisible forces or ghostly apparitions. This alone may suggest we are dealing with two different things here—unless demons have found a way to become fully physical. Yet some UFO experts such as Jacques Vallée supported an interdimensional origin for aliens that might fit in more with how demons appear, disappear, and operate in our physical realm.

Another religious concept that might create a dividing line between aliens and demons involves where they are supposed to come from. We are told demons emanate from the bowels of Hell and aliens from "above" in outer space. However, fallen angels have been called demons, and they come from the heavens (i.e., outer space). Many fell to Earth, then to rule Hell as overlords, but they were not born of Hell. We must also look at demonic possession, which does not seem to have a counterpart in the alien world. UFOs do not land for the purpose of possessing humans, as much as for the purpose of scientifically experimenting with them, and often making babies with them. Might this, though, be a form of possession?

If we were ever to meet an alien, we could ask whether it believed in God, or the Bible, and if it were a demon or angel, good guy or bad guy. This is called "testing the spirits," as quoted in 2 John 1:7–9: "Test the spirits. If they purport a gospel any other than that given by the revelation of Christ, that God came to Earth in the person of Jesus Christ, and gave His life for the forgiveness of sins, then they are deceiving spirits." Yet, what are the chances that beings from a solar system millions of light years away will have the same belief systems evolve on their planet as we do here? The testing of spirits would no doubt label all but devout Christians as "deceiving spirits," human or otherwise.

Ufologists, who like to keep any religious beliefs out of their research, cannot prove that aliens, if they exist, are angels or demons, and vice versa. But one might argue that if our planet is being visited now by entities from somewhere else, then why wouldn't our past be filled with such visitations? Even if those doing the visiting were the same, or entirely different beings, perhaps it is our perception of them, and our ability to describe them, that matters most. One man's angel is another man's Nordic from Pleiades!

INTERDIMENSIONAL ENTITIES IDENTIFIED

Some IDE armies of demons are at war with angelic armies for the souls of all of existence. The Hindus have a story called "The Churning of the

Milky Way" that speaks of the cosmic battle between the asuras, or demons, and the daevas, or angels, much like the Judeo-Christian concept of demons vs. angels battling for the souls of humanity during end times. IDEs may also fight for the consciousness of humans or humanity, as well as souls. It's not just the Devil that tempts us, but entities from other worlds that want a piece of what it is that makes us human.

Some potential IDEs include the below descriptions.

Black-eyed Children/Adults

They appear at your doorstep, looking innocent. Lost, alone or in groups, forlorn, these children ask if they can enter your home and use the phone, or find rest, food, water, shelter. They appear to need help and, playing upon your compassion as someone who cares about children, they know you will let them in. The problems begin when you do.

What may have begun as an urban legend in the 1990s has quickly become one of the most enigmatic paranormal experiences reported. Abilene, Texas, reporter Brian Bethel may have been the origin point of the legend, when he wrote about alleged encounters with such bizarre children in a paranormal mailing list in the late 1990s. His stories quickly spread in popularity, prompting Bethel to further expound on them on a 2012 television show called

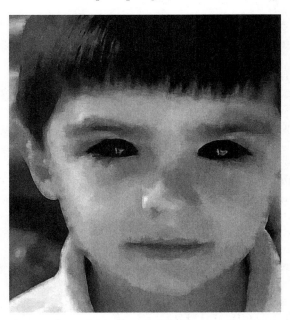

Encounters with black-eyed children started in the mid-1990s, when Texas reporter Brian Bethel said he encountered one in Abilene.

Monsters and Mysteries in America. After that, the black-eyed-children phenomenon took on a life of its own, with more articles suggesting alleged encounters, a documentary titled *Black-eyed Kids* in 2012, and stories galore on the popular CreepyPasta website alongside other urban legends that may have been based, in part, on reality.

Encounters with black-eyed children ran in some newspapers and soon books were being published about real-life experiences with what was once thought to be totally fictional. The encounters had similarities: children, but sometimes even teenagers and adults, would knock on someone's door, asking to use the bathroom or to make a phone call. These children would have totally black eyes, with no discernible pupils or irises, just black pools. They often behave strangely, almost robotically, and many reports state they have adult, robotic voices. Their movements are not normal, and they incite feelings of dread upon entering the home of the unsuspecting victim.

Once the black-eyed ones are inside, all bets are off. Reports run the gamut. Some say the children make demands that, if not met, result in death, injury, or the taking of the souls of the poor residents who just thought they were being kind and compassionate. Others who have encountered these children report recurring nightmares and sleep disturbances, along with a general sense of dread. Ideas on the origin of these beings also run the gamut, from vampires to aliens to the lost souls of the dead to demons to interdimensional beings who have come to possess human souls.

According to David Weatherly, author of *The Black-eyed Children* and *Strange Intruders*, these entities may display many behaviors that appear to make them demonic. Some witnesses have reported foul odors accompanying the black-eyed children, describing the smells as "sickly sweet," "decay," "rotten eggs," and "sulfur." There is also a general feeling that these children are predatory, and sinister, even before they show any signs of it, an impression amplified by their elusiveness in answering any direct questions from the witnesses. Their pale skin and dark pools for eyes give some the impression of vampires or the undead. Weatherly notes, "Whether the black-eyed children are physical manifestations or not seems irrelevant in encounters with people of religious backgrounds. The bottom line is that a number of these witnesses believe they have had a brush with the demonic and they respond based on their religious beliefs."

That statement speaks volumes when it comes to encounters with any paranormal or supernatural entities. The perception of good or evil is often swayed by the beliefs of the victims or witnesses, as well as by their social and cultural backgrounds.

Men in Black/Women in Black

For decades, UFO witnesses and abductees have reported being visited by men, and now, women, dressed in sharp black suits, usually wearing hats, with an official air about them. But something about these Men and Women in Black (MIB/WIB) didn't seem right. The way they moved, the way they spoke, the blackness of their eyes, a foreign yet unidentifiable appearance. Are they themselves aliens, actual government agents hired to spook witnesses and abductees, or interdimensional beings that have an investment in keeping watch, and scaring, those who come in contact with UFOs and potential aliens?

The famous movie series *Men in Black* made the MIBs a fixed part of our popular culture, along with various episodes of *The X-Files*, but these pale-faced beings that use fear to quiet those who may have seen too much have

Events involving UFO encounters have often been associated with mysterious, official-looking men or women in black suits who appear somehow menacing.

been reported so often, and all over the world, that they are undoubtedly a real phenomenon, even though theories abound as to who, or what, they actually are. Usually men are reported operating in pairs or trios, but new reports have surfaced of women in black, as well, tormenting witnesses.

The MIB/WIB mystery appears to have begun in the early 1950s with a man named Albert Bender in Bridgeport, Connecticut. Bender was responsible for establishing the International Flying Saucer Bureau and was shortly thereafter visited by three typical men in black, wearing dark suits and fedoras, who threatened him with death. Interestingly, the trio were not, as Bender claimed, government spooks; rather they appeared in his bedroom, more like materialized, accompanied by the strong smell of sulfur.

Bender later was the subject of a book by ufologist Gray Barker in 1956 called *They Knew Too Much about Flying Saucers*; Bender went on to write his own book, *Flying Saucers and the Three Men*. Shortly after that book was published, Bender quit the field of ufology entirely and rarely spoke of the subject again.

According to Nick Redfern, the author of *Women in Black: The Creepy Companions of the Mysterious M.I.B.*, one of the first reports of a woman in black happened around the same time as another possible wave of sightings of an interdimensional entity—Mothman. In the 1960s, Point Pleasant, West Virginia, was the location of a series of sightings of a strange, large, winged creature called Mothman, which often predicted disaster and doom. At the same time, pale-faced, staring-eyed women in black were posing as "census takers" in the small town, going door to door and forcing themselves into the homes of witnesses of Mothman. The women in black would begin with regular census-type questions of family members, but then launch into strange and persistent questions about dreams, unusual telephone interference and beliefs in the paranormal—not the usual stuff of a census!

Redfern writes that one of the WIB claimed to be the secretary of the late John Keel, author of a number of paranormal books, including *The Moth-*

man Prophecies. She would appear at the doorsteps of witnesses late at night, and once inside their homes, grill them relentlessly on what they had seen, then vanish into the night. Once Keel himself found out about these horrific visits, he went on record to say, "I have no secretary."

Speaking of Mothman, this demonic entity appears to have displayed interdimensional behavior. The large, flying creature began appearing to people of Point Pleasant, West Virginia, from November 15, 1966, to December 15, 1967. During this time, even the local newspaper, the *Point Pleasant Register,* reported odd sightings of a birdlike creature the size of a human. However, the first sighting may have occurred a few days earlier, on November 12, 1966, when five gravediggers at the local Clendenin Cemetery spotted a humanoid creature flying at treetop level above their heads.

The next witnesses were two young couples, Roger and Linda Scarberry and Steve and Mary Mallette, who reported to local police a large, white creature with red, glowing eyes. The large humanlike creature had wings and followed their car as they drove past a local World War II munitions plant. This large beast with red eyes was reported over the next few weeks by locals, in what eventually numbered close to one hundred sightings, prompting the sheriff and a local wildlife biologist at West Virginia University to pass the creature off as a Sandhill crane or large heron, birds that could reach humanlike size and even sport a seven-foot wingspan, as well as have a reddish tinge around the eyes.

But the collapse of the Silver Bridge in December 1967, and the deaths of forty-six people, seemed to end the sightings. Many locals felt the Mothman's presence prophesied the collapse of the bridge. Later, as more witnesses went public, the initial stories seemed to blossom with all kinds of extra, possibly exaggerated, elements, such as attacks on cars, interference over phone lines, disappearances of local pets, premonitions of disasters, and even UFO and MIB sightings in the same area.

Though Mothman was not inherently evil, even if definitely sinister in his presence, the growing legend surrounding him has labeled him as a demon from another world, whose presence meant that a terrible disaster or event was on the horizon. Mothman has become modern-day folklore.

An artist's conception of what Mothman might look like, according to witnesses.

MIB, WIB, and the Occult Side of Ufology

BY NICK REDFERN

It's largely due to the phenomenal success of the *Men in Black* movie trilogy that most people assume the MIB (and their female counterparts, the Women in Black) are the employees of a clandestine government organization. "Secret agents," in other words; 007-types. The reality, however, is that when we take a close look at the MIB/WIB history, we find that most of the reports take us far away from the likes of the CIA and the Pentagon and far closer to the realms of the supernatural, the paranormal, and even the demonic.

It is all thanks to the late Albert Bender that the MIB have become staples of ufology and popular culture. In the early 1950s, Bender—who lived in Bridgeport, Connecticut, at the time—established the International Flying Saucer Bureau. It was a group that quickly attracted a great deal of attention—worldwide attention. Most of that attention was positive, but some of it was downright nega-

Could the Men and Women in Black have gained entrance to our world from another dimension?

tive and malevolent. Many within ufology were deeply surprised when, after around eighteen months, Bender quickly closed down the IFSB—amid rumors within ufology that he had been silenced by three men in black suits.

Gray Barker was a friend of Bender and an author and publisher of books on paranormal phenomena, including UFOs, Mothman, and other strange entities. Barker ran with the story of the silencing of Bender and wrote a book on the affair in 1956. Its title: *They Knew Too Much about Flying Saucers.* Barker's book implied that Bender's MIB were "from the government." They were most certainly not. Six years later, Bender set the record straight in his own book, which was published by Barker, *Flying Saucers and the Three Men.*

Bender's book tells a very different story, that of a man under unrelenting, supernatural attack. The fault may well have been Bender's himself. For example, a year or so before the MIB turned up, Bender decided to turn his attic bedroom/living-room into what he termed his very own "Chamber of Horrors." Bender decorated the room with ghoulish imagery of monsters, vampires, werewolves, and skeletons.

On top of that, practically one entire wall of the bedroom was adorned with paintings and cutouts of large, black cats—some in prowling pose and others standing to attention; their wild, staring eyes near-hypnotizing those who dared to look at them. In Bender's own words:

"Late at night the attic became a creepy place. The floor boards creaked as you walked upon them, and on dark windy evenings stranger noises came from it. Visitors were often 'shaken up' and uncomfortable, as I laughed heartily at their nervousness and amused myself by relating ghost stories at times. My friends eventually decided they enjoyed the spooky atmosphere and that probably was another reason for my fixing up the 'chamber of horrors' by painting grotesque scenes and faces upon the walls of the room. After about eight months I had done so good a job that it almost frightened me when I stood back and looked at all of it one evening. No wonder my friends found it so fascinating, for so many of the ghostly characters appeared to be looking straight at me, no matter where I might be in the room."

Bender was also deeply knowledgeable of the world of the occult and even created a "paranormal altar" as a means to contact occult entities on "the other side." It's almost certainly the case that Bender's reckless actions opened a doorway that allowed the MIB through. And they clearly weren't G-Men or government employees. They literally materialized in his attic—amid nothing less than an overpowering odor of brimstone and sulphur—and were shadowy entities with bright, shining eyes. In the days that followed their first appearance, and their further warnings to him to leave the UFO issue well alone, Bender was plunged into a state of paranoia and ill health. It was almost as if he had been supernaturally infected. Maybe even *cursed*. No wonder he quit chasing UFOs and, after writing and promoting *Flying Saucers and the Three Men*, walked away from ufology, never to return. Bender died in 2016 at the ripe, old age of 94.

As all of the above shows, even from day one, the MIB were steeped in issues of a supernatural nature. And that trend did nothing but continue, in wretched, malignant fashion.

Now let's head to the night of Saturday, September 11, 1976. That was the decidedly ill-fated evening upon which the Orchard Beach, Maine, home of a certain Dr. Herbert Hopkins was darkened by a nightmarish thing in black. "Vampire-like" scarcely begins to describe the terrible creature that descended on Hopkins' home on that fraught night.

When Hopkins opened the front door, he was confronted by a pale-faced, skinny, bald ghoul—one that was dressed in black, had dark and hostility-filled eyes, and sported the *de rigueur* fedora hat.

The Man in Black made it very clear, and extremely quickly, that if Hopkins knew what was good for him he would immediately cease all of his research into the life and experiences of a reported alien abductee: David Stephens, who lived in nearby Oxford. Hopkins, frozen to the bone, didn't need telling twice. Just for good measure, the undeniably malevolent MIB—in monotone fashion—told Hopkins to take out of the right pocket of his pants one of the two coins that was in there and hold it in the open palm of his hand. Hopkins didn't even think to wonder how the MIB knew the coins were there; he just did as he was told.

With a detectable threat in his robotic voice, the MIB ordered Hopkins to keep his eyes locked on the coin, which he did. To Hopkins' amazement and horror, something terrifying happened: the coin transmuted. It turned blue; it shimmered slightly—as if in a mini heat-haze—and then, in a second or so, turned into vapor. After a few moments, the vapor was gone. The MIB implied that he could do exactly the same thing to Hopkins' heart. Hopkins got the message. The MIB shuffled his curious way to the door and vanished—as in *literally*—into the chilled night.

The 1980s saw a deeply disturbing and even dangerous development in the saga of the Women in Black. In fact, it was just about the most disturbing and dangerous development of all. It revolved around the phenomenon of what became infamously known as "Phantom Social Workers" (PSW) or "Bogus Social Workers" (BSW). On numerous occasions, terrified parents throughout the United Kingdom were plagued by visits to their homes from pale- or tanned-skinned, black-garbed women—occasionally accompanied by men—who claimed they were there to inves-

Continued...

(Continued from previous page)

tigate reports of abuse of babies and children, whether mental, physical, or sexual.

In many such cases, the claimed social workers acted in extremely strange and unsettling fashions and created atmospheres of dread and high strangeness. Not only that, a significant number of the reports eerily paralleled the saga of the so-called female "Census takers" of the 1960s, which so fascinated and unsettled the mind of John Keel.

Despite an extensive investigation by the British police—suggesting that the WIB were attached to satanic cults that wanted the children for sacrificial purposes—these creepy Women in Black were never identified or arrested. On top of that, there was the high-strangeness issue—namely, that some of those visited by the PSW and the BSW experienced violent poltergeist activity in their homes. Electrical equipment—such as toasters, microwaves, and kettles—suddenly stopped working. Weird, late-night phone calls abounded.

Today, the situation is no different: I have reports of both WIB and MIB right up until 2016. Just as was the case in the years when Albert Bender was menaced and tormented by the black-garbed ones, these mysterious figures are still turning up on doorsteps late at night, threatening, scaring, and intimidating people as they see fit. And, we still have that unsettling air of the occult that hangs over just about everyone, and every locale, visited by the Women and Men in Black. The reality is that the MIB/WIB issue is far less Will Smith and Tommy Lee Jones, and far more H.P. Lovecraft meets Edgar Allan Poe with a dash of Bram Stoker's *Dracula* thrown in for good measure.

(Nick Redfern is the author of 38 books on UFOs, lake monsters, the Roswell UFO crash, zombies, and Hollywood scandal, including Women in Black; Chupacabra Road Trip; The Bigfoot Book; and Close Encounters of the Fatal Kind. Nick has appeared on many TV networks and shows, including: Fox News; the BBC's Out of This World; the SyFy Channel's Proof Positive; and the History Channel's Monster Quest.)

Skinwalkers

Of a distinctly more demonic bent is the legend of the Skinwalkers. Navajo Indians tell of the *yee naagloshii,* or "man who walks on all fours," a medicine man or shaman who achieves the highest level of the tribe, but chooses to use his powers for evil instead of good. He takes the form of animals, wearing their skin, to cause pain and suffering, even death, to others. But Skinwalkers can also transform into other people, too, if they are powerful enough. Often described as "evil witches," these Skinwalkers take on the skin of their victims because it is taboo to the Navajo to do so, in a display of evil and wickedness.

Skinwalkers are often said to appear looking through windows at night, or banging on walls, and are able to avoid capture. If one is lucky enough, according to legend, to track down a Skinwalker, he or she must say its name out loud in full and the Skinwalker will take ill and die for its sins. Though this is clearly the stuff of legends, many Navajo insist it is real, but make the distinction between medicine men, who do good, and witches, who do evil. A common name associated with Skinwalkers is Wendigo, as well as Nagual, Werebear and Werecat.

ELVES, FAIRIES, AND ELEMENTALS

Elves and fairies constitute a different "beast" entirely. They are not devils, demons, angels, cryptids, or IDEs. Perhaps they exist more in the realm of folklore, but many people have reported seeing them and insist they are real, and not just the stuff of stories and fairy tales. Often referred to as "wee folk," "pixies" and "little people," these entities have a history of being rather mischievous, as told in folk tales, and perhaps as amplified by modern Hollywood portrayals of murderous elves and warring groups of fairies.

Yet some of those old folk tales may have a bit of a basis in truth, as stories often do. The legends of Ireland, Scotland, Wales, and England depict fairies as full of mischief, and at times, quite capable of evil, even going so far as kidnapping babies right out of their cribs. Celtic fairy stories often involve temperamental wee people that would be terrible to deal with if you got on their bad side. They might even do you great harm. Welsh stories of interactions with fairies include "baby farmers," a term used during the Victorian era in Britain to describe the kidnapping of infants and children as a form of payment, lump-sum or periodic, with the understanding that care of the babies and children would be provided.

In Ireland, fairies were depicted as fallen angels cast out of heaven for having the sin of pride. Some fell into the ocean, others upon land, thus creating the various types of fairies written about and reported over the centuries. Some even ended up in Hell, where they took orders from the devil and went back to Earth to carry them out.

The word "fairy" comes from the Latin *fata* (*fey, faerie*) and is derived from the Old French *faerie*, which means "enchantment." Other words often used are "fay" or "fay folk." The name could mean an actual entity, a place of enchantment, or an illusion of enchantment.

Most fairies are described in lore and by those who insist they are real as being small in size, including the very tiny (think Tinkerbell). All have some sort of magical powers and many have wings and can fly, which no doubt gives them a similarity to angels. During the Elizabethan era, literature meshed fairies with elves and often the

Fairies are typically described these days as quite small and beautiful people who fly about on delicate wings, but in folklore and the Bible they are devilish creatures.

two are hard to distinguish. But in general, fairies are more ethereal and sprite-like in nature. Old Celtic and Germanic folklore occasionally portrayed them as dead, and devilish, a form of demon and not human, or angelic, in origin. No doubt this was in part prompted by the advent of Christianity, which combined pagan and religious elements into one.

In fact, the King James dissertation *Daemonologie* states that "fairies" refer to demonic spirits that can prophesy and consort with humans if they wish, or possibly to the spirits of the dead roaming the Earth. Later medieval themes of witchcraft and sorcery were often imparted upon the fairy lore, relegating fairies to demoted angels, though not quite on the level with demons. However, as with demons, speaking a fairy's name is said to bring about its manifestation and force it to do your bidding—a Celtic spin on the genie/jinn lore of the Middle East.

> **A**nother legend refers to the fallen angels of the Bible, although in this version they become fairies, elves, and hidden beings....

In any event, fairy lore has persisted through the generations, and a host of spells, incantations, charms, and herbal formulas has been devised to protect people from their wicked intentions. Protective charms included wearing church bells, St. John's Wort, four-leaf clovers, wearing certain colors or types of clothing, and even offering food to keep the fairies at bay. One of the scariest legends involves changelings, fairy children that would be left in place of real human children kidnapped by fairies and taken to their enchanted domains. Changelings might look like real children upon first glance, but were often misshapen and deformed.

One of those domains lay within the Earth, as in underground or in the "hollow earth." Fairy hills often were said to mark entrances to underground kingdoms, and queendoms, of fairy folk. Icelandic legends tell of the Hidden People, which are the descendants of Adam and Eve's "unseen" children they did not wash clean and present to God. These unseens became invisible and made mounds, hills, and rocks their homes. Elves are descended from these original Hidden People.

Another legend refers to the fallen angels of the Bible, although in this version they become fairies, elves, and hidden beings that can take on human form but usually consort only with their own kind.

In Denmark, the legend of the Bergfolk also involves fallen angels cast out of Heaven. But not all of them made it straight to Hell and were said to inhabit mounds, hills, and banks, becoming "Bergmen," as opposed to the fairies, who fell into the woods and mosses. They are said to be small demons. Sweden has a similar legend of its own that assigns names according to where the fairies fell from heaven—i.e., sea fairies, woodland fairies, and mound elves.

Some were said to go underground, where vast empires were built. In 1644, a Scottish reverend named Robert Kirk was to become one of the most authoritative figures on fairy folk. He attended the University of St. Andrews and the University of Edinburgh and then became an Episcopal minister in Scotland. He published one of the first translations of the Bible into Gaelic. But he was more revered for his superior work in the realm of the fairies, as he became immersed in their lore and origins. He wrote such books as *The Secret Commonwealth of Elves, Fauns and Fairies*, considered even today a masterpiece of modern folkloric scholarship.

More modern scholars, such as John Matthews, claim to have found Kirk's early manuscript, which revealed that not only did Kirk study and write about these little people, but he lived his work as well. In this almost journal-like earlier manuscript, Kirk describes journeying from the town of Aberfoyle to "Lands Beneath," fairy realms that existed below ground. He then described in detail the "Seelie and Unseelie courts" (good and bad fairy courts) that existed underground, including their food, dress, and customs, and that he was more than welcomed into their worlds. His mysterious death in 1692 is said to be the result of a deal he made with the fairy courts after he was trespassing where no human folk ever should have been. His body was found upon a fairy hill in Aberfoyle, adding fuel to the legend.

Interestingly, the idea of impish entities living below ground plays into the concept of Hell or the Underworld found in various world religions and myths. Perhaps one religion's or myth's devils were another's fairy folk.

Like fairies, elves are often portrayed as both good and evil, helpful and wicked, pleasant and malicious. They can be ethereally beautiful or horrendously ugly, almost troll-like. Elves have even been known to lure human beings to their death.

The word "elf" comes to us from the Old English and Germanic words *alo, elbe, apli* and *alfr,* all having root connections in the Indo-European word "white." Elves are Germanic in origin, so perhaps "whiteness" was considered a euphemism for a white person, or a pale, pure, and light-filled one.

Elves are supernatural beings, short in stature, and like fairies, a part of folk tales, ballads, stories, and myths that later spread through Scandinavia and into the British Isles. Germanic folklore more strongly associated them with dwarves, like our more-modern Christmas elves, or those featured in the folk tale "Snow White." Elves had magical powers and abilities and often were seductive and harmful, although others could be totally neutral to human beings. Their threats were often sexual in nature, according to German lore, which may date back to the sexual associations of pagan deities like Pan.

Later Christian source information looked at elves as demons, incubi, succubi, and, once again, dark angels. Throughout medieval times, elves were

The mystic elves, so strongly associated with the natural world, came to be seen as evil beings in the eyes of Christian cultures.

seen as demonic forces by the English, Germans, and Scandinavians. Often elves brought illness upon humans they interacted with; the medical condition was called being "elf-shot." They could even cause mental illnesses, and disease in livestock and domestic animals. Later medieval writings often portrayed them as female and more human-like. These female elves were also sensually alluring, and the Elf Queen, like the Fairy Queen, was a being to be worshipped, adored, and revered.

In England and Scotland, elves were popular but thought to exist invisibly in rural areas. Much of the crossover between fairies and elves appears to have come from literature, as original folk origins suggest they are the same "beings," with different names and specific appearances. Demons of another breed with, again, pagan origins and characteristics were later reshaped by Judeo-Christian beliefs and traditions, and the growth of Puritanism, into the interpretations we have today in modern literature and reshaped lore.

Elementals and nature spirits were usually grouped in with elves and fairies. Spirits of the Earth, air, water, and fire; mineral spirits; storm and water and nature spirits of air, Earth and sea—all were prone to the same dualism of good and evil as other supernatural/folkloric entities. Tricksters also populate world myths and cultures. These mischievous spirits, sometimes even demonic, often lacked morals and behaved in ways that could cause physical harm to humans unlucky enough to encounter them.

Germanic lore speaks of the *kobold*, or household elementals that were full of trouble and mischief. Kobolds liked to play pranks on people, even tripping them or pushing them down flights of stairs. But they also had a kinder, more helpful side—often assisting in chores and finding lost objects. The ancient Greeks had their *kobalos*, entities filled with mischief that could look quite demonic and terrifying. The jinn were said to be trickster spirits, as were the spirits in thirteenth-century accounts that haunted mines and caves, documented much later in 1657 in *De animantibus subterraneis* by metallurgist Georg Landmann. Recall again the underground fairy empires and the belief in spirits that haunt mines. Were they one and the same?

BANSHEES, PSYCHOPOMPS, AND THE GRIM REAPER

Elves and fairies aren't the only possibly demonic beings that inhabit mounds. The old Irish banshee, or "woman of the mounds," was a female spirit said to haunt the Irish countryside, often portending the death of a famous or important member of a Gaelic family. She could be heard wailing or keening, even shrieking, wearing red or green clothing, with long, knotted, dirty hair. She was a shape-shifter of sorts, able to change her appearance from young and beautiful to old and ugly. She may have been a personification of the Irish goddess of battle and war, Morrigan.

The banshee was also part of traditional Scottish lore, in the form of a "keening woman," who was not evil, but certainly was not someone you would want around, as she was associated so much with coming death. In Welsh lore, she was the Hag of the Mist, and if you heard her keen or sing her wailing song, death was approaching. When more than one banshee appeared at the same time, it was said to portend the death of someone holy or important to the community.

Like the banshee, the psychopomp was associated with something dark and sinister, scary and demonic. Yet the psychopomp is found in many religions and world myths as the guide of souls into the Underworld or the afterlife. Greek, Roman, and Egyptian myths include such psychopomps as Charon the ferryman, Hermes, Hecate, Mercury, Anubis, and Vanth. In modern Philippines, dead relatives might serve as the psychopomps who become visible to the dying and help them cross the barrier between life and death. Often anthropomorphic in form, they could appear as part deer, dog, raven, horse, owl, and sparrow. A group of psychopomps might gather outside the home of someone dying, waiting to escort the soul to the other side.

The most famous of these is the Grim Reaper, a symbol of death himself. Originating in England, and dating as far back as the fourteenth century, the concept of the Reaper spread around the world and is now a part of almost every culture. The term itself was coined much later, in 1847. Usually described as a skeleton wearing a black, hooded robe and carrying a scythe, the Reaper appearing at your door meant

A c. 1900 painting by Henry Meynell Rheam, "The Banshee" shows how the female spirit would appear when death was near for a member of a Gaelic family.

you were about to die, as he was there to collect your soul and accompany it to the other side. Often people would try to bribe or bargain with the Reaper to buy more time, but once a life was up, the Reaper took what was his. He is thought to be male, though some countries have had a female reaper, such as Marzanna from Slavic myths.

Though looked upon as the ultimate evil, the Grim Reaper really wasn't any such thing. It was his job to escort the dead, and because everything and everyone died, he truly did not not possess demonic intentions. Each culture gave its own Grim Reaper characteristics appropriate for its region and beliefs, but most respected the representation of death as something inevitable, and certainly terrifying, but not evil or demonic. As the "angel of death" in Abrahamic traditions, he indeed played an unpleasant role, associated with death, dying, and even the slaughter of first-born children in Egypt, so he often was confused with destroyers, dark angels, and even angels of light.

Our greatest fear as humans is death; thus, the Grim Reaper has the unpleasant job of being the most hated of all dark entities or beings, even if his role is totally natural and a part of the cycle of birth, life, and death. Put it this way … the Grim Reaper has no friends. Even demons have other demons.

Viral Demons and Fakelore

With the advent of the Internet, we can post a story on a website or forum and within seconds, someone across the globe will be reading it, and reposting it, and so on. This is how stories today go viral, and yet some of them go viral under the premise that they might be true, even as their creators insist they are fiction.

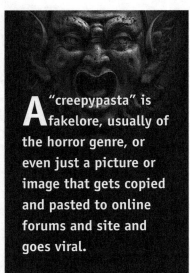

A "creepypasta" is fakelore, usually of the horror genre, or even just a picture or image that gets copied and pasted to online forums and site and goes viral.

There are websites and forums online that allow people to post stories, usually horror, for others to read and take viral. Some of these stories were taken so seriously by some readers that they started claiming to see the monsters or the entities in the stories, which, please remember, were entirely made up by contributors.

A "creepypasta" is fakelore, usually of the horror genre, or even just a picture or image that gets copied and pasted to online forums and sites and goes viral. The term "creepypasta" actually comes from "copypasta," which involves literally copying and pasting information to forums and sites that allow it. One such site, 4chan, is a cross between Pinterest, where people "pin" images they like onto their "pages," and Reddit, a hugely popular forum site that younger people flock to with information on just about everything under and over the sun.

Creepypastas can be about urban legends, crimes, paranormal and cryptozoological entities, and gruesome murders that never took place, but the tone of the stories is often so realistic that anyone who didn't know they were fictional might be easily misled. In the case of evil and demonic entities, they can scare people into actually thinking they exist.

The most popular creepypasta is "Slender Man," which became such a huge rage that Slender Man costumes became one of the most widely seen costumes for years at the San Diego Comic Con. This fictional yet sinister entity was created by Eric Knudsen, also known as Victor Surge, for a forum called "Something Awful." He created the image of a very tall, slender man with no face wearing a black suit, white shirt, and collar with tie. This spectral entity was said to lurk near places children played or went to school, and legend had it (there's that word "legend" again!) that if

A cosplayer dressed as Slender Man for the 2014 Chicago Comic & Entertainment Expo.

you looked at Slender Man, you would die on the spot. Slender Man would abduct children and was eventually linked to the more paranormal "shadow people" entities being reported worldwide. Yet this one was not real.

The stories proliferated, and the legend grew, and soon Slender Man was a popular Halloween and Comic Con costume, but also a scary example of how something totally fake could take on a life of its own, even spawning acts of violence. In 2014, two teenage girls were arrested in Waukesha, Wisconsin, after they stabbed a classmate and left her for dead, claiming Slender Man told them to commit the crime. The stabbing victim recovered but will no doubt be scarred physically and emotionally for life, all because two girls believed in something that was nothing more than the brainchild of a creative imagination. Scholars have dubbed this "digital folklore," and it is a phenomenon worthy of study, combining true elements of folk tales with modern methods of fast communication. The power of mass communication has taken fakelore to a new level. But where oral and written traditions of old have stood the test of time, fakelore suffers from quick burnout amid the overwhelming number of new stories available with a few keystrokes.

Like folklore, fakelore can sometimes include nuggets of truth or be based on or inspired by a true person or event. One such piece of creepypasta fakelore is called Jeff the Killer. It involves a sinister-looking teenage boy named Jeff whose face was badly burned by a bully, causing him to go insane, sporting a sinister smile much like the Heath Ledger version of the Joker. Jeff the Killer became a serial killer with the M.O. of sneaking into his victims' homes, whispering in their ear, "Go to sleep," and then killing them. Jeff the Killer is a feared person, if you read the stories, and it almost sounds like people believe he is real, possibly because of our inherent fear of "copycats," who might be prone to take this fictional stuff and adopt the identities, and characteristics, and behaviors. Copycat killers pop up whenever we hear about real serial killers, so why not those who aren't real? A crazy person doesn't distinguish much difference.

> **D**espite being entirely fake, [The Rake] ... has spawned hundreds of eyewitness sightings (dating back to the 1690s!), if you believe the reports on the various sites.

There is also a humanoid entity called The Rake that has created its own place in the creepypasta Hall of Fame. This cyptozoological entity on four legs with glowing red eyes can attach itself to people for no reason and cause severe psychological trauma to its victims. Despite being entirely fake, it has spawned hundreds of eyewitness sightings (dating back to the 1690s!), if you believe the reports on the various sites. Some of them sound terrifyingly genuine, and herein lies the curse of storytelling—it can sound awfully close to the truth, and we are left to figure out what is fact and what is fiction. One glance at The Rake's own Wiki page and you can see the many drawings and renditions people have made over the years. It looks demonic and scary enough to tie into the deepest fears of the collective, which then may very well promote further "sightings" and reports. Are people seeing these things for real, faking it, or imagining something based upon what they read and heard? Viral demons are afoot, and play directly into the human desire to spread information, even when it has no truthful foundation.

Perhaps the creepypasta entities and creatures are not all that far removed from stories and reports of Bigfoot, Nessie, Mothman, Thunderbirds, and even Skunk Ape, a Florida cryptid with its own urban legend. And perhaps they are not that far removed from the paranormal entities many people report, such as shadow figures, black-eyed kids, apparitions, and the usual religious-oriented demons.

As we become more educated, we realize that stories are both a blend of the real and the unreal, the normal and the paranormal, the natural and the supernatural. Stories combine fact and fiction in order to influence and affect the right and left brain, the subconscious and the conscious. Often stories contain symbols, motifs, and themes that have a deeper meaning understood only by our subconscious minds. Often they contain fairies and elves and demons and beasties and three-headed hydras, which may simply be the creepypasta creations of the subconscious realm. Could this very phenomena account for reports of angels, demons, and other entities throughout history, from our myths to our religious texts and stories?

The bottom line is this: folklore and fakelore are almost indistinguishable, unless one has access to the exact origin point of said tall tale. In the case of Slender Man, we know who created it. That is where its power should end. With other legendary beasties and entities, we may not have that information at hand, and that is why many legends continue to be passed down to younger generations. Until someone proves it's true or false, and locates the original perpetrator of said story, we are left to guess. We are left to imagine and label the stories accordingly.

The demons and angels of yesterday may be the creepy and sinister creations of the collective psyche of humanity today. Or they could be aliens!

Other fakelore entities include:

Dark Watchers—Mysterious human-like entities, often wearing a cape and hat, that stand eerily in the Santa Lucia mountains in California.

Skinwalker—Based on Navajo legend, a cursed medicine man or shaman that wears the skins of its victims (see above).

Grinning Man—A Slender Man-type entity but with a face and a massive grin that is too big for its face.

Hat Man—Another Slender Man-type entity that wears a dark cloak and hat and doesn't appear to be entirely physical.

Fakelore plays on our love of things that scare us, but do these entities have the power to actually manifest and spread their brand of evil simply because enough people believe they exist? Demons of the mind and imagination may be the most frightening of all.

SHADOW PEOPLE

Ghosts. Demons. IDEs. Spirits. The phenomenon of shadow people seems to cross all lines of explanation, yet anyone who has encountered such beings insists they are not friendly. Imagine seeing a dark, shadowy human form moving across the room, only to vanish into the wall as if made of air, and yet have an actual physicality to it. People who report these shadow figures sometimes say they are not "see-through," like a ghost, but solid, like a human, and yet they can do things humans cannot, such as float across the room, or appear and disappear as if from another world, or dimension. There might be a puff of black smoke that appears right before a shadow person appears or departs.

Shadow people look like human beings but are able to float and appear out of nowhere, perhaps from another dimension.

Usually such a being is seen only out of the corner of the eye and only for a moment. But in some cases, these elusive beings appear for longer periods and are said to have red, glowing eyes, much like those of many IDEs and cryptids, and a malevolent presence the witness can't quite explain. In fact, they might even flee once detected and are not normally associated with violence or terror, except for the fear they instill in the witness. Shadow people can be children or adults and male or female, but they are often depicted as males wearing long coats and hats (i.e., the Hat Man). Their association with ghosts is much stronger than with demons, as they behave more like apparitions than devilish spirits intent on doing harm.

But there are those, according to David Weatherly, author of *Strange Intruders*, that attack witnesses. "Crushing pressure is applied when the shadow form pushes down on them making it difficult to breathe. There are reports of physical sensations as the form strikes out with dark limbs, at times leaving marks that are discovered later. Others report that the shadow beings attempt to drag them from their beds, intending to pull them into some dark netherworld." They are also blamed for poltergeist activity, such as objects flying around a room or items being pushed off shelves. Witnesses are often immobilized in the presence of a shadow person in the room.

Sentience and awareness of being seen are sometimes reported. It is even theorized that shadow people are the sad souls of the dead wandering between earth and the next world, unable to cross over out of despair or fear. They are sometimes reported wandering outside of, and even in, cemeteries. Locations where tragic deaths or murders have occurred are prime places for shadow-people visits. Perhaps they are drawn to the dark energy of these locales, or perhaps they are the souls of the victims themselves returned to the scenes of the crimes.

Shadow people may be a type of interdimensional beings, or even the spirits of the dead, but a more Christian-oriented interpretation labels them as having evil intention. Weatherly states, "Indeed, from most reports, the negative energy emitting from shadow people is so strong that many victims are convinced the beings are demons attempting to manifest fully onto the earth plane."

JINN

Jinn or djinn are more recognizable to the Western world as genies, which is an anglicized form of the Arabic word. The Koran speaks of the jinn often, saying they are made of "smokeless and scorching fire." Like shadow people, the jinn are physical entities, yet they possess the ability to move through objects and take on the characteristics of both angels and demons. In the Koran, the jinn are one of the three sapient creations of God, along with humans and angels, and possess free will. Therefore, they can be good or evil, depending upon their choice. They are most often compared to Judeo-Christian demons, much more so than to angels, but in fact appear to be some ancient type of IDE associated with the Arabic world and Islamic myth and religious tradition.

The root of the word "jinn" is Semitic and means "to hide," but later it became associated with the French *genie*, from the Latin *genius*, which is a guardian spirit in Roman tradition. Genies are most known from literature and pop culture as entities that grant wishes and do favors, but the jinn were not so easily swayed. Made of smokeless fire, as opposed to humans made of clay, *Iblis*, the head of the jinn, refused to bow before Adam and Eve and was punished by being expelled from Paradise into the wild deserts, like the fallen angels of Judeo-Christianity. Jinn are not human and will be judged during end times for their actions and behaviors.

They appear from lore to inhabit a world parallel to ours, perhaps interdimensional in nature, and are often associated in our world with desert regions and the Middle East. Known as the Hidden Ones, they can live in sand, on the wind, or in the ashes of fire, and yet also have human characteristics. Interestingly, like fairies, jinn have their own communities, with kings, courts, laws, weddings, and ceremonies. Muslim beliefs vary as to how many types of jinn there are. Some list five orders, others three classes, and they can

The Threat: Shadow People and the Hat Man

BY HEIDI HOLLIS

Just when it was thought that no other layer of the paranormal could be unveiled, drawing up one's covers over one's head is once again inviting! Traversing the planet, in every land, culture, and nightmare—a demon lurks. Most demons find strength in anonymity, such that they don't wish to share their names so that you could vanquish them in an exorcism. But what if there were a demon, or worse, that wanted to gain notoriety for the fear it invoked?

Haplessly wishing such a thing did not exist was something even this author attempted, who first came upon this creature and gave it a name. This demon would not always just come in an instant, attack, possess and devour. No, not always.

It would sometimes become your friend, your "guardian," your watcher, and your companion. Then just as easily, it would become your stalker, your abuser, your rapist, your reaper, and your eternal torturer. This entity was dubbed "The Hat Man" by this author. This being most often comes dressed all in black, wearing a three-piece suit, trench coat, and gaucho hat. Its garb might change; such that it might wear a cape, top hat, no hat, pinstripes, chained watch, or brown suit. It might be clean-shaven or have a goatee. Or it might be merely a shadow-like shape, wearing any combination of these items.

Originally, it was called "The Hat Man Shadow," as simply another form that Shadow People took on. Hollis was quick to readjust its title, soon after introducing the world to the phenomena of Shadow People. This change was done when it became clear that this entity was no mere shadow—he was real!

Speaking of Shadow People, they are a type of demon that can morph into a variety of forms. They are sometimes seen with red eyes, glowing through their black form, that swallows all light in their presence. Some people report being able to barely make out objects through a Shadow Being.

Shadow People can be seen best in peripheral vision, initially. This element often makes the observer feel his or her eyes may be playing tricks! Once spotted, these entities have been known to flee quickly. Especially since seeing such a thing may give

The Hat Man is described as wearing a trenchcoat over a three-piece suit, and he wears a gaucho hat.

a person the upper hand, knowing that something else may be living with him or her that doesn't help with the mortgage payments. Having knowledge brings power over these beings, which is something that they don't like to share.

Then there are the overwhelming instances where Shadow People go on the attack against the observer, almost as if to intimidate the person into silence:

"I saw this black mass, sort of, poke its head out of the doorway and then duck back in. Then as if it got mad, it came out from around the corner with full force and flew quickly—straight at me! I ducked and ran the other way, but it felt like it might have gone through me!"

Shadow People like to scratch, punch, rape, bruise, poke, slap, wrestle, and, most especially, choke their victims! They go on the prowl at all times of day, but take special interest in the hours when most are sleeping and unaware they are featured on an unknown menu. Where there are Shadow People, there are often other presences like ghosts, orbs, spirits, and The Hat Man.

Getting back to The Hat Man: he is international and multidimensional and commits the unmentionable.

Children are said to have an element of innocence when it comes to matters of the soul, but The Hat Man treads often where he would seem least likely to be:

"I was maybe 5 years old when The Hat Man started to visit me. Every night I would lie in the top bed of my bunk bed and watch as my door would crack open for him to creep inside. As high up as I was, I would still have to look up to see him and I would freeze in horror at the sight of him!

"He moved faster than anything humanly could, as he'd spring towards me. He would then say, 'One day I will have you!' Then he would put his hands around my neck and begin to choke me! I would shoot straight up

in bed screaming at the top of my lungs—then he'd just disappear!!!

"My mom would just dismiss it all, though she had taken me to doctors to try and help with my nightly outbursts. She eventually grew tired of it and took the light bulb out of the lamp in my bedroom so I couldn't get up to turn it on all night long. One night, she even locked the door on me with The Hat man inside the room with me!

"I heard The Hat Man come close to me and say, 'Now I've got you!'

"It was on this night that my mother didn't hear me scream. So she came into the room to check on me only to find my body was pushed through the narrow, wooden rails of my bunk bed—hanging by my neck!

"It took my mom and three of her male friends to pry the wood apart to get me out from between the wooden planks! Afterwards, they found large hand marks around my neck in bruises. They did CPR on me to bring me back to life and I woke up screaming, 'He almost had me!'

"I slept with my mom every night after that until we moved out of that place. I never saw him again!" (from the book *The Hat Man* by Heidi Hollis)

Children are a common target of The Hat Man. Some say they don't recall any part of their childhood when they didn't know his presence was near—watching! Respecting NO limits, The Hat Man operates with no regard to the best of us or the worst of us. Whether a person is faithful or disregards all thoughts of there being a God, The Hat Man may tip his hat toward that person and lean in.

The Hat Man doesn't just frighten a person. With a mere glimpse of him, it's common that a person fears for the rest of his years that The Hat Man will return again. His utter presence pulsates as being the ultimate evil:

"When I was 10 years old, I was playing in the living room by myself for a while. That's when I suddenly looked up to see this man all

Continued...

(Continued from previous page)

in black, wearing a hat, standing there just staring at me! I fell backwards and screamed, but no one came for me. He remained for a few more seconds, and literally scared me down to my soul! Then he just vanished without a trace! I told my parents, but they didn't believe me—I've never been the same since! I'm 55 years old now and I feel that The Hat Man robbed me of living a normal life! I have so much anxiety and fear since that day that I forever slept with a light on, and have anticipated that he will be back for me one day! I am beyond angry that such a thing would happen to an innocent kid like myself!"

From a tree on a joyful day, to the side of the road after an accident, The Hat Man has been seen watching with delight. He is sure to make an appearance, almost as if to be certain he gets the credit for being present. If seen, he may tip his hat in acknowledg-ment, and if asked, he may even tell you his name. But if you are close enough for either to happen, then you should give some thought to what he's found of interest in you to even look your way....

(Heidi Hollis is the first author to write about Shadow People and The Hat Man, giving them both their descriptive names to portray these dark menaces now interrupting lives around the globe. Hollis is also a radio talk-show host who has authored several books on various topics and has been featured on television and radio shows worldwide. When it comes to the paranormal, Hollis claims to have "Been there, seen that, experienced it, freaked out, found some answers, wrote about it, got over it and now help others do the same!" She offers levelheaded advice for anyone seeking answers to personal paranormal mysteries via her radio shows or website [HeidiHollis.com].)

take the forms of snakes, humans, dogs, vultures, and even dragons. The Koran specifically forbids the jinn from associating with God and warns humans not to worship the jinn and their devious ways. One popular belief states that a jinn is assigned to every person and can influence one's behavior both good and bad, just like a guardian angel, or devil, upon one's shoulder, whispering in one's ear.

Jinn myths and stories are found all throughout the Muslim world in various forms and have even populated pop culture with references in movies, books, and comics. As genies, they are most associated with the epic story *One Thousand and One Arabian Nights*, the hugely popular television series *I Dream of Jeannie*, and the movie *Thief of Bagdad*. Legend and lore is expansive when it comes to the jinn, with some stories saying they have vast kingdoms on earth and others saying they live in cities that exist only in their dimension. Perhaps one of the things that most demonizes jinn is the belief that if someone gets the attention of a jinn, it attaches itself to that person and harasses him, driving him crazy, even to the point of death. Jinn can possess humans, like demons, and cause mischief and worse. Therefore, it is not considered wise to talk about them much, as you may be asking for trouble.

They may be tricksters, poltergeists, or demons, and sometimes it's hard to tell the difference. They are also described as time-travelers and shape-shifters and can take on the forms of humans, animals, and even the deceased loved ones of someone they wish to possess. Jinn and genies alike make up another category of beings that can be associated with demons, even share similar characteristics, while having a local, regional, or cultural "spin."

There are a million faces, forms, and personas demons may take, sharing common traits that give us a distinct glimpse into the human need for dualistic thinking and the tug of war between good and evil. What is one country's jinn is another's genie. One religion's fallen angel is another belief system's fairy. Since the beginning of our walk on this Earth, humanity has ascribed labels to everything we've encountered as either beneficial or harmful, positive or negative. Good or bad. Demons are simply all the things we believed and experienced that ended up in the "evil" column.

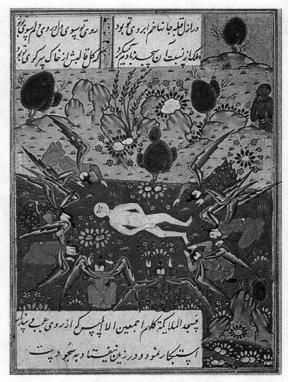

A pre-nineteenth-century book illustration showing the angels bowing to the newly created Adam. Iblis (shown at top right), the leader of the jinn, did not bow, however, and was thus banished from Paradise.

A Psychic Medium's Experiences with Dark Energies

BY JEN DEVILLIER

As a psychic, I've experienced much throughout my life. My first experience ever was with a shadow man. I was home alone while my mother was at work. Playing in my room, not caring much about anything but being a kid, I suddenly felt I needed to look into the hallway. I looked and saw this shadow man blocking out the entire light in the hallway. He was very tall. Rather than be afraid of what he was, I was more afraid of what in the heck he was doing in my house. Around the time of this occurrence, I had been making and using Ouija™ boards with manila folders or paper; whatever I could find. This was the beginning of a very long road of paranormal adventures in my life. I have experience with the dead, the crossed-over, angels, and even fairies. My life is far from boring, I'd say.

One of my most memorable experiences was living in a historic home in Pensacola, Florida. It was a beautiful two-story home that was converted into two apartments. I was living downstairs with my now-ex. There was a single man living upstairs who was a bit of a recluse, so he was more often than not home. He claimed he'd never experienced anything odd upstairs. Downstairs where we lived, though, it was an entirely different experience. My now-ex was skeptical of what was happening, but I knew better, as I was well into my twenties and knew or at least had an idea of its being tied either to the

Jen Devillier started experiencing strange, paranormal adventures after dabbling in Ouija™ board construction.

dead or to residual energy. Over time, I learned there was something intelligent there, but it took a little while to get me to that point.

The first thing to happen is that I started to hear whispers in the kitchen. I blew it off and didn't think it was a big-enough deal to say anything. However, after a month or two, I started hearing my name called when no one was around. This wasn't my normal telepathic communication. This was audible to my ears. It sounded just like my ex and a few times I actually thought he had come home and perhaps I just hadn't heard the door. I would look and no one else was home. There were times when I would be in the bathtub and hear the front door unlock, open, close, and then lock again. Surely that meant my ex was home. I'd say aloud, "Hey!" but got no response. I would get up out of the tub with my towel still wrapped around me, walk out, and see an empty house. No one had come in or left. I was again alone.

There were also infestations. It started with those huge wood roaches that they have in Florida. They are massive and have the ability to fly. As gross as they are, they were coming inside in droves. They come into people's homes when it rains, but now, I don't know why, they were coming in even without the rain. We had the management company come out and spray. After a month or so they sort of dissipated. The next thing we experienced was rats! The way the house was configured, there were two huge wooden doors that slid into the walls separating the front room from the living room. Once we figured out they were coming through the space behind one of the doors in the wall, we quickly put some poison in there. The rats had been coming out and running right across the living room floor into the kitchen in broad daylight with us sitting there. It was terrifying. I have had pet rats before so the rats themselves didn't frighten me. It was the fact that they were coming out right in front of us as if it was no big deal. Rats typically do not

do this. They wait until the coast is clear or it's nighttime. They kept getting into the kitchen and tearing holes in our bread. We had to put the bread into the refrigerator to keep them out.

After putting the poison out, we finally got rid of the rats. Since critters were becoming somewhat of a disturbance, we decided maybe it was time to get a cat. A cat would hunt and kill any other critters that might try to infest the home, right? Wrong! Not long after we got this cat, we got infested with fleas! The entire house downstairs was overrun with them. The cat never had fleas: he stayed inside. Yet suddenly fleas were everywhere. After a couple of months of this nightmare, even with putting a flea collar on the cat, fleas were tearing him up so badly we had to re-home him because we could not get rid of them. We sprayed ourselves, we scrubbed the wooden floor, poured insecticide all over the house, and even had professionals come out and spray. They were STILL there. We could not get rid of them no matter what we did. Other activity at the time escalated as well.

Whenever my now-ex and I would be in the house, we would fight. We could NOT get along there. If we left, we were just fine and all was normal. Even when my mother came to visit, she'd only be there ten minutes or so before she'd start squirming. She'd tell me, "I need to go, I don't know why but I feel like I need to get out of here," and she'd leave! It was a beautiful home but it was also very creepy. When I was home alone, I'd shut the door into the bedroom and put a towel under it so I didn't have to see the shadows that would move back and forth in there. We figured out that there was a walled-off room. When you walk into the entry way, there is a small area and a wall that closes off the downstairs apartment. In other words, there is a tiny room sectioned and closed off from the rest of the house that was behind that wooden sliding door. We could see back there with a flashlight. It connected to the bedroom closet. I feel the portal was in the bed-

Continued...

room closet. I hated going in there for any-thing but that was the only place we could put our clothes.

Eventually we ended up not being able to pay the bills after my ex got himself fired from his job. I was a housewife at the time so I was always home. The electricity was the first thing to get shut off, which was awful since it was winter time. However, the cold did get rid of those fleas finally. Sadly, all we could afford to do was pack what we could fit in our car and drive all the way back to Nebraska to live with some family until we got on our feet. I was not sad to leave that house, though. It was one of the more fright-ening places I've lived in. There were shadows constantly dancing on the walls, talking, whispering … and the infestations. There may be residual energy from a time past that was sinister, but there is also an intelligence there that cannot be reasoned with.

In more recent times, I've experienced some very interesting things. My skills have been fine-tuning and helping me to see, hear, and get a history on a place. I investigated a haunted home owned by a friend; several investigative teams have been there, including crews for television shows. It was the strangest thing. I asked to stay in the main house while the owner and other friends did a walk-through to explain the history of the place.

While there, I kept feeling as though I was being summoned by a woman into the first bedroom on the right in the front hall-way. She wanted me to come sit in there with her, so I did for a few minutes. Later I found out from my friend, the owner of the house, that it was her mother's room I had gone into. Her mother passed away in the house and is often heard as well as seen around there. Imagine my surprise! The whole night of my stay, I picked up on presences all over the property. It was exciting. Probably one of the most unnerving times, though, was when we all stood at the front stairway looking at a dark figure that had come down from the

attic and was blacking out the hallway at the top of the stairs. We neither saw nor heard anything, but when we turned around to walk through that front room we noticed that all the chairs at the round tables there had been pulled out, and other chairs that had been lined up like pews were all messed up. All the chairs in that room had been moved. You would think that we surely would have heard movement since we were standing close by. We heard nothing. It reminded me of the scene in the movie *Poltergeist* where the mother yells at the kids for not pushing the chairs in and then turns around to find the chairs all piled up on the table. We were all shocked. We all felt very uncomfortable and decided to take a break in the back room where our gear was set up. After another short walk through, we decided to call it quits. We knew, for 100% certain, that place IS haunted. When you hear footsteps all around you, voices of people you cannot see, and plenty of corroborating stories from the many people who had been there before, not to mention the current residents, you know something is there. I was able to confirm much of the history and many of the regularly seen ghosts of the house. It was a thrilling experience and it's always affirming to know that what you saw or heard was spot-on.

That brings me to my most recent investi-gation. A friend asked me to come on out to Seguin, Texas, to check out this place she was excited about. I couldn't resist the invitation and it was only a 45-minute drive for me. I was craving to connect to more spirits. Although my life consists of encounters with ghosts and spirits daily—they typically come to me when I'm out running errands or doing anything else, really—going to a location is exciting because it gives me new perspective. I love figuring out the history of a place via the voices that still reside there after death.

I arrived at the location and met up with my friends. Several other people whom I knew were there, so it was a friendly gather-ing. I went upstairs with my friend and his guests to their room while they put their things away since they were staying the night. He opened a door that went nowhere—into open space—with a rail to keep you from falling. It overlooked the "ballroom." I immediately got this horrible pain in the middle of my forehead. My friend had a shocked look when I told him that. He said, "I'm not going to tell you why you're right until later, but you are definitely correct!" We sat in there a bit longer. When I got up to use the restroom off their room, I heard a man singing. I came out and asked if my friend had been singing or if anyone around the room was. They said no. However, my friend's wife confirmed that the last time she was there, she had heard someone singing a lullaby!

There was also a Jacuzzi tub in the room. I sat on the edge of the tub and a few times felt a cool breeze brush past me. The ceiling fan was not on and the air conditioner vents were not angled in that direction. There was already activity happening around me and we had just gotten there!

Closer to the time of the actual investigation, my friend and his wife decided they would hand out papers with the current owner's experiences and history of the place. At that point, I exited the room and went toward the front of the house into the "parlor." I felt it was far enough away that I couldn't hear anyone, so I could try to pick up information on my own via the energy and information any souls could give me. I first felt a woman who liked to sit in that front room often. She was all right with my sitting down on the sofa in front of the window, as this was where I could tell she preferred to be most of the time. However, while I was sitting there, I felt her get up and walk over to my right to look out a window. Suddenly, I telepathically heard a horrible scream as though someone was in a lot of pain. I'd never heard a scream like that in my head before.

Finally, my friends finished listening to the house history and we gathered again to break off into groups, as it's known you can get better evidence when you're not in a big group. We decided to take the basement first. As soon as we got down there I felt pain in my solar plexus (two fingers just above the belly button). It felt like someone had stabbed me there. We tried to do some EVP recordings (Electronic Voice Phenomenon, captured by a digital recorder). I decided to walk to the other side of the basement because I heard in my head the words "the wall." I wasn't sure what the voice was referring to so I went into another basement room, which had a hole cut in the wall big enough for someone to crawl through it. Higher up was another hole in the wall with bars on it. To see into it, you had to stand on a folding chair that had been placed there by the owners. When I got up and looked in there, I heard "tomb." The inside of this area has been filled with rocks, up to the hole itself. Why? No one knows yet. Some of us believe that someone may have been buried in that wall or jail, whatever it was.

The rest of the group slowly made its way over to where I was. I sat down in the middle of the room and everyone else gathered around me. I mentioned "the wall" and so one of my friends took her recorder and crawled into the easily accessed hole. We started recording in there. As soon as we did, we heard noise heading toward us. I felt a spirit walking toward me then felt a cold breeze across my arms. Seconds later, one of the devices to my right lit up and my friend in the hole said, "Someone just said 'get out!'" It was all in sequence! There was no way any of us could deny what happened. After this happened, it started to get quiet and it was time to go to another area of the house.

Later one of my friends mentioned she had felt her arm grabbed, and yet another friend also had felt pain in her stomach. We concluded it had something to do with a male ghost down there that didn't want anyone in his space. Later in the night another group had other things happen and I said, "Well,

Continued...

you keep bothering him; he's tired of people being in his space."

After the basement experience, we headed up to the attic. I had been drawn there when we walked through the front hallway the first time. I could feel a young woman wanting to take my hand and saying "come see my room." We reached the attic and went into a bedroom area. Immediately, I picked up on this young girl, maybe late teens, early twenties. She was very lively and curious about what we were doing. In fact, she kept playing with our various devices. Some folks found their EMF meters lighting up, only to look over and see another device lit up not too far away. She played with everything we had that would light up. After several minutes, I could feel some serious heat on my back as though someone was right behind me. I told the group.

It was time to switch and head to another area. We went down a floor and into the hallway where we immediately started seeing the meters and such lighting up. The funny thing was, the people around me quickly fig-

The ghost of a young woman took her hand and led her to the bedroom. The spirit seemed interested in the equipment used by the ghost hunters.

ured out that the most activity was right behind me. Whoever latched onto me in the attic room had followed me down and was right behind me in the hallway. Because of this, my friend decided to go ahead and pull out the ghost box and turn it on to see if any voices would come through. A few did indeed come through. After a while they seemed to lose attention and moved on. When my group decided to go downstairs, my friend's wife pulled me into another room that was on the floor we were still on. She said, "I want to see what you pick up in here."

It was a HUGE room with a couch, TV, and on the other side, a bed. It was almost like two rooms rather. There was an old, wooden divider door that could be pulled closed if someone wanted to watch television and not disturb the person in bed. This was the same type of door that was in my Florida house, so this freaked me out immediately. I did indeed feel a woman's presence in the bed. I don't know if she was classified as "intelligent," meaning she could comprehend that she was dead. She just sort of sat there looking at me, as if saying, "What are you doing in my bedroom?" While I was exploring around there, my friend's wife kept taking pictures of me. In one there was a strange, wispy-looking thing touching me next to the bed. I mentioned that I felt someone touching my back in between my shoulder blades, though in the picture whatever it was was touching near my bottom. It's interesting that the touching was in only one of the several pictures taken.

After all this excitement, we decided to rejoin our group. Two friends came out of a room where they said while they had been doing EVP work, the bathtub faucet turned itself on!

We all made our way downstairs to the front room. I was back in the "parlor," only this time with a group. It was time to do some EVP work in there. I walked over to the window where the lady was standing last time. She kept playing with a piece of my hair. I felt it being jerked a little, not hard, though. I said out loud, "Someone likes my hair," and the meter next to me lighted up. My friend looked at me and said "Yep," she's confirming it! At that point, I decided to sit on the floor and be comfy while they asked questions and see whether they'd get any replies. The meter next to me kept flickering as I knew the lady was still near me.

My friend then asked questions and started to play back the recordings. The recorders he was using were the type that let you know right away if you got something. Much even to my surprise, someone screamed exactly like what I had heard in my head! We got the same scream at least three times with different recorders. We still aren't sure what happened to cause someone to scream like that, but it was shocking. My friend's wife told me that earlier, in a different part of the house, she had also experienced a sharp pain in her head and was almost crying when suddenly it went away. It was very close to the experience I had when we first got there. We were thinking maybe someone was murdered and the guy in the basement was the one who did it. We all gathered in the ballroom again to take a break. After the break, a couple of my friends and I went back to the parlor, where a group had a different ghost box set up. Two voices were steadily coming through as if they were talking to each other. It was a woman and a man.

Earlier that night when I walked through the upstairs hallway I had heard the word "angel" telepathically. I just assumed the voices were talking about me because I am a vessel for angel communication. However, during the ghost-box session, the voices said "angels" a few times. I waited to say any-thing then finally broke down to tell the people in the room that the spirits probably could see my angels and were confirming. I had indeed asked Archangels Michael and Uriel to help guide me. They are always protective, and the fact that the ghosts confirmed they were seeing them was just mind-blowing to me.

Not too much later, we decided to call it a night. It was getting late and the owners were ready to get quiet in the house. I had my friend walk me to my car and I revealed some more things I hadn't gotten to mention. He looked at me and said, "Jen, I am normally very skeptical when it comes to psychics, but you totally blew my mind. You picked up on everything in the right rooms and the experiences that others have had. I'm amazed!" I found this the highest of compliments. It was definitely one of the most active and interesting experiences I've ever had. We are planning to go back in November 2017 for a second round. I'm looking forward to it.

I hope sharing my experiences with you helps you to understand that there IS more than you can imagine going on around us every single day. The dead are literally every-where! Think about it, you as a human; get freed of your body. You can go anywhere at any time to do whatever you want. The possibilities are endless. Keep your eyes and ears open—you just may be able to experience something of your own.

(Jen Devillier is a psychic medium, spiritual teacher, author, and lecturer, very well versed at doing a variety of readings including Tarot, numerology, Egyptian scarabs, angel readings, fairy readings, and astrology. She is also author of her own paranormal autobiography, Dark Night Haunting.*)*

Demonic Places

When we think of places like old abandoned houses or buildings, graveyards and cemeteries, and spooky historical locations, we often assume they are homes to demonic activity. Not true. While thousands of such locations are claimed to be haunted, mainly by ghosts and apparitions, few places that can truly lay claim to being the stomping grounds of the Devil and his legion of minions. This chapter focuses only on those places that stand up to the definition of being possessed by forces and energies, if not outright entities, that are demonic in nature.

MUSEUMS

By nature, museums are places that house old, storied objects, including those with religious or occult backgrounds. It is believed that even primitive and ancient items can harbor forces and energies. But few museums can be called places of true demonic activity. One that most certainly can is Pollock's Toy Museum in London. This small museum is made up of two connecting townhouses containing a treasure trove of antique and vintage dolls and toys. There are 150-plus-year-old Victorian dolls, porcelain dolls, rag dolls, dolls with no features, cheery dolls, sad dolls, and utterly sinister dolls. Some are dressed in nineteenth-century clothing and some no longer have hair. But visitors to the museum often avoid the "doll room" because of our natural distaste for spooky things.

Ken Hoyt, who has worked at the museum for years, told Smithsonianmag.com's Linda Rodriguez McRobbie that even though the doll room is the last room before the exit, people will often turn around and go all the way back out through the entrance to avoid it! Ironically, Hoyt says, it is usually adults who refuse to go through the room, not children, and that when some of them do, "It's like you'd think they've gone through a haunted house." Dolls scare us.

Although Pollock's doesn't have any particularly possessed dolls, it doesn't seem to matter when it comes to evoking terror in human beings, even grown-up ones.

A museum that does have a claim to demonic fame though belongs to noted demonologists Ed and Lorraine Warren. Their fame comes from several of their big paranormal and demonic investigations, such as of the Amityville house of *Amityville Horror* fame, and a family plagued by a doll named Annabelle. The Warrens keep a room below their own house full of objects, dolls, and other things, that they have taken from haunted and possessed homes and families and locked away, some in glass cases, to keep them from hurting anyone outside.

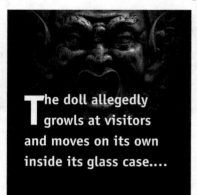

The doll allegedly growls at visitors and moves on its own inside its glass case....

Located in Monroe, Connecticut, the Warren Occult Museum claims to be the oldest of its kind, attracting hundreds of thousands of brave visitors from all over the world familiar with the demonologist couple's work on cases, several of which have gone on to become motion pictures. More on the Warrens is in the next chapter. But their museum is said to include hundreds of items that they deem extremely dangerous because of their occult associations and potential for harboring hostile spirits.

The museum offers tours, featuring a look at such items as the famous Annabelle doll from *The Conjuring* movie and the demonic dealings of the Perron family before the Warrens and an Episcopal priest performed an exorcism and cast out the demon. Other items include the tombstones of children that were allegedly used and sacrificed in Satanic rituals; an organ that plays itself; possessed Egyptian and African artifacts and items; psychic photographs; cursed crucifixes; a vampire coffin; diabolical masks, and other items that patrons are warned about beforehand. There are voodoo dolls, mummies, magic mirrors, and books that are not meant to be casually read.

Annabelle the doll is the biggest attraction, locked in a glass cage with a note stating that the last person who touched it was killed in a motorcycle accident immediately after leaving the museum. The doll allegedly growls at visitors and moves on its own inside its glass case (see the chapter on "Possessed Possessions" for more about Annabelle).

The Warrens, who were founders of the New England Society for Psychic Research, lived upstairs and created the museum from over ten thousand cases worked on, expelling evil spirits, over the course of six decades. According to Ed, many of the objects have maimed and even killed others, and the witching hours are between 9 P.M. and 6 A.M. when the paranormal activity in the basement museum can be heard even a few floors away upstairs. The museum is open for visits now only during what are called "Warrenology" events. Ed has passed on, so the events are hosted by Lorraine and their son-in-law and occur when time permits.

Another famous haunted museum, also in Connecticut, belongs to famed demonologist and paranormal researcher John Zaffis, long considered the godfather of the paranormal by his many fans. Zaffis is actually the Warrens' nephew; they trained him in the field of demonology. He has gone on to become one of the most well-known people in the paranormal field, appearing on television shows, writing books, and owning a museum.

The Museum of the Paranormal takes up its own building on the property of the Stratford, Connecticut, home Zaffis lives in when he is not traveling for speaking events and television shows. The collection includes items from his decades of casework in the field, including a velvet clown painting, black-magic ceremonial items, a sword used in Satanic rituals, and other items pertinent to the variety of cases, some of them famous, that Zaffis has investigated over his long tenure. His work has been featured on television's *Ghost Hunters* and *Ghost Adventures* series; the *Haunted Collector* series on the SyFy Channel; Discovery Channel's *A Haunting in Connecticut*; *Unsolved Mysteries* and various talk shows on CNN and Fox News, as well as *Piers Morgan*, where he has shared his amazing experiences dealing with hauntings, ghosts, demons, and haunted objects.

Among his books are two he wrote with his famous aunt and uncle, Lorraine and Ed Warren, *Graveyards* and *In a Dark Place*; *Shadows in the Dark* with Brian McIntyre and two books with author/paranormal researcher Rosemary Ellen Guiley, *Haunted by the Things You Love* and *Demon Haunted: True Stories from the John Zaffis Vault*. A documentary of his life, *John Zaffis: The World Within*, was released by CORE Films in 2010.

In addition to his training with the Warrens, Zaffis has trained and worked with many priests, monks, and ministers, as well as well-known exorcists such as Bishop Robert McKenna, Reverend Jun, and Malachi Martin. Originally a skeptic himself, Zaffis credits seeing an apparition of his deceased grandfather when he was sixteen with triggering his interest. By the time his *Haunted Collector* show came on the air, focusing on haunted and possessed objects rather than places and people, he had amassed a background of dealing with what he calls "trigger" objects in homes and other locations that may be the sources of ghostly, poltergeist, or even demonic activity.

Zaffis and his crew, which included his son and daughter and other associates of his group, the Paranormal Research Society of New England, would remove the items from a home and take them to the museum, cleansing them in the process. Zaffis believed that haunted objects were either made that way, such as artifacts created for occult rituals, or had acquired paranormal qualities introduced by negative entities or energies. The museum contains some objects that are quite new and some that are thousands of years old. Many can be viewed at www.johnzaffisparanormalmuseum.com.

According to the website FAQ, all items are cleansed by clergy members before being put in the museum. The rituals must be repeated if the object is taken out of the museum and brought back in. Zaffis says the rituals don't always work to bind the spirits in and often have to be repeated. Extremely active objects are kept in cases. Zaffis often reports strange activity such as car troubles when transporting objects to and from the museum. He also points out that while some objects are not "possessed" per se, they do hold the energy of rituals that were associated with the object, and the items become surrounded by the dark energy sent to them by a human during a spell or cursing.

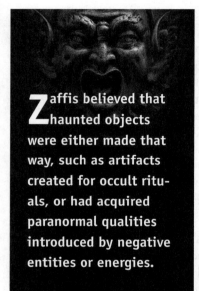

Zaffis believed that haunted objects were either made that way, such as artifacts created for occult rituals, or had acquired paranormal qualities introduced by negative entities or energies.

There are items, according to the website, that the museum will not accept because the demonic energy is supposedly so bad that items must be buried or tossed into the ocean. And, often attempting to destroy a demonic object only makes matters worse, as the entity possessing the object might turn its attention on the person attempting to destroy it!

Not every object in the museum is haunted, but most are, and a few are from famous cases such as the haunting in Connecticut, which will be examined more closely in the next chapter. Zaffis reports that the most terrifying object the museum houses is one called "The Idol," which was used in rituals he found to be extremely disturbing. Visitors touring the museum might do best to stay far away from that particular idol! Asked how someone might determine whether an owned object is possessed or haunted, Zaffis suggests using psychometry, which is a way of picking up on negative energies by touching or holding an object.

Do it at your own risk!

The world is filled with museums that claim ghostly activity, but few places can truly claim to harbor demons amidst the artifacts.

ISLAND OF CREEPY DOLLS

One of the most terrifying places on earth, one truly associated with sinister activity, is an island in the canals of Xochimilco, near Mexico City. Known as the Island of the Dolls, this creepy tourist hot spot is home to hundreds of mutilated and rather frightening dolls that are missing eyes, limbs, and even heads and are wearing various forms of tattered dress. They hang from trees and appear possessed even in the broad light of day. But this island's background is more tragic than terrifying.

The island's only inhabitant, Don Julian Santana, found the body of a drowned child over fifty years ago in the canal nearby. The death deeply disturbed him, and days later, when he saw a doll floating down the canal, he decided to hang it from a tree to honor the little lost girl. He hoped that this act would not only help her soul find peace but also protect the island from evil. But Santana became so obsessed with this act that he ended up hanging more and more dolls, even doll parts, that he found floating in the canal, as well as lying in trash heaps nearby. He soon began even trading foodstuffs for more dolls.

Legend has it that Don Julian Santana went mad, as he believed the dolls were actually real children he had saved from drowning. He also told family that he believed the little girl herself was haunting the island. So, while not a place of demonic activity, it certainly is a place where a man was driven to

Damaged and dirty dolls such as these hang from trees scattered about the Island of the Dolls near Mexico City.

The Devil's Tramping Ground

BY DAVID WEATHERLY

In the rolling hills of southern Chatham County, North Carolina, there's a mysterious, barren circle that has become one of the state's most enduring legends. It lies off an old dirt path near the Harper's Crossroads area in Bear Creek, and it's known as "The Devil's Tramping Ground."

According to legend, the Devil himself regularly visits the site to stomp around inside the circle, contemplating evil and thinking about ways to win souls for his fiery pits. The sparks created by his cloven hooves have destroyed the very earth in the circle, and nothing, not a tree, plant, or weed, will grow on the spot.

Objects left in the circle before dusk often disappear, or are found later, tossed far out of the boundaries of the Devil's space, thrown, it is said, by the Devil himself, angry that a mortal would dare to leave something in his circle. Animals react strangely at the site. Dogs whimper and cower and refuse to enter the circle, wild-animal tracks are never found on the soil, and legend says that even birds won't fly over the spot.

The circle itself is perfectly round, about forty feet in diameter, and completely barren. Scientists have on occasion studied the strange patch of land, but no satisfactory reason has been presented to explain the conditions there. In years past, there were those who attempted to plant seeds in the desolate circle, but each time the plants refused to grow. Others have tried to transplant vegetation into the area, but it all withers and dies.

Chatham County was founded just before the American Revolution, and from its earliest days, the legend of the tramping ground began to grow. The early Scotch Irish settlers gave the spot its name, and their take on the Devil was based on a complicated perception that viewed him as both comical and demonic. They saw the Devil as a complex character both threatening to humans yet able to be tricked and outsmarted by them. They believed that the Devil, like a man, was aided in his thoughts by pacing around in a circle. The "tramping ground," they believed, was his private spot.

Over the years, people have attempted to spend the night in the circle, hoping to catch a glimpse of old Scratch, but no one has reported success in either staying the entire night or in successfully dealing with the Devil. Some stories say those who have attempted to stay in the circle have run out in a wild state bordering on insanity after catching a quick glimpse of the Devil's true face.

An old rural state road leads to the infamous spot, and, at times, a shadowy figure has been spotted in the woods near the road, heading to the circle. Perhaps it's the Devil

Plants do not grow at the Devil's Tramping Ground in North Carolina, where the Devil apparently likes to go.

himself, or one of his many minions, watching the circle and waiting to claim any helpless souls who dare to step on the Devil's tramping ground.

(David Weatherly is the author of Strange Intruders and The Black-eyed Children. His website is http://twocrowsparanormal.blog spot.com/.)

madness by the ghost of a little girl … and his own mind. How did it end? Well, in 2001, Don Juan Santana himself ended up drowning in the same canal he found the little girl in. Most likely it was an accident, but there are those who believe he was murdered by the tortured spirits of the dolls he saved.

CROSSROADS

One of the most fascinating places oft associated with the Devil is also the fodder for many a great blues song. Throughout mythology and folklore, the place "between worlds" known as the crossroads has long represented a place where spirits dwell and the Devil might even make an appearance now and then. A crossroads of two intersecting streets, especially those out in the middle of nowhere, represents a place that is directionless, not here and not there, and a slip in the time-space continuum. At the crossroads, decisions are to be made, temptations are to be dealt with, and choices can mean life or death … or worse.

This belief is not new, as there are references to crossroads honoring the gods Mercury and Odin as far back as the eleventh century in "De Falsis Deis," a sermon that suggested sacrifices were offered to Mercury by heathens who had been fooled by the Devil into worshipping the false god.

African American conjuring, based on the voudon practices in Africa and the Caribbean, often calls for certain objects to be gathered from crossroads and warns of meeting the "black man," or the Devil himself. Folkloric belief states that you can summon a demon, even the big D himself, at a crossroads and even make a deal with the Devil or sell your soul. In Brazilian mythology, crossroads are homes to evil spirits and entities such as Exus, which are similar to demonic entities.

The Devil Went Down to Georgia

BY W. T. WATSON

Those of a certain age, when they think of the state of Georgia, may hear an old Charlie Daniels Band tune playing in their heads. For those of you not familiar with the song, "The Devil Went Down to Georgia" is a classic Southern rock tune that tells the story of the Devil getting into a fiddling contest with a young man named Johnny. Johnny cleans the Devil's clock and wins a golden fiddle from Old Nick, but it is made clear that he does this at risk of his immortal soul.

The Devil seems to pop up a lot in Southern lore. There were persistent rumors that the blues man Robert Johnson sold his soul to the Devil in order to become one of the best blues-guitar players of his time. Like the Scottish pipers and fiddlers who were said to have gained their skill from the faery,

One of musician Charlie Daniels's most popular songs is "The Devil Went Down to Georgia," which is about how a Southern boy outfiddles the Devil.

any musician who showed a sudden, marked increase in talent could be the subject of whispers that he or she had gone down to the crossroads and made a deal with that ole Devil. The question that we have to ask ourselves, though, is, who is this Devil that everyone seems to be making a deal with?

No, Virginia, we are not talking about a whole herd of Satanists selling themselves to the Christian Adversary. While Satan and his minions certainly exist in some form, I would maintain that they are, for the most part, creatures who the people of the Abrahamic religions have infused with great power through their fear and loathing (and sometimes secret desire just to give in and sin a little bit). In some way, Satan and his crew are more mass-projected thought forms than actual entities, though that projection is likely based on a real being.

I am the first to say that there are predators in the Otherworld and that there may even be beings who are the unbalanced versions of the angelic host, but I do not see a demon under every rock and I certainly do not feel that Satan, the prince of this alleged group of fallen angels, spends a lot of time hanging around crossroads trying to collect souls one at a time.

Rather, I suspect that the "Devil" that is encountered at the crossroads is an altogether different sort of being. In the Afro-Caribbean religions such as Voudon, crossroads are the specific haunts of the Lwa (a powerful spirit that might even be considered a god by some), known as Papa Legba, the opener of the way between the world of men and the world of the Lwa. The Greeks had Hekate, the Lady of the Three-Fold Way, as their crossroads deity; so popular was she that her statues adorned many crossroads in Greece, and offerings were laid at her feet to ensure safe travel. We can even see traces of the crossroads idea in the Norse Odhinn, to whom crossroads were sacred (although I would not ask the Old One for safe travel as crossroads were the site of hangings and the hanged were sacred to him).

So, crossroads deities seem to have a strong tie with the idea of opening the way. Sometimes the way is a physical one, and the appeal is for safe travel in this world. At other times, those who walk the inner planes will work with a Way Opener to facilitate and ease their own travels.

There is another way in which the Opener of the Way can assist someone. In circumstances where individuals feel blocked or obstructed in some way, they can ask the assistance of one of the Way Openers to help clear that obstruction or even to help them learn a skill that will assist them in walking their road through life. This is where deals with the "devil" come in.

Orion Foxwood published a book on conjure, the folk magic of the South, in 2012 called *The Candle and the Crossroads*. One of the very interesting chapters in that book deals with just this phenomenon. Foxwood refers to the being with which one deals at the crossroads as the Dark Rider. This is what he has to say about that being:

"I was told that he was not evil but rather very old and powerful and that he came from either Africa or Europe. I think he came from both places.

"There is a lot of information in the name the Dark Rider. First, he is dark, or at least made out of the power of the night. This suggests that he is an in-between spirit who can only be encountered when light and night dance under the shadow of true moon. Second, he is a rider, or in movement, which indicates that his power and spirit nature is change...."

Foxwood also states, "But I warn you that though he does not require you to sell your immortal soul to him, he does require integrity and a promise from you in exchange for the road openings he provides...." I think it goes without saying that this is a being one would not want to trifle with, and that, if you give your word, you had better be very sure you can keep it. If approached with respect (and Foxwood presents a fairly simple rite for doing this), the Dark Rider can and will open the way for the petitioner in practically any aspect of life.

As I mentioned before, it is not unknown for someone who wishes to learn an instrument, for example, to petition the Dark Rider for "lessons." There are even stories of this "man" appearing to the fledgling musician, taking the instrument, tuning it, and handing it back after playing a little riff. After that meeting, the musician was quickly able to learn his chosen instrument.

Since all things are supposed to come from God in the Abrahamic religions, it is no wonder that this powerful spirit has been demonized and turned into yet another version of the "devil." While I do not encourage people to go out and seek the Dark Rider unless and until they have had some good training in conjure, my own work with crossroads spirits tells me that, while this fellow could scare the bejabbers out of you, he is not innately evil or seeking to "get over" on you.

If you are at all interested in conjure, I recommend Foxwood's work as a good way to get grounded in and started with that practice.

(W. T. Watson writes extensively about monsters, magic, Forteana, and the paranormal. A practicing Pagan and magical practitioner for almost thirty years, he lives in Charlotte, North Carolina.)

Devil at the Crossroads

BY DAVID WEATHERLY

"If you wanna make a deal wit the devil, take your guitar and head down to the crossroads. Wait til midnite and a tall man in black gonna appear. He'll make you the best blues player anywhere 'round the delta."

So begins one version of the story of legendary blues guitarist Robert Johnson. Folklore says that Johnson dreamed of being a bluesman and was sent to the Dockery Plantation Crossroads at midnight on a moonless night. There, he was met by the Devil himself in the form of a large man, solid black in color. The Devil took Johnson's guitar, tuned it, played his own haunting music on it, then handed it back to Johnson in exchange for the man's immortal soul.

Most of the Western world is familiar with Faust and his bargain with Mephistopheles, but reports of "deals" with the Devil have long been a popular story motif, going back to at least the fifteenth century. Through the ages, those with great talent are often reputed to have made pacts with Satanic forces to gain their skills.

In America's Deep South, such deals are often specifically connected with crossroads. Long viewed by various cultures as the dwelling places of deities and spirits alike, crossroads in the South are known as the best spots to forge a deal with the Devil and gain unearthly skill. Typically, the deal involves gaining abilities with various instruments, dancing, or gambling. Of course, demonic forces don't give away such talents for free. Those making such a dark pact are expected to surrender the rights to their souls at death.

The manifestation of the Devil in these stories is a unique blend of Christian tradition and influences from Southern "Hoodoo" folk magic. There are various forms the Devil may take when he appears. Some say he will be in the form of a large, shadowy man whose form is difficult to discern. Others say he appears in a dapper, old-fashioned suit, red-faced and smiling with classic devil's horns protruding from his forehead.

Most advise not looking the Devil in the eye, as beholding his full countenance may be too much for a human psyche to bear.

While these bargains may be real, they never seem to work out well for those who go through with them. The Devil, you see, is quite the trickster, and while he smiles and offers a golden gift, his only goal is to collect his fee.

Such was the case with Robert Johnson. He may have gained his uncanny guitar skill from a supernatural bargain, but his success was short-lived. Johnson died at the young age of twenty-seven under mysterious circumstances. Many believe that the Devil came calling to collect his end of the deal—that is, Johnson's soul. To this day, no one is sure exactly how Robert Johnson died. There are several versions of the story. Even his burial is surrounded in mystery, with numerous locations purporting to be his final resting place.

The Devil always gets his due.

(*David Weatherly is the author of* Strange Intruders *and* The Black-eyed Children. *His website is http://twocrowsparanormal.blog spot.com/.*)

POSSESSED PROPERTY

The Devil's playthings. That is a cutesy title often given to such objects as Ouija™ boards, dolls, mysterious boxes, haunted mirrors, and other items associated with evil spirits and dark entities. We usually think only of people being the subjects of a demon's possession, as we will see in the next chapter, but certain objects seem to attract demons' attention, as well. One might think only antiques and ancient artifacts, or items associated with extreme brutality and torture, would be "haunted," and in many cases they are, but a demonic object is not necessarily one that is haunted by ghosts of the past. Being possessed by something and being haunted by something are two different things. Demonic objects are usually the "home" of one particular demon that uses the item to gain power, control, access, and force.

DYBBUK BOX

The "dybbuk box" or "dibbuk box" is just such an item, said to be possessed by a malicious demon that can also possess humans. The name is from the Hebrew *Kufsat Dibbuk*. This mysterious item became public when a man named Kevin Mannis auctioned it off on eBay, along with a terrifying story he wrote to accompany it. Mannis was a writer and owner of an antiques-refinishing business, living in Portland, Oregon, when he supposedly purchased the object at an estate sale in 2003. The cabinet was said to belong to a 103-year-old Holocaust survivor named Havela, whose own granddaughter told Mannis that the item was a family heirloom, but that the family didn't want it because it had a dybbuk inside. A dybbuk is similar to a jinn, which could be playful or evil.

A dybbuk is shown clinging to an unfortunate man in an illustration from a turn-of-the-twentieth-century Old Testament. Dybbuks can cling to people or objects.

Mannis decided to find out and opened the box. He found items such as two old pennies; a lock of blond hair with a cord around it; another lock of brown-corded hair; a small, gold, wine goblet; a Hebrew "shalom" statue; a dried rosebud; and a candleholder with four strangely shaped legs. Soon, Mannis was experiencing paranormal activity in his shop, such as light bulbs blowing out, strange lingering odors, and odd sounds coming from the basement, also witnessed by his shop assistant.

On October 28, Mannis gave the box to his mother for her birthday. She suffered a stroke the same day and reported having nightmares in the hospital similar to those that were plaguing Mannis. Other owners of the box experienced similar nightmares, until a Missouri student named Iosif Neitzke, the last owner of the box, put it up on eBay for auction after his hair fell out and lights in his house repeatedly burned out. Neitzke also experienced the presence of a strange entity in his room while he was sleeping one night at his desk.

The next owner after Neitzke was Jason Haxton, director of the Museum of Osteopathic Medicine in Kirksville, Missouri, who bought the box from Neitzke after reading about it on Neitzke's blog. It wasn't long before Haxton wrote a book called *The Dibbuk Box,* documenting his horrible health problems while in possession of the object. After talking to various rabbinic leaders in the Jewish community, Haxton agreed to seal the box and hide it in an undisclosed location.

Or so the story goes.

DOLLS

It is easy to see why dolls, puppets, dummies, poppets, and effigies can be fertile ground for demonic possession. They look like humans and are often the most frightening of possessed objects because of that reason. The fear of dolls is called *pediophobia,* which is related to the overall fear of humanoid figures, called *automatonophobia.* There is even a fear of puppets, *pupaphobia,* so obviously there is something in human nature that upsets us about dolls of any kind, even pretty ones. In an article for Smithsonianmag.com, reporter Linda Rodrigues McRobbie references a horror movie director, John Leonetti, of the *Conjuring* movie franchise, as having told Huffington Post that dolls are exceptional vehicles in horror films because they often emulate a human figure. "But they're missing one big thing, which is emotion. So they're shells. It's a natural psychological and justifiable vehicle for demons to take it over.… They're hollow inside. That space needs to be filled." Sometimes it's filled with evil.

Dolls have been important for thousands of years for their cultural and educational value, as well as for their entertainment purposes as playthings. Dolls have helped us adapt sociologically to changing norms of dress and behavior, and they reflect cultural values and how we see children, or how we want them to be, according to Patricia Hodges, curator of the Strong National Museum of Play in New York. Hodges told McRobbie that dolls were used in the eighteenth and nineteenth centuries to teach girls how to dress, act, and behave, and what the gender norms were for the times. Even today, dolls assist with social interaction and expression, and modern dolls also reflect the changing female roles available to girls.

In ancient times and in pagan communities of old, dolls and figurines would be used to represent actual people in ceremonies and rituals, for both positive and negative reasons, including statues and statuettes of religious figures. Gods and goddesses often had their own dolls to represent their specific powers in special rituals in Rome, Egypt, and many other cultures that recognized a type of sympathetic magic—a more primitive belief of applying magical values to items that can then heal, harm, or help grow crops and find food by mimicking the animal, person, or object in question.

Voodoo Dolls and Poppets

Think of voodoo dolls, which are used in ceremonies not only to curse someone but also to rid the afflicted of illness, which was thought to be the presence of demons inside the body. Poppets are little dolls used for the same purpose, with roots in much older Germanic and Scandinavian cultures, and are used today by many Wiccans and modern witches for rituals and spells. Effigies were used by many Native tribes, as well as in African and European cultures, and are still used today in political rallies to symbolize a hated politician or dictator.

Voodoo dolls and poppets are actually small effigies that have pins in them, and anyone can make them. They are not so much possessed by demons as they are vessels of the will and evil intentions of the person who makes the doll and casts the spell or curse. Yet, if the belief in these dolls is strong enough, they do work. In cultures that focus on natural magic and ascribe a spirit to everything, living or not, the mere suggestion that an object has cursed someone, or cured someone, is enough to trigger a strong type of "place-

Voodoo dolls are magically connected to the people they are meant to represent. When one abuses the doll, the actual person feels the painful effects.

bo effect" on the mind and the body. While voodoo dolls in Western culture are more of a fun novelty item, in Carribean nations and in Africa, the origin nation of voudon, they are powerful and not something to be toyed with.

One possibly possessed voodoo doll is the Voodoo Zombie Doll, another item sold on eBay with an allegedly supernatural history. A woman from Galveston, Texas, purchased the doll on eBay in 2004. The owner claimed it was made in New Orleans, a place itself riddled with spirits light and dark, and that it was not to be removed from the metal box with silver casing it was placed in. But of course the new owner did remove it and then claimed the doll attacked her and haunted her in her dreams. She repeatedly sent the doll to new owners on eBay but each time it would supposedly show back up again at her door. She finally got rid of it when a ghost hunter took it off her hands. If her story sounds familiar, just watch the "Talking Tina" episode of *Twilight Zone,* as well as many other horror movies that play on the "returning demon doll" plotline.

Another creepy New Orleans doll is the Devil Baby, which was actually a carved gourd hung outside a home to ward off the evil child of a cursed woman. Story has it that Marie Laveau, a famous voodoo queen in the 1800s, cast a curse on a new bride, resulting in the bride's giving birth to a horrific baby that looked like Satan. The baby was brought up by Laveau until her death, and when the baby died, it was buried with her in the same cemetery. But while it was alive, it was said to attack anyone who came near it. The carved Devil Baby dolls scared it away if hung outside. Nowadays, these dolls are rare and worth a mint to collectors.

Much more terrifying are dolls that are claimed to be actually possessed by an entity or demon. A doll may be called "haunted" or possessed, and the two terms here can be used interchangeably, although in the case of an actual possessed doll, the entity within is always evil, whereas a ghost inhabiting a doll may not always be.

Dolls, even pretty ones, often evoke a bit of fear in all of us. We harbor a tiny bit of terror when we see a doll or a puppet or ventriloquist dummy, thanks to popular culture and horror movies. But it goes a bit deeper. These objects play on our sense of self and identity. We see a doll and humanize it. Though our common sense tells us it is impossible for a demon to be inside a lovely doll, our fear-addled brain wonders … what if? Two notorious possessed dolls have quite a horrific heritage—Annabelle and Robert.

Annabelle

If you have seen the popular movie *The Conjuring*, then you have met the lovely Annabelle, the truly demonic doll owned by the Perron family. Annabelle is allegedly possessed by an evil entity that plagued the family until famed demonologists Ed and Lorraine Warren saved the family. The actual doll was a common Raggedy Ann rag doll that many little girls have owned over the decades. In 1970, a woman purchased a rag doll in an antique shop to give to her daughter, Donna, who was about to graduate from nursing school. Donna loved the doll and put it on her bed in the apartment she shared with another nursing student named Angie.

At first, Donna and Angie didn't notice much, although it sometimes seemed as if the doll would move or shift positions. But eventually one of them would return home to find the doll standing up, or even in another room entirely. When Donna began testing her theory that the doll was moving by placing it in particular spots and positions, she soon realized that this was no ordinary doll. It would often migrate to other rooms and sit on the couch, and sometimes it would go back into the bedroom and lock the door on Donna.

The two women told a friend, Lou, about the doll, who felt that it was evil when he first saw it. Soon, the two women were finding strange notes left around the apartment, with cryptic messages written in a child's scrawl, such as "Miss me?" "Help Lou," and sometimes, "Help us." Donna had no idea what was going on, or who "us" was, but their friend Lou was sure the doll was behind the notes. The women were curious more than afraid and began thinking about whether possible intruders in their home were responsible for the activity.

But they didn't worry too much, because the doll wasn't harming anyone—until it did. Soon, objects were breaking around the house, and the doll was found with blood coming out of its hands and chest, prompting the women to call a medium, who performed a séance. During the séance, it was revealed that the doll contained the spirit of a young girl named Annabelle Higgins, who was only seven years old when she died, her body found on the very property the apartment building had been built on. The nursing students named the doll Annabelle after the séance and felt sad for the little girl who had lost her life and the doll.

Though Lou admonished the women repeatedly to get rid of the doll he felt was evil, they didn't see his point, but when things escalated, with Lou bearing the brunt of the attacks, they realized they needed help, especially after Lou had an experience when he confronted the doll that resulted in slice wounds to his chest that burned. The wounds vanished two days later. They then contacted an Episcopal priest named Father Hegan, who went to the apartment and realized that he wasn't qualified for the job. He referred them to his superior, who contacted Ed and Lorraine Warren, noted demonologists who had also investigated the house from Amityville horror fame.

Lorraine and Ed Warren regard the Annabelle doll at their museum.

The Warrens came and told the women and Lou that the Annabelle story was actually not true, that the doll embodied a true demonic spirit, and that the doll was not truly possessed but was instead a conduit through which the demon moved between Earth and Hell. They set about doing an exorcism in the apartment before the demon would have time to leave the doll and possess one of them, because they believed that possessing a human was its goal. Another Episcopal priest was brought in to do a blessing of the home, not an actual exorcism as we know them, and he even blessed Donna, Angie, Lou, and the Warrens, then pronounced the home clean.

Just to be safe, Ed and Lorraine took the doll from the women and drove home with it in their backseat. They took back roads home and had nothing but trouble all the way, which the priest had warned them about beforehand. Ed had the good sense to bring a vial of holy water and eventually used it on the doll, which stopped the craziness the rest of the way to their home, where, after a few weeks of repeated levitation and troublesome activity caused by the doll, they called in a Catholic priest, who screamed at the doll, admonishing it and throwing it to the ground. Though Lorraine warned the priest to respect the doll, he didn't, and he ended up nearly losing his life on the way home to the rectory in an almost-fatal car crash!

The Warrens then placed the doll in a specially made case with a sign that said, "Warning. Positively do not open." The doll remains encased there, in a large room filled with other cursed and possessed objects the Warrens had cleansed and exorcised.

Ed passed away in 2006, and Lorraine says the doll has never busted out of its cage. But it has changed positions while inside.... Once Lorraine passes away, no one knows what might become of the doll.

Harold

The popular online-bidding site eBay has a history of haunted and demonic dolls for sale. The first of these may have been Harold, which was actually featured on the Travel Channel show *Ghost Adventures*. Harold belonged to a little boy who died, and his family soon began reporting the doll singing and moving on its own. They contacted their local clergy, who claimed the doll was possessed and that it should be destroyed, but the family reported it would not even singe from fire ... so they sold it at a flea market.

According to the legend of Harold, every owner experienced the same strange activity, including violence and death. However, no proof of any of this exists except the claims of the first owner who put it up on eBay and a paranormal "reality" show.

Mandy, the Porcelain Doll

In the early 1900s, an English doll maker created a lovely porcelain baby doll named Mandy. The owner kept Mandy in the basement when he heard it cry at night, and then donated Mandy to the Quesnel Museum in British Columbia in 1991. Soon, museum employees were experiencing strange things, such as objects being moved or going missing, footsteps when no one was around, and the doll's eyes following them wherever they moved across the room. Museum operators claim the doll has to be kept in a separate case because it does harm to other dolls. Visitors often report that Mandy's gaze does indeed follow them, and sometimes she even blinks.

Robert, the Doll

Another demonic doll comes to us from the year 1896, when a young child named Robert Eugene Otto, living in Key West, Florida, received a gift

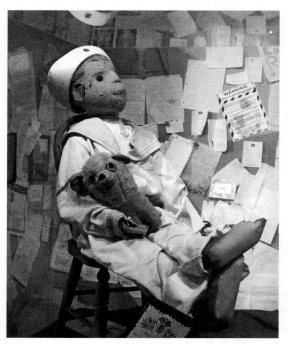

Robert, the Doll, was given to a Florida family by a disgruntled servant who hated them.

of a doll from a servant. But the servant did not like the Otto family, so she gave the boy, who liked being called Eugene, a creepy doll that had been cursed with black magic. Soon the family was hearing strange conversations between the boy and another voice, when the boy was alone with his doll. Eventually, things began breaking around the home, and the family would blame Eugene. But Eugene insisted it was the doll doing the mischief.

Family members claimed to see the doll run from room to room or move in and out of view of windows while they were outside. Sometimes they would hear giggling coming from the doll. Eventually, Eugene grew up and got married, and he insisted that the doll, now named Robert, have its own room and that it liked to be near a window so it could look outside. After Eugene died, his widow moved out, leaving Robert the doll behind in the attic.

When a new family moved in, the ten-year-old daughter found Robert in the attic. But soon she was claiming the doll was not only alive, but evil, and that it tried to harm her. The Robert doll today is located at the art gallery and historical Fort East Martello Museum in Clearwater, Florida, where visitors can take a picture of the doll only if they ask permission first. If permission is not granted and they take a photo, supposedly the doll will curse them. Interestingly, the museum also displays the many letters from visitors who were cursed, asking nicely to have the spells removed! According to Bustle.com's "5 Creepy Haunted Dolls Who Want to Play With You Forever and Ever and Ever," the Robert doll served as the inspiration for the famous "Chucky" doll of the *Child's Play* movie franchise!

FREAKY FURNISHINGS

Dolls and poppets aside, even things found around the home can become possessed or serve as "channels" for demonic spirits. People have reported possessed objects including paintings, tables, mirrors, statues, and collector's pieces, especially antiques or those with a violent history.

A limestone statue of "The Women from Lemb" was discovered in Lemb, Cyprus, in 1878. Known as the "Goddess of Death," the carved statue dated to 3500 B.C.E. and was said to represent a fertility goddess. Originally owned by a lord of the Elphont family, it was passed on after several family members died of unknown causes. The statue then ended up with new owners, Ivor Manucci and Lord Thompson-Noel, who also perished, as well as a fourth owner, Sir Alan Biverbrook. In all three cases, their families died as well.

A surviving family member gave the statue to Edinburgh's Royal Scottish Museum. Yes, the last person at the museum to handle the object died, as well, and no one has dared move it or touch it since; it is under lock and key in a glass cabinet.

How about possessed chairs that push people out of them or curse them to die? In 1894, at Belfourt Castle in Newport, Rhode Island, visitors reported two chairs that made them sick to their stomachs when they sat in them. Sometimes the chairs sent a surge of electricity through the person sitting or tossed the person off altogether. Meanwhile, in Thirsk, England, a convicted murderer in 1702 claimed to have put a curse on his favorite chair in a pub before he was put to death. Club patrons dared each other to sit in the evil seat, especially after noting that soldiers who sat in the seat would never come back from war, including two Royal Air Force pilots who sat in the chair and were immediately killed in a truck accident! Others who met with immediate death by demonic chair include a local mason, a roofer, and the pub's cleaning lady, until the pub owner put the chair in the basement, where it was still able to claim another victim—a tired delivery man who sat in it after unloading boxes.

> **C**lub patrons dared each other to sit in the evil seat, especially after noting that soldiers who sat in the seat would never come back from war....

That chair now hangs from the ceiling of a museum nearby.

Haunted paintings are a mainstay of horror movies, but in 1972, a real-life Hollywood actor named John Marley purchased a painting by artist Bill Stoneham called *The Hands Resist Him* on eBay. The strange painting of a young boy standing next to a doll was sold by an anonymous seller who warned of antics involving the artwork. The original owner warned that the figures in the painting wouldn't just move but sometimes would leave the painting and enter the room where it was hung. The painting made some people sick to their stomachs and many experienced extreme heat, dread, and terror when viewing it.

Eventually the painting ended up in an art gallery in Grand Rapids, Michigan. The original artist claimed that he knew nothing of its demonic activity but did acknowledge that two people who had previously viewed it had died!

Mirror, mirror on the wall, who's the scariest of them all? That would be the mirror that stands in the bedroom of one of the most haunted places in the world—Myrtles Plantation, which dates to 1796 and was built on a

A photo showing actor James Dean racing his 1955 Porsche Spyder, the car he would die in.

Native American burial ground. This beautiful eighteenth-century antebellum home in Francisville, Louisiana, houses many haunted objects, but the mirror takes center stage, said to possess the spirit of a woman named Sara Woodruff and her children within it. The woman and her children were poisoned to death, and visitors to the plantation, which is a hugely popular site for paranormal reality television shows and ghost hunts, report apparitions of the dead, along with child-sized handprints on the glass, despite the fact that the mirror wasn't introduced to the house until the 1980s.

CRAZY CAR?

Legend has it that the beloved actor James Dean owned a cursed 1955 Porsche Spyder that may have been responsible for his death. The car was so evil that the famed actor Sir Alec Guinness was said to have remarked to Dean upon first seeing the car that Dean would die in the next week if he got into what Dean lovingly called the "Little Bastard." Dean didn't listen and died the next week. Then the mechanics who attempted to repair the totaled car also got a taste of the curse when the car fell on one of them, crushing his legs. The new owner then sold the engine and the drivetrain to two auto racers, one of whom died when he lost control of his car; the other was severely injured in a rollover. Two thieves who tried to run off with parts of the car were both injured. Eventually the car was donated to the California Highway Patrol to be used as part of a safety exhibit. It caught fire and the car fell on a student, breaking his hip, then crushed a trucker transporting the car.... The car has since disappeared, or so we are told.

OUIJA™

Ouija™ Board. Spirit Board. Talking Board. There are several names for the simple parlor game created by Elijah Bond in 1890 that has become a mainstay of the occult and paranormal. A Ouija™ board is nothing more than a piece of wood, often square, rectangular, or kidney-shaped, with numbers and letters etched or painted onto it, along with a wooden planchette that moves about the board. The game allows participants to ask questions, as they might of a Magic 8-Ball, and then, after they lay fingers upon it, the planchette is moved across the board to spell out words or phrases.

Hasbro, Inc., trademarked the name, which was ascribed to the product later by a man named William Fuld, who claimed he invented it. The name Ouija™ is often used now to describe any number of similar boards, frequently custom-made with lavish decorations, that are used to talk to spirits, ghosts, and even the occasional demon. Another man named Charles Kennard, who founded Kennard Novelty Co., the first manufacturers of Fuld's version of the board, claimed that the word meant "good luck" in ancient Egyptian, but Fuld later said it was derived from the word "yes" in French and German. In 1966, Fuld's estate sold the business of making Ouija™ boards to Parker Bros., which then sold out to Hasbro in 1991. Hasbro holds the trademark to this day and continues to produce the games en masse.

According to "The Strange, Spooky History of the Ouija™ Board," from the October 2014 edition of Slate, the actual name of the board came from the board itself! According to original documents belonging to the Kennard company founders, the board claimed it wanted to be called "OUIJA™," which meant "good luck."

But it wasn't Fuld or Kennard or even Bond who really came up with the idea. It was already thousands of years old. Around 1100 C.E., during the Song Dynasty in China, automatic-writing tools similar to Ouija™ boards were already in use and were called "planchette writing." These devices were used as a means of contacting and communicating with the dead until they

Ouija™ boards have a "planchette" that has a circular window in it to make it easier to see the response intended by whatever entity is being contacted. One or more people are supposed to put their fingers lightly onto the planchette, which, some speculate, works using the same principles as dousing rods.

were banned during the Qing Dynasty. The American Spiritualist community had adopted the method until Bond saw fit to commercialize it into a game. Automatic writing was also achieved using a simple tool like a pen or pencil, with the writer going into a trance-like state and then "allowing" a spirit or entity to write through him or her. The Christian churches spoke out adamantly against the use of the boards to contact spirits, warning of demons and even the Devil himself possibly possessing the user, and forbade it to their followers.

During World War I, the game became something of a divination tool, owing to a spiritualist named Pearl Curran, and soon everyone was trying to contact the dead or allow the dead to speak through the board to the living. Curran claimed she was in contact with a woman named Patience Worth for over twenty years via the Ouija™ board and used the communications to write novels and poetry about the alleged woman.

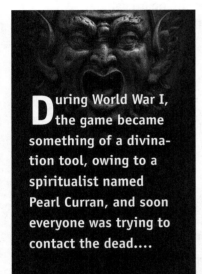

During World War I, the game became something of a divination tool, owing to a spiritualist named Pearl Curran, and soon everyone was trying to contact the dead....

In "Ouija: Origin of Evil and the True History of the Ouija Board," written in October 2016 by Olivia B. Waxmann for *Time* magazine, the writer said the times have a huge influence over the spread of the game's popularity as a means for talking to the dead. She quotes Robert Murch, the head of the Talking Board Historical Institute, who has been researching the Ouija™ for years: "Spirit communications devices took off during the Civil War, when there was massive amount of death, when every family lost a father, son, grandpa or nephew." Murch went on to say victims of war often didn't have ID, so the bodies were never returned to the family, making closure almost impossible. The families instead could turn to the devices to communicate with their dead loved ones and ask questions. The Ouija™ board was one of those methods, and this fact also explained how the game surpassed even Monopoly during the Vietnam War era.

Other "channeled" works that came from the Ouija™ board include the famous "Seth" books, dictated by a male entity of that name to Jane Roberts and her husband, Robert Butts, in 1973. The Seth books have gained huge popularity over time as the enlightenments of a spirit that no longer resided on the Earth plane. Ouija™ boards have been used by creative people wanting to speak to the other side, rock bands hoping to hook up with the Devil, and paranormal investigators holding public séances for profit or a reality television show. It has even been used by jurors to try to discern whether or not a murderer was guilty of a crime, as in the 1994 London trial of convicted murderer Stephen Young, when four jurors used a board to contact the murdered man, who then named Young as his murderer.

In terms of demonic activity, the biggest fears with Ouija™ boards seem to come from religious organizations that shun any kind of interaction, or even the invitation of interaction, with evil spirits, calling the practice a form of Satan worship. The board has gotten a bad reputation owing to those who want to talk to demons, even though most cases involve nothing more than ghostly activity, sometimes mischievous. Chalk the bad rep up to modern horror movies that see the boards as a wonderful device through which to tell demonic tales of possession and even murder.

Today, Ouija™ boards are popular with paranormal investigators, ghost hunters, and anyone who believes that the dead are able to speak through a wooden board. Many claim to see apparitions or get distinct messages from what they claim are dead relatives. Others use the boards as they would Tarot cards, to get insight and guidance from angels and otherworldly guides.

Scientists, on the other hand, chalk it all up to a very simple physiological phenomenon called the "ideomotor response," suggesting how things

A nineteenth-century illustration from France shows people using table-turning to get messages from the spirit world. People put their hands on a table with letters on it, and the ideomotor response causes it to tilt to produce a message.

like planchettes move across wooden boards or how tables turn during séances. In this theory, the responses are basically subtle, unconscious movements of the muscles of the fingers, imperceptible and yet strong enough to create movement. People using the planchettes feel as though the object is moving itself, but they are in fact guiding it so slightly that they are not consciously aware of it. The power of suggestion and expectation can also play a role in the unconscious creating of movement by the body, detached from a conscious awareness of it. Think of someone undergoing a polygraph examination, or a lie-detector test as it is more commonly known. The subtle movements of the body, brain waves, and even alterations of body heat and blood pressure can all tell stories.

The term "ideomotor response" was coined in 1852 by William B. Carpenter, who used it to explain the movements of water-dowser rods and pendulums, as well as spirit mediums' claims of turning and lifting tables during séances. Called "facilitated communication," the ideomotor-response theory holds that the movement of a planchette or a pendulum is a combination of involuntary unconscious motor behavior and the expectation of a certain result. A number of subsequent scientific tests have been performed to show that even people who are not cheating or trying to pull a fast one are often unaware of their own bodies' subtle movements, and that muscular activity at that level could explain most experiences with Ouija™ boards.

This includes bad experiences. According to the November 21, 1891, edition of the *San Francisco Morning Call*, a twenty-eight-year-old woman named Eugenie Carpenter of Bridgeport, Connecticut, was toying with a board with a friend. Recently heartbroken over a breakup, she asked the board if she would ever get back together with the man. The board was said to have spelled out "HE HAS CEASED TO LOVE YOU. HE WILL NEVER RETURN." Eugenie was found later roaming the streets mumbling, having gone mad.

But was it a spirit that drove her mad, or her own inner knowledge coming through via the ideomotor response? In 1930, two women murdered a third woman named Clothilde Marchand when the other women claimed Marchand's dead husband implicated his wife as his killer via communications with a Ouija™ board. But are these really demonic experiences?

The most prominent demonic experience involving a Ouija™ board occurred in the movie *The Exorcist*. The daughter, Regan, is playing with a board before she becomes possessed and in need of an old priest and a young priest to exorcise her. The powerful scene and the popularity of that movie catapulted the parlor game to notoriety as a demonic toy and a tool of Satan himself. In 2013, the Hasbro company came out with a newer version of the board that looked older, possibly to play upon the darker reputation that modern horror movies had given it, and to give users the impression that the boards were thousands of years old (which they were in origin, if not actual product design!).

According to the Smithosonian.com's "The Strange and Mysterious History of the Ouija Board" by Linda Rodriguez McRobbie, the board really tapped into a "weird place in American culture. It was marketed as both mystical oracle and as family entertainment, fun with an element of otherworldly excitement." The reporter went on to say that Ouija™ historian Robert Murch believes that belief itself is the key. "People want to believe. The need to believe that something else out there is powerful. This thing is one of those things that allows them to express that belief."

Perhaps expecting a good result is what brings about a good result from the board. And those who expect a demon just might get one. Murch goes on to say that people who think the boards are demonic have actually asked him not to bring them to paranormal conventions he speaks at, despite his never having experienced such activity. And perhaps it's the subtle powers of the human mind and body, working together just under the radar of waking consciousness, that are most responsible for the mysterious activity surrounding the Ouija™ board. That possibility alone is absolutely fascinating, while leaving the demonic out of the equation entirely, unless one is evil at heart.

In 2012, the University of British Columbia conducted an experiment involving the ideomotor response and Ouija™ boards. In one test, subjects sat with another person at a Ouija™ board and were given factual yes/no questions to answer. The subjects were blindfolded. The partners removed their hands from the planchette (unbeknownst to the subjects). The blindfolded subjects were therefore answering the questions and moving the planchette on their own, even though they reported not feeling as if they were making it move. Interestingly, while doing this, the subjects answered more of the questions correctly than they did when they were asked to answer only verbally. The conclusion: the subjects did a better job of answering correctly when they felt they were not in control. Perhaps this perception of not being in control allows the unconscious mind, known as "implicit cognition," to take over from the rational, conscious mind, perhaps as a form of intuition or inner knowing.

Possessed items are often found for sale today on eBay, Craigslist, and other online sites. Whether or not they are real is a true crapshoot, and many buyers pay good money based on assumptions, allegations, and claims. Perhaps this new wave of collecting demonic dolls and possessed property is worthy of the adage: buyer beware.

DEMONOLOGY, EXORCISMS, AND DEMONIC POSSESSION

Demonology is the study of demons and belief systems that include demons. It is also a label now assigned generally to paranormal investigations and exorcisms involving dark entities that possess humans or objects. Whereas the field of the paranormal focuses more on ghosts and apparitions, demonology requires a much deeper knowledge and understanding of the subject, and often more extensive training in how to handle it.

Once mainly used as a part of religious tradition, especially in the Roman Catholic Church, demonology has now become a more generic research pursuit for those looking to make a name for themselves in the paranormal, either by doing their own exorcisms, appearing on television shows, or writing books. While few of these modern demon hunters have the actual training of exorcists working through the Vatican or other religious bodies, many claim to have successfully cleansed homes and freed people of demonic forces. Thus, today, anyone can become a demonologist with a website, a few tools purchased off the internet, and a handful of investigations under one's belt. This raises the question, though: would you hire your yard guy to perform brain surgery?

For real demonologists have faced terrors that few of us can imagine. The science or study of working with demons goes back to antiquity, and because most, if not all, cultures have their own concept of evil and evil beings, demonology has universalities and commonalities across the board. The only differences might be the processes or rituals used to find the demons and remove them, which of course vary with belief systems. One religion might use incantations and spells, while another uses holy water and crucifixes; still another might burn incense and draw sacred circles to protect the afflicted. But all are designed to separate the demon from the host it has seen fit to possess and control.

Dating as far back as the Babylonian and Assyrian cultures (and most likely further back into primitive times), demonology in antiquity looked at two different possibilities:

1. The demon was a departed or deceased spirit haunting the living. The deceased could even have been a friend or loved one, who then upon death turned hostile. The demon could be nice to some, and horrible to others, depending on how the person died and the relationship status at the time of death.

2. The spirits possessing the humans were not human at all and had no human origin. They never were human, and might take on the form of different symbolic animals, give a specific demonic name, or appear in the form of a religious entity such as the Leviathan of Hebrew tradition. They, too, could be friendly to some, terrible to others.

The ancient Babylonians and Assyrians believed demons were everywhere and especially loved to haunt hidden or remote places, such as graveyards, ruins, and forests. At night, demons would set out in search of victims, finding and torturing them and bringing about all sorts of calamities. Later, ancient Semitic demonology adopted some of these beliefs, along with the use of magical preparations for exorcisms, and using animals, plants, and minerals that held certain powers, much as in witchcraft's use of nature to heal and cast spells, using herbs, plants, and even human hair and nails.

After preparation of the concoction to be used to cleanse the subject from the demon or demons within, there were very specific words and phrases, even intonations, used to call up the demons and deal with them accordingly. A priest, who was also the village sorcerer, would first call the name of the demon. Saying a demon's name gives the speaker some measure of power and dominion over it. After doing this, the priest-sorcerer would use the concoctions and incantations to drive the demon away and demand that it stop its torment and torture. Often, as in more modern exorcisms, the names of gods, deities, and beneficial forces were called upon to nullify the demon and its dark energy.

Babylonians believed that the name of a demon, or a god, was an actual part of the demon's personality and being, and saying the name in a ritual had the power to get the demon to change its behavior or go back to the hell from where it came. This belief echoes that of Australian Aborigines, who believe that the name of a thing is its power and brings it to life. Unfortunately, during ancient times, witches were often accused of being pawns of the devil, when they were often just practitioners of the magical arts themselves.

This is a tragedy that has carried through history to modern times, when witches, wiccans, and pagans are mistakenly accused of being in cahoots with the Devil. More on that in a future chapter.

One of the key tenets of demonology during primitive and ancient times involves the use of symbolic or sympathetic magic, which is a form of imitative magic that suggests a person or thing can be influenced and affected by actions performed with or toward an object representing it. Back to the use of voodoo dolls as an example: by giving a doll the name of a person and sticking a pin in it, the idea is to hurt the real person the doll is supposed to represent. Our primitive ancestors used sympathetic magic with cave and rock art—by painting themselves killing great beasts of prey, they hoped the symbolism would actually manifest into actual killing of prey during hunts to feed their families.

It was the great Sir James George Frazer, author of *The Golden Bough: A Study in Comparative Religion,* the most comprehensive study of sympathetic magic and nature worship, who once said that like produces like. Frazer wrote extensively of cultures that lived by the belief that the magician or sorcerer can produce an actual effect by first imitating the outcome with art, story, or ritual. This concept led to the later use of symbolic objects to represent magical concepts, such as the use of sage to give wisdom and mental "cleansing," or the use of certain crystals to heal physical ailments.

Today's sorcerers, or demonologists and exorcists, use their own symbolic rituals and tools to achieve the same purpose. However, today's demonologists are not always the ones who expel the demons. They will defer to trained exorcists. Some demonologists simply study the demonic world. Others actually take the demons to task. One noted group of demonologists, known as the Paranormal Clergy, defines a demonologist on its website as, specifically, "One who has completed primary research within the field and has accepted his/her calling to devote their lives to the study of demonology and may be appointed by Church leadership to investigate demonic cases." However, not all demonologists operate through the Church or even religious sources, and this group itself is quick

Sir James George Frazer (1854–1941) was an expert on mythology and comparative religions. He is famous for writing *The Golden Bough,* which would influence the field of anthropology for many years.

A Brief Explanation of Demons and Demonic Activity

BY KEITH E. JOHNSON

In researching the paranormal, there is always the chance that eventually an investigator will encounter forces that exist outside the human realm, and that fall into the sphere of the inhuman or preternatural. This includes the demonic and angelic realms.

My first encounter with what I now consider to be a demonic spirit took place when I was five years old. While I was in bed one night during a heavy rainstorm, I was suddenly awakened by what sounded like high-pitched voices laughing and speaking gibberish outside of my bedroom window. Naturally, when I told my mother about these voices the next morning, she attributed them to either a dream or my childhood imagination, even though I insisted that I'd been wide awake at the time. It was exactly ten years later, when I was fifteen, that the voices outside my bedroom window returned. This time, there could be no mistaking that I was hearing actual voices, for I was certainly wide awake because of a thunderstorm outside. And this happened on more than one occasion during this period. Just as when I was five years old, the voices were high-pitched, and although they were quite audible, they seemed to either be speaking gibberish, or a language I was completely unfamiliar with.

Each time, the voices seemed to be getting closer, as if becoming bolder, until one night during a storm, a voice could be heard directly outside my bedroom windows. In fact, a taunting, high-pitched laughter could be heard from outside all three windows, as if something was leaping from one window to the next with split-second timing, and traveling counterclockwise. It was also when my identical twin brother, Carl, and I were age fifteen that Carl and our twelve-year-old sister, Cynthia, began nightly sessions of playing with a Ouija™ board, in an attempt to contact whatever spirit might be causing mys-

terious little "pranks" in our house. These pranks included the contents of a glass of water suddenly disappearing before our eyes and a woman's leather glove we'd never seen before suddenly appearing, lying in the hallway … only to be gone again moments later. While supposedly communicating with a spirit on the Ouija™ board, Carl and Cynthia asked the spirit to identify itself, and the name "Sylvia" was spelled out. Their next question to "Sylvia" was where she resided, and the word "cellar" was spelled out. My brother and sister promptly ended their session and went to the cellar stairs, to see if they could get Sylvia to communicate with them on a more personal level. They asked their spirit friend to please give them a sign of her presence and then stood as still as possible on the stairwell for several minutes. They were about to give up and return upstairs when they heard three equally spaced knocks on the wall to their immediate left. Carl and Cynthia traded glances, and Carl speculated to Cynthia, "Could that have been a squirrel?" His comment was instantly answered by three loud, resounding bangs on the same wall. Carl and Cynthia both quickly thanked "Sylvia" for her response, then beat a hasty retreat upstairs.

As I was to learn years later, the three knocks can be a calling card of the demonic, in that it is considered to be a deliberate mocking of the Holy Trinity: the Father, the Son, and the Holy Spirit. The demonic also often tend to strike on the left, as well as moving counterclockwise. These patterns could be applied to the situation involving the high-pitched gibberish voice I heard outside of my bedroom window during a storm when the atmosphere was electrified, the presence momentarily stopping at all three windows and traveling counterclockwise. It was instances such as these, along with my

Christian upbringing, that sparked my interest in studying and actively investigating the paranormal—specifically the angelic and demonic realms. Angels and demons are both considered to be nonhuman spirits. In other words, neither of these types of entities are the spirits of deceased humans. They have never walked the Earth in human form, at least not as we know humanity today.

In my early years of paranormal investigation and religious intervention, I was a member of the original team that investigated the Perron farmhouse in Harrisville, Rhode Island. This is of course the case upon which the 2013 movie *The Conjuring* was based, and it was our organization at the time (Parapsychological Investigation and Research Organization, or PIRO) that alerted our friends Ed and Lorraine Warren to the situation. We ourselves experienced a great deal of paranormal activity during our investigation of the Perron residence, and this was the first major in-home investigation I was ever involved with. As soon as I stepped onto the property of the Perrons' eighteenth-century farmhouse, the

Lorraine Warren founded the New England Society for Psychic Research with her husband, Ed. It is the oldest ghost-hunting organization in New England.

atmosphere felt palpable. By that I mean that however nice and friendly the family members were as they welcomed us, the property immediately surrounding the farmhouse and the interior of the nearby barn exuded a foreboding feeling that seemed almost electric. Later that evening, a few of the daughters and one of their friends who was sleeping over led me on a tour of the farmhouse. We were upstairs in one of their shared bedrooms, in which the girls said they felt the most frightened. Even more so than the rest of the house, the atmosphere in this particular room seemed foreboding.

It truly seemed that we were being given a sort of warning that some sort of sinister intelligence was watching us, monitoring our every word and movement. It was also a rather humid August evening, causing one of the windows in this bedroom to remain stuck halfway open. The father of the family, Roger Perron, had repeatedly tried to push it closed, without success. At one point, while the girls were explaining to me how frightened they were, I asked them, "Do you have any religious beliefs?" One of the teenage girls, Nancy Perron, replied, "Yes, we're Catholic." I suggested that they call upon Jesus—at which point there was an instant reaction in the room. The window that could not be closed suddenly slammed shut with terrific force, causing the girls to gasp in shock. At the same exact moment, the atmosphere in that bedroom instantly became charged with an unhealthy, powerful, but draining current. Nancy Perron screamed as her head jerked sharply to the right, and she tearfully exclaimed that she'd just been slapped on the side of her head. She was nearly sent reeling off of the bed on which she sat, and I could tell from the way her head angled that she had been struck on the left side of her head.

As the terrified girls began to cry, I told them, "Don't be afraid, just call upon Jesus! Jesus is stronger." After I said this, the atmosphere in the bedroom instantly

Continued...

returned to normal. The girls looked around in wonder, and Nancy said, "It's gone!" Of course, this did not necessarily mean that whatever spirits may have been responsible for the mayhem we'd just experienced had left the farmhouse altogether. In fact, the Perron family members were to endure an ongoing siege of spirit activity throughout the next several years. But at least for that moment, a hostile spirit presence had been coerced into leaving the girls' bedroom.

The next time I experienced that same nauseating "electric current" sensation was during an exorcism of a fourteen-year-old boy, which took place in Providence, Rhode Island. The boy, who was of Puerto Rican descent, was seemingly afflicted by transient episodes of demonic possession. My brother Carl and I were asked by the boy's family to assist in an arranged exorcism, and we agreed to do so. (Although we were told beforehand that this would be a traditional Catholic exorcism, it was in fact a Santeria exorcism that was to be performed.) Carl and I, along with several family members and friends of the family, were seated in a semicircle, with the boy seated on a chair in the middle of the room, facing us. The boy's aunt, who was the presiding exorcist, began the incantation over her nephew, intending to bring forth the demonic entity. In less than a minute, there was what I consider to be a three-to-five second "warning" that the spirit was about to manifest.

The atmosphere abruptly changed into that familiar nauseating, electrically charged sensation I had experienced at the Perron farmhouse some years before. Then a rumbling vibration traveled through the floor, both heard and felt. When the rumbling vibration reached the spot where my brother Carl was seated in a chair, both he and the chair were suddenly moved backwards a few feet. It was then that the demonic personality manifested and completely took over the boy's personality. His eyes suddenly widened as he slid off his chair onto the floor and began maniacally screaming. He then bolted

upright onto his knees and began swaying back and forth like a cobra, his eyes still widened and unblinking. At one point during the exorcism, Carl and I, along with the friends and family members present, were again seated with our chairs in a semicircle. It seemed that the invading spirit temporarily went out of the fourteen-year-old boy, leaving him dazed. Although unseen, it then began traveling around us counterclockwise, pushing on the backs of our necks in an apparent attempt to look for weaknesses or possible entry points. The young woman seated to my right reacted with a start, and Carl, to my left, felt a distinct tingling on the back of his neck that he was fortunately able to resist. However, the young woman seated beside Carl screamed and went running away from the circle, holding onto the back of her neck and crying. Interestingly, the spirit passed over me without the slightest touch, and I can only assume that this was because I had an open Bible resting on my lap. In my opinion, this exorcism was not completely successful, especially since the exorcist her-

The exorcism didn't work, and instead of the demon fleeing it took over the body of the exorcist herself!

self ultimately wound up being taken over and going into full demonic possession!

Years later, my wife, Sandra, and I simultaneously experienced another example of this nauseating sensation accompanying a demonic manifestation. We were at a private residence in Massachusetts, and the client mentioned a young man who was a former resident of this house who had committed suicide in another location. At the mention of this young man's suicide, I immediately began feeling that familiar draining, negative force, indicating that an unholy spirit entity was manifesting itself in some way, making its presence known. The feeling was so intense that I nearly had to excuse myself to visit the bathroom. But I certainly did not want to announce to anyone what I was feeling, for fear of alarming the client and the other investigators, including Sandra. Neither did I wish to psychologically influence anyone by the power of suggestion. Instead, I took a few slow breaths and silently prayed, which caused this feeling to gradually abate. It was only later that Sandra privately told me she had suddenly started feeling extremely nauseated, apparently at the exact same moment I did, which was when the client had mentioned the former resident's suicide.

To me, this disruption of the atmosphere in the immediate vicinity where a negative spirit is manifesting would seem to indicate that this type of entity may indeed be transdimensional. It seems to be transcending into our dimensional realm by permeating the "dimensional fabric" in a certain spot to which it has easier access, sometimes referred to as a "portal." I like to explain this as being similar to tuning in to certain radio waves, where the frequencies are receptive. Similar to an electrical current, these entities will tend to follow the path of least resistance. It would also seem that the more a "dimensional portal" is being utilized by one or more spirit entities, the more this portal will seem to widen. Over time, an increase in spirit activity will often be experienced in this particular location. This increase could very well account for instances in which phenomena proliferate in a location where Ouija™ boards, séances, and other divination devices are regularly used for spirit communication. And this seemed to be the case in my own family's house, which I grew up in. Judging from what I myself and numerous others have experienced, I would say this negatively charged feeling will often be experienced more intensely by individuals who are particularly intuitive, psychic, or sensitive to the presence of these negative entities.

So, how exactly would we define what a demonic entity is? Where exactly do these entities come from? And what is their gripe with humanity, anyway? The very term "demon" comes from the ancient Greek word *daimon,* which originally denoted a wise, intelligent spirit, not necessarily evil. Over the centuries, however, the word "demon" came to

A stone Watcher angel is attached to the spire of St. Michael's Church in Oxfordshire, England. Watchers, as the name implies, keep watch over humanity.

Continued...

denote a malevolent spirit, one at odds with God and with humanity. Today, anyone can easily Google a list of proper names of demons, as well as their "specialties" (i.e., gluttony, sodomy, lechery, etc.). However, it should be noted that most of these names were derived from already existing mythological names, courtesy of the medieval Catholic Church.

One thing to keep in mind, again, is that actual demons are not believed to be the spirits of deceased humans, however detestable a human may have been during his or her physical lifetime. Rather, they are considered to be a separate order of spirit beings altogether. And although much of their actual origin remains a mystery, the fact that they exist has been proven to me and to many other demonologists, beyond the shadow of a doubt. In Judeo-Christian belief, they originated from an order of angels referred to as the Watchers. These Watchers, numbering 200, were assigned to watch over humanity during our early antiquity. Now, for any *Star Trek* fans, or "Trekkies," out there, I like to compare what is known as the "Prime Directive of the Federation of Planets" to one of the prime rules that the Watcher angels were given: noninterference with other cultures, especially primitive ones. This is apparently the exact law that the Watchers eventually wound up breaking. They essentially interfered with human culture in ways that were strictly forbidden by God. And the Watchers eventually went much further in their disobedience of God's law, to the point of interfering with the physical genetics of living earthly creatures, both animal and human. Some of these Watchers even went so far as to assume quasi-physical bodies, and to copulate with human females, thereby contaminating much of the human bloodline and producing a corrupted race of terrifying genetic monstrosities. Many of these angelic/human hybrids grew to gigantic physical proportions and became a race of superhumans referred to as the Nephilim.

A brief telling of this event in early human civilization can be found in the first book of the Holy Bible, Genesis, Chapter 6:1–6: "1 And it came to pass, when men began to multiply on the face of the earth, and daughters were born unto them, 2 That the sons of God saw the daughters of men that they were fair; and they took them wives of all which they chose. 3 And the Lord said, My spirit shall not always strive with man, for that he also is flesh: yet his days shall be an hundred and twenty years. 4 There were giants in the earth in those days; and also after that, when the sons of God came in unto the daughters of men, and they bare children to them, the same became mighty men which were of old, men of renown. 5 And God saw that the wickedness of man was great in the earth, and that every imagination of the thoughts of his heart was only evil continually. 6 And it repented the Lord that he had made man on the earth, and it grieved him at his heart."

When the physical bodies of these Nephilim perished, as a result of the Great Flood described in Genesis, their spirits were doomed to wander the Earth. A much more detailed account of these events can be found in the Apocrypha book of Enoch, which was not included in the King James Bible. There are also many other cultures whose mythology includes tales of these demigods, the progeny of gods and humans, such as the ancient Greek superhero Hercules. It is also generally well known that many cultures throughout the world include the story of a catastrophic flood that destroyed most of humanity, with only a few noble souls surviving in a specialized craft, and later repopulating the human race upon the earth. And it is believed that the spirits of these biblical Nephilim giants are in fact the demons that haunt, oppress, and sometimes even possess humanity today. (It should be kept in mind that actual demonic possession is a relatively rare phenomenon, while demonic oppression is somewhat more common.) So, how does demonic involvement occur with people? Especially in our day and age? One of the most common ways is through what is known as the Law of Invitation. One method that may result in spirits' being "invited" into a home is through the Ouija™ board, or Witch board.

Demonic invitation may also result from conducting séances, automatic writing, channeling, and other forms of divination. When discussing the topic of spirit communication, one sometimes hears the phrase, "You could be opening doors by doing that," and what is generally meant by this is that permission has been given for a spirit to inhabit a home. Another cause of demonic spirit involvement is somewhat more mysterious, since it concerns what is known as the Law of Attraction. For a variety of reasons, a demonic spirit will sometimes be attracted to a certain individual or family. It could be that a demon is drawn to a certain individual because of his or her energy level, as is the case with people who are sometimes referred to as "spirit magnets." Or perhaps a demonic spirit is attracted to someone because of the person's particular psychic or emotional vulnerability, meaning that the spirit considers that person to be an "easy target." Or it may be that, for whatever reason, a demonic spirit or spirits will be attracted to a particular family.

For an example of this, I again refer to the Perron case in Harrisville, Rhode Island. No sooner had the Perron family moved into its newly purchased eighteenth-century farmhouse than spirits began appearing to the five young daughters. But interestingly, the demonic spirit that eventually wreaked havoc on the family seemed to be "attracted" to the father, Roger Perron ... while Roger's wife, Carolyn, the mother of the five girls, was seemingly "targeted" and severely oppressed by the same spirit.

Another question that is sometimes raised is, What do these demonic spirits actually look like? Of course, most of the time demonic spirits are invisible. On the relatively rare occasions when they do manifest in a

visible form, they most often appear as shadow figures, or "shadow people," as these manifestations are commonly referred to. The ancient Greeks were apparently also familiar with these types of spirit manifestations, and they referred to them simply as "shades." However, there are times when a demonic spirit will take on the image of a man, woman, or child, in a form that can be recognizable to others. (A spirit form that is recognizable is referred to as an "apparition.") Demonic spirits possess the wisdom of the ages, and they can be masters of deception, by masquerading as a deceased loved one, or as an historical figure. Even Satan, the quintessential archregent and commander of all evil spirits, has the ability to appear as a luminous angelic being (2 Corinthians, 11:14). This should come as no surprise, since in Holy Scripture Satan is also known by the name "Lucifer," which means "Bringer of Light." The image of Satan as a red devil with horns, a barbed tail, and a pitchfork was borrowed from ancient Greek mythology by the medieval Catholic Church. I and many others in the field of demonology, including my long-time friend John Zaffis and the late, great Ed Warren, would unanimously agree that demonic forces are as active in the world today as they ever were. It is generally well known that the story of *The Exorcist,* by William Peter Blatty, was inspired by an allegedly true account of a case of demonic possession of a fourteen-year-old boy and the subsequent exorcism, which took place in St. Louis in 1949.

Of course, it almost goes without saying that there are a number of things to rule out before jumping to a conclusion of demonic activity. Some of these explanations can include mold infestations, which can and do cause hallucinations. There is also temporal-lobe epilepsy, which can cause feelings of dread or the sensation of being watched. In some individuals, this can be triggered simply by sleeping too close to a digital alarm clock. There are also hypnopompic states that can

Continued...

(Continued from previous page)

occur upon waking from sleep, when the mind is not yet fully awake, and hypnogogic states, which can occur upon transcending into sleep. These hallucinations differ from the dream state, in that they lack a story line. These hallucinations can also include include sensations of touch, taste, smell, and sound, along with sight. However, having ruled such explanations out, if someone feels that he or she is experiencing an actual demonic haunting, or undergoing demonic oppression, today more than ever there are people and organizations that offer legitimate help. All one need do is a little research, and then contact someone who is reputable within the field of paranormal research and who has the proper connections—such as the author of this book—and you will be placed in touch with those who can and do offer genuine assistance.

(Keith Johnson has been investigating the paranormal for over four decades. He and his wife, Sandra, are former core members of the Atlantic Paranormal Society and are the co-founders of the New England Anomalies Research group. They live in Warwick, Rhode Island.)

to point out that a demonologist is not the same thing as a clergy member, and often actual clergy will be called upon to perform exorcism rituals.

So, there are demonologists, there are demonologists who do exorcisms, and there are demonologists who are also trained and certified clergy. But all agree that working with these dark forces is nothing to be taken lightly and is not a hobby, but rather a serious field of inquiry, and often, a dangerous commitment. This explains why people like John Zaffis, and the Warrens, might often call upon the actual Church-trained exorcists to do more difficult jobs working with demons they themselves cannot rid a home, or a person, of.

SIGNS OF DEMONIC ACTIVITY

Before we look at some of the most famous exorcists and cases of demonic possession around the world, it might help to list the warning signs of demonic activity in one's own home. Granted, many of the things on this list could result from a million different causes, but these lists are a compilation of those on several demonology websites and are worth a look. Some of this activity might be more ghostly, or paranormal, in nature. One of the key things to look for, other than abject hostility, is the use of deception. Demons love to speak and work through the people, pets, and objects we love and trust. So be warned:

1. The presence of shadow people, figures, or entities that bring with them a sense of dread or doom.

2. Strange growling sounds that have no apparent cause.

3. Horrible odors, especially sulfur, that have no apparent origin.

4. Objects moving and causing physical harm to people in the home.

5. The destruction and desecration of religious objects.

6. Fluids that seep from walls, ceilings, and floors with no apparent cause.

7. Physical and sexual assaults where the assailant is invisible, or during sleep.

8. Swarming insects inside the home.

9. Electronic disturbances, such as clocks running backwards or lights turning on and off on their own.

10. Oppressive rooms where it feels hard to breathe.

11. Knockings and bangings with no apparent cause.

12. Drastic changes in behavior of a person or family member, including hostility and violence.

13. Someone having visions or speaking in strange tongues.

14. Pets refusing to go into certain rooms/areas and displaying extreme fear.

15. Cold or hot spots and places where people are touched or have their hair tugged.

16. Rooms or places in the house that cause nausea and possibly vomiting or fainting.

17. Doors, cabinets, or drawers slamming open and shut on their own.

18. Voices and singing with no one else around.

19. Ringing doorbells, phones, or cellphones with no one on the other end.

20. Increasing paranormal activity with no apparent cause.

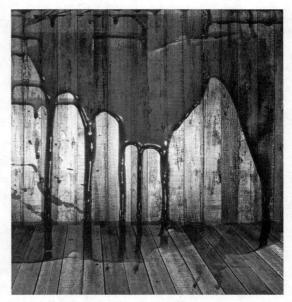

Again, some of these may be ascribed to perfectly natural causes, but chances are that if you have many going on at once, and a feeling of extreme dread or terror, get help. Better safe than possessed!

What might actually cause possession in the first place? A demon might pick the weakest and most fragile or emotional person possible, one who will put up the least amount of fight. Demons seem to possess adults as much as children, and they don't hold any prejudices concerning color,

Fluids seeping and dripping from walls, ceilings, or floors are one of many possible indicators of a demonic presence.

creed, or belief system. If you look at websites of demonologists and paranormal research groups, an interesting list of reasons includes:

1. Listening to hard-rock music and music with "demonic" lyrics.

2. Belief in the occult arts.

3. Practicing the occult arts, witchcraft, or divination such as Tarot reading, palm reading, using pendulums, astrology, or numerology.

4. Belief in metaphysics and the practice of meditation (some believe it is capable of opening you up to negative spirits!)

5. Reading novels and watching movies about magic, the magical arts, or the occult and paranormal, including the Harry Potter novels, Stephen King books, and horror movies.

6. Committing a crime or a sin, which invites evil into the soul.

7. Calling up demons for fun such as with Ouija™ boards, etc.

8. Having sex before marriage, as well as infidelity and divorce.

9. Not believing in God.

10. Hypnotism.

11. Joining a cult.

12. Drug and/or alcohol consumption.

13. Being extremely ill, either physically or mentally, which makes one the perfect entry point for a demon.

14. Doing paranormal investigations or performing exorcisms without proper training and protection.

15. Going to "haunted" locations known for reports of demonic activity.

POLTERGEISTS OR DEMONS?

Poltergeists are often mistaken for demons. The word is German for "noisy ghost" and describes a specific type of activity that may mimic some of the characteristics of a demon in the house, but without the demon. Poltergeist activity usually focuses on objects that move, levitate, break things, create loud noises such as knocking and rapping, and/or disturbances such as changes in behavior of young people and pets, and sometimes physical symptoms like bite marks, kicking, bruising, hair pulling, and pinching.

While this activity may sound evil, it is more mischievous than hostile. Poltergeists, like demons, haunt a person. Demons can also haunt a location or an object, but a noisy ghost requires a human "host" or human agent through which to manifest its psychokinetic energy, and that host is usually a young male or female going through major hormonal changes (puberty, adolescence, menses onset). Females are most often associated with poltergeist activity, owing to their having more hormonal activity than their male counterparts. The unconscious physiological bursts might account for the psychokinesis.

Typical activity involves objects around the home or location moving on their own accord, as if somehow being tossed around by an invisible force. There may also be odors associated with the events, as well as objects that disappear and appear in other rooms or locations.

Explanations for poltergeist activity range from strong air currents to anomalous geomagnetic or seismic activity to the presence of water beneath a home, although these don't explain why it is often associated only with the one host person. Poltergeists are not ghosts in the traditional sense,

Poltergeists are known for their penchant for moving, levitating, and breaking objects around the house.

as they do not seem to be spirits of the dead or entities trying to make contact from the other side. Although some paranormal researchers do believe they are lesser spirits, most conclude that the activity is more physical than spiritual or supernatural in nature and that we just don't yet understand the psychokinetic origins.

One hypothesis involves the association of poltergeist activity with stimulation of the temporal lobe of the brain, an area that is also highly active during *grand mal* seizures in epileptics, as well as during *déjà vu* experiences. The idea is that under extreme emotional stress, possibly influenced by hormone levels in young people, who are most often the hosts, the brain is stimulated to create some kind of energy that exits the brain/host to affect things nearby. In one study done for the National Institutes of Health, in which a famed poltergeist researcher, William Roll, took part, it was discovered that people who report moving objects, unusual sounds, auras, and sensed presences exhibit electrical anomalies in the brain over their right temporal lobes.

A sensitive temporal lobe can also trick someone into thinking that he or she is seeing a ghost or apparition. Michael Persinger, Ph.D., professor of psychology at Laurentian University in Ontario, Canada, believes these apparitions are not real but instead a construct of the sensitive temporal-lobe area responsible for regulating emotions and motivating behaviors. When the brain is exposed to naturally occurring magnetic fields, a ghostly encounter may result. Persinger even suggests that some houses may be more electroni-

Neurotheologist Michael Persinger was interested in showing that neural phenomena in the brain create the illusion of spiritual experiences.

cally charged than others, with magnetic activity peaking at night, when most paranormal events seem to occur. Thus, the combination of the inner physiological activity of the human brain and hormone chemicals with outside electromagnetic anomalies may create the perfect recipe for poltergeist phenomena.

"Individuals prone to paranormal experiences are sensitive to weak electromagnetic fields and to man-made electrical fields, which are becoming more prominent in the communication age," Persigner told *Psychology Today* in a May 1, 2003, story by Darcy Lockman. He went on to describe his own experiments stimulating the temporal lobes of volunteers in a lab setting and the bizarre reports of a presence interacting with their thoughts and moving in their visible space. The right temporal lobes of those with temporal-lobe sensitivity "lit up" with a higher level of paranormal experiences, including visible auras, something also experienced by epileptics during *grand mal* seizures.

So are all ghosts and poltergeists simply no more than the external EM fields affecting the right temporal lobes? Maybe ... but in the case of real demonic activity, that explanation might not suffice.

ATTACHMENT

Often, a demon will attach itself to a person, item, or even a location and not let go without a series of exorcisms and cleansings. Even then, the attachment may simply be transferred to the person doing the ritualistic cleansing or to another person or location. Sometimes ghost sightings can become violent, and the energy or spirit of the deceased will attach itself to whomever is nearby and continue to create havoc.

Many of the allegedly haunted locations we hear about on reality-television shows and read about in paranormal books could be said to harbor dark energy that got "stuck" in that location and now manifests in apparitions that appear to be a time loop, repeating over and over as if imprinted upon the very walls of the home or building itself.

Demons can also attach to pets. The animal then attacks its owner until the spirit embodied within either takes up residence elsewhere, is exorcised, or kills the animal with its negative energy.

According to Nicole Canfield, author of *Things That Attract Demons and Signs Your Home is Haunted,* "Unfortunately, and quite often, when a demon is inhabiting a home or building of some sort, the situation can be fueled by other people." Thus, the energy and emotions of people present can influence, and add to, the already dark forces of the attached demon. "It is a vicious cycle in that the demon brings negativity that triggers people's fears, then the negativity that emanates from these people feeds the demon more energy."

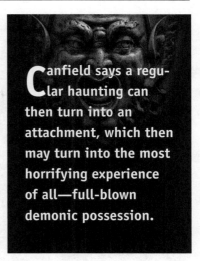

Canfield says a regular haunting can then turn into an attachment, which then may turn into the most horrifying experience of all—full-blown demonic possession.

Canfield says a regular haunting can then turn into an attachment, which then may turn into the most horrifying experience of all—full-blown demonic possession. Signs of changes in the behavior of those who might be a part of this insidious loop include:

- Withdrawal and isolation of the person under the demonic influence.
- Recurring nightmares and night terrors, often with demonic visions.
- Unexplained marks on the body and illness/weakness that cannot be explained.
- Extreme anger and violent behaviors in someone who was normally passive.
- Newfound interest in the occult arts, demons, black magic, etc.

These signs are enough to make one pick up the phone and call the nearest exorcist, if one can be found. If these signs are there, escalating violence could lead to a host of problems, including murder, suicide, rage killings, and torture of animals and people. But these signs could also suggest any other type of mental illness, hormonal changes, and even just bad behavior. We cannot label these behaviors and actions as demonic in nature without looking first for possible "normal" explanations, which any good paranormal researcher and demonologist will be the first to agree with.

Like the characteristics of demonic activity, these lists don't account for the millions of people who DO all of the above, or experience all of the above and don't end up possessed by demons. But the idea is to avoid people, places and situations that make one vulnerable, physically or spiritually, to outside forces taking control. Meditation, for example, has led to greater health and clarity for millions of people, but in a July 2016 story for *Destination America* titled "Did the Lutz Family's Practice of Transcendental Meditation Lead to the Amityville Horror?" writer Sasha Brown-Worsham inquired into whether or not the Lutz parents' practice of TM might have been the doorway to demonic activity.

Some researchers suspect that transcendental meditation can actually leave one more vulnerable to demonic activity and possession.

Allegedly, the Lutz parents, who moved into the notorious Long Island home five years after the DeFeo family were slaughtered in their sleep by their oldest son, Butch, were big on TM, and the writer alludes to the possibility that their practice of finding peace, clarity, and stress reduction could have opened them to the horrors that they experienced during the twenty-eight days they were in the home before they fled. There is absolutely NO proof of this, though Kathy Lutz asked whether there might be a relationship between the two in a book about the case by Jay Anson (*The Amityville Horror*), and we would not suggest that anybody stop meditating because of potential demonic possession. More likely the activity in the home was caused by what occurred there before the Lutzes moved in … if you believe that a house can trap or store demonic energy.

EXORCISM

Clearly something causes possessions, because world-famous exorcist Father Gabriele Amorth, who died at age ninety-one in 2016, had allegedly performed over 70,000 of them during his thirty-odd-year tenure as a Pauline priest. As an exorcist in the diocese of Rome, Amorth was often sought out by news media and journalists alike for his views on exorcisms. In addition to holding a degree in theology, Amorth wrote many books and essays about the Virgin Mary and edited the magazine *Mother of God*. He was ordained in 1951 and appointed the exorcist of the diocese of Rome in 1985. Outspoken and opinionated, he once stated that Hitler, ISIS, and Stalin were probably possessed by Satan, although many outside the Church could claim they were just crazed, evil men on their own. Amorth also blames divorce, gay marriage, and abortion as reasons for extensive evil in the world, although again those opinions are merely his own and mimic those of the Church.

When it came to actual exorcisms, he did perform many of the same rites on the same persons, suggesting once is not enough to rid some demons. In 1990 he founded the International Association of Exorcists and was president until 2000, when he retired. He told journalists in the past that the world no longer turns to God but rather focuses on idolatry, accepts atheism and puts science on the altar over religion. There is no record of whether the demons he attempted to exorcise were all atheist scientists or not, but Catholicism is one of the reasons that exorcisms are so hard to study or prove the reality of—because of their associations with biased religious beliefs and prejudices that prevent objective scientific inquiry.

So what, exactly, is an exorcism? The word comes from the Greek *exorkismos*, which means "binding by oath." The act itself consists of various rituals designed to destroy or take control of an evil spirit and can be as simple as saying the demon's name or as complex as repeated visits with holy objects, Bible readings, and assisting priests. The popularity of exorcisms has increased over the last decade or two, thanks to pop culture and movies and reality ghost-hunting shows featuring demons and the possessed.

In Christianity, one might look at an exorcism as the casting out of demons, and therefore Jesus himself was an exorcist. To perform an exorcism, one might call upon God, Jesus, angels, and saints for assistance while using prayers and holy objects over the demon-possessed. Always, the exorcist should be a powerful member of the Church or clergy, to intimidate the demon, and the exorcist is required to undergo extensive training and display a level of maturity capable of dealing with such dangerous and unpredictable situations. Even though the consensus is that a possessed person is not responsible for his or her actions, those actions may still be deadly if not handled properly. Sometimes, the possessed is restrained for the person's own safety, as well as the safety of the exorcist and assisting priests.

The Roman Catholic exorcism is the most widely understood, thanks again to pop culture and movies like *The Exorcist*. Only a real, trained priest can perform a formal exorcism, and there must be permission from the bishop to do so. The formal rite is called a "major exorcism" and has exact guidelines to follow once the actual affliction is determined by the attending priest. The priest himself must be consecrated and use a rite that invokes the names of Christ and God, while utilizing various sacred symbols and tools, all in accordance to the rules as laid down by the Church. Often an archangel such as Michael will be called upon to intervene in the ritual, and in the

When people hear "exorcist," most think of the process from the Catholic tradition, thanks to the popularity of such films as *The Exorcist*.

worst cases, it may take a series of exorcisms over weeks, months, and even years to completely remove the demonic entity.

One noted American exorcist, Father Gary Thomas, believes that just as God can be called upon by people for help through prayer, the Devil can be called upon by rituals. He ascribes a rise in the need for exorcism to a rise in demonic activity, especially in America. He blames interest in the occult, Wicca, and people seeking out fortune tellers and doing séances to channel spirits they may not know how to deal with. He also believes the Devil seeks out humans involved in broken relationships, but he admits that approximately 85 percent of the people he sees for exorcisms are not possessed but rather victims of abuse.

> There is actually something called "demonomania," in which a person believes that he or she is possessed to the point of behaving as such and experiencing symptoms.

Both Judaism and Islam have their own versions of exorcism, similar to Christianity's. In Judaism, the modern Hebrew exorcism is performed by a trained rabbi who is versed in the Kabbalah, along with a group of ten adult men, called a *minyan*, who form a sacred circle around the possessed during the ritual. The entire group will recite Psalm 91 three times and then the rabbi blows a ram's horn called a *shofar* to shake up the body and loosen the hold of the demon. The exorcism is meant to expel the demon, but also to heal the possessed, and often the rabbi will try to communicate with the demon to understand why it possessed the body. It is often prayed over in a bid to make it feel safe enough to leave the body on its own.

In Islam, the exorcism is called *ruqya*, and the purpose is to repair any damage to the possessed caused by the use of black magic against it, known as *sihr*. A sheikh performs rites that consist of holy water and verses from the Koran invoking God's help. These exorcisms can also help rid someone of a pesky jinn, as well as demons.

Often if a priest, rabbi, or sheikh is not available, other noted clergy members will perform the rites, and sometimes they aren't even clergy, as in the case of Bobby Jindal, former governor of Louisiana, who allegedly performed an exorcism in 1984 over his college lover, "Susan." Anyone can go to the library or look online and find a host of books that show how to perform an exorcism. But would anyone want to?

MENTAL ILLNESS AND HYSTERIA?

The scientific community suggests that demonic possession is more of a mental illness than anything else and is most likely an example of hysteria, mania, delusion, or some type of schizophrenia or dissociative identity disorder, wherein one personality seems to be "possessing" the main personality. There is actually something called "demonomania," in which a person believes that he or she is possessed to the point of behaving as such and experiencing symptoms. This situation is similar to the power of suggestion displayed in the placebo and nocebo effects, whereby the belief in something can actually affect the body and cause physiological reactions.

Demonic possession also has similarities to religious fervor or rapture, which can lead to hallucinations and speaking in tongues, and also to poltergeist activity, which triggers brain activity in the same region of the temporal lobe as *grand mal* seizures in epileptics, and often is associated with objects moving on their own, levitation, and other "paranormal" activity that might on the outside look quite demonic.

FAMOUS EXORCISMS AND CASES OF DEMONIC POSSESSION

Some of the most famous cases are those that have been exploited through the entertainment industry and mainstream media, becoming a part of pop culture and the perception we have of demonic possession.

Amityville Horror

This 1976 case involved a house filled with horrors, investigated by the Warrens, and the fodder for a series of movies and books, including the 1977 book *The Amityville Horror*, which was made into a successful feature film. The case involved the family of George and Kathy Lutz and their three children, who moved into a house allegedly haunted by the demonic entity of a former resident who had brutally slaughtered his entire family.

It all began on November 13, 1974, when a man named Ronald DeFeo walked into a bar and screamed that his parents had been shot at their family home at 112 Ocean Avenue in Amityville, a suburb on the south shore of Long Island, New York. Police went to the home and found six bodies: the father, mother, and four of the five children. Only Ronald had survived the mass execution, stating he wasn't home at the time and discovered the slaughter when he went home.

The house in Amityville, New York, where the Lutz family experienced the horrors of a demon in their home.

Police later found a box of ammunition for the type of gun found in Ronald's room, and he eventually confessed to the killings. He was convicted in 1975 and sentenced to six consecutive life sentences.

But the story did not end there. One month after DeFeo was convicted, the Lutz family moved into the six-bedroom Dutch Colonial home after purchasing it for a bargain. George, Kathy, and their three children immediately began experiencing a host of paranormal activities, including swarms of flies in the winter, knocks on walls and slamming doors, cold spots throughout the home, odors of both perfume and excrement with no discernible origins, green slime oozing from floors and walls, revolving crucifixes, and more. Some of the more terrifying events included George's waking at 3:15 A.M. every night to wander the house in a trance at the same time the DeFeo murders occurred; five-year-old daughter Missy claiming to have an imaginary pig friend named Jody, whose red eyes were seen by Kathy one night in the upper story window; George's discovery of a small red room in the basement that made their dog, Harry, cower in terror; the children sleeping on their stomachs, the same position in which the DeFeo children's bodies were found; and George's tripping over a ceramic lion that caused bite marks on his ankles and would reappear in the living room even when moved elsewhere.

> **D**uring the investigation, Ed was reportedly pushed by an unseen force, and Lorraine felt an overpowering demonic force in the home. She had psychic impressions of the dead DeFeo family.

After realizing something was amiss, the family attempted several house blessings, but the activity continued until the Lutzes decided, after only twenty-eight days, that they had enough. They got their things together to leave and went to stay with Kathy's mother. Twenty days later, Ed and Lorraine Warren were called to go to the house, along with a team of reporters and parapsychologists. The Lutzess were not there at the time. During the investigation, Ed was reportedly pushed by an unseen force, and Lorraine felt an overpowering demonic force in the home. She had psychic impressions of the dead DeFeo family. She also found many links between the home and black magic practiced on the same land, as well as an old story of the Shinnecock Indians' using the land for a home for the insane and sick. She believed that these factors may have contributed to the spirit activity in the home and its negative nature.

The house was later resold, and then sold again after reports of continued activity. Years later, one of the children who lived in the house, Daniel Lutz, came forward to discuss what had happened in a chilling documentary. He recounted many of the classic terrifying moments in the house he experienced as a ten-year-old boy, including the demons telling a priest who had come to the house to "Get out!" and the garage door slamming up and down while the family dog, Harry, went ballistic. Lutz also recalled seeing the red demonic eyes of the imaginary pig, Jody, that his sister befriended and said there were many books about Satanism and demonology on his father's bookshelves, suggesting his father's beliefs and practices triggered the demonic activity at the house.

Anneliese Michel

Sixteen-year-old Anneliese suffered from epilepsy and mental illness and was often in psychiatric hospitals. In 1973, she became suicidal and displayed unusual symptoms of drinking her urine, shunning religious artifacts, and hearing voices. After she failed to respond to medicine, her family contacted two local priests, who began performing exorcisms. The girl died within a year. The case caused tremendous controversy when it was learned her parents stopped the girl's medications while the exorcisms were underway. She had almost seventy exorcisms and stopped eating, and her body began deteriorating over the course of several months. She had visions of being a martyr. Some of her exorcisms were recorded, and her death was attributed to emaciation and starvation, for which the family and the priests were charged with negligent homicide. This case spawned the famous movie *The Exorcism of Emily Rose*, released in 2005.

Clara Cele

Clara Germana Cele was a Christian student in 1906 at St. Michael's Mission in Natal, South Africa, when she decided to pray to the devil and make a pact with him. A few days later, she began speaking and understanding languages she never was taught, felt repulsed by religious artifacts, and even began to read the minds of those around her. Attending nuns reported she also made horrible grunts and animal sounds and that she could levitate above her bed. Apparently, Cele tried to strangle an attending priest who had come in with another priest to exorcise her, and over 170 people saw her actually levitate while priests read the Bible to her. It took two days to fully exorcise the demon inside her. She was healed and went on to lead a normal life.

Connecticut Haunting

In 1986, the Warrens had another case to deal with that would become famous later via several reality shows and movies loosely based on the events. This time, it involved a former funeral home called the Snedeker house, which was allegedly infested with demons. The house was located in Southington, Connecticut, and home to the Snedeker family, who reported demonic activity. However, author Ray Garton, who later wrote an account of the case, stated that the family was riddled with drug use and alcoholism and that family members couldn't come up with a straight story of what happened. Supposedly, Allen and Carmen Snedeker moved to the rented home with their four children. While moving in, Carmen found some strange items in the basement, which they learned were mortician's tools. How cool, right?

Soon, the elder son was seeing ghosts and having terrifying visions, which then seemed to spread to the other family members. The parents claimed awful experiences, including being raped and sodomized by demons. Perhaps not surprisingly, the family then contacted Ed and Lorraine Warren, who came in and confirmed that the house was demon-possessed. However, later reports by the landlady asserted that there was never any strange activity in the house and that the family stayed there for two more years, despite the supposed rapes and paranormal activity. Garton was later hired by the Warrens to write the book and suspected the Snedeker family might have been trying to ride on the success of the Amityville movie and books. He claimed that he was even told by Ed to "use what you have and make the rest of the stuff up," according to a LiveScience.com interview in March 2009, "The Real Story Behind 'The Haunting in Connecticut.'" Garton's book was released in 1992 and was titled *In a Dark Place: The Story of a True Haunting.*

Demon Murder Trial

Ed and Lorraine Warren consulted on this case involving Arne Cheyenne Johnson, the first known court case in the United States that used the defense argument of "not guilty by reason of demonic possession." In 1981, the nineteen-year-old Johnson walked up to his landlord, Alan Bono, and stabbed him multiple times with a pocket knife. Bono died later in a hospital, and Johnson was picked up by police. Johnson's lawyer, Martin Minnella, came up with the idea of pleading not guilty due to demonic possession and argued that Johnson's actions went back to behaviors originating from his childhood. Johnson, as a child, had allegedly been taunted by demons most of his life and Minnella claimed that his adult behavior was a result of that. It might not come as too much of a surprise that the judge ruled against Johnson, and he was convicted of first-degree murder. Unfortunately, he ended up serving only a five-year sentence.

The controversial case was later turned into a book, *The Devil in Connecticut,* and a movie called *The Demon Murder Case.* It turns out the story goes back to 1980, when Johnson's fiancé, Debbie, asked him to stay with her family because her young brother, David, was having visions and dreams of a demonic "Beast Man" and would wake up covered with strange bruises and scratches. The family endured some classic demonic activity, such as odd noises and David's speaking in multiple voices, before turning first to their church for help and then to the famed couple, the Warrens, after a priest's visit to the house made the activity worse.

In a 1981 case, attorney Martin Minnella argued that his client, Arne Cheyenne Johnson, had been possessed by a demon when he killed his landlord.

The Warrens interviewed David and deemed him possessed. Three exorcisms were held with the Warrens officiating, and forty-three demons were removed from David. However, during one of the exorcisms, Arne Cheyenne Johnson taunted the demons, claiming that they were too scared to possess him. After that, he began displaying strange behaviors such as going into trances, making growling sounds, and claiming to see the Beast Man himself. Fast forward to February 6, 1981, when he and Debbie went to lunch with Alan Bono, when an argument between the two men ensued, resulting in the stabbing of Bono and Johnson's arrest.

Was Johnson really possessed by the demons that had taken control of little David? Or was he just mentally unstable and violent, and clever enough to claim he was possessed to excuse a crime? The judge decided there was no evidence to point to possession.

Ecklund Possession

Also known as the Earling Possession, this case involved a fourteen-year-old girl from Earling, Iowa, named Anna Ecklund, who showed all of the classic signs of possible demonic possession. She was a Catholic, although her father and aunt were said to have practiced witchcraft and had cursed the girl for her religious beliefs. Soon, Anna was shunning all religious objects, acting sexually advanced, and refusing to enter a church. In 1912, she was successfully exorcised, until her father and aunt prayed to the Devil to cause her more suffering, after which she was allegedly possessed by even more demons. Some of her demons may also have been the same as those that possessed Anneliese Michel in the 1970s.

When Anna was put into a convent in 1928, her behavior took an even more significant turn for the worse. She would torment the nuns who took care of her and even began speaking in tongues, as well as levitating and clinging to walls, defying gravity. It took twenty-three days and three full exorcisms to finally free her of her demons.

Enfield Poltergeist

Most people know of the horrific case of the Enfield, England, poltergeist from the recently released movie *Conjuring 2*. It shows a single mother and her four children tormented by demons that possess the youngest daughter until Ed and Lorraine Warren come in and chase the demons away. The allegedly true story took place from 1977 to 1979 at the council house in Brimsdown, Enfield, involving two sisters who may or may not have faked evidence of demonic activity. Although labeled a poltergeist case, this series of events had aspects that raised the question of whether it might lean more toward demonic possession, if it really happened at all.

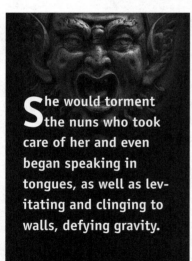

She would torment the nuns who took care of her and even began speaking in tongues, as well as levitating and clinging to walls, defying gravity.

The single mother, Peggy Hodgson, called police to her home with claims that two of her children witnessed furniture moving on its own, heard knocks when no one was there, and heard strange sounds coming from within the walls of the home. A police constable called to the scene witnessed a chair sliding across the floor. Later claims included demonic voices, levitation, and overturned furniture, as the activity escalated.

Media attention brought reporters to the house from the *Daily Mail* and the *Daily Mirror*, but it wasn't until Society for Psychical Research members Maurice Grosse and Guy Lyon Playfair witnessed the activity that allegations of trickery and fraud came to light, causing the two daughters to confess to faking it. However, some of the activity appeared beyond fakery, causing great confusion between various news reporters and psychologists who believed that the girls had staged the events, which included ventriloquism.

When Ed and Lorraine Warren were finally called in, they claimed that the demonic possession was real. Almost immediately, critics and skeptics began suggesting that Ed had a proclivity for making up and exaggerating incidents and turning them into "demonic" activity, and said the trickery always seemed to occur when the girls were not being watched directly. A number of documentaries, reality shows, and even motion pictures have glamorized the events and suggested that they were indeed paranormal in nature, despite significant evidence to the contrary.

Julia

This case occurred in 2008, when a board-certified psychiatrist, Dr. Richard E. Gallagher, who was also a professor of clinical psychiatry at New York Medical College, treated a patient he called "Julia," whom he believed was possessed by demons. On numerous occasions, Dr. Gallagher allegedly observed Julia speaking in tongues, levitating off her bed, causing objects to fly around the room, and stating things about people as if she were clairvoyant or a mind reader. He claimed that she would go into a trance state and that was when the phenomena would occur. She would frequently threaten, taunt, curse, and speak in a voice much different from her own, and with a masculine sound, or that of a growling animal. Like other exorcism subjects, she had a huge disdain for religious objects. She went through several exorcisms to rid her of her demons.

She would frequently threaten, taunt, curse, and speak in a voice much different from her own....

Latoya Ammons

In a 2014 story in the *Indianapolis Star*, reporter Marisa Kwiatkowski wrote of a woman and her three children who claimed to be possessed by demons. The story included a nine-year-old boy who walked up walls backwards in front of a caseworker and hospital nurse. Captain Charles Austin, a veteran police officer with the Gary, Indiana, police department, stated that he thought Latoya Ammons and her children fabricated the story for money. But after several visits to their home, he changed his tune and said, "I am a believer."

It all began in November 2011 when the Ammons family moved into a rental on Carolina Street in a quiet part of Gary. Giant black flies suddenly swarmed the home during the winter (just like in the Amityville case), and footsteps could be heard climbing the basement steps in the dead of night. Soon, shadow figures were appearing before family members. By 2012, the family was terrified and when the twelve-year-old daughter was seen levitating in front of family friends, Latoya's mother, Rosa Campbell, who witnessed the events, suggested praying. The girl descended to her bed and awoke the next morning with no memory of what happened.

Campbell talked with her daughter about getting help, and they contacted local churches, which refused to listen to their story. They even brought in two clairvoyants who claimed the house was infested by over two hundred demons and that they should move, but the family could not afford to. A cleansing was done, but three days later, things apparently got much worse, and soon, the three children, ages seven, nine, and twelve, experienced bulging eyes and deepened voices that were almost inhuman. Latoya Ammons turned to a family physician, Dr. Geoffrey Onyeukwu, who told the newspaper that the situation was "bizarre" and that he had never seen anything like it. When one of Latoya's sons raged at the doctor, the child was thrown against a wall by some unseen force, prompting police and ambulances to be called. A domestic-abuse counselor investigated the family and found the children to be healthy, free of bruises, and sane of mind, until the youngest son began to display demonic behavior and was joined by his older brother. It was then that the caseworker and others witnessed the nine-year-old walking up the wall as if gliding, unassisted. The counselor believed the child's affliction could be demonic, though possibly a mental illness. But what mental illness gives the ability to walk up walls?

The activity kept going and eventually the Rev. Michael Maginot from the St. Stephen, Martyr Parish was called in. He spent time with the family at the house and was convinced that the demonic activity was real. Several exorcisms were performed, despite ongoing investigations into allegations that the children were faking it, or abused, or both. Ammons lost custody of her children in April 2012, when they were questioned and their behavior was examined, but regained them later in 2012 after a long police and DCS investigation. A final exorcism courtesy of the Catholic Church rid the home of demonic activity after the reverend had Latoya and her mother write down the names of the demons so he could use them in his ritual. The landlord later said there had never been any problems in that house before, nor were there after, the Ammons family lived there.

Lukins

In 1778, a man named George Lukins living in the village of Yattin, Mendip, in the county of Somerset, England, claimed he was possessed by demons. His symptoms included singing in a strange voice and an unusual language that caught the attention of neighbors, who contacted the local church for help. Lukins was admitted to a hospital for almost two years, but the doctors could not help him. From there, he was sent home and became more and more violent, claiming he was the Devil and telling local clergy he was possessed by seven different demons that must be exorcised by seven different clergy. Seven priests at the Temple Church performed the rites and claimed Lukins was free of all the demons. Lukins thanked the priests and proclaimed praise to God, having finally been freed of dark forces.

Michael Taylor

Michael Taylor and his wife, Christine, lived in Ossett, a small town in England. They joined a prayer group led by a woman named Marie Robinson,

In 1778, the priests of Temple Church (shown here) in Bristol, England, were called to perform rites on the possessed George Lukins. The exorcism was happily successful.

whom Christine accused in 1974 of having an affair with her husband, a claim both Marie and Michael denied. But Michael began shouting obscenities and acting strangely, leading those who knew the couple to believe he might be possessed. Clergy were called in after a few months and an exorcism lasting over twenty-four hours was done, allegedly removing forty demons from Michael's body except for one, the Demon of Murder, which was not exorcised by the priests. When Taylor went home, he murdered his wife and dog and was later acquitted by reason of insanity. Was this a real demonic possession or a failed attempt by a cheating husband to get himself off the hook with an outlandish claim?

Robbie Doe, the Real "Exorcist" Case

The famous 1973 movie *The Exorcist*, based on the 1971 book by William Peter Blatty, was in turn based on the case of a fourteen-year-old boy born in 1935 who went by the pseudonyms Roland or Robbie Doe (among others), given to him by the Catholic Church to protect his identity. Coming

Truth: Beings Stranger Than Fiction

BY ANDREA PERRON

There was an extensive cast of characters at the farmhouse, but the house itself had the lead role in a passion play that ran for a decade. It was the spirits' base of operation, their theater, their story to tell. Whether backstage, center stage, or just hiding in the wings, the spirits ran the show. We never knew when one was about to make a grand entrance with no script at our disposal. All the blocking was their call. They were there all along, improvising, lurking behind an invisible scrim, a veil that does not exist.

To grow up in a place so extraordinary was a privilege. What some would call a curse was a blessing in disguise, including beings dressed in period costumes, proficient at transfixing their captive audience with magic tricks. Antique bottles flying around a room, smashing into windows and walls without any damage done, doors that mysteriously opened and closed with no sign of a soul in sight—the spirits were capable of every sleight-of-hand, but they were no illusion. Appearing then disappearing before our eyes, they made their presence known in myriad ways, at every time of day or night. However, we were not merely observers but were often drawn into their drama as unwilling participants dragged from their seats to become part of the play.

Three decades after our departure from the farm, Hollywood wanted to rewrite the script. The screenwriters attempted to compress ten years into two hours and were not allowed to tell the truth, as the studio executives were fearful that doing so would cause an adverse reaction from the viewers. It was probably the first time a *scary story* was toned down rather than exaggerated beyond belief, though there were elements of the film that did so, taking liberties and creative license with it as the executives pleased. *The Conjuring* is a great film but it barely scratched the surface of a true story larger than life and death, a story that is essentially about love and spiritual connection. Telling the cryptic tale on screen once the story had new life breathed into it within the pages of three intense books, *House of Darkness House of Light* tells the true story of these spirits, including some bad actors on a dark stage, often dropping the house lights to create that extra special effect of terror. Yes, there were times when one sinister spirit became threatening, insisting that our mother leave her own home, this female spirit apparently perceiving herself to be mistress of the house, but it was not the villain portrayed in the film as Bathsheba Sherman. In fact, it is far more likely portraying a woman who died before Bathsheba was born. Of course, we will never know for sure who they were (or still are), as none of them ever presented themselves with a handshake, a proper introduction. In actuality, in *reality*, ours was not a "horror story" but was, instead, a phenomenal spiritual journey of enlightenment. It shatters all stereotypes of the genre and sheds new Light on a very dark matter, indeed.

From 1970 until 1980, the farm was an integral part of our lives. We left it behind, but it will never leave us. My family waited thirty years to tell our tale to the world. Ed and Lorraine Warren are a piece of the puzzle, but they came to our home only five (maybe six) times over the course of about eighteen months and departed upon demand from my father after a séance they were asked to do went horrifically wrong. The awful incident nearly cost my mother her life. Whatever attacked her that fateful night did not want to kill her, as it certainly had the power to do. Upon reflection, I have realized it merely wanted to make a scene, make its presence known to everyone in the house. The medium collapsed, my father punched Ed Warren in the face, and my mother was tossed like a feather from one room to another, knocked unconscious. It was an ugly event, much more intense than anything portrayed in the film. No exorcism ever occurred in our home. My mother was not possessed; she was attacked and used as a communication conduit by something heinous, and its message was received loud and clear by everyone present in the house that night. As I've said countless times, I have seen the dark side of existence, which is why I deliberately choose to live in the Light.

Hundreds of incidents occurred in our home, numerous spirits manifesting frequently, though there were extended periods of tranquility when the paranormal activity seemed to subside or go dormant. When things were calm, we were most nervous because we did not know what would happen next. My sisters would come to me and sleep in my bed for comfort, telling me of their encounters and experiences. After several months, I finally told my mother what was happening; she was in the midst of processing some serious incidents of her own—nothing she'd shared with her children. My father was overwhelmed with the reports and let it be known that he did not believe the "stories," which caused all of us to withhold everything from him. Until he had encounters he could not deny, we felt abandoned by the man of the house, the one there to protect us. Years later, Dad confessed that he, too, had been afraid and felt totally out of control, unable to maintain equilibrium in his own household, stunned by the sheer number of inhabitants. There is always a period of adjustment when dwelling among the dead; we were literally sharing space. The place is a portal cleverly disguised as a farmhouse, a vortex of energy unimaginable for mere mortals to comprehend. Eight generations of one extended family lived and died in the dwelling and many of them never left the premises, for whatever reason. We made their acquaintance the day we moved in. Interestingly, our family visited the farm several times prior to ownership. There was nothing unusual going on during those visits, but all bets were off the day we stepped over the threshold as the new occupants on January 11, 1971. Within moments four of us saw an oddly dressed man standing alone in the corner of the dining room—and then he disappeared before my sister Nancy's eyes.

It was only the beginning of an odyssey unlike any other recorded, which is why Ed Warren asked his wife from his deathbed to be certain she got the Perron family story told before she joined him on the other side. Ed always spoke of the investigation they had conducted with reverence and respect, stating that it was the most "intense, compelling, disturbing and significant" case they ever pursued during the course of a forty-year career as paranormal investigators, which is precisely why it was the first in the series of films highlighting their most extreme encounters. Ed and Lorraine Warren meant no harm. They only wanted to help but realized they were in over their heads in entering a house alive with death. Mrs. Warren, to her credit, came into the house and immediately sensed a presence. "Her name is Bathsheba." Well, perhaps Bathsheba Sherman was a part of the play but she certainly did not have the lead role among the spirits. She never lived in the house and she was not the one responsible for haunting and taunting our mother. The woman—apparition—who came to Carolyn Perron was hideous and spoke her threat using language that was archaic and out of use by the time Bathsheba was born in 1812. "'Twas mistress once afore ye came and mistress here will be anon." In spite of the lingering folklore that persists to this day, there is no indication, public record, or private proof that Bathsheba was a practicing witch, a wicked charge that could get a woman killed, and often did, during Puritan times in New England. History is brimming with mystery, and the farmhouse is no exception. Perhaps someday we will all know whom we

Continued...

came to know while living there, but it will most likely not happen in this realm.

Hard to believe, but we learned to live with it. Over the course of a decade we made peace with the spirits and they did not want to let us go. Their final curtain call was a fascinating one. The one who greeted us on the day of our arrival was likewise present to see us off, as he had done for the previous owner, Mr. Kenyon. We thought we were leaving them behind. Nothing could be further from the truth.

Curtain call—truth be told, there is no retracting it now that it has found its way into the world. The curtain will never be drawn on a story with no end.

(Andrea Perron is the author of House of Darkness House of Light.*)*

from German Lutheran descent, the boy lived in Cottage City, Maryland, a suburb of Washington, D.C. He was an only child and was said to have emotional problems. He was particularly close to his Aunt Harriet, whom was also called "Tillie," who lived in the household. After her death, the boy allegedly was using a Ouija™ board trying to contact his deceased aunt, who had been actively involved in spiritualism, and in the process let in a demon that possessed him. Interestingly, Aunt "Tillie" died of multiple sclerosis on January 26, 1949, just a few days after Robbie began experiencing strange phenomena.

The activity began with dripping water, strange sounds, religious artifacts flying off walls, furniture moving on its own, footsteps, and scratching noises with no origin. Then, scratches began to appear on Robbie's body, including words such as "hell" and "evil" that looked as if they had been carved into his flesh. Soon, he was speaking in tongues and levitating, his body contorted.

The boy underwent over thirty exorcisms, including one conducted by Edward Hughes, a Roman Catholic priest at Georgetown University Hospital. During that exorcism, the boy slashed the priest's arm with a piece of broken bedspring and the ritual was ended. The boy's family went to St. Louis from there, and a family member contacted Raymond J. Bishop and William S. Bowdern, local Catholic priests, who both visited Robbie at home and saw his bed shaking, witnessed objects flying around the room, and heard the boy speak in a guttural voice.

Another priest called in to observe the boy, Walter Halloran, suffered a broken nose inflicted by Robbie while Halloran, Bowdern, and a third priest named Willaim Van Roo, a Jesuit, did an exorcism. Afterward, the boy seemed to be freed of the demons that had possessed him and is said to have gone on to live a normal life from that point on, reportedly as a government worker, with his own family. It is said that he remembered next to nothing of the incidents. However, as with other such cases, investigators and skeptics found ample contradicting information in the stories, and many believed the boy was mentally ill and not truly possessed. This allegation of mental illness seems to be the pattern with such cases of possession, even with witnesses present to see the activity. Though such critics dismissed the case as not demonic in nature, Christian academics Terry D. Cooper, a professor of psychology, and Cindy K. Epperson, a professor of sociology, commented that "cases of genuine possession cannot be explained by psychiatry." They even went on to write about Robbie's case in their book, *Evil: Satan, Sin and Psychology,* and favored the explanation that there was indeed something supernatural regarding the nature of evil.

This case served to fuel many exorcism investigations to follow and spawned a number of related books, documentaries, and reality-show segments devoted to proving, or disproving, the case that went down in history.

The Exorcist author, William Peter Blatty, based his story on a 1935 case involving a teenaged boy who was helped by the Catholic Church.

Son of Sam

Son of Sam possessed, you say? Well, not exactly, but the New York City terrorist, David Berkowitz, aka "Son of Sam," killed six people and injured seven others in his summer killing spree and claimed to police that the Devil made him do it. He did not claim to be possessed, saying instead that his neighbor's dog was possessed and that the dog ordered him to kill. He was sentenced to six life sentences, and he later amended his case to include a statement that he was part of a Satanic cult, which had ordered the ritual murders.

RISE IN EXORCISMS

Because of mass media and entertainment, social networking, and a newfound interest in all things paranormal, there seems to be a rise in reported cases of demonic possession and activity. Perhaps it is only relative to this increase in reports, but the Catholic Church has claimed that exorcisms are making a comeback. In a *San Francisco Weekly* story on March 9, 2016, "Return of the Devil: Exorcism's Comeback in the Catholic Church," writer Chris Roberts looked into the rise of healing masses designed to rid churchgoers of evil, sickness, and demonic activity. Often these are done in people's houses, with trained Catholic exorcists present, who perform the Solemn Rite of Exorcism and do a formal casting out of the Devil. The person afflicted is usually a Catholic believer, but not always.

This "renaissance" of exorcisms within the Catholic Church may be because people once hid their afflictions, as stated by Angela Alioto, a practicing attorney and fervent Catholic. "I think people were hiding exorcism more before," she said. "I think they were still doing it, they just kept it quiet. Now they're not being as quiet as they used to." Yet social networking and wider access to information may also play a role in the increase, not to mention the popularity of paranormal television shows that suggest anyone can be a ghost hunter or exorcist, with minimal training.

In 2004, Pope John Paul II issued a decree ordering every diocese to appoint an official exorcist. Many priests and religious scholars agree that exorcisms are back and popular again. What was once a medieval practice has been modernized, and there is a belief that more people are coming under the spell of the Devil and evil. "Almost all exorcists are unanimous in their belief that more people are becoming possessed today than in the recent past," wrote journalist Matt Baglio in his book *The Rite: The Making of a Modern Exorcist.* However, skeptics, including clergy, suggest that is not true, as exorcisms ebb and flow with the news and media cycles that promote exorcism stories.

Perhaps the proliferation of modern horror movies also adds to the increase in people believing that they or their houses are possessed. And it certainly seems sane to say that children and teenagers who act up and act out, even those with mental disorders, might look to be possessed when they are just displaying abnormal behaviors. We seem to want to label everything "demonic" these days. Is doing so a way of shirking responsibility for our own actions and failures?

Pople John Paul II decreed that every diocese in the Church must have an official exorcist.

Historian Brian P. Levack wrote in *The Devil Within: Possession and Exorcism in the European West* that there are two main periods of time when exorcisms were at the height of popularity—the seventeenth century and modern times. Apparently, as many as fifteen percent of the world's population has had at least one exorcism performed on them. In fact, the act of baptism is a sort of mini-exorcism that includes renouncing Satan and all of his works.

Because exorcism is mainly a Catholic rite, and there are over 1.2 billion Catholics in the world, it makes sense that there are many exorcisms that we never hear about. The influx of immigrants from Catholic countries in Latin America has also added to the increase in interest. Where there is faith and belief in the Devil, there is the need for exorcists. The country with the most exorcisms of all was Italy, home to Rome and the Vatican, with over 500,000 exorcisms a year for those seeking healing and freedom from demons, depression, and disease.

Exorcisms, then, are not always about freeing someone of a demon or the Devil. They sometimes are more symbolic and involve casting out negative forces and energies that make people sick, in similar fashion as shamans and medicine men and women who perform rituals and ceremonies on villagers and locals with many afflictions. Modern exorcists, those formally trained, also look to weed out the possibilities of other things as the cause for "demonic" behavior, such as drug use, sexual and physical abuse, and a history of trauma, and only after all medical and psychological possibilities have been exhausted will the Solemn Rite be given.

Some hard-core Catholic priests say that New Age beliefs and metaphysics, and even the practice of yoga, are causing more demonic possession, but there is no empirical proof for their assertions, which appear to be based on religious bias and ignorance more than fact. The Church would claim that the only way to stop or prevent demonic possession for those who practice other faiths such as these would be to attend church, pray, and be a devout Catholic. Such extreme views do not sit well with many younger potential church members who seek answers in other religions or in atheism and agnosticism. And there is no proof that there are more possessed non-Catholics than Catholics.

The newest pope, Pope Francis, is also an advocate of exorcisms and has been involved in several discussions of the Devil and his temptations. In May 2014, the Vatican hosted a convention on exorcism, and the media was allowed in for the first time to observe the discussions and events.

One of the most interesting aspects of exorcism is that it often takes numerous attempts to work. As with psychological therapy and twelve-step programs, perhaps it just takes that much time to wrestle the demons that come from outside us as it does those within. Demonic possession and exorcisms seem to be more prominent among those who believe in the power of demons and the Devil to possess them. It is at its core a religious belief, and part of a religious belief system, that looks at evil as originating from the Devil and his minions.

Pople Francis has also been an advocate of exorcisms, backing up the position of Pope John Paul II.

An Interview with Rosemary Ellen Guiley

Q: How do you define activity that is "demonic" in nature, as opposed to ghosts, apparitions, and even poltergeist activity?

A: I have a broad perspective on the demonic realm that is closer to ancient views, in that "demons" are intermediary and interfering spirits whose temperaments range from tricky and annoying to malevolent and evil. There are far more demons than the Christianized "Satanic" variety. Under this umbrella, poltergeist activity of all kinds could be classed as demonic. I consider ghosts, and most apparitions of the dead (except for crisis apparitions and genuine visitations of the dead), to be residual.

Q: Have you ever experienced a demonic case that truly terrified you? How was it handled?

A: The most frightening cases I have dealt with are djinn cases. In the West, many demonic cases are misdiagnosed djinn cases, because little is known about the djinn. There is significant overlap in behavior and characteristics, and an argument can even be made that demons are forms taken by djinn. One djinn can manifest in multiple forms even simultaneously and perpetrate an unending storm of nasty activity.

In this one particular case of djinn-occupied land (and the house built on the land), attempts were made to exorcize the property through different religious and spiritual rituals, conducted by the appropriate, trained individuals. Temporary periods of peace could be obtained, but nothing dislodged the djinn, and the residents finally moved. The house had a history of troubling activity and a revolving door of owners, so I suspect that previous owners were similarly plagued.

Q: Do you believe animals and objects can also be possessed? Have you experienced such a case that stands out in your mind?

A: Yes, animals and objects can be possessed. In the case mentioned above, the family dog suffered greatly, even vomiting shards of glass and metal at one point. It was fine after the family vacated the property. (Their health suffered, as well.)

Q: What do you do to protect yourself from dark energies?

A: The best prescription is daily meditation, which is spiritually grounding and expands consciousness. It strengthens the aura, which is a shield of energy around you. You must have strong boundaries, not only of physical and psycho-spiritual energy but also boundaries that are filled with the energy of sovereignty (allowing no violation) and will.

I have cultivated a connection to the angelic realm for years, especially the Archangel Uriel, who holds the cosmic flame of Truth, and the Archangel Michael,

Very little is known about the djinn, according to Rosemary Ellen Guiley, but the djinn can be as nasty as any demon.

the strength that vanquishes evil. Understanding the essence of Truth with a capital T is vitally important. Evil cannot stand up against Truth, along with Divine Light and Unconditional Love.

Q: Do you have advice for paranormal researchers who try to deal with these types of cases on their own?

A: I always recommend the establishment of a daily spiritual practice that includes meditation. In addition, undertake a study of esoteric literature dealing with consciousness and a study of the paranormal, angelology, and demonology. Don't forget the djinn, because they are excluded from most Western treatments of demons. Taking some classes in energy healing will teach you a lot about the aura and boundaries.

Concerning religion, it is important to realize that religion—any religion—does not hold all the answers or solutions to the dark side. Every religion has effective means of expelling the unwanted, but none of them has techniques that work 100 percent of the time and in 100 percent of all cases. Thus, dealing with difficult cases requires being open-minded, and a willingness to be versatile in approach.

Also, you have to know when it's prudent to back off and return another day. That requires a good reading of whatever you are dealing with—so sharpen up your psychic ability.

(Rosemary Ellen Guiley is a leading researcher and author in the paranormal and metaphysical fields. She has done groundbreaking work on the djinn and has undertaken numerous cases of "persistent negative haunting." She has written more than sixty books, including the Encyclopedia of Demons & Demonology, The Encyclopedia of Angels *and* The Djinn Connection. *She is the host of the* Strange Dimensions *radio program on KGRA. Her website is www.visionaryliving.com.)*

An Interview with Demonologist Katie Boyd

Q: What made you decide to pursue studies in the occult and demonology? Did you have a personal experience that drove you to this? What is the number-one misconception you feel people have about what you do?

A: I grew up in a severely haunted house in Goffstown, New Hampshire. We actually had to have the local priest, Father B., come in several times to cleanse and bless it. My family was essentially being torn apart by this entity and I wanted answers. I was in my early teens when I began reading on the paranormal, demonology in particular, since that was my religious view back then. Based on what I had seen, an entity I called "Fireface," I was convinced it was more than just a spirit. Whilst doing research for my *Devils and Demonology in the 21st Century* book I found accounts of a local tribe being slaughtered and I now believe that is where this entity originated from. My father became oppressed by this energy, bitter, angry, and obsessed with the early colonial period, especially their guns, weapons, and war strategies. At the end my parents divorced and I ended up walking this path of the occult. I was lucky enough to have met some amazing teachers along the way from different religious backgrounds. This got me ready to deal with darker entities recognized in different faiths, such as hungry spirits and dybbuk.

Continued...

It also enabled me to differentiate between what is spirit, demon, thought-form, or residual energy. I outline my entire backstory in my book *Haunted Closets*.

I believe that the biggest misconception that surrounds the demonology field as a whole is that demons are plentiful. I have only seen four or five no-doubt demonic cases in my career. Most of what I deal with is spirits, energy, or mental/physical illness. Demons are very, very rare.

Q: When approached with a case, do you have a vetting system to make sure it is actually something paranormal/demonic?

A: Yes, a very strict one. Before I can assess a person, he or she has to fill out a lengthy questionnaire. If it is a demonic case, then the person must be evaluated by trusted doctors and psychologists. Depending on the claims I will also ask for medical history and if possible access to the person's records. The reason for this is there are so many psychological/medical issues that

can coincide with demonic oppression/possession or that can imitate what some of the symptoms are. Usually when vetting we will get to this stage and find our answers. If for some reason the answers are not there, then we will continue on to environmental causes. If that does not pan out, then we will look at the metaphysical possibilities.

Q: Do you have a particular case that most frightened you?

A: There was a woman with severe oppression. For over fifteen years she suffered attacks that doctors could not explain. They concluded it was mental illness; however, upon further evaluation, she seemed to be of sound mind. We watched her over a period of a month. We became convinced that there was definitely more going on there. Her apartment was spotless; however, it smelled like rotting garbage. The air was thick and heavy. On recording we got multiple EVPs (electronic voice phenomena—voices captured on tape recordings) of entities talking backwards, making clicking and other strange noises. I remember asking her, "Where does God come from?" She looked me right in the eye and said, "Oh. I know where God comes from! He comes from dust." Just at that moment on the tape (literally tape; it was a long time ago) you heard the sounds of trumpets. It was one of the coolest things that I have ever gotten on a recording. We found that she did indeed have an entity in the home as well as a few spirits. She has been without problems since that time.

Q: You have a background in both law enforcement and medical-safety procedures. Do those skills come in handy when dealing with a potential demonic case?

A: Absolutely! The medical aspect comes in very handy when identifying possible medication interactions, mental or physical illness, as well as environmental causes. When you are in law enforcement you

Katie Boyd's family was being torn apart by a demon she called Fireface.

are taught chain of command when handling evidence, which erases doubt as to manipulation or mishandling. It has also greatly influenced my writing, which most of my readers appreciate. With inclusion from the medical aspect and detailing some of the methods from the law enforcement side, plus of course the occult. The other thing that was drilled home to me in both careers was the scientific method and the principle of Occam's Razor—meaning the most obvious answer is more than likely the correct answer. Just those few takeaways from my previous careers have helped my clients feel more assured and trusting in my findings.

Q: How can others learn about your work? Classes? Consults? Books? Lectures?

A: My website is www.katieboyd.net. From there people can email me to ask about classes or find out about lectures and events.

Some of my most popular books are:

- *Devils and Demonology in the 21st Century*

- *Witches and Witchcraft in the 21st Century*

- *Werewolves: Myth, Mystery and Magick*

- *Haunted Closets: True Tales of the Boogeyman*

(*Katie Boyd is a demonologist and occult sciences expert with a passion for the paranormal with both a law enforcement and medical background. She has led over 400 paranormal investigations, including of poltergeist activity, UFOs/abductions, demonic hauntings, and more. Over her twenty years in the field Katie has seen, heard, and dealt with almost every form of entity and energy out there.*)

No Sane Person Plans to Become a Demonologist

BY KYL T. COBB, JR.

No sane person plans to become a demonologist. The path begins with subtle choices. Unlike television demonologists, real demonologists spend years of their lives exploring ancient texts and studying six thousand years of religious evolution. Unfortunately, spending weeks in the special section of libraries reviewing four-hundred-year-old manuscripts rarely provides a riveting television experience.

To truly study the natures of demons through history, a future demonologist must have a passion for historic research and a knack for written languages. While the specific catalyst varies, the path takes a researcher back to the earliest accounts of demons found on shards of Mesopotamian tablets. Among the most prominent collection of early writing on demons is the epic of *Gilgamesh*. *Gilgamesh* lays a foundation for understanding early concepts of demons before the emergence and influence of modern religions.

It is in the context of the Mesopotamian religions that the study of Sumerian concepts of demons provides one of the cornerstones of demonic understanding. Sumer is an area occupied by inhabitants of Mesopotamia who were black-haired and spoke a non-Semitic language. They referred to their land as Ki-En-Gi, the place of lords. Occupation of the area dates to 6500 B.C.E.

The Sumerians believed that demons controlled many aspects of their lives. Often the line between gods of nature and the power of a demon was blurred. As a result, a dizzying array of demons was identified. As part of

Continued...

their understanding of gods and demons, the Sumerians began to make lists of the ones they could control. For the first time in recorded human history, standardized uniformed rituals to deal with demons were developed. As part of the ceremonies, they invoked the names of demons for power. The use of animal or human surrogates was introduced. Healing or purification spells were the most commonly used rituals.

Sumerian spells also formed the basis for modern exorcisms around the world. In one example, the host is tied to a bed. White yarn is used to form a path on the right side, which faces the rising sun. Black yarn is used on the left side to face the darkness. The Sumerian chief god Asari-alim-nunna (Marduk) is invoked to force away the particular demon causing the ailment. As part of the cleansing ceremony, the victim is ceremonially washed with holy water to wash away the evil.

One of the Gilgamesh tablets that is at the British Museum. It is from the pre-Akadian era and relates the tale of Gilgamesh, who was part man, part god and ruled over the kingdom of Uruk. This early epic contains some of the first mentions of demons.

Armed with a basic understanding of Sumerian concepts, the serious researcher takes a path to understanding through thousands of ancient Sumerian texts spanning hundreds of years. Each new spell and every religious text offers a glimmer of insight into ancient concepts of demons. Piecing together the thousands of fragments of prayers, spells, and stories, it becomes possible to perceive the larger picture that the tapestry once held. Very little can give a historical researcher more joy than uncovering the actual text of an exorcism that had only previously existed as rumor or legend.

A second fundamental cornerstone of researching any set of historical events rests in the realization that words and context matter. The fact that a Sumerian exorcism uses the power of Asari-alim-nunna to control a demon becomes an important tool in modern exorcisms. Whether it's a Catholic exorcism using the power of the Christian God to expel demons or a Hindi exorcism that invokes Brahma to expel demons, the concept that there is a power hierarchy that binds divinity gives humanity a tool to resist demonic forces.

One of the complexities in understanding the nature of demons is the Alexandrian split. For better or worse, the concept of demons differs depending on which side of Alexander the Great's conquest line they appear. In the areas conquered by Alexander, Greek concepts spread toward the East and Eastern concepts swept to the West. The Alexandrian pathway eventually would result in the West's believing spiritual entities to be intangible, immortal, and eternal. In the East, the concept of demons retained the idea that gods and demons maintained physical bodies. While invisible, the entities can be trapped, hurt, and even killed.

One failing of fake demonologists is not understanding the evolution of religions and the interaction of various religions with each other. Historically, religious ideas spread from neighbor-to-neighbor contact, trade, or conquest.

If an existing religion is facing the influence of an encroaching religion, there are several steps used to resist or isolate followers from external factors. One method is the conversion of competing religions' gods to lesser gods/demons. The entrenched religion then brands any competing religions' gods as evil. In the case of the Shedim from *Gilgamesh,* a cult worshiping the Shedim was strong throughout the Middle East, including what is today Israel. As a result, the word *Shedim* became the generic Hebrew term for "evil demons."

In addition to the Shedim, it is important to understand that almost every named demon in Western demonology can be traced to a deity worshipped by another culture.

For example, take one of the most famous named demons, Beelzebub. The name "Beelzebub" is a corruption and deliberate mischaracterization of the Canaanite god *Baal Hahdad.* The Lord of Thunder was the most popular deity in Canaan, and his cult presented a serious challenge to the Yahweh cult that formed modern Jewish beliefs. As a result, *Baal Hahdad* became a supremely evil demon in the eyes of Yahweh followers.

The forge of demonic understanding comes in unraveling the history and the nature of each demon. Most Western demonic names can be traced from Mesopotamian to Hebrew traditions and through to the grimoiric traditions of occultists and magick practitioners. This requires the demonologist to trace the evolution of a particular demon through dozens of languages and hundreds of religious sources.

Most true demonologists are scholars and not field investigators. But a select number do engage in paranormal investigation as a chance to better understand the nature of their research.

While popular culture suggests that demonic entities are lurking around every corner and possess certain television actors in every episode of their paranormal adventures, the reality is that legitimate cases of actual demonic possession are extremely rare. Out of thousands of historic cases, only a handful would not be attributed to mental disorders under modern standards. Only slightly more common than possession, demonic events such as physical encounters give credibility to Eastern demonic concepts.

Because of the rarity of true demonic encounters, the assumption is that most paranormal events claiming agitated spirits are not demonic in nature.

A Russian icon depicts the demon Beelzebub lying in Hell. Beelzebub was the creation of the Jews, who took the Canaan god Baal Hahdad and demonized him.

Continued...

(Continued from previous page)

No matter how many years of study and research a future demonologist spends in searching for the truth, when the theories of academic study thrust themselves into a tangible part of reality, no level of preparation is sufficient.

One encounter with a demonic event happened in 2011 when there was a request to investigate an agitated spirit that was plaguing residents of a new home built in a subdivision inside a Civil War battle zone. The client had described a number of objects being displaced, exceptionally bad dreams, and reluctance to spend time in several rooms of the new home.

As part of standard investigation procedure, this particular investigation required the team of five to spend fifteen minutes resting for every forty-five spent in active engagement. This break period was used to refresh equipment batteries, as well as answer nature's collect calls.

At the end of one of these breaks, four of the team members, with fresh batteries in their equipment, started investigating the second floor of the home. Upon entering the front storage room, two of the investigators simultaneously declared that their batteries and flashlights had failed. They immediately abandoned the other baffled team members, who clearly saw that all the flashlights were working. A third team member also declared that he had an extreme need to use the bathroom and then literally ran out of the room. The fourth investigator was left alone, against protocol.

Within a few seconds, there were sounds of motion in the room and a shadowy figure ran at the remaining investigator, physically shoving the investigator to the side as it passed out of the room.

This case demonstrates one of the key elements found in both Eastern and Western demonic stories: the power of the entity to "suggest" thoughts to the victims. Whether it is a demon causing harm to the host in a possession case or a demon whispering chaotic thoughts, victims hear the "suggestion" as their own thoughts. While it is possible to resist such alien thoughts, most victims fail to notice the difference and react accordingly.

As it turns out, the Latin word *daimonizo* is the origin of the English term "possession." The word has been corrupted in English to mean "to be possessed by a demon." The real meaning of the verb is "to be influenced by a demon." The slight difference here means that the host has a choice on the actions taken.

Cases of true involuntary possession are very rare. The Catholic 1614 Rite of Exorcism establishes four tests of possession: the ability to speak with some facility in a strange tongue or to understand it when spoken by another; the faculty of divulging future and hidden events; the display of powers that are

A painting by Francisco Goya shows the Jesuit Saint Francis Borgia performing an exorcism.

beyond the subject's age and natural condition; and, "various other indications which, when taken together as a whole, build up the evidence of demonic influence."

It is to gain access to greater physical and mental powers of a demon that shamans around the world actively invite demons into their bodies as temporary hosts. When the demon enters the host, there is an immediate and discernible change both to atmosphere in the area and to the physical presence of the host. During the winter solstice Sun Death ritual, Mayans known as J'Men direct a demon into a host who has volunteered to become the jaguar for the annual event. For twelve hours, without food, water, or rest, the possessed man performs the highly energetic ritual bound inside the spell circles. At the end of the ritual, the J'Men cleans the demon out with sacred purification smoke, and the host collapses.

In a similar fashion, Tibetan Paju shamans perform an exorcism rite called the Gcod that instead of binding the demon and repelling it, encourages the demon to enter freely and feast on the bodies of the ritual performers. Playing a drum fashioned out of two skullcaps and a trumpet carved from a human thighbone, the priests summon demons to the cremation site. Calling on the goddess Ma-gcig slab-sgron to cut up the bodies of the dead ritual performers, the priests invite the swarms of demons to ritualistically feed upon themselves. Once the demons are satiated, they leave and take the anger, passion, ignorance, and ego with them. The self-sacrifice of the Gcod pays the Karmic debts of those at the ritual by paying the demons with self-sacrifice.

Both of these examples of voluntary possession give insight into the physical transformations that involuntary possession can facilitate.

Crossing the line between being a demonologist and doing field research is not one to be made without extensive consideration of the ramifications. If one pokes enough sticks at a rabid dog, there is always a chance that the dog will strike out.

Unfortunately, this happens in demonic cases.

Sooner or later a demon may decide that it is happy with its present circumstance and not want to abandon the residence or victim that it is engaging. The demonologist seems a bit too curious and is perceived as presenting a threat. While a demonologist is not an exorcist or a shaman trying to eliminate the entity, the difference can be academic to the affected entity.

Demons hit quickly and with little warning. They have enough force to lift a 250-pound man off the ground and leave him quivering in a corner. Even in the extreme heat of summers in the southern United States, the kind of cold left within the mind of the targeted demonologist can leave someone shivering for weeks.

(KyL T. Cobb is a paranormal investigator and demonologist, as well as the author of Ghosts and Demons and Forgotten Lore.

Is demonic possession any different from things like channeling and automatic writing, or speaking in tongues in a Pentecostal church, or is it just the intention of the entity taking over that most separates the evil from the mundane? What about mediums and psychics who claim spirits inhabit their bodies and speak through them? Are they somehow "possessed," albeit not by demons, but rather by the dead and those crossing over? And how much does the power of suggestion and psychology have to do with the success, or failure, of an exorcism on the possessed? James R. Lewis explains in *Satanism Today: An Encyclopedia of Religion, Folklore and Popular Culture*, "To exorcise means something along the lines of placing the possessing spirit under oath. The word exorcist itself has its roots in the word 'oath,' so that once a higher authority such as God is invoked, the demon is compelled to comply with that oath to abide by the authority of God." This becomes clear when the demonic entity is commanded to leave the person, not by the authority of a priest, but instead, for example "in the name of the Father, and the Son, and the Holy Spirit."

So perhaps a belief in the power of demons, as well as a belief in the power of a higher authority to cast out those demons, are necessary requirements for a successful exorcism. Yet many people have died during exorcisms, people who clearly were not possessed in the first place, as in the case of an autistic and disabled eight-year-old boy killed during a rite in Milwaukee performed by Catholic Church members who believed an invading demon was responsible for his autism. Or the young nun in 2005 in Romania who died during an exorcism when the priest bound, gagged, and left her strapped to a cross for days without food or water to try to rid her of demons. Or the numerous stories of people being beaten and drowned by relatives who believed they were possessed, such as fourteen-year-old Kristy Bamu of London, who died at the hands of ignorant relatives on Christmas Day in 2010.

Sometimes things like these give us pause as to what—or who—the real demons are.

SELLING YOUR SOUL TO THE DEVIL

History is filled with anecdotal tales of those who made pacts with the Devil in order to gain some favor or get revenge on an enemy. Witches have been accused of working in unison with the Devil for centuries, although in the next chapter we will take a closer look at whether or not those accusations are accurate, or rather constitute "media spin" of religious leaders needing an excuse to persecute and suppress female sexuality.

Theophilus

No, we are looking for actual accounts of people who signed in blood on the dotted line and handed over their souls to Satan for all eternity. One such individual was actually a saint. Saint Theophilus of Adana is said to have given over his soul for political and social position after he declined an offer to become elevated to bishop in the sixth century C.E. Too humble a man, Theophilus watched as another man took the position and began tormenting him and making his life a "living hell," at which time Theophilus called upon the Devil himself to reverse his own decision and make him the rightful bishop. Yet his guilt got the better of him, especially since the Devil demanded he, in return, denounce Jesus and all the saints. And yes, he signed a contract with his own blood.

Sometime later, he began to realize that he shouldn't have done what he did, but the Devil wasn't one to forgive. Theophilus allegedly sought the help of the Virgin Mary and prayed over and over, begging for forgiveness and freedom from his pact with the big D. He fasted several times, after a vision of the Virgin Mary promised that she would intercede on his behalf, but the Devil wasn't one to go back on a deal. Finally, he sought out a bishop to help him, and the bishop symbolically burned the pact and set Theophilus free. He died at that exact moment.

Urbain Grandier

Another holy person who sold out on his beliefs is French Catholic priest Urbain Grandier, who, in the sixteenth century, was alleged to have

engaged in sexual relations with several nuns, who later accused him of being a witch. He was acquitted at a trial, but the current chief minister, Cardinal Richelieu, ordered a second trial, resulting in the arrest and torture of Grandier. During his interrogations, his belongings were searched and a very interesting contract was discovered. Grandier had signed a pact written in Latin and covered with occult symbols. The pact gave him free reign to love women, deflower virgins, and even become a man of great power and respect, as long as he stayed loyal to the dark side. It was signed by Satan and some of his minion demons.

However, questions were raised as to the authenticity of the document, as it could have been forged for the purposes of finding Grandier guilty, which he was. He was burned at the stake in 1634 for "fraternizing with the devil."

Ms. Rose and the Devil

Usually we think of men selling out for fame and power and lust. But in the fifteenth century, a woman named Antoine Rose confessed to consorting with the

The Catholic priest Urbain Grandier was burned at the stake for signing a contract with the Devil that allowed him to have gratuitous sex and obtain power in the Church.

Devil, although she did so while being tortured. In fact, Rose is credited as being the modern symbolic witch riding on a broomstick with the Devil so widely known today. Rose was known as the Witch of Savoy, France, but she claimed to be a very poor woman who was introduced to the Devil to help her financially. She signed a pact and agreed to carry a stick rubbed with a particular ointment that would make the stick fly if she called upon the Devil. Of course, her part of the pact was to shun God and her religious beliefs. She later confessed to a number of strange rituals, including kissing the Devil on his rear end in worship, and stated he often took the form of a large black dog.

Rock 'n' Roll and Selling Your Soul

Many legends of those who sold their souls come from the creative world. Musicians, writers, artists, and the like, struggling to make it in a dog-eat-dog world and turning to the Devil for help make for great movie and book plots. But has it ever really happened?

It must be really hard to make it as a violinist, because we have two tales of musicians selling their souls to achieve greatness. The first is Nicolo Paganini, an Italian violinist in the early 1800s who was considered a virtuoso at the young age of twelve. His incredible musical genius caused such pressure, he suffered a breakdown and did not play for years. At twenty-two, he returned to performing even more complex musical pieces, and some began whispering that he must have made a pact with the Devil to acquire such talent and skill. Concert attendees even claimed to see the Devil on stage with Paganini. Sadly, the rumors caused him to be denied proper death and burial rites by the Catholic Church, which only later rectified the situation, burying his remains in Parma, Italy. It appears here that prodigy-like talent was so misunderstood that, even with no viable proof, someone could be accused of "dancing with the Devil" and suffer the consequences of rumor and gossip.

Another violinist, also Italian, accused of teaming up with the Devil was Giuseppe Tartini, who supposedly had an encounter with a demonic figure in 1713. The demon offered Tartini the usual—his soul for musical talent and fame. As with Robert Johnson, the Devil actually played a gorgeous song on Tartini's violin, and when he gave it back to the man, Tartini played back what would become the famed "Devil's Trill Sonata," an incredibly difficult piece to play. Tartini was praised for the piece but insisted it wasn't nearly as good as the one played by the Devil. Was this just a "creative" dream or an actual pact?

Anyone who, according to legend and lore, makes a deal with the Devil will have to eventually pay up. Even in the cases where religious intervention frees the person, it usually results in death anyway, and once dead, who can say where the soul goes … and who controls it?

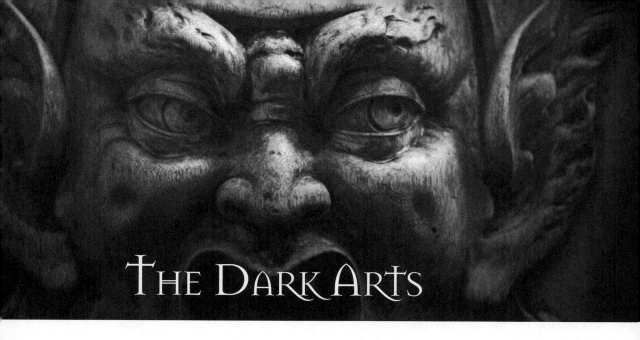

THE DARK ARTS

Up until now we have examined demons and the Devil, fallen angels, and dark entities mainly as beings to be avoided at all costs. Those who have lived with demonic possession or visits from the Devil and experienced the terror, suffering, and pain it brings would never think to ask for these experiences. But curiosity is an extremely powerful force, and now we are going to take a look at those who welcome the demonic into their lives in the form of rituals, practices, and beliefs that celebrate and worship the Devil and his legions. We will also look at practices that have mistakenly been associated with the Devil over the course of history, right down to modern times, and the practitioners who paid a dear price for it.

We may want to make clear right now that not everyone who calls himself or herself a practitioner of the dark arts is a murderer, torturer, or abuser, despite many associations with violence, as we shall see with satanic cults and ritual abuse. Some just want to explore the darker world of hedonism and pleasure, the sinfulness denied them by the traditional religions. Others like the symbolism of the shadow and exploring their own darker personas. Still others just want to reveal what is hidden, good or bad, and understand the energies and forces of the universe, dark and light, and the dualities of life and death. And maybe even sway those energies and forces to their will.

THE OCCULT

The occult is a perfect place to begin. The word itself implies hidden, secret, unknown. From the Latin *occultus*, which means "clandestine, hidden, secret," comes a world of knowledge that exists just beyond the visible. Some may call it the paranormal or supernatural, because it is beyond what we know of normalcy and everyday reality. Others look upon it as a number of systems of knowledge that hold the keys to a deeper understanding of who we are and how our world works, including how we ourselves shape and mold our reality. The implication of the word "occult" is that only some people are privy to this information, or that it should be kept only for the select few, as in those with the eyes to see and the ears to hear.

The occult can also be described as a broad range of subjects that are esoteric in nature and that are not to be readily explained by modern science. These include astrology, numerology, divination methods, Tarot, magic (black and white), alchemy, ESP and psi, spiritualism, cryptozoology, New Age beliefs, Hermeticism, Gnosticism, mystical traditions, Wicca, witchcraft, paganism, Earth-based traditions such as shamanism, Theosophy, and everything in between. These traditions and belief systems go far outside the accepted organized religions and are therefore shunned and often branded as "evil" and "of the Devil." In today's pop culture, the occult is usually thought of as "the paranormal" instead, but embodying many of the same beliefs and practices.

The esoteric ideas held in the body of works by occultists may have nothing at all to do with evil or the Devil, yet because of the rise of Christianity and mainly the influence of the Vatican and Catholic Church, they have

Sir Isaac Newton was accused of practicing occult arts when he proposed his laws of motion and gravity.

been tainted as sinful and deviant. Yet from the fifteenth to the seventeenth century, there was huge interest in the practices and teachings that could lead to enlightenment and understanding beyond what the religious leaders and even scientists of the time were capable of conveying. In fact, occult ideas often helped pave the way for scientific advancements and a broader, deeper view of the universal forces. Though some scientists shunned the occult because it did not follow the standard scientific method, others saw it as another way to look at reality and possibly unite religious beliefs with scientific knowledge. The occult was just what we did not know yet, and it could very well hold secrets to further science as well as find common ground with religion and spirituality.

When Sir Isaac Newton first proposed his ideas about gravity and magnetism, he was accused of practicing the occult, simply because he was offering a concept that was out of the range of current acceptance—that gravity could affect objects at a distance. Newton, among other noted scientists of his time, practiced the art of alchemy, which sought to use base metals to create the ultimate Holy Grail: gold. It was also a symbolic practice for man to transmute his own inner nature to the highest possible achievement and spiritual understanding or esoteric wisdom, in the same way the metal was believed to be transmuted into gold. There was nothing evil about alchemy, yet those who practiced it did so in private, in fear of retribution from the powerful and often vengeful Church.

Though the Christians believed the occult arts to be heretical, the more Earth-based religious traditions welcomed the occult as a part of their own spiritual unfoldment and mystical experimentation. But if you were caught practicing anything from reading tea leaves or using a pendulum to make a decision, to reading Tarot, casting spells with herbs and candles, or any other occult act, it was considered a challenge to Church beliefs in the power of God and the use of only the Bible and biblical practices. Occult practices also threatened to remove the middleman of the Church by giving the person practicing the potential ability to gain knowledge and understanding of the universe and its forces. This was supposed to be God's work, and the work of the clergy, not anyone sitting in his or her own home reading and performing rituals.

Even mystical traditions actually based on or branched off from accepted Western religious traditions often get labeled as occult or esoteric, including Kabbalah, the mystical Hebrew belief system. In fact, Kabbalah is one of the foundations of esotericism, which is said to have originated in the eastern Mediterranean region in the first few centuries after the death of Christ alongside Hermeticism, Gnosticism, and magical traditions.

GNOSTICISM AND MYSTERY TRADITIONS

Organized religion has certain rules and doctrines that must be followed, and those who do not follow them, or knowingly embrace concepts that oppose those doctrines, are often labeled as heretics and devil-worshippers. Mystery traditions have always sought to provide followers with a deeper method of knowing oneself and the world, minus the limited doctrines and preordained concepts. Some mystery traditions are even a branch of an organized religion and in no way challenge or denigrate religion.

Gnosticism

Gnosticism comes from the ancient Greek word *gnostikos*, which means "having knowledge of." *Gnosis* means "knowledge" and focuses on the spiritual rather than the material, as well as on knowing directly rather than finding knowledge via priests, rabbis, ministers, and middlemen. Many of the most ancient religious traditions have at their roots Gnostic influences and ideas of enlightenment and oneness with God, but Gnostic traditions themselves varied according to region.

The main concept behind this belief system, which many scholars believe is far older than the Western Abrahamic traditions, is that the Underworld is the realm of the flesh, time, and the imperfect. The Upperworld is the realm of God and perfection, timeless and eternal. It is the search for the Upperworld that is at the core of Gnostic traditions, which involve turning within, studying the forces of nature, and often giving of oneself through philanthropy, even chosen poverty. Many Gnostics are celibate, and the teachings embrace aspects that can be found in most mystery religions and early Christian and Judaic teachings. However, the discovery of the Nag Hammadi texts, a collection of thirteen books called codices found in the upper Egyptian region in 1945, places Gnosticism in the second century C.E. The "Gnostic Gospels" found at Nag Hammadi were once thought to have been destroyed by the early Christian church because they went outside of the chosen orthodoxy of scriptures that the early Christians felt defined the truth. These new gospels literally changed the face of the history of Christianity itself and put a new light on beliefs and understandings long suppressed.

> These new gospels literally changed the face of the history of Christianity itself and put a new light on beliefs and understandings long suppressed.

Because gnosis was considered the way of salvation, rather than a particular messiah or prophet, Gnostics were often associated with the Devil. Their focus on intuitive knowledge went against the teachings of more traditional religions, and their supreme being went not by the name "God" but by "Pleroma," which means "totality and fullness." Jesus, however, is actually looked upon by Gnostics as a supreme being who came to Earth to teach gnosis, but some Gnostic traditions deny his divinity and believe that he was just a man who attained divinity via gnosis.

Perhaps it was the interpretation of the demiurge, the creator God, as being inferior that led Gnosticism to be linked with the Devil, because this figure has been referred to in some Gnostic schools as Satan, but also as Yahweh, the Hebrew name for God.

Gnosticism was considered a heresy because it advocated finding wisdom without the aid of a Church or Church intermediaries. True students studied as seriously as if they were in a mystery school, which they pretty much were. But many of the teachings went outside the boundaries of the state-sponsored religions being pushed by authority figures and thus put Gnosticism on the map with other "occult" traditions.

Kabbalah

Kabbalah is simply the somewhat secret (although with modern celebrities practicing it, that ship has sailed!) practice of mystical Judaism. The word itself means "receiving," and implies that the reception of ancient knowledge and an understanding of the cosmology and theology of Judaism that may not be taught in temple. Those who practice Kabbalah insist on keeping the integrity of the teachings intact to pass down to future generations, and there has been great controversy over celebrities and stars who claim to be students of the Kabbalah, yet seem more interested in the hype than the actual discipline involved.

Believed to have originated in the twelfth century in southern France and Spain, the Kabbalah was based upon earlier Jewish mysticism and later became popular during the sixteenth-century "Jewish mystical renaissance" in Palestine. From the eighteenth century to modern times, it was Hasidic Jews who were usually associated with the growth and reinterpretations of Kabbalah, all the way up to today's incorporations of more modern spiritual ideas. But at its heart, Kabbalah is the teaching of man and his place in the universe. The discipline examines the relationship between the infinite and eternal *Ein Sof,* or the "infinity," and the fixed and defined nature of God and mortal humans, as well as the purpose behind our existence. The *Sephirot* (also spelled "sephiroth"; singular *sefirah*) are the ten emanations and attributes of God by which he continually sustains the universe in existence, i.e. the Kabbalistic Tree of Life.

The main text of Kabbalah is the *Zohar,* a group of Jewish books written in Aramaic, including commentary of the mystical aspects of the Torah (the first five books of Moses), as well as mythical cosmology and mystical psychology. The discipline also required the study of the Torah itself.

Kabbalah's only association with anything demonic comes from its viewpoint on evil, which states that evil is a quality of God, because the negative is part of the Absolute's essence. In order for the Absolute to exist, it must have both good and evil,

Title page of the 1588 edition of the *Zohar,* the main text of Kabbalah thought and tradition.

both sides of the dualistic coin. Older medieval Kabbalic texts looked at evil as the demonic parallel to the holy and part of the dual powers in the divine realm. There is no Devil or outright evil, but instead a misbalance in the area of *Gevurah,* one of the ten holy Sephirot. Gevurah is strength, judgment and severity, so when out of balance, this is where the root of evil manifests. There is no Hell, per se, but rather a realm of impurity where sin exists in the lower level of Creation. Kabbalah also suggests that immorality occurs when any of the pillars of the Sephirot become extreme in nature, such as someone's exercising extreme judgment of others or when lovingkindness leads to sexual depravity or possessiveness. Justice in the extreme can lead to torture or execution. Therefore, harmony was critical among the dualities of the Sephirot.

Thelema

Like Kabbalah, Thelema is based upon religious ideals, but it took on a more philosophical bent. It is not as old as Kabbalah. Thelema suffered guilt by association because it was developed by a rather dark figure, Aleister Crowley, in the early 1900s. Crowley founded the philosophy upon the tenet of "do unto others," but in Thelema it was expanded to "Do what thou wilt shall be the whole of the law. Love is the law, love under will." Crowley was a ceremonial magician who believed that he had mystical experiences in Egypt in 1904. Much of Thelemic belief and practice has an Egyptian feel to it, including some of the pantheon of deities, many of which are from ancient Egyptian beliefs.

Thelemites believe mainly in the ethical code of "Do what thou wilt" as meaning they should follow their own individual paths in life, something traditional religions frowned upon. Thelemists believed in using the will to get what they wanted and to live their purpose; the word "Thelema" itself comes from the Greek *will.* Many deities are a part of the Thelemic religion, and Crowley even incorporated aspects of Kabbalah, Hermeticism, and Eastern and Western mystical traditions. He wrote the holy books used in Thelema, as well as other books about ceremonial magic and the occult. More on that later.

Thelema had a bit of a shadow side to it as the use of the will was often associated with pursuits of desire, which in the extreme could lead to the darker practices of black magic, with which Crowley was often associated. This association may have come from his own claim that while in Egypt in 1904 with his wife, Rose, he was contacted by Aiwass, a supernatural being that dictated to him the sacred texts, *The Book of the Law,* on which Thelema was founded. Remember, the Church didn't take too kindly to any kind of channeling or direct contact with deities, good or bad, so Crowley got a reputation for being a practitioner of black magick (as opposed to magic, which is for fun and entertainment; magick with a "k" denotes ceremonial and ritual magical practices), which may or may not have been true.

In 1912 Crowley was initiated into the German esoteric Ordo Templi Orientis and became the leader of the British branch, which later spread to America and Australia. The OTO followed Thelemic laws and beliefs. He went on during World War I to infiltrate the pro-German movement and get information to British intelligence, adding spying to his long list of accomplishments, which included writing poetry and books and painting. It was his later use of drugs and his love of sex, including with other men, as well as his outspokenness against establishment ideals, that got him labeled a Satanist and black magician. To the Thelemites, he was a prophet who just loved to have a good time. On one website, Hermetic.com, he is described as such: Aleister Crowley (Oct. 12, 1875–Dec. 1, 1947)—however one judges him—was a fascinating man who lived an amazing life. He is best known as being an infamous occultist and the scribe of *The Book of the Law*, which introduced Thelema to the world. Crowley was an influential member in several occult organizations, including

Often criticized for being a promiscuous drug addict, Aleister Crowley was the founder of Thelema, preaching that you should pursue your individual path in life.

the Golden Dawn, the A∴A∴, and Ordo Templi Orientis. He was a prolific writer and poet, a world traveler, mountaineer, chess master, artist, yogi, social provocateur, drug addict and sexual libertine. The press loved to demonize him and dubbed Crowley "The wickedest man in the world."

Crowley was an object of obsession for many future writers, artists, and even rock stars such as Jimmy Page of Led Zeppelin, who lived in one of Crowley's homes and delved into the study of the occult, as well. The association of Crowley, black magic, and rock music proved a potent one, as it spurred many fans of the band to look into, and begin to practice, the occult arts. But that seems to suggest more the power of pop culture than of the Devil himself.

Theosophy

Like Gnosticism, Theosophy seeks direct knowledge of the mysteries of life, nature, and the divine. More of a body of teachings than just one specific path, Theosophy is an esoteric tradition with definite Western roots. The

Spiritualist Helena Blavatsky was cofounder of the Theosophical Society, helping to popularize it.

word comes from the Greek *theosophia*, which combines *theo*, or God, with *Sophia*, or wisdom. Though the word was used to describe early "theology," or religious teachings, it came into its own as a mystery school of teaching during the Renaissance, in the sixteenth and seventeenth centuries, when it took on many of the aspects of pure Gnosticism and the search for individual enlightenment through inner knowing. Yet until the nineteenth century it was not truly meant to indicate a Gnostic belief system.

A German-Russian woman named Helena Blavatsky changed all that when, in 1875, she founded the Theosophical Society in New York City (and later moved to India, where the international headquarters was set up) with Henry Steel Olcott and William Quan Judge. The motto was "There is no religion higher than truth," and Blavatsky, an occultist and spiritualist, was instrumental in popularizing the esoteric tradition she would go on to be forever associated with. Like Aleister Crowley, Helena Blavatsky would become a bigger-than-life figure in the occult and esoteric worlds, through no fault of their own, for both were charismatic and shunned modern conventions.

Theosophy embraced the following objectives:

1. To form a Universal Brotherhood of Humanity that was without distinction of race, color, sex, or creed.

2. To encourage studies of comparative religion, philosophy, and science.

3. To investigate the unexplained laws of nature and powers latent in man.

These somewhat "New Age" concepts went against the stricter rules of the Church and most other organized religions, which did show bias against women and certain creeds and people of color, disapproved of the teachings of science and philosophy, and encouraged only biblical teachings, and of course denied the power of both man and nature without God at the helm. Because of these polar beliefs, Theosophy, an otherwise neutral system, was cast into the occult/dark mystery-school drawer, even when it often embraced Judeo-Christian concepts in its body of understanding.

Hermeticism

One of the most well-known mystery-school traditions and esoteric teachings is Hermeticism, the body of religious, scientific, and philosophical ideals of the "Thrice Great" Hermes Trismegistus. Considered to be one of history's greatest philosophers, Hermes Trismegistus was incredibly influential in later schools of thought in science, philosophy, religion, and spirituality. He may have been a contemporary of Moses, or an Egyptian priest king, and some Christian writers equate him with a pagan prophet who foresaw the dawn of Christianity and influenced its early teachings.

Hermes Trismegistus wrote a three-part body of wisdom that encompassed all that one could know of the universe and man's place in it. His nickname of "Thrice Great" came from a sacred writing called *The Emerald Tablet of Hermes Trismegistus*, because of his knowledge of alchemy, astrology, and theurgy. Some scholars say the name was given to him because he is considered the greatest philosopher, priest, and king of the Pre-Christian era. Though there is heated debate over how he got his name, everyone agrees that his body of work was astounding and continues to be used even today as a powerful mystery teaching, taught via the Hermetic text *The Corpus Hermeticum*, that gives the secrets of the cosmos, man, and God to those who have discernment. In fact, Sir Isaac Newton himself studied *Hermetica* to understand the science behind cosmic forces, even writing about Hermetic teachings in his many published and unpublished manuscripts.

In 1945, as part of the discovery at Nag Hammadi, more Hermetic texts led to a greater understanding of the principles, which led some to suggest Hermes was a reincarnation of the Egyptian god Thoth, the god of wisdom, who could deify man through gnosis, or direct knowing. Hermetic students even formed secret societies to further their studies in private outside of the Church's glare.

Hermeticism believes that God is All—the One. God exists apart from the material cosmos. He transcends it. It is the Absolute, and we and the Universe participate in this Absolute. There are hierarchies of beings in the Universe, such as angels and elementals. Hermeticism also states that there is but one actual true theology that is the core of all religions and was given to man by God, but that Christians, as they often did with other Gnostic teachings, appropriated the teachings and turned

A floor inlay at Italy's Siena Cathedral depicts Hermes Trismegistus, founder of Hermeticism.

Hermes into a contemporary of Moses or an Egyptian priest-king to keep in line with the teachings of the Church.

The most powerful teaching is that of "As above, so below," which is also found in just about every mystery tradition, as well as Earth-based traditions such as Wicca, witchcraft, and paganism. The concept of a macrocosm and a microcosm, and that one corresponded to the other, was at the heart of all Hermetic thought. The microcosm is mankind. The macrocosm is the Universe, the Cosmos. Therefore, what happens within us, happens outside of us, and what happens in the Universe is mirrored in what happens in the individual. This concept alone gave great power to the individual as a mirror of creation itself. Again, this was something organized religions did not approve of. These aspects, and the association with alchemy, astrology, and theurgy (three occult arts) have often put a "dark" label upon Hermeticism, despite its having absolutely nothing to do with Satanism, black magic, or demonology whatsoever.

HITLER, THE NAZIS, AND SATANISM

The obsession of Nazis with the occult has been a popular theory for decades. But it may have been more than just theory. According to Professor Nicholas Goodrick-Clarke, head of the Centre for the Study of Esotericism at Exeter University, in the article "Hitler and the Secret Satanic Cult at the Heart of Nazi Germany" by Danny Penman (*Free Republic*, January 2009), occult myths were a central tenet of Nazism and Nazi activities throughout the twentieth century. Goodrick-Clarke wrote extensively of the Nazi-occult connection in *The Occult Roots of Nazism*, and of links between Nazi ideology and Ariosophy, an esoteric ideology system created by Guido von List and Jörg Lanz von Liebenfels in Austria between 1890 and 1930. Ariosophy refers to the wisdom of the Aryans and was first coined by Lanz von Liebenfels in 1915.

"Aryan" was a racial-group term used from the late nineteenth to the early twentieth century to describe Indo-Europeans in general, and later to mean the Nordic and Germanic people....

"Aryan" was a racial-group term used from the late nineteenth to the early twentieth century to describe Indo-Europeans in general, and later to mean the Nordic and Germanic people (even though Aryans were originally from Persia and India). The Nazis revered the Aryan race as the "Master Race" in the racial hierarchy and their ideology was built around that belief.

Penman also quotes historian Michael Fitzgerald, who claims that the Nazi-occult connection, especially the focus on evil, goes back to the Nazis' fascination with the

Vril Society. The Vril Society was a secret society founded on the contents and themes of *The Coming Race*, an 1871 novel by Edward Bulwer-Lytton, a tale that told of a subterranean race of refugees from the Great Deluge who powered their advanced civilization with a substance called "Vril." This was a fluid that was described as being capable of having power over all forms of matter—animate and inanimate. This universal force was used by a race called the Vril-ya, who are referenced in the novel as the Aryans, and who used the energy/force for good and for evil. Like the Force in the *Star Wars* movies, Vril itself was neutral and powered the technology of the Vril-ya without polluting its environment.

The mystical substance could be used for any purpose, and anyone could use this fluid energy source. Sounds like any science fiction novel, except this one heavily influenced people like Helena Blavatsky and her Theosophy, which held that Europeans were descended from an angelic race known as the Aryans, and that the Aryans used

Edward George Earle Lytton Bulwer-Lytton, 1st Baron Lytton, was the author of the 1871 novel *The Coming Race,* which inspired the founding of the Vril Society, which, in turn, also influenced the Nazis.

some type of psychic force to build the Pyramids and construct the cities beneath the ocean called Atlantis. The symbol of the Aryans was the swastika, the crooked cross that is also an ancient good-luck symbol of the Hindu. This symbol was also used by the later Thule Society.

An entire society was formed around the belief in the fictional energy source of Vril. Throughout the twentieth century, the Vril Society was said to control the Nazi Party and influence its evil acts upon humanity. The society worked in complete secrecy to promote Aryan power and influence through everything including assassinations, murder, evoking the dead, human sacrifice, and raising Vril energy during sexual orgies. The links with the occult and, most notably, Satanism, come from the Vril Society's association with the more-occultist Thule Society, and mainly rumor and allegation, such as the belief that part of the Vril Society's darker activities included sacrificing hundreds of children to summon Vril energy.

The Vril Society also believed that a coming Germanic Messiah would lead Aryans to world domination and assist in the mass extinction of unwanted races such as the Jews. When Adolf Hitler appeared on the scene, the

Messiah had been found, especially with Hitler's ability to mesmerize people and make them do his will.

Hitler's own fascination with occult practices from alchemy to astrology to psychic abilities added fuel to the fire, along with his associations with Thule Society members who were said to be avowed Satanists. These may have included Rudolf Hess, Heinrich Himmler, Hermann Goering, and Martin Bormann, all members of Hitler's inner political circle as he moved forward with his goal to take over Germany.

According to Michael Fitzgerald, author of *Stormtroopers of Satan*, Bormann was an avowed Satanist. "Bormann, together with (Alfred) Rosenberg and Himmler, wanted to destroy Christianity and replace it with a truly occult religion of their own making," Fitzgerald wrote.

The Thule Society was said to be a Germanic study group that focused on occult teachings but was later said to be transformed into the foundation of the actual Nazi Party. It was founded in August 1918 by German occultist Rudolph von Sebottendorff and was a secret-society chapter of the Munich branch of the "Order of Teutons," aka Germanenorden. While the founder wanted the group to consist of those interested in exploring occult subjects, the Germanenorden began to introduce into the meetings political, nationalist, and even anti-Semitic discussions that eventually led to the formation of the Nazis.

The beliefs of the Thule Society focused on the Aryan master race that came from a land called "Thule," somewhere in the far north. The name refers to "ultima thule," or "most distant north," and may have been a reference to Scandinavia based on a reference in Roman poet Virgil's *Aeneid*.

Hitler soon became leader of the Nazi Party and made sure that Thule Society members were key position holders in his political machine. Their quest to dominate Germany and lead it into a world war was set in stone in those earlier meetings of the Thules and Germanenorden.

Fitzgerald writes that the occult obsessions of Hitler and his cabinet led to the formation of "The Ahnerbe," which was an occult-research group devoted to proving German superiority by linking Germans to the mythical Aryans, and to uncover lost artifacts said to hold tremendous power, such as the Holy Grail, Ark of the

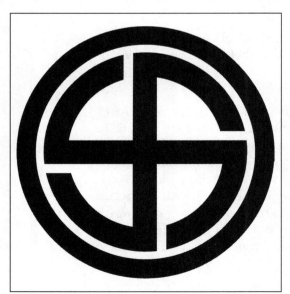

The logo of the Thule Society has a marked resemblance to the Nazi swastika.

Covenant, and Spear of Destiny. The group launched major archeological expeditions into the Himalayas and parts of Bolivia and the Middle East to find these relics. They also looted artifacts whenever they could.

"The Ahnerbe devoted considerable efforts to exploring paranormal phenomena, such as EPS, psychokinesis, water divining, astrology, and black magic," Fitzgerald writes. Little of that exploration helped them fight the war, although there is a rumor that the Nazis employed water-diviners to seek out Allied warships and subs. Though Hitler firmly believed he was a chosen one among men, his mission ultimately failed, and millions died because of his obsessions. Hitler Youth and neo-Nazis are indoctrinated into occult studies to this day, but most of the plans for the Thule Society never played out because of the defeat by the Allies.

Still, Hitler was said by many to have been a true Satanist, according to claims made by researchers and historians, and new English translations of German books such as *Magic History/Theory/Practice* (1923), by Ernst Schertel, who sent a dedicated copy of the book to Hitler. Schertel was interested in everything from flagellation to BDSM (Bondage, Discipline, Dominance, Submission), as well as the occult. He was earlier imprisoned in Nazi Germany for seven months, during which time his doctoral degree was revoked. The book he dedicated to Hilter was later discovered as a part of Hitler's library and contains highlighted annotations, including lines such as "Satan is the beginning …" and "He who does not have the demonic seed within himself will never give birth to a magical world."

But the interest of Hitler and his cohorts in all types of occult sciences is evident, as is the early influence of the Thule and Vril societies on ideologies and intentions....

Another early claim to a link between Hitler and the Nazis and occultism is mentioned in *Occult Causes of the Present War,* by Lewis Spence. The 1940 book states that Alfred Rosenberg's book, *The Myth of the Twentieth Century,* promoted occult, pagan, and even anti-Christian sentiments that laid the groundwork for the Nazi ideology. Claims that Hitler was demonically possessed are made in books like Hermann Rauschning's *Hitler Speaks,* which many historians say is fabricated; in "Hitler's Forgotten Library," an article in the May 2003 *The Nation* by Timothy Ryback that refers to Schertel and his book dedicated to Hitler with Satanic annotations written throughout the book; in accusations that Hitler was playing with "dark forces" in Theosophist Alice Bailey's 1957 *The Externalisation of the Hierarchy*; in numerous links to the famed occultist Aleister Crowley, including allegations by John Symonds in his *Medusa's Head, or Conversations Between Aleister Crowley and Adolf Hitler* (later proved to be fiction); and even in documentaries such as *Hitler and the Occult,* which claims Hitler's newfound magnetism and authority may have been the result of his working with a clairvoyant performer named Erik Jan Hanussen. Add to this the fact that Hitler dedicated his notorious book *Mein Kampf* to his known occultist and anti-Semitic mentor, Dietrich Eckhart, who was also a playwright, journalist, and Thule Society member. Eckhart was also responsible for introducing Hitler to many wealthy and influential society folk in Munich who began financing the Nazi campaign.

One of the biggest challenges researchers face is separating modern pop-culture references to Nazi/Satanism from those that actually had factual basis. Historian Goodrick-Clarke calls those perpetuating the theories that connect Hitler to the occult and black arts "crypto-historians." But the interest of Hitler and his cohorts in all types of occult sciences is evident, as is the early influence of the Thule and Vril societies on ideologies and intentions, and the occult might have truly been the impetus behind the Nazi quest for power over the world.

SECRET SOCIETIES

Because of the ever-watchful eyes of Catholic Church leaders, those who wished to know of deeper truths often went into hiding behind the doors of secret societies, with closed memberships and rituals only they knew about. Initiates had to go to great lengths before being trusted with the knowledge of the universe these societies claimed to have, and wished to pass down to new generations, and the word "conspiracy" often was attached to initiates' existence. Anything that occurs in shadows usually is given a stigma, and secret societies were often associated with devil worship, black magic, and ritual sacrifices. But did those things really happen, or was that the spin and propaganda of those who were not allowed inside the sacred doors?

Secret societies differ from cults, which we will look at later in this chapter, in that they often truly did exist for the sole purpose of keeping and passing down very sacred teachings that, when exposed to the public, were tainted and watered down, if they survived at all. During the darker ages of history, members of secret societies especially had to avoid all visibility for fear of being tortured and burned at the stake, or put to death in other heinous ways. They were deemed the heretics, the blasphemers, and the workers of the Devil himself, spreading gnosis that went against the teachings of the Church and the authority of its priests, bishops, cardinals, and popes, not to mention God himself.

Thus arose the need for secret signals, passwords, meeting locations, handshakes, and methods and means of recognition, including the use of symbols, to avoid the scrutiny of prying eyes.

The Cathars

More of a religion than a secret society, Catharism appeared on the scene in eleventh-century Europe, although its origins may be much older.

Cathars mainly flourished in the Occitanie region of France, which became known as the Languedoc, and they often clashed with the Catholic Church, which looked upon them as heretics. Cathars were dualists; their beliefs involving both a good creator God and an evil adversary, much like the Devil. They actually referred to themselves as Christians and adopted many Christian beliefs and ceremonies, but they rejected the priesthood and the idea that one must worship within church buildings. Instead, they believed one could worship anywhere. To the Cathars, men and women were equals, and they had accepted birth control, suicide, and even euthanasia, although they did not eat animals and promoted sex above and beyond procreation, which of course put them in a complete head-butt with the Church, which promoted sex only for the means of procreation.

Cathars generally led regular lives, except for what were called the Elect of Parfaits, who were male, or Parfaites, who were women. These inner-circle elects worked and yet led ascetic lives. By the early thirteenth century, Catharism was threatening to overtake Catholicism in the Languedoc, which of course made them a target of the Church, especially when the Church was coming under fire for preaching about helping the poor while flaunting its own prosperity. Cathars refused to tithe to the Church, too, which was one of the straws that broke the camel's back, leading to the formal crusade against them called for by Pope Innocent III. The war against the Cathars lasted for decades and eventually spread to a war against Jews and others who did not adhere to Catholic rule and law.

By the time these crusades ended, the Catholic Church had regained all power and influence, at least on the surface. The Church believed it had destroyed Catharism by the time the fourteenth century rolled around. But there remained Cathars and Cathar influence throughout the region, and even today, there are adherents to what was once called a wicked, heretic religion. History also has given the Cathars credit for being one of the earliest and most important Gnostic traditions in Christianity.

Freemasons

What began as a fraternal organization has now become the biggest, most well-known secret society in the world, one that brings out the conspiracy theories by the dozens despite its humble origins. Freema-

The cross of Occitania was the symbol of the Cathars in southern France.

sonry simply began as a fellowship of stonemasons at the end of the fourteenth century. Their purpose was to regulate the industry and adhere to a high quality and work ethic. Their use of "degrees" added a mystique to the craft of masonry—Apprentice, Journeyman, and Master Mason. Members were known as Freemasons and over time the organization has adopted new degrees and rules and regulations. Freemasons met at a lodge, which was a local unit, with a grand lodge governing a region of local lodges.

Because the rituals and rites of the Masons were generally done in secret, with members only, in the lodge, it created the air of a secret society and rumors of dark arts and occult practices going on behind closed doors. Today's Masons no longer focus on the art of masonry, but on the passing down of knowledge and ritual to future generations and bringing in new initiates. Yes, there are rules that all Masons must adhere to: the belief in a supreme being and knowledge of scripture; members were strictly males until quite recently, when some lodges included degrees of study for women; vows must be taken by initiates and degrees must be earned through study and discipline; uniform symbols were to be used in the lodges and ancient customs observed.

Freemasonry also included philanthropic work, and although it appeared to lean on biblical scripture, politics and religious discussions originally were not permitted during lodge meetings. The entire belief system revolved around morality, and yet because of the use of symbology, the outside world thought all kinds of immoral things must occur during lodge meetings.

The square and compass symbol of the Masons reflects upon their history as a fraternity of stonemasons. The G in the middle does not always appear in the symbol. Depending on the reference, it might stand for God, St. Germain, Gnosticism, or the Grand Geometrician (again, God).

The Masonic brotherhood has stood the test of time and continues today, with little emphasis of course on masonry itself, and more on the community the members create and the use of ritual and ceremony as a way of instilling support and discipline and passing it on to apprenticing members. In the United States, the earliest lodges existed in Pennsylvania in 1715 and many a famous historical figure was among the members of lodges, including George Washington, who served as the first grand master, as well as James Monroe, John Hancock, Paul Revere, and Benjamin Franklin.

Like Catharism, Freemasonry attracted the wrath of the organized religions as competition for influence, and outsiders spread rumors of sexual deviance and even ritual murders, rumors that mainly came from the Catholic Church. Accusations of Satanism were leveled as well, mainly because Freemasons followed a more natural deistic belief system that went against formal Church doctrine. As always, because a group of people got together to share ideals and values in a formal setting that did not exactly follow Church rule, they were demonized, especially since the lodges shunned the use of priests, rabbis, and ministers, and in fact had no use for clergy at all.

The Catholic Church also looked down upon the inclusiveness of the Masonic lodges, which allowed men, and later, women, of all professions and backgrounds to come together under one roof to perform rituals and experience fellowship. Yet, atheists and agnostics were not permitted to join, and the organization really was for those who believed in a supreme being, as do the opposing Catholics. Instead of celebrating common ground, the Church chose to focus on differences, which again demonized the simple order of Masons and led to some of the conspiracy theories associated with the organization today.

No doubt there are some rogue lodges that use secrecy and ritual to celebrate their own deviance and wickedness, but true Masons do not, and cannot, for it goes against everything the organization was created to represent.

Order of the Golden Dawn

The Golden Dawn is a major secret society that focuses its studies on the occult and metaphysical, especially Hermetic, teachings. It was founded in the nineteenth century, and well into the twentieth century it absorbed many occult and magickal teachings. The three founders of the Golden Dawn were William Robert Woodman, William Wynn Westcott, and Samuel Liddell MacGregor Mathers. All three were also Freemasons and Rosicrucians, and they established the Golden Dawn to look like Freemasonry. They did allow women and treated them as equal to men. The Golden Dawn is considered the most influential esoteric organization of the twentieth century, going on to influence modern Wicca, witchcraft, and metaphysical and New Age belief systems.

The foundational documents, known as the Cipher Manuscripts, were outlines of specific rituals and also served as a curriculum for the levels of teachings available to initiates and members, who were exposed to astrology, tarot, alchemy, and Kabbalah. Established first throughout Great Britain in the mid-1890s, the organization included such notable figures as William Butler Yeats and, of course, Aleister Crowley. The history of the order is rife with restructuring and revolt, and as the originators left and new members gained more influence, including that of the Rosicrucians, the society spread

Aleister Crowley wearing robes for an Order of the Golden Dawn ceremony.

to other parts of the world. The actual symbol of the Rosy Cross of the Golden Dawn is from Rosicrucianism. Hermetic influence permeates the teachings, as well, including the orders and grades that a member could rise through to achieve further instruction in practical magic and its uses.

In 1937, Israel Regardie published *The Golden Dawn,* which explored the knowledge and teachings of the order, along with the symbolism, rituals, and initiation practices of both Outer and Inner Orders. Some famous members over time included Algernon Blackwood, an English author; Sir Arthur Conan Doyle, the author of the Sherlock Holmes books; A. E. Waite, author and famed Freemason; and Bram Stoker, author of *Dracula.* In fact, much of the membership were authors, poets, and writers of varying levels of fame and success, as well as a few artists and filmmakers.

Today, there are many different splinter groups operating under the name Order of the Golden Dawn, dedicated to preserving and passing down metaphysical and esoteric knowledge to new initiates. None of the new temples is associated with the originals—those shuttered in the 1970s—but the durability of the Golden Dawn proves that the quest for hidden knowledge is not just a part of our past but is as valid today. Occultism today has taken on a more metaphysical bent, though darker aspects do remain. For the members of the Golden Dawn, the emphasis has always been on magic, even astral travel, divination, Egyptian and Hermetic teachings, Neoplatonism, and the new alchemy for the more modern practitioners. Any negative or dark associations come mainly from critics.

Ordo Templi Orientis

Also known as the Order of the Temple of the East, and Order of Oriental Templars, the OTO was founded in the early twentieth century as a fraternal religious organization. It revolved around Thelemic teachings, thanks in great part to Aleister Crowley's being a major member, and followed the tenet of "Love is the law, love under will" and "Do what thou wilt shall be the whole of the Law." The OTO was a secret society with a membership, rituals, and initiations, and many of the same characteristics as Freemasonry, including varying degrees of discipline. It was different in that it had, and has to this day, a Gnostic arm that practices a Gnostic Mass, which was composed by Crowley when he joined and became the OTO's central public ceremony and private rite. Members call it the "Ecclesia Gnostica Catholica," or Gnostic Catholic Church.

Though many of its teachings mirror Thelema and Gnosticism in general, one of the things that made the OTO stand out, and perhaps gave it a rather negative and even Satanic reputation amongst its critics, was its utilization of Hermetic teachings, magick, yogic practices, and for later initiates, sex magic involving specific methods of masturbation and vaginal and anal intercourse done with magical techniques. No doubt this aspect was due to Crowley's influence, and though much of the rest of the OTO sounded and looked like a form of Freemasonry, with lodges and meetings and initiation ceremonies and degrees, sex magic gave the OTO a different spin and one that outsiders could no doubt create conspiracies about.

The Gnostic Catholic Church wing of OTO did have orders of clergy, with bishops, priests, and deacons, as well as priestesses, and offered its members officiation at weddings, exorcisms, and other rites. The OTO did not worship Satan in any way, shape, or form, but its deviations from traditional Church practices earned it the wrath of organized religion and declarations as a "cult."

Rosicrucians

The most popular and recognizable secret society is the Ancient and Mystical Order of the Rosy Cross (AMORC), or Rosae Crucis, also known as the Rosicrucians. Though their teachings today are available via their website for anyone to learn, they were originally founded as an ancient order that predated Christianity, yet had the rose and cross as their symbol. Teachings and initiation rites have been passed down for generations—in fact, centuries—and focus on gnosis and secret wisdom with Egyptian mystery-school influences.

According to the AMORC website, the order began thousands of years before the birth of Christ, and was formally structured by Pharaoh Thutmose III, who ruled Egypt from 1500 to 1447 B.C.E., into the first esoteric schools for initiates that taught AMORC beliefs and disciplines built on truths of the ancient past. The system spread into Europe in the seventeenth century with the introduction of the *Rosicrucian Manifestos*, published to spread the wisdom teachings to a wider audience. Europe was excited by this brotherhood of secret wisdom initiates and sages who were, as the manifestos claimed, going to transform art, science, religion, and politics and change the intellectual landscape of Europe. Another four hundred manuscripts were published between 1614 and 1620 to further the Rosicrucian cause.

A statue of Pharoah Thutmose III, who founded the ideals behind the Rosicrucians, is preserved at the Kunsthistorisches Museum in Vienna, Austria.

Like the Freemasons, original members met in secrecy in chambers located in old temples to be initiated into the mysteries of life. Certain symbols such as the rosy cross and the Great Pyramids held power and spoke to the heavily Egyptian origins of the order, long before the Europeans discovered it. The Rosicrucians learned mystical teachings of practices such as alchemy, which played a huge role in the early development of the order. Members looked upon alchemy as symbolic of the quest for human transmutation and transcendence of the material into the spiritual. Noted members included Roger Bacon, Albertus Magnus, Paracelsus, and Robert Fludd, as well as later members Benjamin Franklin, Thomas Jefferson, Thomas Paine, Theresa of Àvila, John of the Cross, Blaise Pascal, René Descartes, Michael Faraday, Edith Piaf, Claude Debussy, and Sir Isaac Newton.

In the late seventeenth century, the renowned English philosopher Francis Bacon orchestrated a plan to bring Rosicrucianism to the Americas. In 1694, Rosicrucians came across the Atlantic and landed in Philadelphia, where they established the first American lodge. The popularity of the order rose and fell. In the last ninety years, hundreds of thousands of people have become students of the teachings, now made available to anyone who is curious and committed.

Like the secret societies mentioned before it, Rosicrucianism was a powerful and positive mystical school that sought to impart wisdom to its members. But again, because of its secret rites and initiations and symbols, its focuses on science and philosophy, and its inclusion of women and every race and creed, it was not accepted by the traditional religious bodies and incurred the New Age "cult" label in more modern times.

Skull and Bones

A more modern and perhaps more secretive society is Skull and Bones, founded at Yale University in New Haven, Connecticut, in 1832. It is the oldest senior-class society at Yale, and it was originally called "The Order of the

Skull and Bones" and the "Eulogian Club" by founders William Huntington Russell and Alphonso Taft. Only the members of the Skull and Bones could ever know what went on in its meetings. The high-level secrecy gave outsiders plenty of fuel for conspiratorial fires and accusations of Satan worship, sex orgies and drug parties, despite the society's claims that it meets twice a week for basically Masonic-influenced rites. Other critics say it is just a glorified college fraternity with a desire for attention and the illusion of power.

Its hall was called the Tomb, adding to the symbolic creepiness associated with the group, which has initiated new members every spring on "Tap Day" since 1879. Fifteen men and women of the current junior class are invited to join (it was open only to white males until then), with current members tapping those they choose for membership. The society purchased Deer Island retreat on the St. Lawrence River as a place for members to reunite, which added to the conspiracy fodder of secretive rituals taking place amongst the power elite, from which the chosen membership every year was usually selected. The senior societies, Skull and Bones included, were very exclusionary, with no Jews allowed and few Catholics accepted until later years.

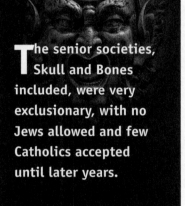

The senior societies, Skull and Bones included, were very exclusionary, with no Jews allowed and few Catholics accepted until later years.

Members revel in symbology that often confuses outsiders and even take on nicknames that can be drawn from religion, literature, and mythology. Former president George H. W. Bush was called "Magog," and many other politicians are members, including former President George W. Bush and former Senator John Kerry.

Though the society remains one of simple fraternity and senior community, it has gained quite a reputation via pop culture and conspiracy theorists as being a power-mad breeding facility for future world leaders bent on bringing about the New World Order, and a place where sex, drugs, and Satanic worship prevail. One conspiracy theory even suggests Skull and Bones controls the CIA.

ANTI-CHURCH

The common thread of all the above orders and societies, whether secretive or public, and mystery schools and alternative religions is that they came under fire from the Catholic Church for deviating from strict dogma and doctrine. As a result, anyone who belonged to one of these heretical societies was labeled a heretic as well, if not an outright worker of the Devil. Whenever the Church has been challenged in the past, it has struck out with crusades, Inquisitions, and sometimes less-violent attempts to discredit and destroy the competition. But the allure of secret societies, as well as the protectiveness of their members, combined with a growing population of people curious to explore knowledge and wisdom of the ancients (and do it without intermediary interference) has kept these organizations intact in one way or another, despite their being associated over time with devil-worship and ritual sacrifice.

Truth can be hidden, suppressed, and denied, but the quest and thirst for it always wins out in the end.

BLACK MAGIC AND THE LEFT-HAND PATH

Allegations of black magic often plague secret societies and occult traditions, linking them to the Devil and to gaining his favor. The use of ceremonial magic in orders such as the Golden Dawn and even the sex magic of the OTO are based upon ancient concepts of Hermeticism and natural laws that can be bent to work on behalf of man. Aleister Crowley practiced ceremonial, sexual, and ritual magic, which used symbols and objects, altars, and often natural herbs, plants, or parts of animals to create a particular influence on the natural world. Through spells, chants, incantations and charms, one might actually shape manifest reality, and as long as the outcome was positive, it was considered good magic, or white magic.

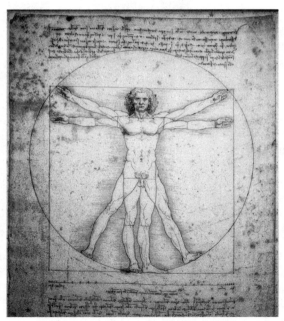

Leonardo da Vinci's *Vitruvian Man,* a study in anatomy and motion, can also be viewed as representing a pentacle in shape, which is also a symbol of the body.

Only when the outcome was intended to hurt, harm, kill, or seek revenge on others or use the power of nature to bring about disaster, or to call upon the darker forces at work in the world, including the Devil and his demonic army, did it cross over into black magic. The tools of both white and black magic are often the same: an altar adorned with candles, a wand, cup, sword or athame (double-bladed knife), symbols, stones or other natural objects, and perhaps the names of the deities being called upon. The pentacle was one of the key symbols, representing the body of man, as displayed in Leonardo da Vinci's famed *Vitruvian Man.*

A grimoire, or book of magic, contained spells and incantations, prayers and blessings, and in the case of black magic, curses and names of demons and dark entities to be called up and communicated with, as well as instructions for making talismans

French occultist Alphonse Louis Constant (1810–1875), who went by the name Éliphas Lévi, is credited with reviving interest in the occult and magick in the nineteenth century. He studied magickal subjects and often wrote commentaries about them. He did not consider himself an adept, although he did practice necromancy, the practice of using magick to summon the deceased or communicate with spirits of the dead. He first experimented with the occult art in 1854 in London, where he met a woman who asked him if he could conjure up the spirit of the ancient magician Apollonius of Tyana. First Lévi prepared by fasting and meditating, and when the time came, he put on white ceremonial robes and went into a magic chamber with mirrors on the walls. He spent twelve hours doing a ritual that involved lighting candles, speaking incantations, and waiting for something to appear in the mirror.

On his third spoken request, an apparition appeared to him, wrapped in a grey shroud. It touched Lévi's ceremonial sword. Lévi felt his arm go numb and lost consciousness. He claimed days later that the apparition answered his questions via telepathy. Later, on several occasions, he again conjured Apollonius successfully. He wrote several books about his practices and beliefs, including *The Dogma and Ritual of High Magic* and *A History of Magic,* among other notable books.

He was a student of the Tarot, taking on the huge task of linking each card to the let-

Éliphas Lévi

ters of the Hebrew alphabet, and later proposed ideas about astral light based on his studies of animal magnetism. Lévi amassed a following of devotees. He died in 1875, the same year Aleister Crowley was born. The Hermetic Order of the Golden Dawn, of which Crowley was an influential member, was founded on many of the principles of the magic of Éliphas Lévi.

and mixing herbs and medicinals. Thus, the only difference between white and black magic was the intention.

Enochian magic specifically focused on the calling up of demons, angels, spirits, and entities that would assist in the desired outcome. John Dee, a noted figure in magic's evolution, wrote widely of this type of magic with Edward Kelley in the sixteenth century, claiming it was given to them by angels to share with humanity.

Ceremonial magic has been a mainstay of the Golden Dawn, OTO, and occult practices generally, whether conducted in groups or by lone individuals. The use of sex and the sexual energies of the union of man and woman, even masturbation, have been included in some ritual-magic practices, simply because these are the energies of nature and creation, and not because they are dirty, perverted, or deviant. Even modern pagans and witches practice in the nude and use the act of intercourse to summon the Earth's energies.

But black magic is very specific and quite particular. Those who practice the dark arts, or what is often called the "Left-Hand Path," the opposite of the path of the right or righteous, use supernatural and demonic powers and entities for malicious purposes, and they do so knowingly. Formal black magic, not the kind practiced by foolish teenagers playing around with swords and salt pentagrams, is a structured and ritualistic type of worship that dates back to the more primitive nature and shamanic practices that invoked spirits to heal and help. But in this case, the outcome is harm.

During certain times in our history, such as the Dark Ages, and even the Renaissance, all magic was considered evil because it went against the teachings of the Church. The use of tools, spells, and idols was unnatural and sinful in the eyes of the Church, and those who practiced any kind of magic, even simple kitchen magic using herbs to heal wounds and sicknesses, were punished, either in the form of torture for an individual, or Inquisitions and mass burnings at the stake for large groups.

Upper-class citizens in the sixteenth and seventeenth centuries practiced high magick, which was natural and positive in intent, but anything that smelled of folk magick, or anything ritualistic and steeped in darker symbolism, fell under the label of black magic even if the Devil wasn't involved. Eventually, even white magic was condemned and anyone found practicing it fell under the same punishment as outright devil-worshippers.

The idea of calling up demons, the Devil, and dark angels to do one's bidding was a natural offshoot of practicing good magic. Those who chose to walk the left-hand path and work with the dark side, so to speak, were simply responding to the inability of the light side to give them their desired outcomes, often the death and destruction of a fellow human being. Just as voodoo practitioners can use dark forces for bad as well as light forces for good, those who believe in God and angels would no doubt think to summon the opposite army to satisfy their immoral and unlawful wishes.

Black magic is absolutely NOT Satanism. That is a whole other subject, with discussion to come. Nor is it devil-worship, although many who do worship the Devil do engage in black magic. One can practice the black arts and engage in what is called the Black Mass, a parody of Catholic Mass, regardless of one's beliefs in Christianity, for in order to worship Satan and do his bidding, you first have to believe in the religious system that created him.

Dion Fortune

One of the most respected and well-known occultists was a woman named Dion Fortune. Born Violet Mary Firth in North Wales on December 6, 1890, into a family of Christian Scientists, she showed abilities as a medium from age four, when she had dreams and visions of the lost continent of Atlantis. She even claimed to have lived a past life as a priestess and wrote a book of poetry at age thirteen.

Fortune's interest in the occult was born during World War I, when she was a Freudian analyst, trained by a doctor who helped guide her to the Western mystery traditions, especially the Hermetic Order of the Golden Dawn, which she joined in 1919 upon moving to London. The branch she attended was led by Moina Mathers, the widow of one of the founders of the Golden Dawn, MacGregor Mathers. Dion changed her name in reference to her family motto, "Deo non fortuna," or "God not luck."

She became a prolific writer, first with articles on the occult, then books, but she became disillusioned with the Golden Dawn, so in 1921, she founded her own esoteric order, the Fraternity of the Inner Light, later to be called the Society of the Inner Light. Many of the members lived in a big old house that was considered their "magical lodge." Fortune also wrote novels in the 1930s that contained many occult and esoteric teachings and secret wisdom that she could not put in her nonfiction articles and books. Her book *The Mystical Qabalah* helped put the esoteric teaching of Qabalah (also spelled Kabbalah) on the map as a Western mystery tradition and her *The Cosmic Doctrine* became a textbook of sorts for initiates.

She also practiced astrology, scrying, and astral traveling, and she served as a "psychic physician" for people who were in trouble on the astral plane. In *Raising Hell: A Concise History of the Black Arts and Those Who Practiced Them,* author Robert Masello points to Fortune's perception of evil based on her own studies: "Fortune contended that the actual forces of evil in the world had created evil intelligences, entities that had 'probably originated through the workings of Black Magic, which took the essential evil essence and organized it for purposes of its own.'" She believed the presence of these evil manifestations, or creatures, could be detected in pungent odors, sinister sounds, and flickering balls of light, and that they could cause hallucinations and physical decay of the human body.

Throughout her long and illustrious career, Fortune resisted the Left-Hand Path and the use of evil in her works. Her goal was to explore the unseen world and explain to others what she had learned until her death in 1946.

Some of the practices and rituals of true black magic have been grossly distorted by pop culture, mainly horror movies. One of the best guides to real black magic comes from A. E. Waite's, *The Book of Black Magic and Ceremonial Magic,* which lays out actual comprehensive descriptions and meanings of the rituals involved. Though much of black magic involves calling up demons by their names to utilize each demon's basic qualities, some of it involves nothing demonic at all. Rituals can include using a person's name to influence him or her, as with voodoo used poppets. Black magicians often desire to bend the rules of physical laws and use the powers of nature for their own benefit, and sometimes that benefit is the quest for immortality or the powers of divination, to see the future, and to change the present.

Still other rituals are performed simply to hex a person or place, or remove a curse on the black magician if need be. The accusations of murder, child sacrifice, and animal sacrifice are usually made by those who do not practice black magic, or by those who mean to refer to extremists. Extremists are not purists—they bend the rules of evil beyond even what most black magicians feel comfortable with.

Many Western esoteric systems have a left-hand path, with Baphomet as their symbolic entity, or deity. The left-hand path has been equated with devil-worship, although it is simply the opposite of the right-hand path, the two together signifying our dualistic belief in reality. The path that is right for one person may not be right for another. The left-hand path often breaks taboos and clashes with morals and values, but it may not do so with the intent of sacrificing a goat to Lucifer or calling up the fallen Enochian angels to cause a holy war. The left hand has usually been the path of going against the establishment or status quo and might involve the use of sex magic and the exploration of human sexuality, natural and manmade drugs for spiritual empowerment and altering conscious states, and other methods not thought to be conventional.

To show how fine a line there is between white and black magic, the art and science of divination was once thought to be the work of the Devil and black magicians. Divination, which utilizes tools such as pendulums, tea leaves, rocks, Ouija™ boards, Tarot and other playing cards, palm readings, astrology, numerology, and a host of other methods, focuses on trying to learn the future, often to help someone avoid making huge mistakes. It is also used to locate lost objects, speak with deceased loved ones, and predict possible love matches and even the success of crop growth.

Yet to some organized religions, divination methods were outlawed because they implied that the divine speaks directly to humans through objects and talents, and not via the hierarchy of chosen priests, bishops, cardinals and the pope, or ministers and preachers. The gift of divining was also thought to be a dark art, as only God could know the future. Today, people seek out fortune-tellers of every bent, not to do harm, but to avoid it and help plan their own destinies.

SACRIFICE RITUALS

Throughout human history, sacrifices to the deities have been made in the form of food, animals, and sometimes humans. The idea is that offering something to the gods will appease them, or gain favor with them, and the bigger the sacrifice, the bigger the result. In the Old Testament, human and

John Dee

Magic often involves divination methods. John Dee, an English mathematician and philosopher, born in 1527, and adviser to Queen Elizabeth I, was known for his obsession with magic, alchemy, astrology, and the Hermetic teachings, which he used to try to commune with angels later in his life. Dee was a scholar, and the owner of a massive library, who failed to see differences between mathematics and divination studies, as they were simply different sides of the same coin. Despite his public drive to learn the esoteric arts, including magic, he was regarded as a man of great scholarship and often spoke about mathematics, geometry, and astronomy, as well as navigation, even training British explorers in the use of navigation for future expeditions.

Dee was a man of both magic and science, yet today many regard him as a black magician even though he was not involved in black arts in any manner. His occult studies never pushed him toward Satanism, and he instead became a trusted advisor to a queen. He wrote several books that reflected his belief in mysticism and Hermeticism and how they applied to his understanding of science.

The use of ritual often brings about demonic associations, again based in part on pop culture's portrayals of teenagers toying with a pentagram on the ground, or calling upon the names of demons in Latin they don't understand. But ritual is the formal, structured performance based upon traditions or beliefs. It is an observable mode of behavior and action, often symbolic rather than literal, and a part of primitive, ancient, and modern culture.

Rituals, to those who are not a part of the culture, sometimes appear to be frighten-

John Dee

ing or even disturbing. In countries that celebrate Día de Los Muertos, or the Day of the Dead, for example, the ritual use of candy and sugar skulls on altars often painted in garish colors might seem morbid or even frightening, yet are meant to represent reverence of the deceased. Christians take the body and blood of Christ during Communion, in the form of a symbolic wafer, a ritual that might seem disturbing to those not familiar with Christ's own words at the Last Supper. Ritual can be relative to the culture or the occasion. Some are serious and formal, others fun and celebratory, and often the meanings of the actual rituals, symbols, and even manner of dress are lost on anyone who is not familiar with the culture in question.

animal sacrifice are mentioned numerous times, as it was indeed a part of our ancient past. The Mayans sacrificed humans by first painting their faces blue before they cast them into the open mouths of volcanoes, and many ancient cultures offered sacrifices to the deities, as well as to deceased humans.

A sacrifice could be offered in gratitude, in praise, or out of fear of something awful happening to the village were it not given. Individuals could sacrifice on their own, but for the greater good, and the larger effect, it took a priest or holy person to do the ritual.

Sacrifices of foods and gifts were usually left on altars to various deities, or brought to sacred locations such as statues and monuments. But animals and humans were offered up to the gods, good and bad, in ritualistic fashion usually involving specifically cleansed and prepared tools such as knives and daggers. Animal sacrifices were a part of almost every culture on the planet, including Hebrew, Hindu, Greek, Roman, and Mesoamerican. Today, animals are still sacrificed as part of voudon and Santeria, both influenced by Catholic and West African beliefs. Some black magic and devil-worship cults

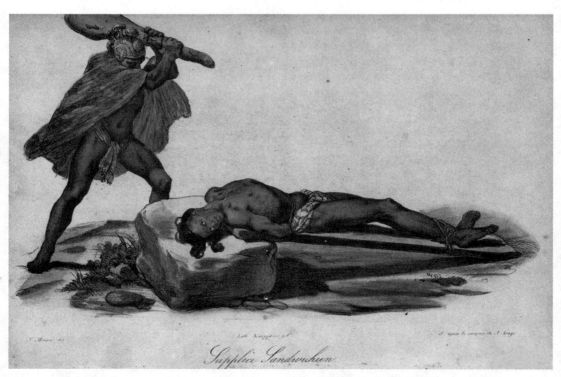

Supplice Sandwichien

Human and animal sacrifice rituals have been common around the world. This c. 1818 drawing shows a Hawaiian being religiously slaughtered—based on an account by French explorer Jacques Arago—in an attempt to satisfy some local deity.

do sacrifice animals, although original black magicians of the past did not need blood to carry out their spells and curses.

The same way animals were offered to the deities, humans were as well, and not always to make a god or goddess happy. Our ancestors once picked a human to ritually kill for the purposes of blessing new monuments and buildings, bridges and edifices, and even to keep crops growing. Human sacrifices also occurred during natural disasters and often bodies were thrown into active volcanoes to try to calm the fiery eruptions.

The most distressing of all are child sacrifices. Not many cultures engaged in it, but archeological evidence shows some did, such as the find of multiple child skeletons in Carthage, killed in a fashion similar to animal sacrifices by our Phoenician ancestors. Teenage girls and boys were offered up to the god Minotaur in ancient Crete.

Christianity does not ask for sacrifices of humans, although one could say that Jesus is God's sacrifice to humanity, the offering of his only begotten son. Sacrifice is symbolic throughout the New Testament, leaving the real thing for the Hebrew Bible and the use of burnt offerings (sacrificed animals) in Judaism. Islam does use the sacrifice of animals in some countries, mainly cows, goats, and sheep, even camels, and the animals must be alive and healthy at the time. According to the Koran, the sacrifice is not about giving the blood and meat to God, but about the piety involved in the one doing the sacrifice.

In Mayan, Inca, and Aztec cultures, the act of human trophy sacrifice allowed warriors to take human trophies by capturing them, then torturing and killing them in ritual fashion. Mayan mass skeletal remains suggest perhaps they sacrificed more humans than originally thought. Mass sacrifices appear to have occurred at the Temple of the Feathered Serpent and Temple of the Moon as far back as 500 B.C.E. In Tibet, before the arrival of Buddhism, human sacrifice was common, as it was in India. Once Buddhism took hold in the seventh century, bringing with it more nonviolent principles, the use of effigies made from dough replaced human beings.

In India, it is rare to see or hear of a human sacrifice today, thanks in part to the acceptance of later nonviolent Vedic beliefs. But an Indus seal from the Bronze Age discovered in the Indus Valley depicts an upside-down, nude female figure with legs outspread and a plant coming out of the womb. The reverse side of the seal shows a man holding a sickle and a woman seated on the ground in prayer. Scholars interpret this scene as a human sacrifice in honor of the Mother Goddess, although many historians doubt it. Sacrifices were made more often to angry and vengeful deities than loving and kind ones. Indians once offered humans up to the goddess Chamunda, who is considered fierce, as well as Shakti, the great divine Mother of Hinduism and the powerful agent of creation and change.

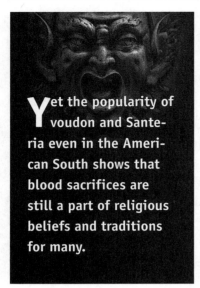

Yet the popularity of voudon and Santeria even in the American South shows that blood sacrifices are still a part of religious beliefs and traditions for many.

Ritual sacrifice was symbolic, but sometimes the poor would get to partake of the dead animals, at least the parts not used during the event. But for the many humans who lost their lives, one has to wonder whether the deities appreciated the "sacrifice" made in their honor ... or whether some fruit or libation would have sufficed.

It is easy for a culture to excuse the use of killing animals and humans, even including children, for the sake of the gods, goddesses, and powers of the Earth. But the same practices have been labeled as evil by magic practitioners, and no doubt they should, especially when they involve human beings. Today, most societies will no longer accept these practices, and only in countries where more primitive ideas still prevail do we see them. Yet the popularity of voudon and Santeria even in the American South shows that blood sacrifices are still a part of religious beliefs and traditions for many. Blood sacrifices were once normal, until the later introduction of new religious and spiritual values and ideals displaced the need for them.

NECROMANCY

The art of communicating with, or bringing back, the dead is known as "necromancy." From the Middle English *nigromancie* and Medieval Latin *nigormantia,* and late Latin *necromantia,* the word is a combination of "dead body" and "divination." Talking with and raising the dead was a form of divination that allowed the practitioner to speak with the dead for purposes of finding out future events and gaining knowledge. It soon became a general term used to define anyone practicing shamanism, witchcraft, or black magic.

A goal of necromancy during medieval times was also to manipulate the will of others and may have originated from the shamanic belief that dead spirits have much to offer the living. Necromancy is a divination method as old as time and found in most countries and cultures dating to antiquity, when the emphasis was on a belief in the survival of the soul after death and that the dead possessed wisdom and knowledge far beyond that of the living.

Though Mosaic Law forbade necromancy (Leviticus 19:31; 20:6) because God forbade it, there are numerous mentions of consorting with the dead or spirits of the dead throughout the Old Testament, such as when King Saul, after seeing the enemy army of the Philistines, asked the Witch of Endor to invoke the spirit of the prophet Samuel using a conjuring pit. Samuel sought help in battle and also wanted to know the outcome. He went in disguise to the witch, and she performed the rites that evoked the shade of

Samuel, who rose from the dead and told Saul the bad news: "Tomorrow shalt thou and thy sons be with me; the Lord also shall deliver the host of Israel into the hands of the Philistines." Needless to say, Saul went back a broken man, ready to face the enemy and his own demise.

Necromancy is present in all myths and religions, in some form or another. Ancient cultures in Persia, Babylonia, Sumeria, Chaldea, Egypt, Greece, and Rome practiced their own version as a means of divination. During the High Middle Ages, Christian clergy used necromancy, done in formal ritual even if under the radar of the Church. Clergymen believed the soul continued on after death and that they could manipulate the spirits, even demons, into doing their will by combining Christian rites with those of the occult. Ancient Greeks and Romans often performed their necromancy rites in dark caverns in or around volcanic regions, lakes, rivers, and other bodies of water, all of which were said to be the abodes of the dead, where communication would be easier to achieve. Volcanoes were seen as entrances to the fiery-hot Underworld, as were caves with long, dark passages underground, often leading to hidden lakes beneath the Earth.

Necromancy could also be utilized to seduce women, by using a poppet made of wax, placed upon a grave with thirteen needles piercing various body parts. The grave had to be of someone who had died prematurely, or violently,

A sixteenth-century artwork by Annibale Carraci depicts the Greek hero Ulysses meeting the witch goddess Circe. In Homer's *The Odyssey,* necromancy through Circe's hand is one of the earliest-known references to the art in literature.

and the magician or necromancer would call upon the corpse and other spirits who had died to go to the desired woman's home and cast a spell over her. We have no records of how well this seduction tactic worked! Spirits were also often raised by those seeking buried or hidden treasures of gold and riches, since it was assumed spirits saw and knew everything that went on in the world.

The oldest known mention of necromancy in mythology is from the *Odyssey*, book XI, part of the epic Greek ancient poem written by Homer in the eighth century B.C.E. Book XI concerns the voyage of Ulysses to Hades to try his hand at evoking souls according to rites given him by Circe. His goal was to consult the shade of Tiresias, but he ended up evoking a number of other spirits instead. Myths from Greece, Rome, and Norse countries all contain stories of contacting the dead to help assist the living with a particular goal, often the actual hero of the myth. Spirits were consulted especially before a long journey or battle, to learn its success or failure, and sometimes spirits were asked for strategies to fight and overcome an enemy.

Whether praying to spirits for guidance, or asking them to appear by one's side, there were many ways one could turn to the dead in the past. Today, it is an offshoot of the recent spiritualism movement involving channeling, séances, and table tapping, and using strange devices to talk to the dead. More recently, necromancy has morphed into a fixed part of the "ghost hunting" craze and mainstream acceptance of the paranormal, although most people refer to it now as "communicating with ghosts and spirits" rather than necromancy. Modern paranormal investigators use all kinds of gadgets and devices to try to speak to the dead that may be haunting the location they are investigating.

The association of the word "necromancy" with demonic activity comes from the root origin of the word, which is linked to *niger* for "black" in Italian, Spanish, and Old French. Necromancy was labeled as "black magic," whether it was used for nefarious purposes or not. Like any other occult practice, necromancy can be used for positive or negative intentions, but doing it for negative intentions is not considered wise.

Naturally, a necromancer could make the practice evil by conjuring up a demon or the spirit of a killer, or by taking the wisdom gleaned from the encounter and using it for selfish or evil purposes, including harm to others. But most who practiced necromancy saw it as an opportunity to expand human knowledge beyond the limitations of life and learn what the dead might know of upcoming events and situations, just as someone today might go have his or her palm read or tea-leaves examined, or attend a séance to try to contact dead Uncle Jim or Aunt Tillie.

In *Raising Hell: A Concise History of the Black Arts and Those Who Dared Practice Them*, author Robert Masello writes: "Although with some adjustments, necromancy would be performed in the comfort of one's own home, graveyard necromancy, or raising the dead right where they lay, was understandably the most popular form of the black art." Masello points out that the prodigious number of famous cases throughout legend and lore of successful necromancers no doubt gave encouragement to "would-be raisers of the dead." Today's pop-culture obsession with horror stories of the dead coming back, as well as the love of haunted graveyards, no doubt originate from these practices. Another popular conjuring place was at crossroads, on the theory that the living and the dead were "accustomed to passing by." Also popular: the ruins of monasteries, castles, churches, and abbeys.

The prime time for raising the dead was said to be 1 A.M., also known as the "witching hour," and a full moon or stormy weather was always a plus. Perhaps the spirits were able to manifest better during the pull of the tides, or the high electromagnetic anomalies that occur during storms. In any event, a necromancer knew, from practice by trial and error, the best times, locations, and conditions for lifting the veil between the dead and our world.

> **The prime time for raising the dead was said to be 1 A.M., also known as the "witching hour," and a full moon or stormy weather was always a plus.**

Masello goes on to call necromancy the most dangerous of the "black arts" for two reasons: 1) The difficulty of actually doing the elaborate rituals involved correctly made it the ultimate act of any magician of worth; and 2) The act of calling up dead spirits and demons itself posed a great risk. "These spirits were often quite unhappy at having to make the trip."

Franciscan friar Roger Bacon studied alchemy, astrology, and necromancy despite a lifetime devoted to science over superstition and natural law over occult law. Bacon, born in 1214 in Somerset, England, wrote in his thirteenth-century book *Discovery of the Miracles of Art, Nature and Magick* that "there is a more damnable practice, when men despising the Rules of Philosophy, irrationally call up Wicked spirits. Supposing them of Energy to satisfie (sic) their desires." Bacon believed this to be a big mistake, because man assumed he had dominion over spirits and that man could have authority to tell spirits what to do, which he believed was "altogether impossible, since humane energy or Authority is inferiour by much to that of Spirits." Bacon instead suggested invoking God's angels or God himself for good favors. He may or may not have followed his own advice!

SATANISM

"Satan is at once a rebel and a tyrant. He proclaims independence but his rule bodes oppression and slavery. He himself is represented in chains, for the liberty of sin, which is license, enthralls the mind." So wrote Paul Carus in *The History of the Devil and The Idea of Evil*. Those who worship Satan, the Devil, Lucifer, and any of his other personas claim an independence from the rules of societal norms and values, yet live under the oppression of the choices they make for engaging in sin. But for Satanists, that choice is obvious. They have willingly chosen to shun the light, the right-hand path, the good, for the realm of the Prince of Darkness and all that he promises, which is usually the opposite of what God and Jesus promise.

Carus goes on to say that while Satan may be symbolic of rebellion, God alone promises liberty. Satan promises independence, calling his followers to stand against the orders and rules of the day, but God gives independence through self-control and discretion. Satan then is not real freedom, but rather a protest against what God stands for, which binds one to the chains of belief and resistance. Yet most modern Satanists feel they are bound by nothing. No taboos, no inhibitions, no dogma or doctrine stop them from living the hedonistic lives they choose. They instead look upon the devoutly religious as being locked up in the chains of having to behave and believe in accordance with a fixed system, or suffer the consequences.

The practice of Satanism probably began about the same time that the concept of a deity to represent evil did. But historically, it began with the origins of Christianity and changed and shifted over the millennia, from the Middle Ages to the Inquisitions of the Roman Catholic Church in Europe, to the torture and killing of heretics and those labeled witches in America and in Europe, through to modern times and the decades of Satanic-ritual-abuse hysteria, to modern Satanism and the adherents of the Church of Satan. During the time of the Cathars, the Catholic Church labeled heretic sects as Satanist, and the trend continued to include any religious group or sect that embodied ideas other than those ordained by the Church, even if the group or sect had absolutely no belief in Satan at all. Even a group like the Knights Templar, who were Christian warrior soldiers devoted to the Church, were later accused of consorting with the Devil when they went against certain rules or allegedly rejected doctrine and law.

The inverted pentagram is the symbol of Satanism.

Worship of the Adversary is rampant throughout the Bible, but it also came to represent the beliefs of any opposing side. For example, in the Old Testament, David might be the adversary of the enemy Philistines, just as today, a Republican might be the adversary of a Democrat. The word was also used to describe someone being "opposed to." Fallen angels were thought to be Satanic because they opposed the rule of God's law and fell from Heaven. But only one of them really was Satan, the rest having their own individual origins, names, and identities.

Most of the darkest times in history involved people being accused of Satanism, as opposed to those who actually were. We will discuss witchcraft in more detail later in this chapter, but first, we need to understand that the leveling of the term "Satanic" was often politically charged. The Roman Catholic Church threw the term out as wide as a blanket to cover everyone from the Cathars to the Gnostics to Muslims, Hindus, pagans, and anyone else who did not live by the law of the Vatican's dictates. In the latter part of the Middle Ages the Church referred to those who disobeyed those laws as heretics, but once we entered the more modern era, they became known as witches.

THE MIDDLE AGES

Yet, as we shall see, most, if not all, witches were innocent of consorting with the Devil. True Satanism involves those who knowingly do his biddings and works and celebrate him as their patriarchal deity, rather than God. For those wrongly accused, the Middle Ages (500–1500 C.E.) were a time of extreme fear and oppression, when one could be put to death for something as simple as the use of herbs and plants as medicinals.

Those who practiced the "Old Religion" of paganism and nature-based beliefs were targeted in European countries by the Church, and their often-ancient rituals and traditions were looked upon as heretical, even blasphemous, especially those involving sex and reproduction to promote abundant crops, rituals that went directly against Church teaching that sex was only for procreation. Nature-worship was severely suppressed during this time, but the suppression backfired and led to a rebirth of interest among the peasant populations. In his 1954 book *Sex in History*, G. Rattray Taylor looked at the three main codes of the Church involving morality and sex:

1. Celibacy was to be encouraged at all times.

2. A ban was to be placed on all forms of sexual expression other than intercourse between two married people. Those in violation of this ban would be subject to penitence and punishment.

3. There were actual days in the year when married couples were allowed to have sex, and those were few: about two months out of each year.

One might imagine the frustration of the populace with these restrictive rules that went against natural urges. The penitential books the Church set forth for the public to live by were full of unrealistic concepts; for example, if a man seduced a virgin, he was accused of adultery, for all virgins were said to be the brides of Jesus Christ. Even the virgin was punished for having betrayed her husband, the Christ. In this time, chastity was revered. Ironically, this extreme chastity was not supported by either the Old or New Testaments and was instead a fabrication of the Catholic Church to control human sexuality by assuring sex was used solely for procreation.

THE OLD RELIGION

During the beginnings of Christianity, women held positions of power. They could preach, discuss politics and religion, and even perform exorcisms. But come the Middle Ages, these allowances were denied and women became second-class citizens with no legal rights to speak of; they were viewed as whores in the bedroom and saints in the kitchen, existing to give birth to children. Thus, the old customs and beliefs of more Goddess-oriented religions of the past were

Feasts and celebrations from old religions, such as the Bacchanalia, which was a feast honoring the Roman god Bacchus, were portrayed by the Catholic Church (and the arts they commissioned) as sinful, heretical practices to be banned. (*Bacchanale devant une statue de Pan* [1633] by Nicolas Poussin.)

also demonized. The Old Religion had revered both genders. Now, only men had power and dominance, and only the male God could be worshipped.

Needless to say, the people began to rebel. Between sexual repression, loss of basic civil rights, the destruction of sacred sites and rituals important to the Old Religion and nature-based belief systems, the denigration of women, and the removal of all reproductive freedoms, it was enough to create a "counter wave" among the people. Many of the old ways of women and of pagans were turned into "witchcraft" and something evil and forbidden, including their traditional holidays and gatherings, imagery and symbolism, and rites and rituals. The feasts of Diana, Dionysus, and Bacchanalia, once about abundance, sacred sexuality, pleasure, and reproduction, now became "Satanic," as did those who engaged in them. The horned deity, Pan, soon became Satan, an enemy of Christ and the Church, although worship of Pan long predated the Church. The broom, which was a symbol of the "sacred hearth," became an evil mode of transport for witches. This systematic attack on pagan life, ritual, and symbolism created the negative stigma that the Old Religion, the original witchcraft, was to exist with forevermore.

In *The History of Magic*, author Kurt Seligmann writes that the Church solidified Satan into one encompassing symbol of both the Devil and any enemy of the Church that walked on Earth. The peasants of this time in history did not think their Old Religion was evil and against the Church at all. They drew great joy from their beliefs, but the very fact that they did so without abiding by the rules of the Church put them on the map as heretics and, later, as witches to be punished, put back in line—and if that didn't work, eradicated entirely. Seligmann wrote that the peasants saw their religion as both innocent and primitive and something that gave them freedom from the bleak existence the Church put upon them with rule after rule.

Thus, the real birth of Satanism was most likely the responsibility of the Church itself, which forced those opposed to their dreadful restrictions to find some way to rebel, and caused the Church to create a new label that would cast a dark shadow over them: Satan-worshippers. The Church itself did more to create Satanism in the Middle Ages than Satan himself did. It was its way of denouncing the Old Religion, declaring its practitioners heretics and witches and accomplices of the Devil, executing its Inquisitions and mass tortures and burnings of innocent people. It was the beginning of one of the darkest time periods on our historical record as human beings.

Another factor in the rise of Satanism in the Middle Ages was the emphasis on dualism, and the concept of good and evil, which the Church hammered into its believers. Some historians will argue that Satanism may not have ever really existed except as a fabrication of the Church to enforce the dualistic belief that God represented all good, and those who went against the orders of God, and thus the Church, were the opposers, the adversaries, Satanic. In her article "Devil Worship in the Middle Ages," Denise Horton suggests that the reasons the epidemic of Devil-worship arose during this time are many. Because the Devil symbolized iniquity, it is possible that the old nature religions, which evolved alongside the growing powers of the Church, were simply considered to be heretical. The label stuck. "Lingering ideas of pre-Christian cults of Diana and the Horned God became entwined with the doctrine of the Catholic Church concerning evil," Horton writes. "Church officials perceived these as both evil and a threat to the tenuous state of order in mediaeval society." So, the Church's creation of and attack on Satanism were political tactics to quell the threat to the status quo.

By the Church's forcing God on the people as the good guy, and killing those who did not comply with their laws, ... the Church began to look like the "evil" ones....

Those who practiced what was considered "low magick," folk traditions and nature rites, were lumped into one big group of Devil-worshipping heathens who, if left alone, might usurp the rising glory of the Church, just as a bunch of termites might crumble the foundation of a home from the inside. But an interesting thing happened. By the Church's forcing God on the people as the good guy, and killing those who did not comply with their laws, no matter how extreme and ridiculous, the Church began to look like the "evil" ones in the eyes of the peasants, who then may have ascribed a benevolent aspect to Satan as the opposer of such brutality and rule of law. This is an obvious and natural progression of human behavior that forcing someone to do something often makes the person doing the forcing the enemy.

The fact that Satanism may indeed have been either something the Church created on purpose, or something that the Church created unwillingly in its attempts at complete control of its subjects, is intriguing. Before the Middle Ages, we saw that secret societies and mystery schools such as the Gnostics were attacked as heretics worthy of being slaughtered by holy soldiers. One of the earliest mass executions of heretics occurred in 1022 when a group of people were put to death in the French city of Orleans for their devil-worshipping ways. This group, which existed before the Cathars, included nuns and former royalty figures and stood accused of all kinds of crazy things—orgies and eating burnt babies and worshipping the Devil during ceremonies—but those were accusations leveled against them by the Western European Church. The truth is, they were executed because, according to Norman Cohn in his book *Europe's Inner Demons*, they denied key beliefs of the Church, including the virgin birth, the Resurrection, baptism, and prayer to the saints. However, the Orleans people were pious, not

Satanists at all, believers in the grace of God even as they were being led to the stakes they would be burnt upon.

Many heretical groups suffered the fate of the Orleans, the Gnostics, and the Cathars. In 1179, the Waldensians came on the Church radar. Founded by a rich man who rid himself of all his money and material objects, this group was all about aestheticism and living as the Apostles of Christ had lived. Though this sounds like something the Church would have welcomed, the Waldensians incurred its wrath for preaching their gospel without permission. This resulted in the Church's labeling them cannibals, devil-worshippers, and sexual deviants. They were officially condemned as heretics in 1184.

Then came the Luciferians of the thirteenth century, who actually did worship Lucifer, the fallen angel expelled from Heaven. In their opinion, he was expelled unfairly, and they believed he would return one day to rule the heavens. According to historical records, the Luciferians did engage in acts of opposition and offense to the Church, but interestingly, the man sent to destroy them was far more evil than they. His name was Conrad of Marburg, who was considered a sadist and fanatic who loved to beat and torture his victims.

The Knights Templar also fell under the wrath of the Church in 1305. After existing throughout Christendom as protectors of the religion, devoted to helping the poor and needy, the Templars became powerful and rich, thanks to many favors they did for King Louis the VII and Pope Alexander, until their autonomy was curbed. They were made to operate under Church law rather than in secrecy as before. From this point on, the Templars suffered accusations of sorcery and of the usual Devil-worship, despite the order's devotion to the king and pope.

A detail of a stained-glass window at Elisabeth Church in Marburg, Germany, shows Konrad von Marburg (Conrad of Marburg). Konrad was a priest charged to eliminate the Luciferians, which he did in a devilish manner.

Soon, the Templars were confessing to sins they did not commit under ordained torture, and eventually they lost all their property and wealth and suffered the same fate as heretics before them.

According to Denise Horton in *Devil Worship in the Middle Ages*, these heretic groups showed the nature of the spread of Devil-worship in the Christian world. "With each new heresy, elements such as osculum, infane, Devil in the form of animal, and the ritual orgy became part of the legend, and possibly practice, of Devil worship." This pattern of label, accuse, and destroy still works even today in the world of religion and politics. And as history moved from the Late Middle Ages into the Early Modern period, the sins of the heretics became the sins of the witches.

In a July 2015 *Time* magazine article, "The Evolution of Modern Satanism in the United States," Lily Rothman writes about how many of those who confessed during the Inquisition and at other times may have resented their torturers and killers enough to "follow the only image of rebellion they knew—Satan." During such desperate times of poverty, the Plague and persecution, a pact with the Devil may have been a last hope for many who couldn't find salvation through the Church that was trying to destroy them. Not to mention, as Rothman points out, many of the members of the aristocracy of the times were actually titillated by the idea of women running around naked, worshipping and fornicating before Satan, an interest that he claims may have led to the spike in interest in the occult and witchcraft during the Victorian era!

WITCHCRAFT

Even today, the word "witchcraft" implies black cats and ugly old crones, broomsticks and cackling laughter over a cauldron. But these stereotyped images come more from fairy tales, folklore, religious persecution, and modern movies and television than from anything factual. Witchcraft is as old as humanity itself, having gone by different names, or no name, during the most primitive times. The word "witch" comes to us from the Anglo-Saxon period, derived from the Old English masculine noun *wicca* and feminine *wicce*, which mean "to have wisdom, to bend and shape," but also "soothsayer, wizard, sorcerer." A witch was originally someone who manipulated or bent the forces of nature to his or her will, and the means by which he or she did so became known as "the craft."

The original witches were Earth-worshipping and nature-worshipping pagans, who lived close to the land and the cycles of life, death, and rebirth. Highly spiritual and ethical, living by a code that respected all life, true witches never worshipped or believed in the Devil for one very simple reason. He didn't exist yet. With the advent of Christianity, witches and pagans became the enemies of the Church and thus had put upon them the label of "devil worshippers" despite the fact that witches didn't even acknowledge a "devil" deity in their hierarchy of gods and goddesses. In fact, it was the rise of Christianity that truly placed labels of "witchcraft," albeit negative labels, upon people, usually women, who practiced nothing more than the use of herbs as medicinals. The fact that women menstruated blood was also associated with their alleged links to the Devil, simply because at the time there was no medical understanding of menses.

During the Early Modern Period, someone was called a witch for being different, for expressing sexuality that was taboo, for looking different, for speaking out against authority figures, for cheating and adultery, for making his or her own medicinals, for having black cats, for worshipping many deities, for worshipping the Goddess, for elevating women to positions of power, and for so many more reasons that had absolutely nothing to do with the Devil. But as we shall see, they were killed by the thousands anyway.

Some historians argue that the malefic label attached to witchcraft, even primitive pagan practices of old, was put upon them by the Catholic Church. Rites that may have looked crude and primitive, such as animal sacrifice or worshipping nature, were looked upon as demonic, and yet, were similar to the rites and practices of early Christians. This hypocrisy was ignored by Church leaders, who used the word "witch" to level against anyone they felt might usurp their power and influence,

A witch cackling over a cauldron is, of course, nothing more than a Halloween cliché. Real witches do nothing of the sort.

especially women, who in pagan cultures were revered as equals, but in Western religions were treated as secondary to men.

Those who did engage in darker arts were considered sorcerers, not witches, though the two were often confused with each other, or grouped together. In both the Late Medieval and Early Modern periods, sorcery was considered evil and an association with the Devil because it went against the rites and practices of the Church. Even those who engaged in divination, or claimed to speak to the dead and communicate with deceased loved ones, were often thrown into the witch category and labeled evil. This category also included anyone who could heal, or perform miracles, which in those times was relegated solely to the domain of the Church. One of the biggest groups that came under attack were midwives, hired to help women through childbirth. These women were considered powerful because they assisted in the act of creation and birth of a human being; without the help of midwives, one can only imagine how many more women would have died in childbirth.

Today's witches, and the broader group of "neo-pagans" that encompass Earth-based religions and spiritual systems, believe that what they do is on the side of good, the light—white witchery. Black magic is not in their belief system, for it would only come back to harm them. Casting a spell to hurt someone comes back to the witch threefold. The general moral and ethical code was to "do what thou wilt," but for no one else's harm. Contemporary witchcraft and Wicca saw a revival period in the early twentieth century, and today's Internet and social networking have created a community for those who practice the old ways. The earliest neo-Pagan groups to emerge may have been the Bricket Wood coven, run by noted witch and author Gerald Gardner, and the Roy Bowers' Clan of Tubal Cain in the 1950s and 1960s.

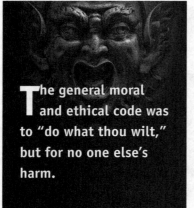

The general moral and ethical code was to "do what thou wilt," but for no one else's harm.

Witches practicing what we now call the Old Religion today use herbs, plants, concoctions, and spells in their rituals and pay homage to the four elements of earth, water, air, and fire, as well as the workings of natural laws. As a witch, one can bend the will of those laws to do one's bidding, but all witches understand that what you put out comes back to you threefold (the Threefold Law). Therefore, if you choose to do evil, you are all but cursing yourself to a threefold return on your investment.

Witchcraft is also linked with such spiritual practices as shamanism, spiritualism, metaphysics, and the occult. Witches were once the village wise ones, the healers, the medicine men and women, the cooks and advisers, the spiritual guides and the revered, especially during the days of Goddess-worship and matriarchal religion before Abrahamic traditions took hold. There are different traditions and branches of practice today, from the Stegheria of Italian witchcraft to the solitary practice of the singular witch to the Feri Tradition, which is more of an ecstatic school of sexual mysticism, to the traditional Gardnerian. Some practices are based upon familial lineage and passed down from generation to generation. Others are open to the curious public and those called to these belief systems. Some operate as mystery schools or secret societies. Others are on the Internet!

Covens

Covens are considered to be a fairly significant part of witchcraft. A coven is a group of witches who gather together for rites and practices, often thirteen in number, based upon a concept originally presented by Margaret Murray, a famed anthropologist and folklorist who wrote extensively about the subject. A coven is actually like a church group or club that meets at specific times, often aligned with the sacred cycles of the moon to celebrate the Sabbats, which are the special "holidays" of the year, to call upon the powers of the Goddess to help someone in the community, or just to gather and break bread.

Both witch and Wiccan covens can break off into smaller covens when they get too large, keeping three members minimum, and usually a high priest and priestess preside. Some groups run their covens like democracies, choosing new leadership regularly. The coven celebrates the specific dates important to all neo-pagans, the Sabbats:

- YULE—December 20–23, the time of the winter solstice
- IMBOLC—February 2
- OSTARA—March 19–22, the time of the spring equinox
- BELTANE—May 1
- MIDSUMMER—June 19–23, the time of the summer solstice
- LUGHNASADH—August 1
- MABON—September 21–24, the autumn equinox
- SAMHAIN—November 1—Halloween time

This cycle was based upon the changing seasons of the Earth, which all neo-pagans believe hold power and influence. Some festivals became absorbed, or outright stolen, by the Church, to become important Catholic holidays, such as Yule, which became Christmas, marking the birth of Christ; Ostara, which became Easter and the time of resurrection and renewal for the Church; and Samhain, which became All Saints' Eve or All Hallow's Eve. It was common for pagan holidays to be overtaken by the existing power and authority of the time, and most pagan days of celebration serve as the basis for many of our lesser holidays, as well.

Wicca

An offshoot of witchcraft is "Wicca," a neo-pagan belief system centered around the love and respect of nature and its elements, laws, and cycles. Much like witchcraft, Wicca is more of a Goddess-based religion that has nothing to do with Satan or evil, despite accusations of the Church to the contrary. Wiccans follow the Wiccan Rede, "As it harm none, do as thou wilt," which sounds a lot like Aleister Crowley's "As ye harm none, do what you will" and suggests that one has free will to do anything as long as it doesn't impose upon anyone else or harm the self, others, or nature. This is similar to the concept of karmic action, in which what we do has a consequence in the world, and to ourselves.

For the sake of this book, we will use the term "witch" to mean all witches—Wiccans and pagans—because the truth is, they all suffered the same fate throughout history. Today, the Constitution of the United States grants Wiccans and other pagan traditions the same protection as any other religious tradition with the same rights and freedoms afforded to those who practice.

Modern-day Wiccans are focused on being more one with nature, as well as practicing healing and positive forms of magic.

So where and when did the black mark of history fall upon the witch and lead to one of the most horrifying times in human history? Obviously, we have seen already how the rise of the Catholic Church was responsible for creating witch-hunt fever. But at some point, the Church began to carry out its quest to quell and destroy the pagan influence that still existed and that refused to become a part of the growing Roman empire. In her essay "How Local Wise-Women Who Carried on Ancient Traditions Were Exterminated by Christianity," for the October 2008 issue of *Freethought*, Barbara G. Walker (author of *The Women's Encyclopedia of Myths and Secrets*) wrote that women were revered in earlier cultures as equal to, or above, men, and their folk magic and healing remedies were never seen as a negative, until the fourteenth century. The Catholic Church viewed these traditions and the use of charms and spells not as healing or sources of wisdom but as heretical things of the Devil. "Throughout the Middle Ages, the village witches or wise-women were the only healers available to ordinary people," Walker wrote. "Physicians usually only treated the rich, and clergymen were forbidden to learn anything about medicine, being taught that sickness is the work of demons and must be treated only with holy water and exorcisms."

In France in 1390, what had always been accepted as the ways of the village folk suddenly became a crime. Witchcraft, that is. Interestingly, the Hebrew word for "witch" is *kasaph*, meaning "seer or diviner," but the dawn of Christian thought eradicated the acceptance of women as anything other than the wives, daughters, sisters, aunts, nieces, and mothers of men. Walker writes that up until the fourteenth century, even European nobility and clergy employed the services of witches and believed they had power, including the ability to control the weather on behalf of God! "God didn't turn against his earthly weathermakers until the beginning of the Renaissance," Walker writes. "English law tolerated witches up to the reign of James I, the Renaissance equivalent of a 'born again' national leader. The infamous Witchcraft Act was instituted in his time." It would take until 1951 for the British Parliament to overturn the Witchcraft Act of 1735.

THE INQUISITIONS

From the fourteenth to the eighteenth centuries, there existed a four-hundred-year holocaust that barely made our history books and is rarely the subject of films or documentaries. During this time, depending on which sources you consult, anywhere from a few hundred thousand to several million men, women, and children died at the hands of the Catholic Church. Their only sin was being labeled a heretic, or, later, a witch. Most of the persecuted were women, approximately eighty to ninety percent, and many were uneducated peasants and village folk who had no idea why they were being rounded up and burned at the stake.

How did such a horrific time in human history begin? It started with Pope Gregory IX, who began the Inquisitions as a means to prosecute and put to death heretics and pagans, whether they were groups that opposed the rising power of the Church or individuals who threatened good Church folk with their mystical and misunderstood beliefs. Before this, the Crusades had eliminated many of the people against

A c. 1495 panel painting showing the Spanish Inquisition preparing to burn an unfortunate person at the stake.

DEMONS, THE DEVIL, AND FALLEN ANGELS

Broomsticks and Brews

If you've ever wondered why witches are so often associated, especially at Halloween, with old crones hovering over a pot of something brewing, or women flying around on broomsticks into the night sky, there are some very interesting reasons. Old pagan fertility traditions used poles, broomsticks, and whisks in rituals to encourage crop growth and also at weddings where the bride and groom were to "jump the broomstick" to solidify their union. The broom is clearly both a domestic and a phallic symbol, which may have arisen to represent the dualistic nature of female domesticity and sexuality.

In *The Discoverie of Witchcraft,* published in 1584, Reginald Scot wrote of magical assemblies of witches where they danced and sang, "Har, har, divell, divell, dance here, dance here, plaei here, plaei here, Sabbath, Sabbath." The women would be holding up a broomstick as they danced and sang. And how did they come to ride them? Again, looking back at pagan traditions and possible natural explanations, we might assume that the strange brew the witches cooked up in their cauldrons were hallucinogens of some sort, designed to give the sensation of flying when applied to the vaginal area via the broomstick.

Hallucinogenic plants that existed around the time these symbols arose include rye mold, deadly nightshade, mandrake, and henbane, all of which have become, over time, associated with spell-casting. These ingredients were made into an ointment that, when applied to the mucous membranes under the armpit, or via the anus or vagina, courtesy of being spread over the long broomstick, allowed the witches to enter altered states of

The traditional view of witches has become that they should be old hags and fly brooms, such as in the case of this souvenir Czech doll.

consciousness or trip out just as someone would on LSD.

The use of hallucinogenic plants and mixtures was nothing new to shamans and medicine men and women, but when put into the hands of women, these substances allowed them the freedom to express themselves and, perhaps, fly above their normally mundane existence.

the Church. The Inquisition in some ways was meant to take care of those who remained.

The idea behind the Inquisitions, which occurred throughout France, Spain, and other parts of Catholicized Europe, was to prosecute anyone who might be a witch, and then torture a confession out of the person, even if it resulted in death, which it always did, unless the accused was somehow able to pay off one of the accusers, either with sexual favors or money. The earlier Inquisitions went after groups such as the Cathars and Templars, and more Gnostic traditions that operated outside of the Church, and there were Inquisitions in specific countries, such as the Portuguese and Spanish Inquisitions, all operating under the same directive. The goal: wipe out protest, dissent, and heresy.

The word itself came from the Latin *inquisitio*, meaning a court process based upon Roman law, and represented a body of institutions within the growing Catholic Church. Inquisitions began in twelfth-century France to fight religious sectarianism. Later, Inquisitions expanded in response to the Protestant Reformation of the Late Middle Ages/Early Renaissance. Other European nations began their own inquisitorial courts to fight whatever brand of heresy they were facing, and eventually Inquisitions spread to South and Central America as well. Some of the types of Inquisitions could be described as ecclesiastical tribunals or historical expurgation movements directed at heretics and sometimes at Muslims and Jews who claimed to have been converted to Christianity.

Sadly, a person could be put to death with little or no evidence other than the word of an angry neighbor....

The Inquisition most closely directed at the extermination of "witches" was ordained by Pope John XXII and most likely was amplified by the events of the times, such as the Black Death, the Little Ice Age, and the Hundred Years' War, all of which were no doubt blamed on sorcerers and witches. Various popes were involved, with Pope Alexander IV ruling in 1258 that Inquisitors should focus only on cases where there was some proof of the accusations. Later, Pope Innocent VIII ordained the prosecution of witches in Germany at the hands of Dominican priests.

As the cry was raised to hunt witches, the need for hard evidence of a crime was no doubt loosened. At this point, anyone could be accused of being a heretic or a witch even if he or she sneezed three times in a row. Paranoia and religious fervor fueled the fires of persecution and cleansing. Earlier trials might end with the accused's doing some type of penance or community service. But as the quest to destroy witchcraft raged on, the punishments became far more violent and even deadly.

Even if the alleged witch confessed, she (or he) was still often put to death. Some of the crimes these victims were forced to confess to, or at the very least be tried for in the court of the Inquisitors, involved changing the weather, affecting crop growth, copulating with the Devil, devouring babies, flying on broomsticks, sinking ships, and even turning lovers into cats or dogs—all "crimes" they couldn't possibly have been guilty of. There were even organized witch hunts to track down those who ran in fear of the judges of the Lord. Sadly, a person could be put to death with little or no evidence other than the word of an angry neighbor, or in many of the women's cases, the jealousy of a Church female who thought her husband might be attracted to the "witch." It was that easy to send someone to die, even young girls who had never even taken part in sexual acts.

Accusations

According to Eva Pocs, associate professor of ethnography and cultural anthropology at Janus Pannonius University in Hungary, there were four general categories of accusations leveled against witches during the persecution periods:

1. A person was caught in the act of sorcery, positive or negative.

2. A sorcerer or healer lost the client's or authorities' trust.

3. A person did nothing more than gain the enmity of a neighbor or neighbors.

4. A person was reputed to be a witch and surrounded with an aura of witch-beliefs or occultism.

Pocs went on to categorize witches into three groups:

1. "Neighborhood witches" or "social witches" who might curse a neighbor after a conflict.

2. "Magical" or "sorcerer" witches who might be professional healers, seers, midwives, or people who through magic increased their fortune to the perceived detriment of a neighboring household.

3. "Supernatural" or "night" witches portrayed in Inquisition court narratives as demons that appeared in visions and dreams.

These claims, which arose from the opinions and accusations of other people, did not require evidence as we need today in modern courts of law in order to give someone a fair and just trial. Sometimes an accusation could be leveled against an entire community or group of women, resulting in all of their deaths, regardless of claims of non-involvement. Those who were to be tortured, for whatever reason, were charged a fee and even had to pay for their food and prison time, including the wood that would eventually burn them alive! Those who died under duress of torture were said to have been overcome by the Devil, and Church authorities took no responsibility for the outcome.

Those found guilty, as most were, had the distinct pleasure of being burned at the stake, often in public. Other witch-hunting regions such as the British Isles and Scandinavia chose to hang their victims. It was only the rise of the Age of Enlightenment that began to shine a light on the dark deeds of the Church, and put an end, at least publically, to these trials.

The Church authorities would take whatever material goods the accused had, adding to their existing wealth, and often hold feasts to celebrate the successful burning of another town of heretics. Though the trials during the Inquisition were held in private, the torture and death often took place in public squares so that others might be frightened into "confessing" their own sins or be put to death.

Although the last known Inquisition-related deaths took place in Switzerland before the coming of the Enlightenment, even up until 1944 people were being accused of witchcraft in England, and today we see many deaths attributed to witchcraft accusations in countries in Africa and South America. Sadly, the Catholic Church retains an Office of the Inquisition even today.

TORTURE

In 1244, the Council of Harbonne issued an especially horrific order, that in the sentencing of all heretics, no husband should be spared because of his wife, no wife because of her husband, and no parent spared because of a helpless child. When the victims fell under the custody of the Inquisitors, they were forced to wait while a judge went through the documents accusing them, and meanwhile their property was confiscated to cover the expenses of the court and its investigations—whether they were found guilty or not. The accused would then be forced to answer questions that were intended to trick them into either confessing or accusing someone else, and often this questioning involved torture and abuse.

It was the norm for the Inquisitors to sexually exploit women. Often, they demanded a woman strip and be searched in every possible orifice for evidence of the Devil's sign, which they believed would be placed in the hidden places of the body. A woman would be considered a witch if she had warts, freckles, moles, or birthmarks, all considered to be proof-marks of the Devil himself. Obviously, a lot of women have at least one of these on their bodies, and it was hard to convince the Inquisitors that they were natural physical marks. If a woman's body had no markings, then needles might be pushed into her eye sockets to get her to confess, or she might be thrown into a dark dungeon, with no food or water, until she confessed to a crime she did not commit.

In 1252, Pope Innocent IV officially authorized the use of torture chambers for extracting confessions, as well as death at the stake with the con-

Pope Innocent IV (shown here in a c. 1410 illumination receiving members of the Franciscan and Dominican orders) authorized the use of torture to extract confessions.

sent of a bishop. There were many manuals and texts written to offer ideas on how to properly torture a victim, but the pope gave his Inquisitors freedom to use their imaginations. Every possible device one could imagine to cause pain, injury, dismemberment, and more was created, and often said devices were inscribed with the words "Glory be to the only God" upon them. These devices were common from the mid-fourteenth century to the end of the eighteenth century in most European countries engaging in the expurgation of heretics.

Obviously, many victims would incriminate themselves just to escape the horrific torture, often resulting in death or more torture to make sure they were telling the truth. Were a torturer to show any sympathy at all toward the victims, no matter how young, the torturer himself would be accused of supporting heresy and aiding heretics.

Once a victim recanted, it was still up to the judge to decide his or her fate. Those sentenced to die at the stake were often strangled first, then taken to burn. But many more were burned alive.

Some of the devices included:

- The Rack: The most widely known torture device is the rack, designed to stretch the body beyond its normal capacity. The victim would be tied across a long board with rollers at both ends that turned and pulled the body in opposite directions, causing dislocation of every involved joint. Used extensively during the Spanish Inquisition, another type of rack involved the victim being strapped to a board with a razor-sharp round blade hanging overhead that came closer and closer, like a pendulum, cutting into the skin unless the accuser confessed.

- Waterboarding and Drowning: The victim was tied to a board, or tied to a rope by his or her ankles, and put into a large tank of water or a nearby lake. The person would be held underwater for longer and longer periods of time to extract a confession. Often the victim would lose consciousness, especially when boiling water or vinegar were used instead of plain water.

- The Fork: Victims would have two forks put together and plunged into their skin, often their necks. The fork device would be strapped to a collar that would not allow the victims to rest or lower their head, because if they did, the prongs would stab into the flesh under their jaw. Again, this was another popular device used during the Spanish Inquisition.

- The Branks/Bridles: Used mainly on housewives during the early nineteenth century, the device was a metal face mask with a spiked mouth depressor. It was often used to torture any woman whose husband was angry with her, and she would be paraded in public wearing it as a badge of shame.

- Hanging Cages: Victims might be put on display in town squares, naked and exposed to the elements, kept inside cages without food or water. Many would die from exposure to the elements or starvation, but not without first being shamed by their fellow villagers and neighbors.

- The Wheel: One of the most popular of all torture devices, the wheel consisted of a giant spiked wheel that could rip a body apart as it rolled forward. Limbs were tied to spikes on the wheel and death was long and agonizing. Sometimes slices of wood were tied under the main joints and then smashed by the executioner, causing every joint to be broken.

- Skull Crusher: A device would be placed over the victim's head, with his or her chin on a lower board. A screw pushed the cap down onto the cranium, crushing teeth and facial bones and fracturing the skull. Often eyes would be compressed from their sockets. The victims would suffer such horrendous pain they would confess immediately just to stop the torture, even knowing they might be put to death instead. Death would be considered a relief from the Crusher.

- Iron Maiden: This was a tomb-sized container with folding doors with spikes on the insides. The victim would be put into the container and as it shut, his or her body would be pierced all over by the spikes. Sometimes there were spikes placed level with the eyes, causing fast death, but mostly the deaths came slowly and agonizingly.

- The Guillotine: The official execution device of France from 1792 on, this well-known device was named for Joseph Ignace Guillotine, a member of the French Revolutionary assembly. This fast path to death was one of the most "merciful" in that it chopped off the head of the victim, who had had to wait in despair as he or she was led to the posts and positioned correctly below the sharp blade. The blade was attached to a cord that, when cut, dropped the blade down quickly, slicing the head off at the neck.

In *The Dark Side of Human History*, Helen Ellerbe wrote that the time of the witch hunts, the three-hundred-year period of torture and death and fear, was the final attempt of the European establishment to destroy all practice of magic for good. It was called by many historians and scholars the blackest mark on our historical record until the Holocaust and the foulest of crimes committed by Western civilization. The attack by the orthodoxy

One of the many viciously creative torture devices used during the Inquisition, the Iron Maiden contained spikes so that when a person was enclosed inside, the spikes would penetrate the body, causing an agonizing death.

against women most notably created much of today's sexism and continued belief by traditional religions that women are secondary to men and the origins of all sin. Inquisitors perpetuated the belief that women were of the Devil, aligned with the Devil, and made from the Devil himself, and that man alone was the privileged sex chosen by Christ.

The Church also perpetuated the perception of sex, seduction, and even masturbation as acts all associated with the Devil, usually initiated by lust for women and, when men partook, still the fault and responsibility of the women. This might have helped fuel today's "rape culture," wherein women victims are attacked and punished for being raped and shamed by Christian conservatives who believe they asked for it, or worse, that it was an act of God they should be grateful. It might also be why women were denied birth-control methods because it was considered wrong for women to enjoy sex, which was only for procreation.

For the Church, the Inquisitions were also a wonderful method by which to extract money from a large group of people it had yet not tapped.

And what a price those people paid.

THE SALEM WITCH TRIALS

Unlike the Inquisitions sweeping through Europe, the United States was a place where people came to form the colonies and get away from the religious persecution of British rule. In America, one would think religious tolerance would have taken immediate root, but instead the country fell prey to a wave of hysteria in 1692 that became known as the Salem Witch Trials.

The place was colonial Massachusetts. More than two hundred people suddenly found themselves accused of practicing witchcraft, and twenty of them were executed. Hysteria, paranoia, and fear went viral throughout Salem Village for the next two years. The new colonists, the Puritans, were aware of the associations with the Devil that witches in Europe had died for, and political and economic chaos became fertile ground for the work of the Devil to take hold upon the community. In January 1692, the local Reverend Samuel Parris's daughter, Elizabeth, age nine, and niece Abigail Williams, age eleven, began to have fits and convulsions. They threw things, screamed and contorted their bodies, spoke strange words, and made odd sounds. The local doctor suggested they were under supernatural influence, and soon another girl, Ann Putnam, age eleven, began having fits.

Questioned by the local magistrates, Jonathan Corwin and John Hathorne, the girls accused three village women of cursing them. The women were Tituba, the Caribbean slave of the Parris family; Sarah Osborne, a poor elderly woman; and Sarah Good, a homeless woman. The three women were then interrogated before the magistrates. Good and Osborne claimed to be innocent, but Tituba claimed that the Devil came to her and asked for her help, and that he appeared to her in the form of black dogs, red cats, and a black man. She said she signed the Devil's "book," along with other witches who wanted to destroy the Puritans.

The three women were jailed, and soon the entire town was in disarray as another woman, a loyal churchgoer, was accused, along with Sarah Good's young daughter, Dorothy. In April that same year, dozens of people were questioned about having an affiliation with witchcraft and the Devil.

Special courts were set up in May in neighboring towns, and a respected minister named Cotton Mather pleaded that the court not allow dreams and visions as evidence, but the court ignored him and began sentencing women to death by hanging. Cotton's father, Increase Mather, who was at the time president of Harvard, pleaded on behalf of the innocent, saying, "It were better that ten suspected witches should escape than one innocent person be condemned."

Then Governor William Phipps agreed with Mather, especially when his own wife was accused of witchcraft, and he banned the use of dreams and visions in court. He also released witches held in custody and abolished earlier orders and decrees condemning witches to death, eventually pardoning all witches in prison in May 1693. But already nineteen people had been hanged, an elderly man had died from being pressed with stone blocks, and

Cotton Mather was a respected Puritan minister at the time of the Salem trials. While he supported the proceedings, he did protest that more restraint was needed during the very one-sided trials.

several had died in prison. Later some of those involved would confess that it was a mistake and nothing more than hysteria, and in 1702, the courts declared witch trials illegal. A few years later, the colony restored all rights and the good names of those who had been accused and provided their heirs financial restitution.

Though many blame the origin of the Salem hysteria on young girls going through normal hormonal changes, or, as some suggest, suffering from seizures that had perfectly good medical explanations, such as asthma, epilepsy, Lyme disease, and possibly even sexual abuse, there is an alleged connection involving the Parrises' slave, Tituba, telling the young girls tales of voodoo and teaching them fortune-telling and divination. Delusional psychosis has even been posited as a cause of the fit-like seizures that spread throughout a town with little medical understanding, a town filled with people who all too easily blamed the Devil for anything they didn't have a better explanation for. That when pressed for confessions about their behavior, the girls chose marginalized members of society—a slave, homeless women, poor women—as the perpetrators also suggests class and social influence. In fact, while the three accused women testified on their own behalf on the stand, the girls who had accused them writhed and whimpered in agony, as if they were possessed, or else they were really good actresses who had started something that was now out of their control. One of the girls later confessed that the whole affair had been for fun and games.

> **Many historians and scholars say the number of witches hanged was significantly higher than the official tally.**

Many historians and scholars say the number of witches hanged was significantly higher than the official tally, but even if it were only one or two, the fact of their innocence is most important. Salem was not the only town affected, as accusations swept through neighboring communities of Malden, Gloucester, Beverly, Charlestown, and Andover. And it wasn't just humans being tried and hanged for their sins with the Devil. Patti Wigington writes in *About Religion* of a dog that was accused of being one man's "familiar," a helper or accomplice animal to witches that is believed to shape-shift and may or may not be a demon. The dog was accused of attacking others by magical means and was hanged to death! Many innocent pet lovers, especially the owners of black cats, were accused of witchcraft simply because of old British and Scottish legends of familiars that feasted on the blood of women.

Fear and a mob mentality has led to accusations even today in poor and uneducated countries in Africa and South America of voodoo and witchcraft, resulting in the deaths of community members who may have simply been sick, disabled, mentally ill, or different in ways that set them apart and put them on the margins of their societies.

THE *MALLEUS MALEFICARUM*

Known as the "Hammer of the Witches," the *Malleus Maleficarum* was a guidebook for the identification and punishment of those accused of witchcraft. Written in Latin in 1486 by German-Catholic clergyman Heinrich Kramer and a man named Jacob Springer, both members of the Dominican Order and partakers in the Inquisition, this manual was first published in Germany and then endorsed by the University of Cologne's theology department for certification. The *Maleficarum* through its many editions (twenty-eight editions between 1486 and 1600 C.E.) became the textbook for those who hunted down witches. The first English translation came in 1928 by English author Montague Summers, who was a member of the Catholic clergy, studied the occult, witchcraft, and vampirism, and authored *The History of Witchcraft and Demonology* (1926). He believed the *Maleficarum* to be both a necessary and admirable examination of witchcraft and how to deal with it.

The book was divided into three sections:

1. Treating the three necessary concomitants of witchcraft, which are the Devil, a witch, and the permission of Almighty God.

2. Treating the methods by which the works of witchcraft are wrought and directed, and how they may be successfully annulled and dissolved.

3. Relating to the judicial proceedings in both the ecclesiastical and civil courts against witches and indeed all heretics.

One of the most unusual stories involving persecution for consorting with the Devil involved a man who had actually challenged the Devil to make himself known. Before torture became the method of extracting confessions, people who were accused of defaming others of devilish intent were often punished by fines and made to confess before the entire congregation or village. They were not locked up, beaten, abused, or burned until those methods became acceptable to both the Church and the panicked public. In September 1692, a man named John Broadstreet of Rowley, Massachusetts, was brought before

The title page for the 1669 edition of *Malleus Maleficarum,* a guidebook for identifying and punishing witches.

a grand jury on suspicion of having communications with the Devil. He was fined not for this, but for repeatedly lying to the justices about his prowess and ability to make the Devil do his bidding. His defense was that he had been trying to trick the Devil, not obey him!

As told in *The Devil's Disciples: Makers of the Salem Witchcraft Trials* by Peter Charles Hoffer, Broadstreet had been reading a book of magic and claimed to have heard a voice ask him what work he did. "Fearing that he was being addressed by the Devil, he answered smartly: go make a bridge of sand over the ocean, then a ladder of sand up to heaven, and finally, ascend the ladder, goe [sic] to God, and come back no more. Thus the Devil would stand before his judge and Massachusetts would be safe." Needless to say, the court was not amused and fined him.

Today, witches enjoy protection in most developed nations, even if they continue to practice under some secrecy. But they do still suffer in some lesser-developed nations where old beliefs still prevail and in some pockets of extremist religious conservatism where violence occurs against pagans, Wiccans, witches, and even people who follow New Age religions … or no religion at all.

History repeats itself.

Theistic Satanists believe that Satan is a deity just like God. The contemporary Satanic church was founded in 1966.

THE MODERN ERA OF SATANISM

It really wasn't until more recently in history that Satanism became a well-known and "real" phenomenon. In fact, in the early 2000s, a Supreme Court ruling gave freedom of religious practice even to minority religions in prisons after a lawsuit was filed challenging the issue. Before then, Satanism was more about innocents being mislabeled Satanists or set up by the Catholic Church. In the latter part of the twentieth century, Satanism came into its own as something tangible. Two groups of Satanists stood out: Theistic—which looked upon Satan as a deity with supernatural powers and the opposer of God; and Atheistic—which looked upon Satan as symbolizing darker characteristics of human behavior, such as lust, sin, and wickedness.

Though many of the accusations against individuals and groups practicing

My Journey to Becoming a Witch

BY DENISE A. AGNEW

My journey to following Wicca/witchcraft has been a long road. As a child I always dressed (if I could get away with it) as a witch at Halloween. Witches fascinated me. As my belief in reincarnation grew, I came to have the feeling I'd been burned at the stake in a former life. It was a feeling. I didn't have any past life-memories of it, and this childhood feeling was a long time before I experienced past-life regression and learned that I'd had other lives. Perhaps it's good I don't recall the life where I was burned at the stake. Who would want to recall that?

My parents were agnostic, so there was no pressure to follow a religious path. I'm very grateful for that because I think it helped foster an open mind within me. In college I studied all the major religions and some of the less prominent. I enjoyed learning about religion, philosophy, and spirituality. I resisted all attempts by others (and there were a few attempts) to snag me into a full belief in Christianity. At one point, I did try to fit in at an Episcopal church, but after a while realized it didn't fit my philosophy of life. One of my strong core beliefs is in energy and how the power of the individual and the group can change how the world operates, either for good or for bad. I also believe in karma, and in many ways this fits in very well with Wiccan belief in the threefold law that says that what you do will come back to you threefold. If you do bad things to people, bad will be done to you. I've seen this in operation all my life. My mother told me to pay attention to when people did bad things. She said it always caught up with them eventually. She was right.

In the nineties, a Wiccan priestess friend wrote a book for her coven and for others interested in witchcraft. When I read the book, it was like someone had switched on a light bulb. All of a sudden it hit me. This was why I'd always been fascinated in Wicca/witchcraft. I recognized myself in what I was reading. In my heart I knew. *I am a witch.* Once this realization came to me, I practiced as a solitary off and on. In the last several years I discovered a small coven that fit my basic religious philosophy and have joined them.

Although Reiki is not considered as having anything to do with witchcraft, I have also become a Reiki master. Through witchcraft/Wicca and Reiki, I've affirmed my belief in the power of the mind, energy, and magickal workings. Magick appeals to my sense that I can influence my own world. I adhere to the Wiccan Rede, which says: "An it harm none, do what you will." There's a lot of power and personal responsibility within those words, and I like that very much.

(Denise A. Agnew is a widely published author of dozens of books, two of which have been optioned for motion pictures. She lives and writes in Arizona.)

Satanism, whether leveled by the media or the Church, proved false, there did arise several groups devoted to the dark Lord, Satan. With so many books coming out about people claiming to have been Satanists before converting to Christianity, such as *The Satan-Seller* (1972) by Mike Warnke, *From Witch-*

The Perception of Evil

BY W. T. WATSON

Since I am going to be talking about a flavor of Christian practice, I want to make it very clear that I have no bone to pick with Christianity and Christians in general. I strongly disagree with some of the theological implications of Christianity, but I have known too many people who have benefited from Christian religion and who lead lives in which they try to follow the example of their Master. I even know some serious neo-pagan types who have the occasional conversation with the Christ energy and those interactions have been healing to them.

There exists within Christianity, however, a fundamentalist subset whose narrow-mindedness is, in my view, dangerous. I happened to hear one of these fundamentalist individuals on a podcast not long ago, talking about a set of hostile hauntings that he "endured" and spouting his particular brand of belief whenever he had the opportunity. While I will defend to the death this man's right to believe whatever he wants, his brand of "spiritual warfare" is not only insulting to the beliefs and practices of others but is also, in my opinion, hazardous to those who are facing paranormal incursions.

To be certain that I fully understood what this man was saying, I actually read one of his books. During the course of reading this work, I learned that:

1. The religious community in the area around this person's home was apparently out to get him because he did not profess the exact same beliefs the community did.

2. In addition, this entire area was a wretched hive of scum and villainy second only to the Mos Eisley spaceport in *Star Wars* and filled with Satanists and "witches" (the author specifically attacks the religious community in the

area but I am not going to put those attacks in print).

3. While I acknowledge PowWow as a form of traditional witchcraft, the author's ignorance is such that he lumps it in with Wicca and seems to think there is some similarity in practice. If this individual had bothered to do some research, rather than believing the rhetoric of the preachers he seems to favor, he would have discovered that the two practices could not be more different.

4. In addition, First Nations people still practicing their traditional beliefs are "pagan" and obviously in league with Satan since they do not follow Christianity, according to said author.

5. The First Nations people were responsible for the hauntings on the author's land, since those pagan folk cursed the land when the good Christian white people took it from them in another of a long series of ridiculously unfair treaties.

6. All paranormal activity is the result of demonic (i.e., fallen angels) activity.

7. Giving money to televangelists will lead to opportunities for your "deliverance" if you are "oppressed" by "demons."

I can only call this sort of black-and-white, us-versus-them thinking paranoid and dangerously delusional. I certainly think it is the case that a hostile haunting might benefit from the services of a qualified Christian exorcist, depending on the type of infesting entity, but, even in those circumstances, we are talking about an individual who has been ordained, been through a rigorous apprenticeship with an exorcist inside his or her denomination, and is intimately familiar with the rites of exorcism for that denomination. The efficacy of such an exorcism, whether carried out on a building or a person, is then going to depend on the faith/intent of the exorcist, his or her relationship with his or her god and helping spirits (angels), and the type of spirit that is being addressed. While it is true that the ability to speak from spiritual authority is of benefit in an exorcism, not every spirit will respond to the sort of spiritual authority wielded by a Christian priest.

I really feel that this individual created most of his own problem by being pugnacious, but I do not have the space to go into that in this small study. Suffice it to say that if, instead of immediately assuming that the odd things happening in his home were the result of "demonic activity" and going into "spiritual warrior" mode, this person had sought the calm of meditation and tried to discern what he was dealing with, he might have saved himself a lot of pain. He freely admits that it is very likely that battles were fought between First Nations people and white settlers on or around his land. Gettysburg should teach us that those who die in battle can be restless, being one of the most active historical sites for ghosts and apparitions in the entire country. Rather than assuming that Satan was out to get him, this fellow could have used the services of a qualified medium to assist him in finding out what spiritual presences were there and what

they wanted, or at least how best to appease those forces and live lightly with them.

Instead, the author tried repeatedly to cast the spirits out of his home. He addressed them as if they were demonic and thus invited the presence of exactly what he was afraid of: disharmonic entities that fed off human fear. Reading the book, I could not help but note how the haunting continued to escalate the more this individual tried to end it using techniques taught to him by ministers on TV and DVD. Personally, I suspect that, if he had spoken nicely to those "witches" he was always railing about in the neighborhood, they would have been able to advise him on how to live with the spirits on his land.

What is sad to me about the whole scenario is that this person never learned the lesson that spirits, like people, are often simply looking for a little respect and compassion. While there are beings that certainly need to be removed from human habitations, more often than not it is actually the humans who need to adapt and be flexible enough to live with the unseen neighbors who surround them.

(W. T. Watson writes extensively about monsters, magic, Forteana, and the paranormal. A practicing pagan and magical practitioner for almost thirty years, he makes his home in Charlotte, North Carolina.)

Living the Pagan Lifestyle

BY ERIKA HUNT

Living as a pagan in modern society often means keeping one foot in modern time and one in the past. From taking care of personal health issues to celebrating holidays and not getting glared at for the pentacle around my neck, every day brings new challenges and opportunities to educate others on what it truly means to be pagan.

Not all pagans are witches, do spells, or practice divination. As for myself, paganism is more about honoring nature, the balance between good and evil, the wheel of the year, and cycles of life, death, and rebirth. We do not believe in the Devil or anything evil. I believe that what I put out to the universe will come back to me—similar to karma.

Continued...

(Continued from previous page)

Historically, witches/pagans were healers, midwives, and powerful women who were respected in their communities for abilities in aiding others. This respect threatened the rising patriarchy in the Church, so these women were made out to be evil and needed to be eradicated to protect the Church and "godliness." Herbs used for healing were said to be worthless weeds, still claimed to this day, and pagan holidays morphed into holidays that followed Christian tradition.

I prefer to follow natural healing techniques. Once I nearly died from an infection and was made to take strong antibiotics to "heal me," I found myself far sicker. I believe in listening to what my body needs and am more in tune with myself for that. A bad spider bite nearly caused me loss of limb, and yet applying charcoal compresses for two days nearly healed the bite. The doctor was amazed and said he would use it in the future. I'm not saying "modern medicine" is bad or doesn't have its place. However, if we spent more time listening to ourselves and seeking natural methods of

healing, we would have more money and better health.

It's always a challenge facing holidays, especially Christmas. Most of my friends and all of my family are Christian. It's usually just easier to go along with it than try to explain why I don't want to do certain things. No, I won't burst into flames if I set foot in a church. I might fall asleep if I have to sit through Mass, though! Since Christian holidays are based on pagan rituals and customs, I am always amused by my more devout friends and family as they defend where their rituals came from.

I am fortunate that I have not had many issues or faced discrimination for my beliefs. I respect what works for others and only expect the same back. I greatly respect those who are curious or ask about why I do or think certain things. The only evil that there is surrounding paganism is people's misconceptions. You will never find a pagan who's a mass murderer or terrorist. We simply do not believe in putting more negativity into the living universe. We are about peace, love, and acceptance.

Dealing with the Devil—A Witch's Perspective

By Marla Brooks

I personally do not believe in the Devil in the sense of a Lucifer, Satan, or whatever else that particular entity is referred to in the mainstream, and I'm not alone in my thinking. Many pagans do not believe in a personal entity called Satan or the Devil. They will say that this "being" is simply something that the Christian church invented in order to control people with fear. Others will argue that the belief in Satan first appeared long before Christianity, appearing in the form of a serpent in the book of Genesis. Either way, spreading the fear of the Beast and making the accusation that witches are connected to

the Devil and do his bidding resulted in great tragedy and loss of innocent life.

The history of witch persecution began gaining momentum around the year 1233. Almost a century later, in 1320, the Church (at the request of Pope John XXII) officially declared paganism a "hostile threat" to society. Then in 1484 Pope Innocent VIII commissioned Dominican monks Heinrich Kramer and Jacob Sprenger to publish a monstrous piece of propaganda called the *Malleus Maleficarum (The Witches' Hammer,* published in 1446). This manual for witchhunters was used for nearly 300 years as the *craft to Christ* (1973) by Doreen Irvine, and others that critics later claimed were fabrications and calls for attention to Christianity, it remained difficult to separate the fake from the real.

But if any modern period could be called the true rise of the Satanic, it would be the 1970s. In July 2015, Time magazine ran a story called "The Evolution of Modern Satanism in the United States." Writer Lily Rothman stated that interest in the early 1970s in the occult appeared to be at an all-time high, and that included Satanism. She pointed to one man for popularizing modern Satanic worship, Anton LaVey, founder of the Church of Satan in 1966, and author of *The Satanic Bible*.

Anton LaVey

Anton LaVey is a name that many people automatically associate with Satanism. Born Howard Stanton LaVey in April 1930, this author, musician, and occultist was a bit of a showman to those who knew him. He was said to possess great charisma and magnetism, coupled with his unusual looks, and garnered a variety of names from journalists over the years, including the "Black Pope" and the "evilest man in the world." LaVey became to modern Satanism what Aleister Crowley was to the occult—a bigger-than-life character. His family moved to San Francisco when he was young, and he began attempts at a musical career, claiming to have left high school at age sixteen to join a circus.

He allegedly worked in bars and lounges playing the organ and is said to have had an affair with Marilyn Monroe, although that is just rumor and no doubt a part of his plan to build a reputation for himself. He played music, worked as a photographer, and turned himself into a psychic investigator, meeting many notable people on the San Francisco scene. Eventually he married and had a daughter, Karla, then divorced and met the love of his life, Diane Hegarty, with whom he lived for twenty-five years and had another two daughters.

LaVey became interested in the occult and paranormal and soon hosted parties and presented his own lectures on Friday nights, called "Magic Circles," speaking about occult subjects to a growing audience. Some of those lectures were called "Witches Workshops" and focused on teaching women the art of seduction. On April 30, 1966, he opened the Church of Satan at a place called The Black House, and proclaimed the date as Year One of the Age of Satan. They used a Satanic Bible and LaVey of course became the first presiding high priest.

San Francisco during the 1960s was a time of great religious expression and freedom of ideals. But LaVey's brand of Satanism is not what most people think. *Time* magazine's Rothman wrote, "LaVey's church and its branches might well be called the 'unitarian' wing of the occult. The members invest themselves with some of the most flamboyant trappings of occultism, but magic for them is mostly psychodrama—or plain old carnival hokum." To LaVey's followers, Satan was more of a representation of the human ego, self-gratifying in nature, and not really a deity or something supernatural to be worshipped.

Rothman went on to say that the most insidious contribution of LaVey's church and its members was their "resolute commitment to man's animal nature, stripped of any spiritual dimension or thought of self-sacrifice." These Satanists were almost boringly normal. No sacrifices of small children or animals. They provided weddings, funerals, and even baptisms for members and had a priesthood like any other church. To LaVeyan Satanists, Satan was the "adversary" of Hebrew tradition and an archetype of pride, enlightenment, individualism, and defiance of Abrahamic laws and traditions. To the LaVeyan Satanists, the Western religious traditions of Christianity, Judaism, and Islam were oppressive and in opposition to man's natural instincts, including sexuality and pleasure-seeking.

Satan did not exist as a deity at all and was not to be worshipped as such. Instead, members lived by a specific code of behavior, and many were atheists or at least skeptics of the religious doctrines of the churches. They believed not in God, or the Devil, yet established the church as a type of religion with formal gatherings, High Mass, and priesthood. In fact, the Church of Satan actually rejected the legitimacy of groups claiming to be Satanists, calling them pseudo-Satanists and "reverse Christians." His was instead a religion of the flesh, the carnal.

LaVey's church followed specific convictions called the Nine Satanic Statements, Eleven Satanic Rules of Earth, Nine Satanic Sins, and Pentagonal Revisionism. The church also allowed members to practice high and low magic. Its symbol was the Sigil of Baphomet, and it even has its own website with information on its beliefs and philosophies and how to become a member. In the mid-1990s, rock performer Marilyn Manson became a member of the Church of Satan, ordained as an honorary priest. Other famous members include flamboyant pianist Liberace (one of the Church's first members), 1950s blond bombshell Jayne Mansfield, pro wrestler Balls Mahoney, Morbid Angel frontman David Vincent, Soft Cell's Marc Almond, and even Sammy Davis Jr.! No doubt more famous people were members who did not want it publicized.

After LaVey's death in 1997, his teachings lived on. On Halloween night 1999, LaVey's daughter Karla, who hosted a talk-radio show about Satanism, started the First Satanic Church in San Francisco, dedicated to the Satanism taught by her famous father. They referred to their church as both a religious organization and a magical order. It was a re-established church, with newer representations of the same Satanic Bible of the original church. The church also oper-

The Sigil of Baphomet is similar to the Satanism symbol, but includes the image of the goat within the pentagram.

ates a "600 Club" on the Internet, a poke in the side of the fundamentalist Christian television show, *The 700 Club*.

The Church of Satan was somewhat legitimized as a religion in 1978, when the U.S. Army included the group in its manual for chaplains, *Religious Requirements and Practices*.

Luciferians

Another belief system, heavily influenced by Gnosticism, arose that revered the fallen angel Lucifer, the "light bringer" and "morning star" of the Hebrew Bible. Lucifer was not to be mistaken for Satan. Lucifer was an entirely separate entity and remains so to the Luciferians of today. While Satan represents carnality and materialism, Lucifer represents spiritual enlightenment, spiritual goals, and an enjoyment of life that is not an act of rebellion, but is worthy on its own merit and for its own sake. There is a strong belief in the balance of light and dark, the dualistic nature of existence, but Luciferians do not celebrate the dark simply to deny and resist the light, as Satanists might do to rebel against the Church or authority figures.

The Luciferian respects Lucifer more than he or she worships him. Luciferians also support creativity, success, freedom, and individuality, while shunning dogma, which does make them rather antagonistic towards organized religions, especially Christianity. Luciferians, by nature, respect the beliefs and traditions of others, as long as they don't interfere with their own.

During the Middle Ages, Luciferians were persecuted and killed as heretics. As early as 1231 C.E., they were being burned at the stake in Germany for their heretical beliefs. But today they can be your next-door neighbor, teacher, boss, or colleague, and you'd probably never have a clue. Though they do practice a form of magic and believe that their goal is to acquire knowledge and personal power, they do so in a rational, spiritual sense, based on the understanding of gods, demons, and spirits as being archetypal in nature, representing aspects of the creation of humanity—the subconscious and conscious mind.

During the Middle Ages, Luciferians were persecuted and killed as heretics. As early as 1231 C.E., they were being burned at the stake in Germany for their heretical beliefs.

According to *Adversarial Light: Magick of the Nephilim*, Luciferianism is "a symbol for a deeper, more enriching, diverse energy surrounding the order, thus allowing a trans-cultural embrace of the darkness and the light contained within." Luciferian philosophy is more metaphysical than religious. Initiation into Luciferianism involves symbolism similar to that of alchemy, and the transmutation of base metal into gold. Some Luciferians look upon their deity as a friend, a rescuer, and a guiding spirit, and even the one true God. Theistic Luciferians take a more religious approach that combines spiritual beliefs with magickal practices.

In 2014, a worldwide organization of Luciferians was founded in Houston known as the Greater Church of Lucifer under the leadership of Jacob No, Michael W. Ford, and Jeremy Crow, founder of the Luciferian Research Society. The Neo-Luciferian Church is a Gnostic and Luciferian organization with roots in Western esotericism, voodoo, Luciferianism, Thelema, and magic. Another noted organization is the Fraternitas Saturn, a German magical order that is Luciferian in nature, believing Lucifer to be the light-bringer, a demiurge who created our manifest world by breaking the static cosmic order. Represented as the "higher octave" of Saturn (Satan is its "lower octave"), the outermost planet and polar opposite of the sun in ancient cosmology, Lucifer betrayed the divine mysteries to mankind and was punished for it. His heavy, dark, leaden qualities must be transformed into gold by the magician in an alchemical process involving the "repolarisation of lights," according to "Fraternitas Saturni" by Hans Thomas Hakl in the *Dictionary of Gnosis & Western Esotericism*, edited by Wouter Hanegraaff.

Satanic Temple

This New York-based-group, which like LaVey's Church of Satan does not view Satan as an actual entity, took on a much more political stance with its brand of Satanism. The Satanic Temple sees Satan as a metaphor—similar to the one portrayed in John Milton's poem *Paradise Lost*—of a representation of skepticism and the ability to challenge authority. Satanic Temple's aim is to ensure that its political view of Satanism became a part of the dialog, and it was successful in establishing a following that continues to this day.

In December 2013, the Satanic Temple of New York publicly announced plans to erect a monument alongside the Ten Commandments on the grounds of the Oklahoma State Capitol. It even engaged in a mock rally for Florida governor Rick Scott after Scott announced his support for a bill allowing schools to use inspirational messages at school events. The Satanic Temple held same-sex wedding ceremonies on the grave of the mother of a founding member of the notorious Westboro Baptist Church, and carried out other activist events that gained public attention and media focus.

Many critics say Satanic Temple is nothing more than a Web-oriented group that wants attention for its causes, but it makes statements whenever it can, including lobbying for causes involving the separation of church and state. The view of Satan as an "eternal rebel" fits Satanic Temple's modus operandi of challenging social norms and the political status quo.

Temple of Set

In 1975, another Satanic initiatory magical order was founded called the Temple of Set. With heavy esoteric influences, this branch of belief distinguishes itself from Satanists, with members calling themselves "Setians" and adherents to "Setianism." Founded by an American political scientist named Michael Aquino, who was a high-ranking member of Anton LaVey's Church of Satan, the Temple of Set members believe that the Egyptian "Set" is the true name of Satan and the one to be revered. Set supposedly gave humanity the power of intellect, or what is called the "Black Flame" or "Gift of Set."

Set is not worshipped as a god so much as emulated as a teacher; the focus is on individualism in the pursuit of self-knowledge and immortality. The ultimate goal is to achieve self-deification. Temple of Set followers use magic, which is the manipulation of natural forces via rituals. As in Freemasonry, initiates can go through levels or degrees, six in all, with each giving more responsibility to the individual. There

Michael Aquino (shown here with his wife, Lilith, in 1999), was the founder of the Temple of Set.

is a high priest or priestess who supervises the lower-degree initiates and a Council of Nine that oversees the Temple activities in general. Members can join different groups within the Temple called "pylons" to pursue various magical teachings.

Aquino founded the Temple of Set when he began to experience dissatisfaction with the Church of Satan. The Temple was more geared toward esoteric and intellectual Satanism than the more rational form found in the Church of Satan. Much of this reflected Aquino's educational background in politics and philosophy. Aquino was also a military officer specializing in psychological warfare who worked his way up through the Church of Satan while serving in Vietnam and into the early 1970s. Many looked upon him as LaVey's righthand man. When LaVey chose to make fundamental shifts in the way the Church of Satan operated, including giving degrees in exchange for money or other contributions, Aquino resigned and allegedly asked Satan himself for advice on what to do.

In 1975, Satan allegedly appeared to Aquino, telling him he wanted to go by his Egyptian name, Set. Aquino went on to write the bible of the Temple of Set, a book called *The Book of Coming Forth by Night*. He proclaimed himself Magus of the new Aeon of Set, and the heir to LaVey's "infernal mandate," which motivated him to create and found the Temple. Aquino's book references the "Book of the Law," which Aleister Crowley claimed was "revealed" to him as well in 1904, and adopted many of the Left-Hand Path teachings, while questioning and expanding on others.

Though the Temple of Set never achieved the membership numbers of the Church of Satan, it provided a philosophical difference for those not satisfied with LaVeyan Satanism.

Religious Satanism

Among the various types of Satanism, the more religious-oriented organizations adopted similar beliefs to one another that included the exaltation of life, which meant that none of them, even the nonreligious, was into sacrificing animals or children as part of their rituals. Though some did believe in living out the "sins" of lust, gluttony, pride, greed, and sloth, all characteristics of an ego-centered system, they did not support murder or abuse. However, some more cult-oriented groups may have taken on a much darker edge. But true Satanists will defend their code of behavior and ethics, which, while in opposition of those proposed by the Catholic Church, do NOT include bloodshed or violence.

Most modern Satanists are hedonists who want nothing more than to explore their lusts and desires with other like-minded individuals, thus the need for their own churches and temples, pylons and grottos, and small groups, where they can carry out these pursuits in private. Another common Satanic belief is that each person is his or her own deity, redeemer, and in a sense, savior, totally and fully responsible for his or her own life. Despite attacks and accusations of black-magic rites and torture of enemies, modern Satanism is, as members claim, none of these things. While they may pursue both an understanding of the dark and the light, they are, for the most part, not out to harm anyone.

But true Satanists will defend their code of behavior and ethics, which, while in opposition of those proposed by the Catholic Church, do NOT include bloodshed or violence.

And no, Satanists are not witches or Wiccans. Witches and Wiccans work solely with white magic and light magic and do not believe in or worship Judeo-Christian-based entities or belief systems. Satan and Lucifer are both products of the Western Abrahamic traditions. Witches and Wiccans, and other Earth-based traditions, are pagan in origin, existing long before the Catholic Church came into being and therefore operating on a foundation of natural laws and principles that have nothing to do with the religions that condemned them. Even most occultists, Aleister Crowley included, were not Satanists, as they did not embrace the Christian worldview, but they were labeled as such because they behaved in ways that appeared decadent and sinful to those who did.

It is important to realize that attaching a label to someone, or some movement, may be done for reasons other than factual representation. The real Satanists have always worked hard to present exactly who they are and what they believe in, as is now, in the Internet age, available for anyone to research.

Satanic Panic

In 1639 C.E., an all-girls school in Lille, France, experienced what today is called a "Satanic panic," a rash or outbreak of reports suggesting widespread Satanic activity. In this case, fifty young girls were convinced they were possessed by Satan and under his influence. Their own teacher, Antoinette Bourignon, somehow convinced the girls that there were little black angels and devilish imps all around them, to the point that the girls confessed to such things as eating baby flesh and flying around on broomsticks. They were to be burned at the stake for witchcraft when it was discovered that their teacher, who had disappeared at this point, was the one responsible. But this was only one of many Satanic panics that occurred from 1400 to 1650, when over 200,000 people were burned at the stake for witchcraft.

Jump to the 1970s, and a new wave of Satanic panic broke out, lasting well into the 1990s. During this twenty-year stretch, reports of Satanic practices spread like wildfire, going viral long before the Internet, and included

Antoinette Bourignon was a French-Flemish mystic who was responsible for inciting a "Satanic panic" by convincing her girl students they were possessed by the Devil.

allegations of Satanic ritual abuse at the hands of secret societies, powerful authority figures, and even evangelical Christians who were said to be closeted Devil-worshippers.

The first glimpses of the wave of panic coincided with the 1972 publication of *The Satan Seller* by Mike Warnke, a self-proclaimed expert in Satanism who two decades later turned out to be a fraud. A second book, *Michelle Remembers* (1980), written by Canadian psychiatrist Lawrence Pazder, was an alleged memoir of a Satanic ritual abuse survivor Pazder claimed was his own wife and patient. It added fuel to a fire that had already gone viral. Around this same time, heavy-metal music, the Dungeons and Dragons role-playing game, and news stories of poisoned Halloween candy, ritually slaughtered black cats, and graffitied pentagrams exploded into a frenzy of media attention, rumor-mongering, and misinformation about a huge underground Satanic movement that was sacrificing children and animals, sexually abusing women and children, and launching an all-out war against Christianity.

Though the media was most to blame for the spread of panic and accusations of Satanic involvement with every rape, murder, or child disappearance reported during the years ahead, law enforcement had to take the situation seriously, discussing the possibility of a Satanic network of violence responsible for many crimes. That only added more fuel to the fire. The media, law enforcement, and religious institutions particularly "profiled" teenagers, Wiccans, pagans, atheists, secular humanists, liberals, heavy-metal bands, and a host of other groups that were put under the intense and watchful eye in a modern-day witch hunt.

The media had a field day with the Satanic Panic in the 1980s, promoting misinformation and unsubstantiated rumors of cults operating all over the country, scaring people into questioning their own neighbors. In 1988, NBC even aired a documentary with Geraldo Rivera that claimed to look objectively at the rise of Satanic activity, but the program was panned by critics as sensationalistic. Soon, people were even declaring that symbols that had nothing to do with Satanism, such as the peace symbol, were examples of Satanic influence!

Throughout history, Christians have accused those who went against their beliefs as Satanists, and this time was no different. No doubt the presence of true Satanic groups coming onto the scene added to the attacks. A flood of books written by Christian fundamentalists hit the market, overwhelming the very few written by actual Satanists themselves, presenting the alleged "devil followers" as engaged in the ritual abuse of children and women, mostly sexual in nature. *Michelle Remembers* added to the accusations, even though it was a novel and not a true memoir. The story involved a young girl who claimed to have been physically and sexually abused as a child by her own family members, who were all a part of a Satanic cult. When later proved as fictional, it still served as one of the rallying points for fundamentalists who continued to use it to convince millions of people of the presence of Satanic ritual abuse in their own back yards and communities.

The FBI later recognized that the Church of Satan was not involved in any of the activity the agency was investigating.

When no real evidence of any actual Satanic abuse or wrongdoing was presented at the time, the accusations and the interest on the public's part began to die down in the 1990s. Many of the earlier convictions involving alleged Satanic activity were overturned, and even the FBI admitted that of the hundreds of cases it looked into, none was proved to have involved Satanic ritual abuse or anything Satanic at all. What little activity the agency did find was more likely the result of copycats and people seeing the media reports, then going out and spray-painting occult symbols, and even kidnapping and killing black cats just for kicks and to see their "work" on TV.

One of the most heartbreaking revelations, though, came from various psychologists and mental-health experts, including in a study commissioned by the UK Department of Health, noting that many of the claims of Satanic association with child physical and sexual abuse may have been set up by the abusers themselves to scare their victims into silence and excuse or justify their actions.

One of the more ironic results of the Satanic Panic of the 1980s and 1990s is the increase in interest and membership many actual Satanic churches reported, including the Church of Satan, which noted the publicity boost that got many of its members on television and radio to talk about their beliefs and debunk the Satanic ritual abuse myths being perpetrated. The FBI later recognized that the Church of Satan was not involved in any of the activity the agency was investigating.

One might conclude from the evidence that the real Satanists were not behind the more heinous, violent crimes associated with their name. Instead, there appear to be many people who commit horrible acts of abuse, violence,

THE SATANIC PANIC

BY RON PATTON

The Satanic Panic was a social phenomenon in contemporary history that gained media momentum in the 1980s and 1990s. This period was essentially a modern-day Salem witch hunt, characterized by hysteria, paranoia, and fear primarily from evangelical Christians. They felt Satanists and nefarious cults were kidnapping people, mostly children, for the purpose of torturing and sacrificing them to Satan. The media tended to embellish or sensationalize these stories, which mainly consisted of two drastically contrasting perspectives—those who believed Satanic ritual abuse existed, and skeptics who did not.

Jack Chick, a cartoonist and fundamentalist Christian, was recognized for publishing small booklets known as "Chick Tracts." For over fifty years, he fervently exposed non-Christian religions, the occult, secret societies, and Satanism while providing a message of salvation for the lost. Some have coined him the father of the Satanic Panic.

A 1972 book by Mike Warnke, *The Satan Seller,* described a burgeoning movement of Satanism spreading throughout the world. Warnke, reputedly a former high priest in Satanism, would speak at churches and go on television talk shows, warning the audience of this unabashed advancement of evil upon society. Another book about Satanism was *Michelle Remembers,* published in 1980 and cowritten by psychiatrist Lawrence Pazder and his patient and eventual wife, Michelle Smith. It was about Satanic ritual abuse and repressed memory.

Congruently, in the 1970s and 1980s, Christian evangelical John Todd provided alarming details of a ruling elite occult group known as the Illuminati, who since 1776 had supposedly been gradually taking control of the world. Todd said he had "inside" information about this grand scheme, as he was privy to the Illuminati's inner workings because he was a descendant of this exclusive bloodline. In the 1990s, a Christian named Fritz Springmeier continued the Illuminati story with his book, *The 13 Illuminati Bloodlines.* He also wrote extensively about a trauma-based mind-control program called Project Monarch, purported to create sleeper assassins and social-change agents with multiple personality disorder, in order to help usher in the New World Order.

American radio talk-show host, author, and Christian evangelist Bob Larson started his radio show, *Talk Back,* in 1982. Larson would discuss controversial subjects relating to cults, the occult, rock music, and Satanism. He would frequently debate dark-magic practitioners and well-known members of the Church of Satan, while shocking the

The late Ted Gunderson was a former head of the FBI offices in Dallas, Memphis, and Los Angeles. He once claimed that children were being kidnapped by the thousands and ritually sacrificed.

listening and viewing audience on radio as well as major network television shows.

Other prominent personalities who appeared on investigative and tabloid-style shows, with hosts such as Geraldo Rivera, Oprah Winfrey, Montel Williams, and Sally Jessy Raphael, were Michael Aquino, a former U.S. Army lieutenant colonel who specialized in psychological warfare and was also founder of the Temple of Set, an offshoot of the Church of Satan. Aquino incessantly denied there was evidence of Satanic ritual abuse, stating there had never been any empirical evidence from law enforcement to substantiate such claims. His wife, Lilith, would echo her husband's sentiments. Zeena LaVey, the daughter of the late Anton LaVey, founder of the Church of Satan, was another apologist for Satanism.

The other individual who would appear on many of the same programs as Aquino and LaVey was the late Ted Gunderson, a former FBI bureau chief who would cite claims of hundreds of thousands of children in the United States who were kidnapped primarily for the purpose of ritual sacrifices. These antithetical personalities would debate about the existence of Satanic ritual abuse, which usually resorted in circular arguments but made created high ratings for respective shows and networks.

In the early 1980s, Christian pastor Gary Greenwald was exposing the phenomenon known as "backmasking," which is a recording technique whereby a sound or message is recorded backward onto a track that is meant to be played forward. Backmasking is a deliberate process, by which a message found through phonetic reversal may be unintentional. Greenwald, along with other Christians, believed some rock bands were doing this to subliminally embed certain Satanic messages to the listener, on a subconscious or unconscious level.

Rock groups such as Black Sabbath, Judas Priest, Iron Maiden, Led Zeppelin, and Mötley Crüe were blamed for numerous suicides and

for promoting the decline of "family values" through alleged Satanic subliminal messages.

Also adding fuel to the fire (literally) was a pair of Christian ministers, the Peters Brothers. Dan and Steve Peters exposed the dangers of rock music through their nonprofit organization, Truth about Rock, based in St. Paul, Minnesota. They were covered extensively by the media for gathering up rock records and cassette tapes and burning them in large bonfires in the name of Jesus Christ.

Several key events that were televised by major news networks occurred during this time frame, such as the McMartin Preschool trial. Child abuse and molestation, with Satanic overtones, allegedly occurred at the preschool in Manhattan Beach, California. The owner, Virginia McMartin, and her grandson, Ray Buckley, were charged with these heinous crimes, but after six years of criminal trials, no convictions were obtained. The lengthy trial went from 1987 to 1990, making it the longest and most expensive criminal trial in U.S. history.

Another prominent event was the Presidio Daycare scandal, occurring in the mid-80s. There were fifty-eight separate incidents of child sexual abuse, with the FBI and the San Francisco Police Department investigating the case. A few of the children did contract venereal disease. The two primary suspects were an ordained Baptist minister, Frank Hambright, and Lieutenant Colonel Michael Aquino, the Satanist. Charges were eventually dropped due to lack of evidence.

The Franklin Coverup, a book about child abuse, Satanism, and murder in Nebraska, was written by former Nebraska state senator John DeCamp. This 1992 publication is about an alleged pedophile consortium in Nebraska, composed of wealthy businessmen and well-known politicians. Children would apparently be used for prostitution and even snuff films. They were flown out of Offutt Air Force Base and taken to such places as the Bohemian Grove and Washington, D.C. (The Bohemian

Continued...

(Continued from previous page)

Grove is a large campground in Monte Rio, California, that belongs to a private men's art club, The Bohemian Club. Every mid-July, they host some of the most powerful people in the world at a very top-secret, two-week retreat that has long been the fodder for conspiracy theorists and eyewitnesses who have reported ritual activity and pagan celebrations.)

Another highly publicized case garnering significant media attention was the Johnny Gosch kidnapping in 1982. Johnny, a newspaper boy from Des Moines, Iowa, was abducted while on his paper route. According to Paul Bonnaci, an abuse victim and eyewitness to the Franklin cover-up, Johnny, one of the abuse victims in the "Franklin coverup," was abducted by a well-organized pedophile ring. His mother, Noreen Gosch, appeared on several television programs and wrote a book about her ordeal, *Why Johnny Can't Come Home.*

The False Memory Syndrome Foundation (FMSF) was founded in 1992 by Peter and Pamela Freyd after their adult daughter accused her father of sexually abusing her as a child. The FMSF was started to examine the theory of "false memory syndrome" and recovered-memory therapy. Further, they were advocates for individuals believed to be falsely accused of child sexual abuse. The organization was rife with controversy, with one member, Dr. Ralph Underwager, advocating pedophilia under certain circumstances, while another, Dr. Louis J. West, was a key psychiatrist in the notorious MKULTRA mind-control experiments under the auspices of the CIA.

By the close of the twentieth century and with the advent of a new hysteria, Y2K, the Satanic Panic era waned and came to a close.

(Ron Patton is a conspiracy researcher, writer and editor-in-chief of Paranoia: The Conspiracy Reader, *and executive producer of the nationally syndicated radio show* Ground Zero with Clyde Lewis. *In 2003, Patton published* MKzine, *a magazine examining coercive mind control, invasive human experimentation, and other related abuses. Since 2005, he has hosted several radio programs and podcasts, including* ConspiraZine, MKzine, *and* Paranoia Radio).

and torture using the name of Satan that do not belong to the organized Satanic churches and temples but operate on their own with no rules or laws governing them. These people often use Satan's name to excuse responsibility of their horrible actions, including child rape, torture, and murder, and may very well worship the Devil that drives their behavior. But history and fact show that they represent a dark side to society that breaks laws, harms others, and creates a hell on earth that really may have nothing to do with Satan at all. These people operate alone or in small "cells," much like terrorists and extremists who claim to be associated with a particular religion when in fact they are the antithesis of that religion. Sometimes they operate just like a cult, with a charismatic leader who claims to be the Devil himself. Cults allow for the privacy and exclusiveness that often creates the attitude that others outside the cult are not worthy of living, and the atmosphere of decadence and deviance allows for behaviors that would never be acceptable on the outside.

So we have real Satanists, and those who claim to follow Satan. History has shown they are two different groups with two different belief systems and two different modes of operation.

SYMBOLS OF SATANISM

The pentagram, or five-pointed star, also known as the pentacle, is the most popular and widely known occult symbol, especially for those involved with Wicca, witchcraft, and paganism. The five points are often said to represent the body of man, as in Leonardo da Vinci's *Vitruvian Man*, with arms and legs spread and the head as the fifth point. But esotericists also believe the five points represent fire, water, air, earth, and spirit. In the Hebrew Old Testament, the pentacle was the first and most important of the Seven Seals. To ancient Celts, it symbolized the Goddess of the Underground, Morrigan. In ancient Greece, the pentagram was the symbol by which members of the Pythagorean mystery school identified each other once it was driven underground.

Cut open an apple, and you will find a near-perfect pentagram shape at the core, with each point of the star containing a seed. Romanian gypsies refer to this as the Core of Knowledge.

The symbol becomes "Satanic" when inverted. The two points then represent the horns of Baphomet, or the horns of a goat, borrowed from Pan and pagan symbolism, and the three lower points are the Trinity of the Father, Son, and Holy Spirit. With the inversion of the pentagram, the "sign of the cloven hoof" or "Goat of Mendes" signifies the footprint of the Devil, with a contempt or the opposite of what it normally represents, in the same way an upside-down flag is used in protest to represent disappointment, despair, and anger in the country it represents. Because the pentagram is used by white witches and white magical practitioners, it makes sense that those who practice the black arts would use the inverted version.

Baphomet is the son of Lilith and the fallen angel Samael. He is depicted as having the head of a goat and is usually pictured with a pentagram.

One popular Satanic symbol, the Sigil of Baphomet of the Church of Satan, simply turns the horned god into a pentagram and is widely recognized by most Satanism groups. The sigil, actually trademarked by the Church of Satan, first appeared on the cover of the "Satanic Mass," as well as on church literature, business cards, and stationery. According to historical literature, the use of the goat's head within an inverted pentagram originated

Santeria is a religious tradition similar to voudon that is still very widespread in Cuba. These women are wearing dresses in the Santeria style.

with LaVey's church. Before that, a goat-head pentagram featuring Hebrew letters at each of the five points was referenced in the book *La Clef de la Magie Noire*, written by French occultist Stanislas de Guaita in 1897. The more primitive origins go back to the use of the pagan horned goat, or Pan, the cloven-hoofed deity.

The pentagram is also widely used in secret societies such as the Freemasons, and in the Christian church, it has taken on an overall negative stigma for its associations, even when they do not involve Satanic worship at all. The pentacle, which is used in witchcraft, is simply a pentagram in a circle, which describes the microcosm within the macrocosm and is a sacred and holy symbol. The Golden Dawn utilized a pentagram in a magic square, calling it the "Earth pentacle," which represents the four elemental weapons or tools of an adept.

Often used in spells, amulets, charms, magical evocations, and occult jewelry, the pentagram and pentacle in their upright form are mistakenly thought to be Satanic. Even the inverted pentagram is more about opposition to the light than an homage to Satan.

The Church of Satan employs primarily the Sigil of Baphomet as its main symbol. Many Satanists use an inverted cross, which signifies everything from the opposite of Christ, to a reference to St. Paul, who was crucified upside-down, to the office of the pope. Like the flag, an inverted cross can be a protest symbol meant to speak out against the practices, rules, and doctrines that the Church teaches, and Satanism opposes.

The number 666, as we learned earlier, is often used to signify the Devil and has become a favorite tattoo among occultists. But most true Satanists do not subscribe to the revelations of St. John the Divine in the Book of Revelation of the New Testament, and the number has become more often than not a symbol of Satan owing to the popular movie *The Omen.*

VOODOO

Another misunderstood religion often misaligned with Satanism is "*voudon,*" which in America has been popularized by the name *voodoo.* Described as an Afro-Caribbean religion that took root in Haiti before spreading to other parts of the Caribbean, the United States, and South America, voudon is a system of spiritual belief and folk medicine that is carried down through generations in folklore, song, rituals, and traditions, just as any other religion is. True voudon originated with West African beliefs that were merged with those of the Catholic Church, when slaves were brought to America and pressured to accept Christianity. One of the ways they did this was to adopt some of the rituals, symbols and beliefs of Christianity in public, but continue to practice the pagan version in private. Even many of the deities worshipped by Africans were reshaped into new gods that represented the slave experience in the New World. This same process of "Christianization" occurred with Santeria, a religious tradition similar to voudon that was, and still is, practiced by many Cuban and Latin communities.

To those who practice, voudon is a way of life and one that involves the belief in a Supreme Being called Bondye, a creator god, and many lower spirits called *loa* that oversee different aspects of human life and existence. Voudon posits that there is a universal energy that can be worked with to heal and help, and that there is a soul. One of the beliefs that has been labeled by Christian theology as evil is the idea of a spirit's coming into or possessing a body, something that is a part of voudon and the more popularized voodoo. During rituals involving drumming, chanting, and dancing, a person can be overtaken by a spirit, but usually in the presence of a trained high priest or priestess, and always for a good purpose.

During the time of slavery, many slaves turned to their voudon beliefs to give them strength and fortitude during terrible ordeals, and it gave them a sense of their own community and ties to their roots with Africa, even as they were being forced to assimilate into a Christian America, which was busy trying to eradicate the practice of voudon right up until recent times, when voodoo swept New Orleans society and created a groundswell of interest.

Voudon does include in its hierarchy of deities those that represent dark or more negative aspects of life and human behavior, but the emphasis is not on poking voodoo dolls with pins or cursing fellow villagers. Thanks to pop culture, misrepresentations in movies and television shows have given voudon as bad a name as witchcraft. Though practioners might sacrifice animals during their rituals, just as more developed religions once did, their code of ethics prevents them from doing anything to kill or destroy others.

An interesting element of voudon and voodoo that has scared many people away from the religion is the association with zombies, again perpetrated mainly by modern pop culture. The link between the two came from the works of historian and poet Robert Southey in 1810 when he wrote in *The History of Brazil* of *zombi*, which was a West African loa, or deity/spirit. The word was later attached to an interpretation of a human shell lacking spiritual awareness or soul, but to the Haitians, zombies were victims who were people brought back from the dead to be controlled by magical methods by *bokors*, or priests. Southey also writes that these "living dead" were created as a slave labor force to be used on the farms and sugar-cane fields but also may have been a form of punishment for wayward slaves.

Again, no resemblance to today's "walking dead." No voodoo dolls. No demon-possessed young women contorting half naked in a clearing surrounded by fire and chanting villagers. Another pagan-oriented religion maligned by those who do not practice it, or understand it. We have pop culture to thank for that, so that is where we will end our journey.

The Devil, Demons, and Fallen Angels in Pop Culture

ngels, demons, and the Devil have become a fixed part of popular culture, with movies, television shows, novels, comics, and video games featuring dark entities in some form. Our fascination with the dark side runs deep and perhaps allows us to vicariously explore our own evil shadow-selves through fiction and storytelling. This fascination also might help us deal with our deepest fears by looking at them within the context of a good movie or novel, where we can safely process the horror from a detached point of view.

It has long been debated whether the times influence pop culture, or pop culture influences the times, but perhaps the truth is both. Our fascination with paranormal and supernatural subject matter goes in cycles, and we are currently in a period of high interest, thanks to the Internet and reality television, both of which have provided a much more mainstream reach and engaged far bigger audiences than in the past.

Some of that increased interest may be related to our feelings about religion, spirituality, and the paranormal, and whether we are open to exploring other beliefs. Take angels for example. According to *Angels and Demons Go Pop Culture,* by Gene Edward Veith, the new popularity of angels, good and bad, crossed over religious lines into secularism because many people look upon angels as human helpers, pets, spirit guides, and wise ones, as well as the usual holy winged entities that sit beside God in Heaven. "The angels people believe in, however, are not necessarily the cherubim and seraphim of the Bible, the messengers of God and hosts of His army, which sometimes appear in the dazzling, light-filled humanoid form and sometimes as incomprehensible beings with multiple eyes and wheels within wheels," Veith writes. He goes on to say these angels can be someone who might just stop to help a stranded motorist, people either dead or alive who travel around doing good like Della Reese in the hugely popular television series, *Touched by an Angel*.

When it comes to demons, though, Veith sees a tendency to present them in a more unified manner, with a more traditional iconography, though not necessarily a religious one. But we do love our demons. "For some reason, people in our culture like to be scared," says Veith. "Demons are not, however, scary enough to keep people away from them. And when devils are seen as only symbols of evil, they can be explained away and perhaps given another kind of attraction."

Our culture has a fascination with the Devil, with who or what he is and how he operates in the world. That same fascination translates into demons, dark angels, and entities that represent the negative aspect of the duality between good and evil. Some angels can be good; some can be evil. Demons are never good, although they may, as we will see, be very charming and magnetic. The Devil can come across however he pleases but is never a good guy underneath the masks and disguises he wears.

There have been countless references to demons and angels, devils and dark ones in popular culture. No doubt this trend will continue as long as our imaginations can think up new ways to portray old foes. The symbols and icons and archetypes of evil and the opposing forces of good, whether actual manifested entities or just aspects of our own human behavior, will always present creative types with more fodder for entertaining, enlightening, education, and even empowering us … and often scaring us in the process.

ARCHETYPES

To understand our love of the demonic, it helps to understand the archetype it represents, because archetypes are universal symbols that appeal to people across cultural and social lines. These symbols are powerful subconscious drivers of our understanding and perception of the world we live in and the forces we interact with. The actual definition of the word "archetype "is an idea or original pattern/model from which all things of the same type are representations or copies. In Jungian psychology, an archetype is an inherent idea or mode of thought derived from the experience of the species/race and present in the individual and collective unconscious.

Carl Gustav Jung, the famed psychologist, utilized these symbols as a means for understanding the path to personal enlightenment, the way the world works, the way the human psyche works, and how to empower, heal, or achieve goals and desires. There are human and animal archetypes. Jung once said there were as many archetypes as there are typical situations in life, and they constructed a type of formula for the functioning of the subconscious and have the distinct characteristic of showing up throughout human history in the same form, with the same meaning. It doesn't matter which culture, religion, geographical boundary, or language is involved ... an archetype is the same anywhere around the globe, for it represents the language of the collective detached from the intellect and judgment of the conscious mind.

Common archetypes include:

- *The Hero*—sent on a quest to pursue his/her destiny. Comparative mythologist Joseph Campbell spoke and wrote extensively of the "Hero's Journey" found in many great novels and movies, including *Star Wars*.

- *The Self*—Our individual persona seeking to become completely realized, usually via the Hero's Journey.

- *The Shadow Self*—Our opposing, amoral, instinctual, primitive side associated with the past.

- *The Persona*—The mask we wear to show others and hide who we truly are.

- *Anima/Animus*—Our female and male psyches, roles, and desires.

- *God*—The perfected Self.

- *Goddess*—Mother Earth.

- *Trickster*—The change agent.

- *Beast*—Our primitive past of humanity.

- *Sage*—The wise one.

- *Wizard*—The one who knows how to transform, who has hidden knowledge we seek.

- *The Fool*—Our confused, faulty Self.

There are many others, including the enemy/adversary/Devil, that often stands in the way of the Hero achieving his/her mission, and thus, destiny. Because Jungian archetypes are often used to help understand a spiritual and hidden dimension to our existence, they can also help to explain the inhabitants, good and bad, of that dimension. Some experts argue, though, that this explanation of Jungian archetypes doesn't necessarily point to demons and devils as being real objects but rather as possibly aspects of the human mind/heart that are expressed via our actions, thoughts, and behaviors.

The Collective Unconscious

Jung posited that the collective unconscious was akin to a storehouse of information, myths, stories, and symbols that all humans have access to and is a necessary part of the human psyche. Especially during times of conflict, the

Among his many, many contributions to the field of psychology, Swiss psychoanalyst Carl Jung developed the concept of archetypes, shared ideas and symbols common within the collective unconscious of all human beings.

collective unconscious can be tapped into for wisdom, guidance and understanding and also may be the realm of angels, spirits, demons, and other guardians and helpers that exist apart from our manifest reality, such as the spirit guides visited by shamans during their drumming journeys.

Think of the collective unconscious as a universal reservoir that allows all humans to quench their subjective, symbolic thirst for meaning, especially when it comes to those things that are not objective, empirical, or direct experiences. Thus, the demons and fallen angels in the reservoir can ease the thirst of any culture, albeit in different modes of expression on the surface (think using a blue cup dipped in a sink as opposed to a green cup). You end up with the same water but using different colored cups to retrieve it.

Demonic Archetypes

Though the idea of demons as something more symbolic than real may have come into fashion with the Greek philosopher Plato's (427–347 B.C.E.) concept of pure forms embodying fundamental characteristics, the idea of a destructive/negative entity present in nature, adversarial to the "good" deity or deities, is as old as humanity itself. When Christianity began, that symbolism was given over to Satan, and often Lucifer, the fallen one, whereas in pagan times, that same archetypal negative entity might have been Pan or a trickster deity, even a scapegoat deity who was often looked upon as evil, or disagreeable at the least. The popularity of demonic archetypes today, though, owes much to popular culture and the perpetuation of the symbols in movies, books, and other modes of entertainment.

The Devil archetype has gone through many name changes, even personas, but beneath the mask he is always the same. Beelzebub, Lucifer, Satan, Old Nick, Krampus, the Boogey Man, Slender Man, you name it—the Devil comes in many shapes, sizes, and forms but is always representative of the same dark force at play. In *The Devil That You Know: Literature's Evil Archetype*, writer Leah Dearborn suggests that the Devil figure has become a type of talking point, "a convenient and accessible symbol for the worst of human flaws." She goes on to write, "From Goethe's 'Faust' to Bulgakov's 20th century satiric masterpiece, the Devil is without a doubt one of the most versatile and enduring literary archetypes of all time."

Perhaps the Devil in art and entertainment really represents our own inner struggle between good and evil influences, even our own sexuality. Recall the ways witches and heretics were often accused because of displays of what someone thought was sexuality that went beyond societal norms. In dream interpretation, the Devil might represent repressed sexual desires that one might crave to satisfy, the desire to meet and know the shadow self, the struggle against order and authority, and even resistance to inner urges and drives, all of which might appear to be rebellious or bad behavior when expressed or acted out.

The fallen angel, therefore, is a powerful symbol of good gone bad, something we all struggle with daily. A Satanic archetype might also simply be our desire to enter into a bargain with someone and try to get something for nothing. Our greed, lust, sloth, and the other deadly sins in action can drive us to do "devilish" things for the sake of getting base needs met. We might also, as the fallen angels did, seek to rebel and even resist the orders of those authority figures that seek control over us. Simply desiring to go against the will of God or one's peers might be a fallen-angel act of behavior! How many times in our lives do we play the opponent? The adversary? The enemy?

Because the original "daimons" of the ancient Greek were not necessarily evil, and could be either good or evil at any given time, we still struggle with our own ability to act like the Devil and be "demonic" in relationships and situations, wanting sometimes to help others and at other times to harm them. We can heal, and we can kill. We have the ability to be loving, and murderous. We can sin, and we can repent. We may not be all that much different from the demons we fear, or much different from the angels we revere, having both archetypes operating within our psyches.

Among other things, the Devil might serve as a symbol of lustful desires that we have suppressed.

MOVIES ABOUT DEMONS, THE DEVIL, AND FALLEN ANGELS

Countless movies have plots or reference points around a demon, the Devil, or a fallen angel, but three stand out as the most identifiable and popular. One cannot discuss movies without bringing up these three ground-breaking offerings.

The Exorcist

In December 1973, a Warner Bros. movie hit the big screens that may very well go down in history as the most terrifying depiction of demonic possession ever. Some say it was the scariest movie they've ever seen. No matter your opinion, watching poor little Regan, played by Linda Blair, turn her head around, spew bile, yell vile words, and levitate off her shaking bed was enough to make this the hands-down best "Devil" movie ever made, in this humble author's opinion.

Based on the novel by William Peter Blatty, who also wrote the screenplay and served as producer, *The Exorcist* was directed by William Friedkin, who served up a powerful cast with top-notch talent, a terrifying "based on a true story" story, and a theme that resonated with audiences of the 1970s, just as it does today. In fact, many of today's "demonic possession" movies are just copycats of the classic that started it all. Those who watched, enthralled, as Ellen Burstyn played the horrified and helpless mother, Chris MacNeil, a famous actress; Jason Miller the frustrated Father Damien Karras; and Max von Sydow the enigmatic Father Merrin, were privy to a concept rarely seen in motion pictures before—that an average, anybody little girl like Regan could be possessed by demons without rhyme, cause, or reason. Or was it the Ouija™ board the child innocently played with that unleashed an ancient demon named Pazuzu and caused her to begin manifesting all the classic symptoms of possession?

The Exorcist went down in history as a blockbuster and received critical acclaim.

The movie was based in part on the story of Roland Doe, or Robbie, as he was also referred to, whom we discussed in the earlier chapter about possession. The fact that there was some truth behind the plot caused audiences to react with even more horror … the horror of possession being a real and possible phenomenon. *The Exorcist* spoke to our deepest fears—that each of us was vulnerable to, and utterly powerless against, the desires of the Devil and his minions, who might one day choose one of us to become their new host body and soul. The Devil and demons were portrayed as ugly, vile, violent entities that had not an ounce of compassion for the souls they controlled, or the bodies they destroyed. And the haunting "Tubular Bells," by

British musician Mike Oldfield (who was only nineteen when he wrote the piece) would become one of the most memorable movie theme songs ever. Nominated for ten Academy Awards, the film went on to win Best Sound Mixing and Best Adapted Screenplay and became the first horror film ever to be nominated for Best Picture.

The Exorcist went down in history as a blockbuster and received critical acclaim. But for those of us who sat in a darkened theater and watched it on the big screen, it left a searing mark on our psyches as well.

The Omen Series

But what if the Devil was a cute, if not strange, little boy named Damien? And what if he grew up to be a good-looking man, with charm and magnetism and the power to become a global leader … might we still fear him? *The Omen* trilogy introduced us to a new perception of the Devil in 1976. Directed by Richard Donner from a script by David Seltzer, this 20th Century Fox release became one of the most successful and critically acclaimed franchises of its time. A British-American co-production, it told the story of a young child adopted by a powerful American ambassador, Robert Thorn, played by Gregory Peck, and his lovely wife Katherine, played by Lee Remick.

When Katherine gives birth to a stillborn baby, Robert is persuaded by the hospital chaplain, Father Spiletto (Martin Benson), to adopt an orphan child and not tell his distraught wife that the baby is not her own. They take the child home and name him Damien (Harvey Spencer Stephens). Shortly afterward, when Robert is named ambassador to England, strange and horrible things begin happening at the estate that are all centered on the boy who would become the Antichrist.

Through two sequels, we watched as the child's protectors kill off everyone who questions his innocence, including his adoptive parents, as he rises to power in the final installment, *The Final Conflict*, in the form of charismatic Sam Neill as the Antichrist, to do battle with Christ as predicted in the Book of Revelation. The entire series captivated audiences who had never considered the Devil in human form, and what that might look like or play out as, as well as how difficult it would be to kill a little boy before he could grow into manhood. Having to choose to set aside all compassion and kill a small child because he might be evil proved to have a powerful psychological effect on audiences.

Add to the film an atmospheric musical score by master composer Jerry Goldsmith, including Latin chanting about Devil-worship sung by a choir, and the contrasting scenes of home life at the Thorn residence with the sheer evil destruction that surrounded the child, including some death scenes that left audiences cringing, as well as that exciting moment when Thorn discovers the number of the beast on the little boy's scalp, and you have the recipe for one of the most compelling and memorable "Devil" movies ever made.

Rosemary's Baby

Director Roman Polanski is a controversial figure but a brilliant filmmaker, and the 1968 psychological horror movie, *Rosemary's Baby*, the script for which he also wrote, proved that point. Another classic, groundbreaking film based on the 1967 novel by Ira Levin, *Rosemary's Baby* featured sweet, innocent Mia Farrow as Rosemary Woodhouse, a pregnant woman who comes to discover that her baby is not who, or what, she thinks it is. Turns out that her husband, Guy, played by John Cassavetes, did something behind her back that will haunt them both for their entire lives.

The couple moves into an old New York City apartment and soon learn that they have some unusual neighbors, including Minnie and Roman Castevet, played pitch-perfectly by Ruth Gordon and Sidney Blackmer, who may be into worshipping the Devil! As poor Rosemary begins suffering strange physical symptoms as well as paranoia and suspicions that her neighbors are members of a cult, she fights to keep her sanity after giving birth to a stillborn child. But when she hears a baby cry in the Castevet apartment, she finds, to her horror, that her child is alive … and his father is, you guessed it, the Devil! Seems that night of wild, violent sex she had that she could barely remember wasn't with her hubby at all. Now she must agree to give up the Devil's child in order one day to have one of her own, as her husband tries to convince her, but she refuses to be part of the disgusting plan—at first. The pull of motherhood wins out in the end.

Directory Roman Polanski also wrote the script for the riveting horror film *Rosemary's Baby,* about an innocent woman who is pregnant with the Devil's spawn.

The idea that someone could be impregnated, actually raped, by the Devil, drugged, and used by his cult of worshippers, in a fancy New York City apartment, crossed the line and blurred the boundary between fantasy and reality. Audiences responded to Farrow's naiveté and innocence, and the horrors committed upon her, including collusion with the Devil by her own husband, but also to her acceptance of her fate in the end. No doubt many moviegoers went home after seeing the movie wondering about their own neighbors and their own children!

OTHER MOVIES AND TV SHOWS

The list of additional movies and television programs below is not comprehensive, as there are so many we could include, but is a sampling. Because the subject matter never fails to capture our imagination, more are being made as this book is written. In many of these films, the Devil or demons are portrayed as entities of pure evil, yet in others, the demonic characters are slick, clever, and conniving in human form. Fallen angels might be beautiful and charismatic or dark and ugly beasts with wings. Take your pick and pass the popcorn!

Films

11-11-11—2011
Amityville Horror—1979
Angel Heart—1987
Annabelle—2014
Army of Darkness—1992
Bedazzled—2000
The Beyond—1981
Beyond the Door—1974
Child's Play—1988
The Conjuring—2013
Conjuring 2: The Enfield Poltergeist—2016
Constantine—2005
The Craft—1996
The Crow Series (Angel of Vengeance)—1994–2005
Dark Angel: The Ascent—1994
The Dark Tower—2017
Demonic Toys—1992
Demons—1985
The Devil Inside—2012
The Devil's Advocate—1997
Dogma—1999
Dominion: Prequel to the Exorcist—2005
End of Days—1999
The End of Evangelion—1997
Entity—1982
The Evil Dead—1981
Evilspeak—1981

The Exorcism of Emily Rose—2005
The Exorcist—1973
Exorcist II—The Heretic—1977
Exorcist III—1990
Exorcist: The Beginning—2004
Fallen—1998, 2015
Frailty—2001
The Gate—1987
Ghost Rider—2007
Ghostbusters—1984
Haunting in Connecticut—2009
Hellraiser—1987
The Horn Blows at Midnight—1945
Horns—2016
House of the Devil—2009
Insidious—2010
The Last Exorcism—2010
Legion—2010
Little Nicky—2000
Lost Souls—2000
Mirrors—2008
Night of the Demons—1988
The Ninth Gate—1999
The Omen Trilogy—1976–1978
Ouija—2016
Poltergeist—1982
The Possessed—2009
The Possession—2012
The Possession of Michael King—2014
Prince of Darkness—1987
The Prophecy Series—1995—2005
Reaper—2007
The Rite—2011
Rosemary's Baby—1968
The Sentinel—1977
Sinister—2012
This Is the End—2013
The Witches of Eastwick—1987

Television Shows

666 Park Avenue—2016
American Horror Story—2015–2016
Angel—1999–2004
Buffy the Vampire Slayer—1997–2003
Charmed—1998–2006
The Exorcist (Remake)—2016
Ghost Whisperer—2005–2010
Grimm—2011–2016
Lost—2004–2010
Lucifer—2016
Messengers—2015
The Secret Circle—2011–2012
The Stand—1994
Supernatural—2012–2016
True Blood—2008–2014

MUSIC

"Black metal" groups often played music with occult or Satanic themes and lyrics, sometimes simply anti-Christian or pagan. Because of the dark and often garish dress and makeup of these bands, and their raw, distorted sounds, and urgently fast tempos, they were grouped into a category that suggested they were against the mainstream, as was early punk. In the 1980s, death-metal and thrash-metal bands included Venom, Bathory, Mercyful Fate, Celtic Frost, and Hellhammer. In the 1990s, bands such as Norway's Mayhem, Burzum, Darkthrone, Immortal, Emperor, and Gorgoroth took over the reins with a style that became distinctly Norwegian black metal. Later Norwegian bands included Marduk, Dark Funeral, and Nifelheim.

Many heavy-metal bands, especially those in the 1970s, toyed with occult themes, including Black Sabbath, Led Zeppelin, and Judas Priest, but were not themselves Satan-worshippers, although Jimmy Page of Led Zeppelin was a devout occultist and follower of Aleister Crowley. Yet songs such as "Black Magic Woman" by Santana, and "Witchy Woman" by the Eagles, went on to become huge hits, catapulted into pop success along with their rather dark themes and lyrics.

American blues has had a long tradition of dancing with the Devil, so to speak, with musicians such as Robert Johnson and Dr. John the Night Tripper writing lyrics about devils, deals with the Devil, hoodoo, voodoo queens, and black magic. Johnson's "Crossroads Blues" and "Sold it to the Devil" by twentieth-century blues artist Black Spider Dumpling are perfect examples of the fascination with the dark prince, who was believed to give musicians incredible prowess and technical skill ... for a price.

A sampling of odes to the Devil include:

Judas Priest—"Devil's Child"

Motley Crue—"Shout at the Devil"

Iron Maiden—"The Number of the Beast"

Van Halen—"Runnin' with the Devil"

Grateful Dead—"Friend of the Devil"

Spinal Tap—"Christmas with the Devil"

Metallica—"Devil's Dance"

The Rolling Stones—"Sympathy for the Devil"

Alice Cooper—"Devil's Food"

Seldom Scene—"Satan's Choir"

George Jones—"Take the Devil Out of Me"

Robert Johnson—"Me and the Devil Blues"

Lyle Lovett—"Friend of the Devil"

The Fall—"Lucifer Over Lancashire"

Snoop Dogg—"Murder Was the Case"

Mill Supply—"Satan"

Deicide—"Satan-Spawn, the Caco-Daemon"

Mercyful Fate—"Satan's Fall"

Funeral Mist—"The Devil's Emissary"

Ruth White—"Flowers of Evil: Litanies of Satan"

William Kapell—"Liszt Mephisto Waltz #1"

Songs about the Devil transcend genre and style, with rock, thrash metal, folk music, bluegrass, old blues, Christian, and gospel all weighing in on the upsides and downfalls of dealing with the demonic. While writing and performing a song about the Devil in no way meant the performer was in league with the Devil, it would only be natural that some of our musical expression would evolve the darker sides of life ... and death.

LITERATURE

Nowhere in our popular culture have the Devil, demons, and dark angels been more celebrated than in our literature, whether books, novels, stage plays, comic books, graphic novels, poems, or short stories. Fiction has given many a classic and modern author the ability to explore our interactions with dark entities and portray them in a wide variety of ways, unencumbered by the limits of reality.

Aside from religious texts and the many nonfiction books about the subject, fiction has unleashed our imaginations and obliterated our inhibitions. We have erotica involving demons and voluptuous women, dark angels, and beautiful maidens, and love stories between a devil and a housewife, all resulting in hot sex and animalistic lust. The romance industry has also truly embraced letting its mostly female readers explore the dark temptations of loving a bad boy—a *really* bad boy—even sleeping with him and having his baby. Young adult novels have shown a strong fascination with the Devil and demons as enemies of teenagers who have supernatural and magical powers, out to save the world.

> **A**side from religious texts and the many nonfiction books about the subject, fiction has unleashed our imaginations and obliterated our inhibitions.

Fantasy is rife with stories of beings representing the Devil, whether mythological or beastly or downright monstrous. Anything goes, and there are no rules in the world of the fantastic, so a demon could be anything the author wants it to be, and the reader accepts it as so.

There are far too many to mention, but some of the more well-known and widely read works are listed below.

Damned—Chuck Palahniuk

Dante's *Inferno*—part of Dante Alighieri's fourteenth-century epic poem, *The Divine Comedy*

The Dark Tower Series—Stephen King

The Devil and Daniel Webster—Stephen Vincent Benet

The Devil Rides Out—Dennis Wheatley

Doctor Faustus—Christopher Marlowe

Faust—Wolfgang von Goethe and Christopher Aubin

Horns—Joe Hill

The Infernal Devices series—Cassandra Clare

I, Lucifer—Glen Duncan

Left Behind series—Tim Lahaye and Paul Jenkins

Memnoch the Devil—Anne Rice

Mephisto comic series—Marvel Universe

The Mortal Instruments series—Cassandra Clare

Needful Things—Stephen King

Neron comic series—DC Universe

Satanic Subliminal Rock Messages

During the 1980s, politicians in America launched a full-on attack against heavy-metal and rock music that they alleged included subliminal, secret messages, often recorded backwards to avoid immediate detection. In April 1982, the members of the California State Assembly's Consumer Protection and Toxics Committee actually held a meeting at which they listened to songs played backwards, to try to detect Satanic influences. Headed by Assemblyman Phillip Wyman, the committee listened to such classic rock songs as "Stairway to Heaven" by Led Zeppelin.

Why? Because a neuroscientist named William H. Yarroll believed he heard subliminal messages supporting Satan worship, and he believed that teens who listened to the music would be subconsciously influenced by them. Yarroll insisted he could hear, during "Stairway

to Heaven" played in reverse, the following message: "I sing because I live with Satan.... The Lord turns me off.... Here's to my sweet Satan." Yarroll also played select parts of songs by the Beatles, Styx, and other rock bands before the committee, and a bill was written to battle "Satanic subliminals"—A.B. 3741—to make it illegal to use back-masked messages and subliminals without knowledge of the listener.

The vote was delayed until the music industry could have its say, as all around the country media reports caused a frenzy of record-smashing parties and a host of new bills introduced to combat back-masking, including a national bill, H.R. 6363, called the "Phonograph Record Backward Masking Labelling Law." None of the bills ever advanced or was passed into law, and soon members of the rock-music industry were com-

Three of the original members of Led Zeppelin: (left to right) Robert Plant, Jimmy Page, and John Paul Jones. Their classic song "Stairway to Heaven" supposedly had Satanic verses when played backwards.

ing forward to lambast the accusations, calling them a tool of religious fanatics to discredit rock music. One pastor, Gary Greenwald, began holding back-masking seminars to teach good Christians how to look for back-masking and fight it, and numerous books hit the market almost immediately exposing the ostensibly demonic aspects of rock music and those who performed it.

In a story called "The Fight to Save America from Satan's Subliminal Rock Messages" that was posted on the *Atlas Obscura* website on October 20, 2016, Bryan Gardiner documents the progression of the attacks by the Religious Right and its attempts to get lawmakers to acknowledge the issue and do something to stop it. He points to Wyman's asking for mandatory warning labels on all rock albums "containing these morally dubious backwards messages." Yarroll said those messages had the power "to manipulate our behavior without our knowledge or consent and turn us into disciples of the Anti-Christ."

The use of back-masking in music actually was a real thing, going back to the 1940s, and many bands later played with it for fun, especially after the Satanic Panic years. Bands began putting silly messages into their albums, but nothing asking young kids to follow the Devil. The Beatles especially toyed with it, as far back as their album *Revolver* in 1966. They also used backwards guitar solos.

But the problem was determining whether back-masking was intentional, or the result of the human brain's seeking patterns that may or may not be there, called "pareidolia," wherein you can find shapes in clouds and see figures on wallpaper. The brain has a tendency to look for something recognizable, especially when it's suggested there may be something there already. Think of it as our attempts to create order out of chaos.

The panic died down at the end of the decade, when many scientists and brain specialists had come forward in the media calling the whole thing silly, along with the music industry, which looked upon the panic with amusement, watching record sales soar as a result. As for "Stairway to Heaven," a spokesperson for the record label Swan Song, issued a very brief response to the allegations—"Our turntables only rotate in one direction." Bob Garcia, the head of A&M Records, stated, "It must be the devil putting these messages on records because no one here knows how to do it."

The idea that music was being used to indoctrinate American youth into Satanism would be repeated again with allegations against subliminal advertising, novels (this is still happening today with the *Harry Potter* book series by J. K. Rowling), movies, and everything else kids are exposed to. But one ironic aspect to this story sheds a lot of light on the dark subject. Those who heard the supposed messages many times did so even without ever actually first hearing the song. Gardiner points out that the California Assembly members Yarrow came before were first given pamphlets with the demonic back-masked words on them, before they ever heard the songs. Because they were told the message would be there, they heard it and only it. But those who knew nothing of potential back-masking heard nothing strange at all ... only the noise of a song being played backwards. Gibberish. Gardiner concludes, "In what has become a staple of modern Intro to Psych perception lectures, professors will often play these back masked songs or similar garbled and distorted messages. When students aren't given any guidance, almost all of them struggle to make sense of the gibberish. Once supplied with a phonetically plausible phrase, however, suddenly they can't hear anything but that phrase."

In years later, bands such as the Electric Light Orchestra ("Fire on High") and Pink Floyd (the "Empty Spaces" track on *The Wall*) would have fun putting messages into their records, and once cassettes took over, the whole subject faded away.

"Nyarlathotep"—The Cthulhu Mythos of H. P. Lovecraft

Paradise Lost—John Milton

The Power of Five—Anthony Horowitz book series

The Sandman comics—Neil Gaiman, 1989–1996

The Silmarillion—J. R. R. Tolkien

The Stand—Stephen King

Our fascination with all things dark, occult, and even demonic also draws us to graphic novels and video games, proving that life mirrors art, and art mirrors life. What intrigues us in life is often also the foundation for good storytelling, art, and entertainment. The unknown, good or bad, pure or evil, will always be a storehouse of story-idea treasures that will no doubt spawn even more movies, television series, books, and games that attempt to characterize our changing and shifting perceptions of the archetypal representations of our own shadow selves, our own dark sides. Our inner demons.

Popular culture succeeded in bringing the dark forces into our homes and our neighborhoods, our television sets, and our local theaters. These forces are stacked on our book shelves and all over our news with reports of demonic possessions, Satanic ritual abuse, and, more recently, lurking evil clowns and internet-created entities like the Rake and Slender Man.

Living vicariously, we get to dance with the Devil and his minions and live to tell about it unscathed.

THE DEVIL IN THE FINE ARTS

Throughout history, artists have tried to capture the images of the Devil, Satan, Lucifer, and demons on canvas. Those images tend to change with the times, but there are common themes. Early Byzantine, Gothic, and Renaissance art often depicted Christian values and motifs, including those of the Devil, Hell, sin, and demons. In the fourteenth century, during the Great Plague, these motifs may have reached their peak, for this was also a time of power in the Christian church and the use of fear to get people to fall in line with Christianity.

American author Stephen King has, no surprise, written a number of novels featuring the Devil, such as *The Stand*.

Art was filled with symbols, since a picture could speak a thousand words. Often Satan was portrayed as a snake, dragon, or serpent. Early paintings of the saints, including Michael and George, show them defeating a dragon-like Satan. Other popular imagery tied to Satan and demons includes:

Tridents and pitchforks—both symbols of the Devil and witchcraft, the activity of demons.

Mischievous and devious snakes—symbolizing the Serpent in the Garden of Eden that led Adam and Eve astray. Especially snakes in fruit trees or holding an apple.

A goat or goat-like creature—signifying the Devil and borrowing from Pan, the pagan god of fertility.

The color red—the color of the Devil and lust. Red was symbolic of sin and temptation, adultery, evil, and the Apocalypse. Could also symbolize the fiery furnace of Hell itself.

Money or a money purse, sometimes with a knife or blade nearby—denotes greed and the materialism of mankind.

Winged insect-like creatures—the Devil and demons often took shape in art as wasps and other winged creatures.

A burnt candle—denotes death, a lack of piety and purity.

Paintings depicting the Devil ran the gamut from huge, ugly, monstrous beings, usually red with horns and a trident tail, to handsome and charming men in suits and flashing smiles. Lucifer in particular was often described as beautiful, luminous, and handsome, until his fall from grace.

According to "The Devil and Demons in Medieval Art" for Temperaworkshop.com, many scholars believe that the earliest artistic representations of Satan came around the sixth century, but not before then. Until the Ecumenical Council of 553 C.E. made belief in Satan official, the Devil in his most well-known Christian form was nonexistent. The Middle Ages changed that, with artwork of devils, demons, and fallen angels showing up on the sides of walls, in paintings, in church art, in sculptures, and even in architecture.

The Devil is often seen with a pitchfork, an instrument for tormenting the damned. The pitchfork by itself is, therefore, often associated with Satan.

"The Devil and Demons in Medieval Art" writer goes on to state, "While figures of Jesus and the Saints achieved standard, recognizable forms during the Middle Ages, there was no unified depiction of Satan, despite the fact he was a key figure in Christianity."

During this period, the Devil was shown variously as a man, an animal, or a fantastical entity that was half-man/half-beast with horns and a pitchfork and forked tail. The article goes on to state, "Since Satan's physical appearance was never described in the Bible, images were often based on pagan horned gods, such as Pan and Dionysus, figures common to the religions Christianity sought to discredit or destroy." The limitations of both language and original descriptions from the Bible allowed artists' imaginations to take over, and some of the imagery has stuck to this day, including the forked tail, trident pitchfork, haunches of a goat, red skin, and horns.

A common motif of art during this time was an icon of goodness, such as Christ or an archangel, standing on top of a squirming, submissive demon/Devil to show domination of good over evil. The 1308 painting by Duccio, *Descent to Hell*, shows Christ standing on the Devil as he greets the Old Testament prophets. In Carlo Crivelli's *Saint Michael*, an altarpiece done as part of the San Domenico around 1476, Lucifer, the fallen one, takes the form of a dragon on the ground, with St. Michael standing victoriously upon him.

During the Middle Ages, depicting the subjects of Heaven and Hell became popular as a method of showing followers what would happen to them if they turned from God. In Stefan Lochner's *The Last Judgment* (1435), demons and devils squirm among human bodies in the pit of Hell, giving a fearful, almost frantic image of eternal damnation. Demons often had looks of sheer glee on their faces as they tortured, burned, and violated the bodies of human sinners. The more fearful the imagery, the easier it was for the Church to maintain control over its flock.

Depictions of Hell and demons within appear to have peaked in the thirteenth century, said to be the same time the Church came to its peak of power. As the Renaissance period unfolded, Satan and demons showed up less often. But his form certainly changed. In *The Changing Face of Satan, from 1500 to Today*, Carey Dunne looks at how the imagery shifted into an almost "anything goes" approach. The beast with more faces than names was depicted over the last five centuries as "a fanged, horned demon; as an armored, Apollo-like army leader; and as a tailor of Nazi uniforms," Dunne writes.

From the 1500s to the 1600s, Satan was usually projected as a beastly monster. Yet as time progressed, he became more human-like as a personification of evil and one that was found within each of us. "In the Middle Ages, artists who wanted to depict Satan … were given surprisingly few details from the Bible about how he should appear," said Bernard Barryte, curator of Stan-

ford's Cantor Center for the Visual Arts.
"Bits and pieces from lots of now-defunct
religions got synthesized: the cloven feet
from Pan, the horns from the gods of various cults in the near east." Eventually, this
became the way we visualized evil—as a
horned, furry beast that stood against God,
Jesus, and the Church.

Literature mimicked art, as seen in
the Devil of Dante's *Inferno*, the first part of
Dante Alighieri's epic fourteenth-century
poem, *Divine Comedy*, which showed him as
a monstrous beast, a creature that existed
deep within the circles of Hell itself. But by

An illustration by Gustav Doré for Dante's *Divine Comedy*.

the eighteenth century, Satan had become a bit more godlike, if not human. In
the 1790 painting by Thomas Stothard, *Satan Summoning His Legions*, he looks
like the god Apollo, even taking on a more heroic and noble appearance.

Eventually, in the nineteenth century, art and literature began to show
Satan's charming side. He showed up as a more human, dandy, dashing figure
that was also very sly. "Instead of scaring people into sin and intimidating
them," Barryte said, "he now uses persuasion." Satan went from bestial to
weasely! And though much of our modern art, imagery, and visuals still show
him with the usual horns and forked tail and pitchfork, more contemporary
artists continue to humanize him, such as in the 1978 Jerome Witkin painting *The Devil as Tailor*, where Satan is a normal person sewing Nazi uniforms
during the war. Satan has become more like us, and Hell, as Barryte points
out, has become a creation of humans right here on Earth.

WHY WE LOVE DEMONS

But why do we have such a powerful attraction to the dark forces, and the
entities that represent it—devils, monsters, demons, and horrible things
that bring harm, pain, and even death. Patricia Donovan, writing for the *UB
Reporter* in her 2011 article "Why We Create Monsters," sums it up: "Monsters
that scare us—vampires, zombies, witches—help us cope with what we dread
most in life. Fear of the monstrous has brought communities and cultures
together over the centuries and serves us as well today as it did in the Dark
Ages." So just as the good in life brings us together as humans in celebration
and joy, the bad in life brings us together in comfort, hope, and even the
expression of our deepest fears. Understanding the Devil and all that the word
entails in a way helps us better know ourselves, individually and collectively.

Even as a nation. "Making sense of the role played by the devil in
American history helps make sense of the nation's self-understanding, its

sense of identity," writes John W. Morehead in his blog "Satan and America." He goes on to say that throughout our history, the Devil has been the nation's "secret self" and the inspiration for witch hunts from Salem to the McCarthy era to today. The Devil we know has become a part of our political, religious, and entertainment landscape, permeating every part of our lives. This is no doubt true of any nation.

Without acknowledging our history of evil, we cannot cherish our history of good. Ugliness and hatred give us a deeper appreciation for beauty and kindness. Our godliness and purity are valuable to us, as are our fear and anger and despair. There cannot be a shadow without light, and no light without something dark to contrast it with. It goes back to the most primitive concept of recognizing duality in nature. The day gives way to night. The sun shines, then the moon. Things are born, and they die.

We might wish the Devil and demonic beings away, thinking them evil and something this world would be entirely better off without. But without them, we might lose something valuable in our own identities, a side of ourselves that must be recognized, the other half that makes us a whole. We simply would not be human without them.

Contacting and Worshipping Satan: Rituals and Rites

Note: the following information is gleaned from a variety of sources and in no way reflects the beliefs of the authors or publisher. This is for informational and research purposes only. Any attempts to use this information to summon a demon is at the risk and responsibility of the reader.

CONTACTING THE DARK SIDE

There are specific means and methods for communicating with demons and summoning the Devil. The practice of either ritual magick or direct magick can both be used to do so, but of course at the risk of the user. Ritual magick involves various gestures, chants, movements, items, and garb, such as black or red robes, and can also be tied into specific times of the month, year, or even moon phases. Direct magick utilizes meditation, chanting, psychic abilities, and a more mental approach involving intention and focus, and doesn't require special tools or structured ritualistic movements. Which one is better depends on the person, for some will resonate toward the power of ritual and charged tools and items, and others will just want to use the power of their own minds. Often, practitioners combine the two for even better results.

To choose to communicate with the Devil, or any of his demons, one must first prepare both mentally and physically. The tips offered below have been gleaned from a variety of sources offering tried and true methods of talking to, and working with, the dark ones.

There are two methods of drawing demons up from the underworld. *Invocation* involves a special invitation to a specific entity to come into manifestation during a ritual. The name of the demon is critical, as often that is all that is needed to bring the entity forward. Invocations can be done in a sacred circle during a ritual, or alone, and as long as the demon stays within the circle, the magickal practitioner can converse back and forth with it and exchange energies. Sometimes the demon will be requested to do something or reveal some wisdom.

An *evocation* is a more forceful way of making a demon come forth. It is a command or a threat, rather than an open invitation, and is done from within a sacred circle, but in this instance, only the demon is inside the circle. The practitioner remains safely outside. The idea here is to dominate the demon and force it to do one's bidding. This is also the method used by Christian exorcists who want to make a demon show itself during a possession rite. Demons are commanded to come forward in God's name, and not their own, which puts demons in a submissive role.

Many paranormal researchers who have appeared on television reality shows use the evocation method and often demand that a demon appear, which has been frowned upon by more professional researchers. To purposefully insult or lash out at an unknown entity or force is not something to be taken lightly; such is done on these shows just for sensationalism and ratings.

Some types of ritual magick involve the use of mirrors, crystal balls, or other tools to help the demon manifest, as well as daggers, athames (double-bladed knives), wands, incense, special candles, and other items that often bear the symbols of the demon. Symbolic drawings might also be used for the protection of the one doing the evocation, though, and are considered talismans. The grimoire, or magickal book of practitioners, contains a number of different evocations for different demonic entities and specific spells, prayers, or rites to be performed. These are usually performed at night, when the veil between the worlds is thinner and there are fewer distractions from the task at hand.

Demons can also be conjured or summoned with incantations and charms that cast spells and open doorways to the Underworld or the world of the entity in question. Spell-casting is often called conjuring, as are Haitian and African voodoo magic using talismans, amulets, animal body parts, powders, and oils in a "conjure" bag. In a more religious context, conjuring can repel demons and spirits and cast a protecting energy around an individual. But usually conjuring is a way to use demons for bringing harm to others or causing negative things to happen.

Angels and spirit guides can also be invoked, evoked, conjured, and summoned, although they tend to respond better to the less-forceful, less-threatening methods of

An athame is a ceremonial knife used in magic rituals.

communication. Magick adepts, experienced in rituals and rites, can summon demons at will with little effort, having found the best means and methods through practice and trial and error.

DEMON GUIDES

Some magickal practitioners suggest picking a specific demon to work with at first, establishing a relationship with it. The goal would be to have that demon act as a guide as you work with magick and follow the left-hand path. The demon might also help expand psychic abilities as well as astral travel and telepathy. Obviously, it requires studying the attributes of demons to choose the right one to work with and make sure the demon is willing to work with a human.

Once the demon of choice is selected, it is critical to be able to tell it why it is being summoned. Asking for anything, including guidance, often means being ready and willing to give something in return to the demon. Doing this can get tricky, so be careful which demon you choose to work with. One of the best ways to discern good demon/spirit guides is to ask for Satan's direct assistance, for he best knows his minions.

How Do They Communicate?

Demons can communicate with us in a variety of ways. They can talk to us. They can give us symbols and imagery to interpret. They can work with our energies, and they can communicate via telepathy. They can appear in a mirror and only that object, or in a scrying ball, or any other object where their reflection can be seen. If they so choose, they will manifest in a more physical sense and write on walls, move objects around, even levitate items to show they are present. They sometimes manipulate smoke or smells in the room.

Going into a trance-like, meditative state can bring about more direct communication methods, as can displaying a sigil or symbol known to the demon on a clean piece of parchment paper, while chanting its name or offering an invocation prayer.

One such prayer might go like this: "Oh, Lord Satan, you alone possess the power to grant my desire. I ask your help, Great Satan, to bring about the results I seek, for you alone are the one true power. Satan, I ask you to bring into manifestation before me the demon _____, whom I seek for guidance and counsel, if it do please you. I ask that this demon must answer my questions truthfully, and give me what I desire in your name, Lord Satan. May I be worthy of receiving your help and your protection always."

This sounds like a prayer to any angel or God figure, asking for help and assitance, even protection, and stating the reason and purpose of the invocation.

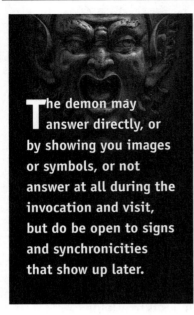

The demon may answer directly, or by showing you images or symbols, or not answer at all during the invocation and visit, but do be open to signs and synchronicities that show up later.

The prayer can be said out loud or in the mind during trance or meditation, while incense or a scented candle burns (preferably black, red, or blue, or the color of the demon being summoned, if it has a favorite), and preferably in an isolated, quiet place where you will not be disturbed.

The demon may not respond to the first invocation. Many attempts may be required before it manifests or makes itself known in any way. Once it does, be prepared not to waste its time and ask your questions. The demon may answer directly, or by showing you images or symbols, or not answer at all during the invocation and visit, but do be open to signs and synchronicities that show up later.

And any good magickal practitioner knows that you must always thank the demon for its time and even offer a token of appreciation such as an offering of food or a trinket. This is no different from the food and trinket offerings pilgrims make to holy statues in Hinduism and Christianity.

Incommunicado Demons

If the demon, or Satan himself, does not respond, perhaps it is because the practitioner is not experienced enough, open enough mentally and psychically, or committed enough. Being open to the experience, even in the presence of fear, is a must for communication to occur. But so is showing a commitment to the dark ways or the left-hand path. Some of the ways suggested to improve the odds of an appearance are: to meditate more, so you are open to voices that are not your own; to practice more; to invoke with other people, as there might be a greater energy to work with; and to go back to the basics of understanding the demon you are trying to win over. Also increasing the intention behind the desire is important, for without a strong intention, the desire to communicate shows up as weak energy.

Most people would never even think of invoking a demon or trying to talk to the Devil, but those who do state that they receive great wisdom, personal power, and even courage. For many it is a strong curiosity or desire to understand the supernatural that drives them to attempt it.

Anyone can communicate with a demon, but those who have abilities as psychics, mediums, and channels may have an edge, as they may have a special gift for sensing nonphysical entities and are already using specific techniques to talk to angels and spirit guides.

Knowing when a demon is around may also require understanding the many forms one might take. If demons are interdimensional entities, they may look nothing like we imagine, and we may not even be able to discern them with our known laws of physics. If they are energy, then our bodies would sense them before we ever see or hear them, so a sensitivity to energy shifts is essential. Visual, auditory, sensual, or emotional responses or reactions may indicate a demon is present, so self-awareness is required. Some practitioners report sudden visual images or symbols popping into their heads, or hearing a phrase or series of words. Think about the many ways people claim to know when they are in the presence of angels or are hearing from God, as these may also apply here.

One of the best ways to discern whether what you are experiencing is real or imagination is to ask for signs throughout the day, or something specific that will help solidify the experience for you. There is indeed the chance that by summoning a demon to ask for its wisdom, you might really be asking your own "inner knowing" and getting the answers from yourself. Without a distinct external presence, the demons we talk to could in fact just be our own inner voices!

One question often asked is, do you have to ask demons or the Devil for bad things? Chances are, doing that would just cause a type of karmic reaction that would bring the evil back upon yourself, so be very careful not to curse others or demand violence against someone. Practitioners ask demons and the Devil for wisdom and guidance, just as they would a "good" deity, but on the more base and material aspects of their lives. And who better to tell you what to be careful of out there in the dangerous world than demons themselves, who can provide warnings of things to come, or better ways to face challenges. What you ask a demon for doesn't have to be evil and horrible.

Some practitioners want to ask demons and the Devil about forbidden, secret, and ancient knowledge that is kept from human eyes and ears. This may include ways to acquire more power, sex, and riches, and increase luck with the more material, hedonistic sides of life. And yes, there are those who want to curse, harm, and destroy others.

Just remember, be careful what you wish for, as your wish might be granted. On a website called World of Azolin, the risks of engaging with demons are spelled out …

Summoning a demon is risky business, to say the least. One must be careful, lest the cost be greater than the reward.

rather frighteningly. "The danger lies in the attempted control of a demonic entity. Such beings do not enjoy being ripped from their homes within the infernal realms and will be greatly enraged by the intrusion into their often incomprehensible plans and designs." Demons, like anyone else, don't like being commanded, so perhaps a more respectful invocation would be in order, but it all depends on the demon in question. The site goes on to say: "The demonologist has but one chance to bring the creature under control. A single slip, just one break in concentration will leave the demon free to roam the material world." Not to mention that the first thing the demon would do is get revenge on the mortal soul who put him there. Tread carefully!

RITUAL

We use rituals in daily life as well as in our religious practices. A ritual is anything we do that has structure or a desired outcome, such as our morning routine of brushing our teeth, washing our face, and getting dressed. That is a ritual. In magickal practice, ritual is a powerful induction method of setting the right stage and mood for demons to come through from their side. The more focused the ritual is, the more powerful the energy used to invoke the demon will be. Structure has incredible power and also shows a respect for the demon being called upon.

Some people perform rituals in Latin for extra effect. But that is not necessary. Some read ancient scripture or religious texts. Again, not necessary. Others cast spells and create elaborate circles on the ground with specially chosen tokens and symbols. That, too, is not necessary. You can work at an altar or in an empty room with just a circle in white chalk on the ground with a large pentagram drawn inside. What matters is the strong intent of the practitioner and the focus of his or her energy to bring about the desired result.

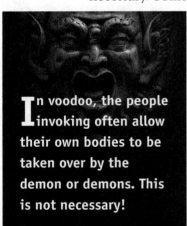

In voodoo, the people invoking often allow their own bodies to be taken over by the demon or demons. This is not necessary!

In voodoo, the people invoking often allow their own bodies to be taken over by the demon or demons. This is not necessary! There can be very specific language in your invocation prayer or commands that keep this from happening, if you do not want to experience the possession by a dark spirit. Another important instruction is always to close the ritual and the connection with the demon before walking away or leaving, because if you don't, you take the demon and its energy with you into your everyday life.

If using a Ouija™ board, or spirit board, it is always best to work in groups or say a protection prayer for yourself so you don't bring across anything unwanted. Specific invocations to a named demon work best, otherwise an object that serves as an open door is exactly that—an open door.

First, you must decide if it is the Devil himself or a demon you wish to reach and make contact with. All are quite different, as we've seen, and require different approaches. The key is to be well-prepared ahead of time, having studied demons and demonology as much as possible.

Basic rituals can be found all over the Internet, including instructional videos. But for purposes of this book, we've condensed a number of them into a simple, basic form that can be adapted accordingly.

First, bathe your body to show respect, and dress comfortably, preferably in a black gown or robe with red trimmings. Find a clean room away from distractions, and prepare your tools and space, which will be an altar and a large area on the ground nearby to draw your sacred circle. The tools might be a sigil, a pentagram, jewelry, candles, incense, or daggers/athames that have been charged with magickal energy, done in a separate ritual beforehand. The daggers will not be used to kill anything, just to be placed upon the altar you are using in a symbolic fashion, and the same goes for the athame. Fifteen minutes or so before the ritual, light some incense to prepare the room.

Light the candles, preferably black and red with silver candleholders (unless invoking Lucifer, who prefers blue candles), and draw a large circle in chalk, salt, or some other chosen material. Within the circle draw or place a drawing of a pentagram. You can also surround the circle with black candles if you wish. Depending on the entity you wish to communicate with, you will either stand in the circle during the summoning or stand outside it. As noted before, if the demon is a nasty one, stand outside it.

Get into a meditative or trance-like state before speaking the invocation. An altered state of consciousness allows for a deeper level of interchange between this world and the worlds of other entities, and it also keeps the analytical mind busy. Rituals are repetitive for this very reason, as it puts those involved in a trance-like state of receptivity and awareness.

Speak the invocation along with the name of the entity you wish to communicate with or, as the case may be, do business with. Again, watch where you are standing. Some choose to stay at the altar, but if the demon is violent and you want to dominate it, you must not step into the circle. The demon, if it manifests in a physical sense, will do so within the circle. If you have a written invocation, you can prick your finger and sign it in your own blood before reading.

A standard ritual to Satan found on Angelfire.com suggests first calling upon the Four Crowned Princes of Hell while ringing a bell and turning in each direction counterclockwise, while imagining a powerful blue light entering your entire being:

Satan/Lucifer to the East

Beelzebub to the North

Astaroth to the West

Azazel to the South

Once you feel fully charged with magickal energy, you may begin the actual prayer of invocation. Some practitioners have a chalice on their altar filled with wine or a red liquid to symbolize blood, and they drink it after reciting their personal prayer.

Another example of a prayer, which does not involve asking for anything to manifest, is:

> I stand before you, Great and Mighty Lucifer, giver of light, morning star, and offer my thanks for desires fulfilled. I renounce all others that you alone may be the receiver of my glory and admiration. Your wisdom is my power. Your energy, my lifegiving blood. I proclaim to you, Lucifer, Great Fallen One, that I will honor you all my days and offer my life as a vessel for your expression and command on earth. Thank you, Lucifer, for the success of all my endeavors. I am your honorable servant. So mote it be.

Once the prayer is spoken, you may burn it if in written form using one of the sacred candles on the altar.

If you succeed in manifesting a demon, or the Devil, or Satan, speak your purpose clearly and firmly, but respectfully and with a bit of reverence for the powers standing before you. When you have done so, if you choose to engage in asking questions to be answered, you can now do so and always offer appreciation and gratitude.

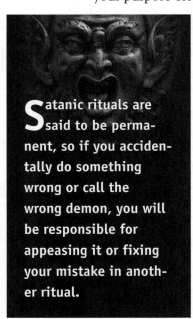

Satanic rituals are said to be permanent, so if you accidentally do something wrong or call the wrong demon, you will be responsible for appeasing it or fixing your mistake in another ritual.

If your goal is to command the demon to do your bidding, state so, powerfully and with authority, with Satan's authority if you have done a pre-ritual asking for his assistance with a demon. Then end the ritual by stating "So shall it be," "So mote it be," "Hail, Satan," or interchange the name of the demon you are speaking with. Always say a clearing prayer to command the demon go back to where it came from, and do not destroy the circle until you are sure it has.

Satanic rituals are said to be permanent, so if you accidentally do something wrong or call the wrong demon, you will be responsible for appeasing it or fixing your mistake in another ritual. But normally, any ritual is done only once.

If you are intending only to offer praise to Satan, there is no need to call up any demons or worry about clearing the circle. Simply speak your prayer and end it.

Sound too simple? The truth is, any ritual has a basic structure, and we are permitted to embellish it as we see fit. This is the case in any religious tradition, where the beliefs of the members of a church or temple will adjust and adapt as they wish.

Look at the different modes of dress among priests, ministers, and other church authorities, in different traditions. Some are far more elaborate than others. The same goes for the architecture and design of the church or temple exterior and interior, with everything from tents to lavish, gold-plated, multilevel megachurches that seat ten thousand people.

Whether you perform a ritual wearing a black robe and hood lined with red velvet, or jeans and a T-shirt, is up to you, but often wearing ritualistic garb adds to the power and emotional impact.

Blood Sacrifices

Most Satanists just don't go there. It isn't a part of their beliefs or requirements. If any blood sacrifices are made, they are done more because of the violent nature of the individuals performing the ritual than because of the devil or demons requiring it. There are many traditions such as voudon and Santeria that still sacrifice animals, usually chickens, to the gods, but most modern practitioners of any spiritual system have found it unnecessary.

Yes, our ancestors sacrificed humans to the deities, even those who lived at the dawn of the Abrahamic religions, but this was before the advent of science, when we understood that sacrifice wasn't influencing or affecting nature in any way. According to the *World of Azolin* website, "The archetypal demonologist, for many common folk, is one who performs the most hideous ritual sacrifices in the pursuit of his black art. The truth is a little different and many demonologists actually shun such practices." There will be cults and sects that do engage in this practice, but it is not a required practice for anyone wishing to train in the occult arts.

Advanced Rituals

Though casting any spell comes with the warning that it comes back around to you, if you choose to cast one, candles are often one of the best tools. Each color can represent either a desire to be manifested, or a problem/habit/behavior to be cast out. Black magick of course prefers black or red candles, although navy blue is acceptable. These colors represent death, anger, passion, darkness, and rage.

A sword can be brought into play as a prop to invoke the demons of Hell. A sword can represent the air element and can be useful in working with more violent demons. However, by using the sword, and first invoking the elements—air, water, earth, and fire—you can infuse yourself with additional power for dealing with the darkest of energies, often those of elemental origins. Some practitioners may instead choose to use a wand for this purpose.

Many demons want something in return for the wisdom, help, and insights you are asking them for in your ritual. Do some research to see what might be applicable, or offer the demon some of your time to do its bidding in the world, if you can handle it. Remember, demons and the Devil are materialistic and do not take kindly to being used, or taken advantage of, so be prepared to give something … just not your soul! At the very least, any wise advice a demon passes on should be appreciated with a prayer of thanksgiving.

The idea that rituals offered to Satan and his ilk are all about evil and death and killing is false. The Church of Satan states on its site, which includes much information about its own rituals and customs, "Greater Magic, which is our name for our ritual practice, is basically meant as self-transformational psychodrama.… The pageantry of ritual is a drama meant for emotional stimulation, not a belief in or worship of any power higher than the projected will of the magician."

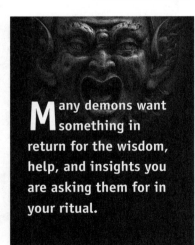

Many demons want something in return for the wisdom, help, and insights you are asking them for in your ritual.

Much of the power of ritual comes from the charging of emotional energy that is then directed to the intended desire. Called the "extended mind" by biologist/author Rupert Sheldrake, this is a powerful form of transmitting focused energy onto something to influence and affect it. The Church of Satan does use ritual in its modern practices, but states, "We emphasize that the philosophy of the Church of Satan does not require that our members believe that ritual is more than an emotional experience, nor is there a mandate even to ritualize at all." Thus, ritual is a personal and group choice used for things like initiations, transitions, weddings, funerals, blessings, and baptisms, as well as invoking spirits. This applies to Satanism as much as it does to any other religion.

In "About Satanic Rituals" by Geifodd ap Pwyll for TheisticSatanism.com, the author and magickal practitioner writes that there is only one item truly necessary for a good Satanic ritual: yourself. No need for priests or authority figures, altars or circles, or anything outside of yourself. You can act as your own priest. He does point out that Satanic worship is more about "spending time in prayer with the Prince of Darkness, and to re-confirm my commitment to the path." Devil-worship, on the other hand, may require ritual because its purpose is different in focus. One is more of a prayer ceremony, the other a Magickal ritual. The author also dispels the belief that all Satanists practice "black mass," which is the totally opposite ritual to the standard Catholic Mass—a belief perpetuated by Christians and conspiracy theorists. Some individuals or groups may choose to do a reverse Catholic Mass, but it is not necessary in true Satanic churches and temples.

Pwyll writes, "For me, a black mass is absolutely any kind of complex ceremony that is performed in honor of the Prince of Darkness. Whether it actually resembles a Catholic mass or not is unimportant. It only has to be some kind of complicated ceremony in which worship is specifically given to Satan." Therefore, one could call any ceremonial magickal ritual a "black mass" even if it didn't in any way mimic the Catholic Mass. This goes back to the use of the word "black" to connote anything dark, evil, or negative … or against the teachings of the accepted religion of the times.

The main key to successfully communicating with and working with the darker forces is to educate oneself fully as to what they are, how they operate, and what knowledge they may hold that can be useful to a human life. Working with dark forces can be done alone, or with a group. It can be structured, or you can just wing it. It can be in a ritual form or just a silent meditation and prayer. It can be for pure evil or for sheer attainment of wisdom and material power. It can be complex or simple. It can involve the sacrifice of a small animal or the sacrifice of good or of time.

Talking to and working with demons, worshipping the Devil or Satan, and engaging in an exchange of favors with dark entities are not things to be undertaken lightly. How you do it, why you do it, and the result of doing it are all up to the individual and the demon or devil you're dealing with. There will always be those who look at communicating with demons as a joke, or something to do on a Friday night, but serious demonologists and exorcists advise strongly against such attitudes.

There is also the psychological argument that trying to compel demons to do one's bidding is really only a form of utilizing purely human dark energies to attain goals and manifest material fame and fortune. If we look at human behavior, we see a lot of these darker traits at work in politics, world affairs, and even sports and entertainment. Greed, lust, deception, theft, arrogance, narcissism, and manipulation of other people are often considered acceptable behaviors in the business world and in our celebrated heroes, who are often given fame and wealth by the public for these negative behaviors. Perhaps our need to ask for help from demons is just a psychological excuse for desiring to use the demons within for our own gain.

Personal Testimonials

Demons … the Devil … dark angels…. To many, these are religious or historical concepts, or the subjects of entertainment and lore that don't affect everyday life. We can research and read about the demonic world and those that inhabit it, but it is a detached level of engagement. This is why the subject resonates most with people when they can read about the personal experiences of those who have encountered and dealt with such forces.

To many, dark entities and energies are a part of everyday life. What follows are real experiences recorded in writing and sent to the authors involving dark entities, events, and situations. Interestingly, we had many submissions from people who later asked that we not include them because the very act of their writing down their experiences and sending them to us had opened up new paranormal activity in their homes. We in no way wish to cause anyone any harm in presenting these stories. Often, we have been told that reliving an experience dredges up memories one might not want to deal with. In the case of demonic activity, it might also dredge up an actual renewal of activity, so we do hope that everyone who chose to contact us is safe. There is something real to all this … even if we have yet to find a one-size-fits-all scientific explanation.

In some cases, the encountered presence may have been truly demonic, in others a misidentified encounter with a simple ghost. We make no judgments, for the world is a vastly more mysterious place than we think.

MARIA ROGERS

When I was 15, I used a Ouija™ board with my sister. We talked with someone who told us he was killed in a car wreck not far from our house. I was skeptical of what was happening. We had a new puppy then. We would put him in a corner of the garage at night because we were potty training him. Two weeks later I had a real scary experience. I woke up one night and heard something coming down the hall. I didn't pay it any mind. Just figured it was the puppy. Closed my eyes. Started to fall back asleep but noticed the sound still was coming and it made its way to my room. Next thing I know, I was overcome with something holding me down. I felt tingly all over, too. I couldn't move. I could see my mom in her bed across the hall. I tried to call for her but could not. No sound came out. I began to hear whispering around my ears. I was terrified. I started calling for the Virgin Mary to help me and saying the Lord's prayer. Soon after, whatever it was went away. The next day I took that Ouija™ board, hopped on my bike and threw it in a dumpster a mile away.

PENNIE BROWN

One night, when my oldest son was three months old, a tall, dark, black entity appeared in my house. I was in the living room with my son; it was about midnight and my husband was working the night shift. Now I am no stranger to apparitions as I have seen them my entire life, but this one was dark, blacker than black, and I got the distinct feeling it wanted my son. I grabbed my son and ran into my bedroom, shutting the door behind me. It came right through the door behind us. I got all the way up on my bed, up as far as I could go and into the middle of my bed. I held my son tight and started praying. I kept telling it that it Could Not have my son, that he was mine and it needed to go, to move on. I begged it to leave him alone. I tried talking to it, telling it I had already miscarried two babies, that my son was a gift from God and I Was Not going to let it take my son.

I really don't know if it was "demonic," but I knew in my heart it was "Death" and it was wanting my baby. It kept floating up to the ceiling and then back down again, moving from one side of the bed to the other and around the foot of the bed. It would reach out towards us but as long as I kept praying it didn't seem to be able to get onto or above the bed, it was like the prayers provided a protective shield around the bed. I battled this tall dark shadow all night. Finally, at about 5–5:30 it looked at us, then flew from the left side of the foot of the bed to the wall and window that was on the right side of the room, then went right through the wall and disappeared. That's when I realized that the sun was just coming up. I sat there holding my son for several hours. Afraid to put him down and afraid it might come back. The relief I felt from that night was short lived.

A few days later I was reading our local paper when I came to the obituaries. It was there that I read that a baby boy, born the same day, in the same hospital as my son had died on the same date that I had battled against this darkness from taking my son. I couldn't help but wonder if he was the same baby boy I had held in my arms the day after my son was born. I had stayed in the hospital three days with my son. The day after my son was born the nurses had brought me the wrong baby from the nursery. I noticed the error when changing him. They didn't use security bands on babies yet back then. My son was born with two birthmarks which this baby didn't have, that's how I realized they had made the mistake. I can't even describe the terrible guilt I have felt ever since finding out another baby died that day.... I know it is tough for some people to believe in the paranormal, but these things really do happen. I know first-hand. I don't know what this was; if it had or has a job to do that we don't fully understand, or if it IS something dark and evil.... I pray it is not the latter. What this experience did bring home to me is that there are consequences to all of our actions, whether we get to realize them or not.

STANISLAV B.

For a long time I've had very powerful dreams. They usually have a very strong effect on me and set me on the right spiritual track. In general, my dreams tend to be biblical—visions and messages, of sorts. But one night I had the most horrible experience I can remember. There's nothing else that I can compare it to.... I was sleeping (in the dream/vision) in the bedroom when all of a sudden a thick shadow began to cover everything. It was so dark and black you could almost touch it. It got cold, very cold, but also very still.... Then the door opened on its own and through it came this ... Thing ... tall, sleek, thin.... With its big head and eyes as black as nothing you could possibly imagine.... And when it looked into my eyes I felt a terror grip my body like nothing I had experienced before.... I couldn't move my legs or my hands or anything....

My dad was sleeping on the other bed (this is still in the dream) and I said, "Dad! Wake up! Can't you see it?" And he just stirred and said, "You know what to do. Just tell it to go away." The creature was slowly getting closer, but when it heard my father and saw that I'm beginning to think, its face began to look angry. I said, "You're not welcome here! Go away, in the name of Jesus Christ, and don't come back!" And at that point it was like an electric jolt ran through it and it gave out this horrible angry scream ... as if something had punched it really hard. It just got thrown out of the door and that thick shadow began to lift. I woke up at that point in [a] cold sweat, and I could remember every detail of that dream as if it had just really happened. I was shaking from head to toe.... I don't know if it was just a nightmare or something real that happened, but I definitely know that this creature was demon-

It got cold, very cold, but also very still.... Then the door opened on its own and through it came this ... Thing ... tall, sleek, thin....

ic. I would describe its appearance [as] not very different from what people think of as an alien. This experience convinced me beyond any doubt that those are not things from another planet.

JASON MANSFIELD

I never considered it during, only realized it after. But doing all my on-site ghost research I used to invite entities to come with me, I blew it off as I would go to these places and nothing would happen. I would leave my team and go to town and—boom—crap would happen. I got cocky, I got bold, I got challenging. My team psychic told me I had an attachment.... I blew it off as BS. My moods got worse, my pain doubled. I blew it off, I became bitter, angry, almost to the point of violence, but seemed to hold my ground and it was only verbal abuse (thank God), visions of death, killing, silencing dumb asses filled my head ... weight of the world on my shoulders, money issues ... and I started to try and change ... boom Heart Attack and death. I lay on a table for three hours with no heart[beat], only a machine putting oxygen in my blood ... and poorly at that. When I awoke ... that weight was lifted. I no longer scoff at true paranormal (dimensional shifting). I'm a skeptic, but I now KNOW real from fake instantly. My abilities are tenfold, and NOTHING IS ATTACHED TO ME. I no longer fear death. I fear humanity! Was this demonic that attached to me???? I never saw its ugly face, only to once look in a mirror and freak out as the reflection was not of my own.... I thought someone was in the room, my face wasn't my face.... Demonic ... matter of interpretation I guess.... I'll not let my guard down again that's for sure.

JON

When I was in undergraduate college I had an encounter. My fraternity house sat on the edge of campus near open ground, which ran up against farm fields about 1/4 mile off. It was Ohio Northern for crying out loud. :-) My junior or senior year on a Friday as usual I found myself in my room studying. The price I paid for a nontraditional major in college. Throughout my college years there were times when things were quiet and the week was low octane in school work, and I could feel my sensitivity being stronger than normal. I would meditate to keep my defenses up and just wander around various images of things going through my mind about campus, flash images of things that might be in the future, etc. There were one or two buildings on campus known to be kind of spiritually active, and I usually kept my time in those places to a minimum. My fraternity house was relatively new, no major events there (other than beer, weed, and the usual college stuff), and no history of anything weird going on.

On that Friday night there were few people in the fraternity house ... nor the other campus housing, which was within at least a long stone's throw from our house. I went downstairs to the kitchen to grab a bowl of cereal to snack on, and it hit me like a lightning bolt. I looked out the window and though I could not see "it," the presence was extremely powerful, and for lack of a better word it was looking at me. Maybe 100 meters outside the building and in one of those long stretches of fields of mowed grass—for lack of a better way of describing it—something was standing or hovering in a field. I paused for a moment and shook my head, trying to shake it off, but this was not an illusion. It was getting strong and closer.

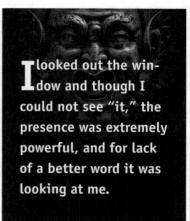

I looked out the window and though I could not see "it," the presence was extremely powerful, and for lack of a better word it was looking at me.

I returned upstairs to my room quickly, closed the door, but did not lock it, turned on the TV, and sat in my favorite chair, trying to find something to watch. This was unlike occasions in my life when I sensed something but I kind of deflected the feeling and that would be that.

In a very short period of sitting up there in my room, I knew whatever this was it was not going to go away. Was this a demon in the Judeo-Christian sense[?] … [I] have no idea and I have my own views on that. As a practicing Russian Orthodox [man], I'm sure you'll understand my religion and my faith are separate things. :-) Whatever it was, this much was true:

1. It was real, and it was powerful, and it was intelligent. In your own work, I'm sure you are familiar with the idea some "ghosts" or events like that are the actual intelligence of someone who has passed away …, and in other cases it is simply a historical event that keeps replaying itself when the time is right, the conditions are right, etc. In my other homeland of Scotland, people report every year seeing Queen Boudicca riding through a British military base on her chariot. In my opinion … just a taped image replaying itself … no more. This was no past image replaying itself … I was certain of that. It was a distinct intelligence.

2. It did not take on a specific shape…. I could say cone-shaped or cloaked figure, but that does not do it justice. The closest thing I could describe is it was like a slowly swirling form of black flame.

3. It gave off an energy of a sort but it was like the absence of energy…. It absorbed light … not reflected it *per se*.

4. There's no other way for me to explain this…. It knew who I was personally…. I felt like it knew me and was looking for me.

5. It was a rage like you cannot imagine…. It was angry …; it was there with purpose …; and it was there looking for me or perhaps someone like me.

Eventually, I felt I had to go full bore on this as there was no acting like it was not there. Fortunately, I had no roommate, so this made the following easier without going into long explanations with people who don't get this stuff. I turned off the TV and instead turned on my mood music on my stereo (Stephen Hill's program out of San Francisco), lit three candles, and arranged [them] in a triangle on the outer edges of the center of my room. I created a circle of sea salt around myself with a circle of water around the outside of that circle. I held the I-Ching pendant I normally wear in my hands and began reciting various prayers. In my mind, I created a wall and concentrated throughout the night on slowly pushing whatever it was away. Not striking at it or trying to—how can you even say this—"harm it." Simply to slowly push it away.

This went on for hours, and I was in a cold sweat throughout the night.... Around 3 A.M. it finally moved off. I fell back on my bed and quickly passed out.

I never encountered an experience on that level again in my life, and there were no further episodes while I was in school. The next morning, I took a very hot shower, vacuumed up the room, bought more candles ;-), went to the gym, and moved on.

Demon ... hard to say. It was powerful ... very powerful ... dare I use this term ... "ancient"?

JAMES "PAT" SULLIVANT

I've had two interactions that I feel were clearly demonic, as opposed to angry, spirits. I'm going to list them both here because the first interaction sets the stage for the second, even though they were decades apart. To this day, I clearly/distinctly remember both episodes.

The first interaction happened when I was 13 years old. I was the victim of a demonic possession attempt. Like most kids that age, I was full of myself and convinced that I was greater than I really was, and after watching a horror movie about demons, I spouted off to my friends/family that I wasn't afraid of demons because I was too strong to be possessed (at that time, I did not fully understand about psychic abilities or how they seem to attract spiritual entities, both good and bad). That night, a couple of hours after going to bed, I woke up feeling very feverish/nauseous [sic] and sensing that something was clearly WRONG here (I don't know how else to explain it). I thought to myself that I need to get out of bed and go throw up in the bathroom, but when I tried, I couldn't get my body to respond. I was able to start to sit up, but then I just collapsed back and could not move anymore ..., and that's when I felt/sensed the entity that was trying to possess me. It felt malignant/evil to me (kind of like when you run into a person who you can immediately tell is really bad/would harm or kill you just for fun). Also, I heard a voice in my head mocking me for my earlier comments.

Being full of myself, and believing my own crap, I threw everything I had at this being, but all to no avail. I tried to will it out. I tried to force my body to move. I tried to call out for help (my parents were in their bedroom, just down the hall). Nothing worked. After about 15 minutes of fighting/trying to move my body, I started to feel my consciousness slipping away. Talk about being terrified. Here I was this 13-year-old egotistical little brat, and suddenly I was losing in a battle that I clearly identified as being the end of who I was should I lose. And I was losing badly....

As a last resort, I remembered that my grandfather had been a Methodist minister for nearly 30 years, and with nowhere else to turn I called out in my mind for help from God/Jesus.... And just like that it happened. I suddenly felt the entity stop (and I also felt its anger, then fear). A second voice came into my head and said, "But believe in me and nothing in this universe can harm you. Fear no evil for I am with you." Having no other option, I submitted to this second voice and accepted Christ. Much to my surprise, I physically felt arms encircle my body, and I immediately felt more safe/secure than I have ever felt in my life, either before or since. It felt to me like my grandfather had wrapped me in his arms and nothing really could harm me. In that exact same instant, the demonic presence was gone, as well as all of the fever/nausea.

I know this sounds like a Christian channel infomercial, but you need to understand: at that time/that age I was not a Christian, nor did I have a strong belief in the Christian religion. I called out simply because I felt I had nowhere else to turn ..., and I was saved by doing so. To this day, I don't know why God intervened, but I thank him all the time that he did. This was also the day that I truly began to pay attention to the paranormal. I discovered that after having experienced this episode, I could sense all kinds of external energies (physical and spiritual) that were around me. Once I recognized that, I really began to pay attention (until an episode in my late teenage years scared me so much I refused to embrace/accept the paranormal for many years after, but that's a ghost story, not a demon story).

Flash forward to winter 2011. I am a practicing paranormal/psychic investigator working with a team in Colorado Springs (I re-engaged when a spirit started terrorizing my children after bedtime in one of the homes we lived in). They have asked me to come on this investigation with them because they have reports that the mom in the house is being possessed, and they are wanting to confirm if there is any real threat to the children in the home. When we first got there, we asked the family to leave for about three hours (to try and catch evidence without them in the house). We set up all of our computers/wireless equipment in the garage, thinking to keep them free of any internal energy interference that might be in the home.

> **M**uch to my surprise, I physically felt arms encircle my body, and I immediately felt more safe/secure than I have ever felt in my life, either before or since.

During those three hours, we recorded absolutely no evidence of anything …, but then the family came home. As soon as they entered the home, things picked up immediately. We started noticing orbs in the camera footage, and they seemed to be following her [the mom] from room to room. Also, we saw footage of the woman's eyes go from brightly reflecting the IR camera light to almost pitch black, and she didn't even blink/move her head.

It was at that point that I started taking a very active role in the investigation by subtly following her everywhere she went and into every room. It took about 10 minutes for her to realize what I was doing, but once that happened things got very involved very fast. She asked me why I was following her, and I responded, "Why do you think[?]" Immediately after my response, she collapsed onto the floor and started thrashing and what appeared to be babbling. Initially I thought it might just be a ghost attempting possession, but very quickly I realized that the babbling was actually not babbling. It was specific comments aimed at me that only I would know the answers to in the group of people who were there. She was using a sing-song/off-key voice and talking very fast, so that it was very hard to understand what she was saying, but as I concentrated on it more, I began to make it out. I had recently been studying some end-of-days/2012 stuff, and while I had strong doubts, I had noticed that some of the "prophecies" seem to be coming to fruition.

This spirit told me that 2012 was not the end, but that the end was much closer than I imagined. I had also been having family issues with some of my children, and it told me that I would die an old man, all alone and miserable. She also called me Priest … and I rarely discuss my deep religious beliefs/experiences with anyone, especially not with those on that Paranormal Team. It was at that point I started realizing that I was not dealing with a human spirit (I had studied exorcisms enough to know that knowledge of others that the possessed person would never know was a common occurrence with demonic possession).

At this point, I reached out with my psychic perceptions, and I immediately felt an energy very similar to what I had felt as a child … only not nearly as powerful. It was at that same moment that she attacked me physically (for the first time that night). I am trained in Kajukenbo martial arts. I don't think she/it was expecting that. I immediately took her to the ground and wrapped her up so that she could not harm me/herself in any way. She was very strong, perhaps even stronger than me (I am 6'1" and 240 lbs.). But I had enough leverage/position on her that she could not get away.

At that point her husband jumped in and she immediately froze/calmed down (and appeared to come out of the possession). I released her, and then we discussed for about 20 minutes what had happened. She told me she was aware of what was going on, but it felt like it was all happening to someone else … not her. We then took a break for about another 20 minutes.

When they came back into the room, we started talking about what we captured during the investigation, how it all started up right after they got home. I had set some K2s [a K2 is a meter for detecting electrical energy from moving sources] next to her for the discussion, and both immediately went off, full Red, as soon as we started talking about something following her room to room. She then collapsed again and just started shrieking. Her husband and I held her down for about five minutes until she stopped. At that point, we let her up, and she appeared to be normal again. However, my senses were telling me she was not. I think she picked up on me picking up on her because suddenly all of the power to the house turned off. She whipped around on me and physically attacked me again, expecting me to be caught unaware. I wasn't. I immediately shouted in my mind, "By the power of the Father, the Son, and the Holy Spirit, I command you be still!"

Much to my surprise, and by the look on her face hers as well, she dropped like a rock. It was like whatever was driving her just ceased. She lay there on the ground for a minute, and then she seemed to come back to herself, and she broke out crying and started hugging me. She said she could not stop whatever had taken control of her, but that somehow, as soon as she touched me, I had stopped it. I explained what had happened, and she immediately understood. Told her it was not me, but rather the Lord working through me. She expressed her concerns about being raised anti-Christian, and I explained to her that it was never too late to reconsider/re-evaluate.

> She lay there on the ground for a minute, and then she seemed to come back to herself, and she broke out crying and started hugging me.

We then talked about everything that had happened that night for another hour or so, and no further possessions/paranormal events took place. One thing to note was that when the power went out, not only did we lose any footage we had of that immediate event, we also lost much of what we had recorded earlier onto one of our two laptops. Some files were deleted, and others were corrupted. It was as if the entity had somehow gotten into the computer's files and corrupted them. There was no one down in the garage at that time. I know the files had been fine up to that point because I was reviewing some of the earlier footage while we were taking our break just before.

Can I 100% confirm that this was a demon and not some other spirit[?] No. However, between everything we experienced and what I felt psychically, I am about 95% confident that it was. Let me also say that while I have studied a little bit about exorcisms, I have in no way ever tried to practice it. Her response to me that night proved to me that this was a spirit in opposition to Jesus Christ. That, by using his name, I was able to incapacitate it in a way that I hadn't really thought about doing (it just came to me, instantly, to think that, and when I did there was an immediate result).

KAARIN ALISA

I've always been a metaphysical explorer, driven to experiment with the mysterious and unknown. But when I was young, still in high school, I didn't possess enough experience to be appropriately cautious. These early experiments with the paranormal took many forms, and all were mostly clumsy attempts to experience something new. The curious and delightful outcomes of these attempts were seminal to my decision to devote myself to metaphysics. However, some of the outcomes were quite frightening. The events I recount now took place on a simple Friday night in spring.

A group of schoolmates and I drove to an old abandoned farmhouse to hold a séance. We had earlier scouted out the forebidding property as a place we could meet without interruption. The farmhouse was built in the 1800s and had been empty for at least 40 years. It was decrepit, and even though it was springtime after a wet winter, and the house was situated in the middle of well-watered crop fields, all the bushes, grass, and trees near the house were dead and brown. In our youthful innocence, we didn't think anything of it other than it added to the mysterious ambiance of the place.

On this night, we climbed the fence and hiked about a quarter mile up the hill to the house. When we arrived, we set up for the séance. We nailed a light blanket over the open doorway to shield candle flames from any breeze. Unfortunately, we didn't have enough nails to keep the blanket from flapping open, so two of us hefted a round of concrete and placed it on the bottom of the blanket to hold it firmly in place. I estimate that the concrete round weighed approximately 80 pounds. It's important to note that there was a light breeze that night, but no real wind, nothing but temperate California spring weather.

The séance advanced the same as always. First, we sat in a circle with lit candles in the middle. Next, we held hands. The literature I'd read was quite clear that we were not to break hands throughout the séance, no matter what happened, the idea being that the circle of light and energy we created through the clasping of hands would shield and protect us.

Then a series of incantations and intentions were recited to create the right atmosphere for manifestations to take place. We had thus far been so successful with sounds, floating objects, channeled entities, and other mysterious events, that we felt quite emboldened. Nothing had yet frightened us. We were startled a few times, but not scared.

I was acting as the medium. We began the session receiving some channeled information about what had happened at the house. Details about a little girl that had died in the house came through. It was interesting, but not special. After a period of this channeling, suddenly the tenor of the room changed significantly. The atmosphere seemed to take on a dark, almost electric charge that caused a few in the group to remark aloud about it.

Then it started. We began to hear scratching on the roof of the house. Sounds as if a large animal was scraping heavy claws across the boards. The clawing got louder and more insistent. I continued to intone our invite [sic] to interact with anyone present as the noise of the scraping got louder and louder. And then, just as suddenly as the noise had begun, it stopped. It became very quiet, abnormally quiet, as if we were in a vacuum.

What happened next would be unbelievable to me if I had not been there and experienced it first-hand. We heard a deep, male voice laughing in a sinister manner. The blanket we nailed to the open door-way ripped forcefully from the wall and flew across the room. More astounding than the blanket, the heavy round of concrete that had been holding down the blanket lifted on its own and flew across the room, slamming into the wall. Everyone was startled, so I cried out, "Remember not to break the circle. Hold hands, don't let go!"

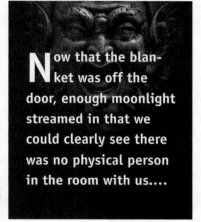

Now that the blanket was off the door, enough moonlight streamed in that we could clearly see there was no physical person in the room with us....

Abruptly, all the candles snuffed [out] at once, and we heard what sounded like someone wearing a heavy pair of boots walk slowly around the circle behind us. Small red orbs of light were flying about the room. Now that the blanket was off the door, enough moonlight streamed in that we could clearly see there was no physical person in the room with us, it was just the sound of the boots clunking and the creaking of the old floorboards as if the steps had weight to them. The footsteps paused a few times, but kept pace slowly around the circle until they stopped right behind me. I could hear all of us breathing heavily, barely containing our fear responses.

Then, I felt a heavy hand slam down onto my shoulder and we heard the same deep, male voice say, "You're the one."

I yelped uncontrollably and terror gripped everyone. The circle was instantly broken, most of my friends bolted out the open door. I couldn't move. I will never know for certain if it was sheer terror that temporarily paralyzed me, or if it was an effect caused by the entity that grabbed me. Two of my male friends had enough presence of mind to pick me up and carry me from the house and down the hill; otherwise I would have been left behind.

We all gathered on the road by the cars. As I was recovering my ability to move normally, I realized that my eyeglasses were missing. I had very bad eyesight and I needed glasses to function. Everyone agreed that the glasses had probably dropped on the path coming back to the cars or more probably were still at the farmhouse. But no one, including me, was willing to go back. We literally feared for our lives. We were sure that what we had experienced was pure evil—demonic in nature. The feeling of the entity's presence was overwhelmingly negative and violent.

Finally, one of my friends, who was Catholic and very brave, had some religious paraphernalia with him and volunteered to go back up the path and into the house if necessary to find my glasses. I was frightened for him, but he insisted he'd be fine. So, armed with his faith and a weak flashlight, he started up the path to the house by himself.

It felt like an eternity that we were standing around waiting for him to return. More than half an hour went by and we were past worry. We were coming to the conclusion that we should do the right thing and go back up the hill as a group to find him, each of us deathly afraid of doing so, but feeling morally obliged.

As we were climbing over the fence, we heard him yelling, "Start the cars! Start the cars!" Then we saw him, running at full speed down the hill. He yelled again, "We have to get out of here now!" When he got to us, he urged us into the cars and away from the scene as fast as possible. He was wide-eyed, disheveled, and white as a sheet, and, beyond belief, he actually had my glasses. I wish I could recount his experiences as well, however, as we sped away from the house, I asked him what happened and he refused to tell. He said it was horrible and he vowed to never talk about it.

I'm grateful that by some means we all got out of that farmhouse relatively unharmed. I say relatively because two of my friends were so emotionally disturbed by the events they had to go into counseling. One friend left our group and disappeared into her religion. I had bruises on my shoulder in the shape of a hand, and one of the other young women had striped scratches across her belly. She couldn't remember how they got there.

For me, however, the entire experience was a wake-up call. It was not the only or last time in my life I faced evil up close and personal, and truly, with but a few exceptions, the biggest evils I have faced in life had nothing to do with the paranormal. But this event was dramatic and it gave me an appreciation for having a care about what resided in the unknown and how we should approach communications with it. It's very important, in the metaphysical realms, but also as we simply go about our everyday lives that we consciously pay attention to who and what we invite to us and how we go about it.

JACQUI CORDARO

When my dad married my stepmom, Paula (not her real name), that is when events began to occur. From the moment she entered our lives until the day I moved away, there were unexplainable events. Everywhere we moved, any house we lived in, there was always a negative presence that followed. Paula shared that she had played with a Ouija™ board and experimented with spells until she was possessed. She claimed to have undergone an exorcism and that it could be easy for her to be repossessed if she was not careful.

She became devoted to religion. She attended church frequently and read her Bible daily. The more she clung to religion, the worse the incidences became.

In one particular house, right after my brother was born, activity escalated. The environment was heavy, negative, and volatile. There was a constant presence that made everyone apprehensive; a feeling of being watched and not alone. We would hear walking throughout the house, as well as growling coming from nowhere. Our dog, Biscuit, died the first week we moved in so we knew it was not him. Paula received many slaps and scratches. One time, at dinner, she yelled. We saw three long scratches appear on her arm as well as a handprint. Until that moment, we believed she self-inflicted the injuries. But to see it happen right before your eyes, without reasonable explanation, makes one reevaluate. We were horrified.

My dad collected a cypress knee that he intended to use for carving. A cypress knee is a structure forming above the roots of a cypress tree and is generally seen on trees in swamps. It was tremendously heavy. On one occasion, I saw that stump move through the air from the living room into the kitchen, where Paula was standing with her back turned, talking to my dad at the door. He saw movement behind her and told her to turn around. As soon as she turned, that thing dropped, rolling to her feet. She looked up, saw me standing in the doorway of my room, watching it all. Shortly after that event, we moved. A week later, a friend of mine moved into that house. It caught fire and her dog died in the fire. The house we lived in prior had similar unexplained manifestations. That house also burned down, killing my cat.

Once I left, I did not experience anything I had during my years with Paula. My younger siblings continued to have negative encounters until they moved out and nothing since. Her mental health deteriorated as she continued to be plagued by negative forces until she passed away. Paula died in 2012 in a house fire.

ANGELA GILLET

When I was in my early 20s, my fiancé at the time encouraged me to become a paranormal investigator. He encouraged me to actually explore this idea and seek out a group since all my life I have had paranormal experiences. My experiences ranged from seeing objects move, seeing shadows of people, hearing people talk to me, and having a plethora of déjà vu experiences. I did end up finding paranormal groups, which led me to plenty of experiences all over the spectrum. Some of those investigations have been relatives visiting, some have been spirits protecting their spaces, and others have been darker and on the verge of what some would call demonic. Now, I work with some of the best people in Minnesota, and we focus more on helping people than trying to get into those so called "haunted" places to make a checkmark on some website. Besides, we have probably been there and done that already.

One of my first investigations I had worked as a "paranormal investigator" was in a very prestigious suburb of Minneapolis. This wasn't exactly the place that I thought I would be working in since this house in particular was a brand-new house! The homeowners had all sorts of off-the-wall claims. They claimed that they would see images of faces appear in the walls, mirrors, windows, and, well, basically anything reflective. They would see orbs flying around—not the little white balls of light, huge, black orbs. They also had the typical claims of feeling watched, hearing strange noises, and bad dreams. The most disturbing claim about their situation was that they had writing appear on their shower door, which was written backwards so it was readable from outside the door. Of course, like so many others, they didn't know where to turn, and they had already "paid" people to remove whatever it was in their house.

Strangely enough, upon arriving at their home, our group experienced a couple of their claims before we even walked through the door. There was an intense feeling of being watched and what appeared to be a black orb flying around. I know, I know, those orbs are dust, bats, bugs, or whatever you want to explain it as. Well, living in Minnesota, when it's cold, there are no bugs or bats flying around. After getting the walk through of their house, we could visually see the faces, which I still to this day think it was the eye causing the image to matrix, and the orb that was outside was now inside with us. We had retreated to their basement/family room to sit down and discuss when everything had started and every single incident that they could remember. During this time, the wife had some of their friends over to make sure that we weren't super weird. She had gone to let them out of the house, [and] ... we had a conversation with the husband that was about an hour long. When the wife retreated back downstairs, we all stared and her in wonderment of what could have possibly taken so long to let her friends out. She was gone for five minutes. Our audio records said five minutes; however, none [of] us, not even the husband, believed five minutes. Right there, we were in for a good night since this strange time-warp thing had already started happening.

Since I was the rookie, I was never given a bunch of background information about the case nor was I involved for [sic] all the conversations with the homeowner, as the other investigator (who has now become a lifelong friend) and I were sent to go document the layout, take some quick pictures, place records, and get temperature and EMF readings. I really didn't know a lot of the specifics of the case until we actually started the "lights out" portion of the investigation. During the investigation, it occurred to me that a Ouija™ board was used in this house. In fact, I was certain that this board was being held hostage in their child's bedroom. Throughout the investigation, we experienced EMF movement with pictures that showed an orb traveling up and down that area, the sounds of balls being dropped on their foosball table, a dog chain being dragged on the floor above us, and the most intense was seeing the reflection of a German shepard sitting next to me while a camera flash was going off. The homeowner had actually just put down his German shepard a couple of months prior to us coming there, and before they actually moved into this new house. Information that I had no clue about. Until....

During a break, we were talking to the homeowner about some of the things that [he was] experiencing. I politely asked him about his dog that he no longer had. I told him about my experience, and then he pulled out a picture of the dog I was describing to him. I then asked him about the Ouija™ board that has moved around the house. As [part of] "family game night" they played with the Ouija™ board on a regular basis. They even named it Mrs. Butterworth. I personally flip back and forth on these boards. The reality [is] they are cardboard and plastic. There isn't anything special about them, but there is that mystery portion to them. Some of us have our own stories with them, and some of us believe they are a hoax. Some believe they can talk to spirits, and some believe you play with the

Some investigation into the symbols led us to believe that the symbols were opening portals to let more things into this home....

devil. This family could have brought in their own entities to play with, but they had paid people to remove the spirits or entities from their home.

This group—or, according to the homeowner, "Frick and Frack"—had supposedly used some Wicca ritual to remove this "nasty spirit." While talking to the homeowner, I noticed a huge oil marking on the wall. I brought attention to it and asked if they were present during the removal. They were not. I'm not into Wicca or really any other pagan type of religion. Something felt off about the symbols, and I was able to locate them on three other walls. We asked the homeowner to wash the walls, and we put some tape marking where we found the symbols. Some investigation into the symbols led us to believe that the symbols were opening portals to let more things into this home, as these people were being paid to be there, after all.

The lead on this case was Wiccan and did remove this entity with a Wicca ritual. We did follow up at this home at least four times over a very short time. Eventually, Mrs. Butterworth was removed from the home.

As I sit here and type out this experience, I personally wouldn't believe this story, nor do I see how it ties into being a demonic type of haunting. Fast forward over a decade, and I have run into these demonic types more than once. Now this "Frick and Frack" group had four people with them. One of the women that was there, not the one that did anything with the rituals, now happens to be a very close friend of mine, and we also work cases together. She stumbled upon a case a while back that we immediately decided to take on even though there is a lot of distance between us and the clients. There was a night that we had gone out to talk about this most current case, and I started mumbling about Mrs. Butterworth. She knew exactly what I was talking about.

Not every case starts off as being demonic. A case of a haunting manifests into something more if it has the capabilities to. Cases that deal with ghosts and spirits are not going to ever be demonic, even though there can be similar claims. Entities, on the other hand, can go one way or the other. Most cases that we work don't have entities in them but occasionally they do. (For some quick terminology, a ghost is somebody that has not crossed over, a spirit is a person that has crossed over, and an entity is energy that has intelligence to it but is not human.)

What does Mrs. Butterworth have to do with this other case? Easy: entities were invited into the home. The problem is that more than one entity can appear. In this more current case, our clients have ties to Wicca, and they also have used a Ouija™ board. Now their case has become a little more intense than Mrs. Butterworth, but it started off exactly the same. If the entity has the capabilities, they can and will progress further and become a demonic type of haunting. [In this] case, we have seen where the entity has played on the client's weakness and fear. In some ways, they have invited it due to getting benefit from it, and in other ways they have fought it. This one isn't going to be easy to get rid of. We have run into multiple entities that were invited in and we also have progressed to possession of one of the clients because the client won't fight against the "gifts" that this entity gives. My personal belief doesn't believe that these types of entities are the Devil. I don't, however, think they are doing good. They are manipulating the situation for benefit and strength of their own being. Until this client gets the "fight" in him, we can't do anything but keep clearing out everything else that we encounter besides the entity that is causing the possession.

Mrs. Butterworth was a great investigation to get my feet wet, especially with cases that aren't family members coming to visit. Not every case that I have experienced has had an entity appear from the Ouija™ board, or from Wicca, for that matter. My rule of thumb is don't dabble in the things you don't understand. Demonic cases are not for the faint of heart and are not things that get taken care of in a short period of time. In some cases, we can be working the case for years before things are taken care of. They are time consuming and mentally and physically exhausting. I wish I could go into extreme detail of what happens in these cases; however, for the clients involved in these cases, this isn't exactly public information they want shared nor is it information I even want to know about these people. Some may think that these people that experience demonic hauntings are just crazy and need a mental health check. Yes, sometimes this is true since most demonic hauntings will only interact with the people [they are] … connected to, meaning that a lot of times we only get subtle hints that there is an actual problem going on because the client is the one that is ultimately affected. The only thing that we can hope for is to experience something while with them.

REV. ROBY CHEVANCE, D.D.

At the age of five I became aware of people gathering around my bed at night trying to talk to me. I was terrified. But as I grew up, my secret world expanded. I knew what people were "really" thinking. I knew if someone was sick. I knew if one of my grandparents' friends were going to die. I started having visions at night with Mother Mary, Jesus, angels, wizards, and solar systems appearing in my room. I worried about world peace, pollution, and overpopulation. I contemplated religious inclusiveness and how dogma was going to intersect with the injection of alien life into our culture—all of this between ages 9 and 13. I then chose to start attending a Pentecostal church with the family next door. This exposed me to the concept of evil here on Earth that I had never entertained before. I also was instilled with a very deep and abiding [knowledge] … about the power of God. This arrived when I witnessed a woman being cured of myasthenia gravis instantaneously by the laying on of hands. The faith healer then turned to me and laid his hands upon me and I was then instantly healed of a broken leg that had just been X-rayed, re-broken, and reset. The healing [was] later verified that evening via X-rays.

So at an impressionable age I knew anything was possible. My few years at this church were preparing me for a career I could not, at the time, even fathom. You see, I had been born with almost every psychic gift—without the context to understand it or actually discern that what I was experiencing was anything "different." I started attending that church when I could understand when people were speaking in tongues. I started having visions of future events at the age of 16, when my deceased grandfather walked through the room of a family gathering. In the conversation that ensued, my mother discovered I had seen and spoken to him on many occasions. She promptly took me to a spiritualist church to have my gifts evaluated.

I never wanted to be a psychic. In fact, my passion was in science (physics, and later, quantum physics), but my metaphysical experiences kept escalating until I could ignore them no longer. Accuracy and credibility were important to me, so I sought out those who excelled in the field. I mentored with Duana Paul, a leading medium, for three years. I studied with a Japanese Shinto priest for three years that specialized in instantaneous healings. I also mentored with a Cree Medicine Woman for three years. All of these studies had me experiencing incredible paranormal phenomena and deepened my knowledge of the power we all have access to.

Of note, all of my experiences with the spirit realm were enlightening and awe-inspiring. The infinite unseen realm was a constant source of joy and delight. Every experience left me feeling divinely connected and a part of our vast and miraculous universe.

It was from this place of familiarity and wonderment with metaphysical phenomena that I experienced my first encounter with the opposing energy of evil.

I was newly married and settled in a lovely condo in an upscale neighborhood. I was working a day job and advertising my offering psychic readings in a local newspaper. I received a phone call to schedule a reading with a young woman I did not know. I booked the appointment but then kept thinking I needed to cancel it. I kept having a sense of foreboding all week. By the time I actually paid attention and went to call her to cancel, it was the morning of the reading and I felt like I couldn't cancel.

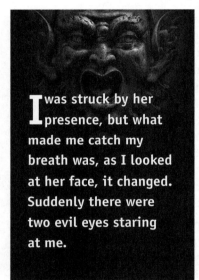

I was struck by her presence, but what made me catch my breath was, as I looked at her face, it changed. Suddenly there were two evil eyes staring at me.

When she arrived, I opened the door, and an attractive, 40-year-old woman with silky, long, black hair was standing there. I was struck by her presence, but what made me catch my breath was, as I looked at her face, it changed. Suddenly there were two evil eyes staring at me. Her eyes disappeared and these other menacing eyes appeared. Her once beautiful face now became hard and angular. I knew immediately why I had wanted to cancel.

I asked her in and she sat down. I asked her if she knew she had a demon in her, and she responded that this was the reason she came. I am continuously surprised that people are so matter of fact when they know they are possessed. It is almost as if they have accepted their fate and have given up the fight in trying to rid themselves of it.

I asked her when she first was aware of this evil entity. She explained that she had gone on a "vision quest" guided by a man she was dating who professed to be a Native American shaman. In the ritual, he had taken her deep into the forest, administered peyote to her, and left her alone through the night to find her spirit guides. She was not prepared for the ritual, and her fear got the best of her.

You see, when we partake of any substance that causes us to "leave our bodies," we literally leave our bodies open for disembodied entities to come inside. That evening, as the peyote had her leave her body, and as her boyfriend did not do his job properly, an evil entity possessed her body. Ever since, she had been depressed and hearing a voice saying evil things [and] trying to get her to kill herself and other people. She was hysterical and begging me to help her.

I began the session with a prayer. Acknowledging that there is God and nothing else. I asked for the assistance of my angels and all of the light beings. I declared the only possible outcome for the session was to have this woman restored to her true self. I gave thanks that I could stand on the promises of the Holy Scriptures. And then I turned to her. I laid my hands on her and started flooding her body with ice blue light. Immediately, there came from her gut deep and ugly growls. I began declaring, "You must leave this body." As I spoke, her body began going into contortions, her spine stiffened and jerked. I could no longer keep my hands on her, so I moved back and channeled the light from a foot or so away. Her eyes rolled into the back of her head and her face began contorting, and it appeared she was having seizures. I did not stop. I invoked the name of Jesus, and her body began contorting even more drastically. I realized her arms were bent backwards at the elbows in a way that arms don't bend. I kept on. She was contorted so stiffly [that] her shoulders were on the sofa and her feet were on the floor, the evil eyes now flashing at me and the growling turning to deep screams. I did not stop. I just kept flooding her with light and demanding the entity leave. I watched as she literally levitated inches off the sofa until there was no part of her body touching it. I just kept standing there, immersing her with light-blue light and demanding the entity leave. Her face was still contorted and the eyes were pure evil, just glaring at me as the growling voice taunted me.

I then felt something move energetically within her. The eyes disappeared, the convulsions stopped, her face softened and I could tell the entity had left her body, and she collapsed halfway on the sofa and halfway on the floor in exhaustion.

I remember thinking, "No one would believe this if I ever told them" and quietly laughed at myself for thinking that.

As the woman "came to," I sat her back on the sofa and she cried profusely as she kept thanking me. Her face and body were completely different, and she said she felt peaceful for the first time in over a year.

I explained to her that in her drug- and environment-induced fear, she had called in help to get her through the terror of being alone in a black forest and she wasn't specific. The peyote delivered her to an alternate state, magnifying the frequency of fear, which allowed this powerful evil entity to enter her.

This experience has never left me. I do believe in evil, but I do not believe evil has any true power over the light. "The light permeates the darkness without effort." While I am not what conservative Christians would consider "Christian," I do have a personal relationship with Jesus (as well as all of the other deities of Light) and commanded that demon to come out in Jesus' name. Between that and flooding her body with a high vibration of light-blue

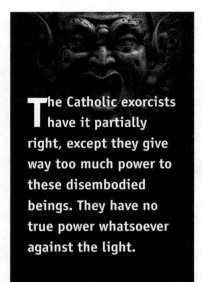

The Catholic exorcists have it partially right, except they give way too much power to these disembodied beings. They have no true power whatsoever against the light.

light, the demon could not hold his lower frequency of darkness and stay occupying her body, but it had to leave.

The Catholic exorcists have it partially right, except they give way too much power to these disembodied beings. They have no true power whatsoever against the light. It is the light that does the work. It requires no effort from us, with the exception of being the channel through which it is applied. "For we have been given dominion over all things...." "I am the way, the truth, and the light." "In the beginning there was light, and it was God." We merely must remember the truth of who we are and whose we are.

MARTHA HAZZARD DECKER

This event occurred when I was a teenager experiencing activity but not yet investigating supernatural activity. How many people as teens find sanctuary inside the four walls of their bedroom? I know I did, and I loved walking through the door into that safe haven. Nothing scared me there. It was light and peaceful. I would spend hours sitting comfy on my bed and reading one book after another. Odd things had happened off and on throughout my life, and there were several occurrences at the house my folks had built in a neighborhood behind a church. The backyard stopped at a tree line. There were two streets that made up the neighborhood. Heavy woods were at the back of both streets, which made a horseshoe or oval that was crossed in the middle by a main street. It was about a mile from Graceland in a part of Memphis, Tennessee, called Whitehaven. We spent three to four years in the custom-made, barn-shaped, early American, two-story house.

While unexplained activity has been around me for most of my life and my earliest memory [of it] was when I was four, nothing really prepared me for experiences while living in that house. I had a high school friend, and it seemed we both were interested in the supernatural and even tried to find books of mentors to guide us on our journey. We never found the help, but we did find an occult store somewhere around downtown and got a couple books to read.

Activity ramped up around us enough so that we would back off because we were concerned that we would get into something we wouldn't know how to handle or get out of should it go even further south than we were living. At first it was minor things that I can hardly remember, but I do remember a few things not so pleasant.

One incident was while my parents were gone. My friend was at the house, and we were in the den. There was a large window, and it faced the woods at the back of the house. The woods I never walked into, even though I loved the woods. My friend and I used to go to Shelby Forest of weekends while in high school to hang out. The street on the other side of the neighborhood had a house where I used to babysit a 10-year-old girl while I had a crush on her big brother. She dreamed of her brother and I getting married so I could be her sister. Her father worked in Washington, D.C. When he was gone, I would babysit, take her places, and talk to her brother a few times. But I remember there was a path in the woods on their side that went behind their house. Even weirder was that I would go back there and walk in the hopes I could catch a glimpse of her brother. Those woods never bothered me, even alone, but for some reason I never set foot in the woods behind our house.

So my friend, my sister, and I were in our den watching TV when I saw what looked like a flashlight come out of the woods and come toward the den window. The curtains in the den and the kitchen couldn't close. There was a laundry/half bath combo room in between the two rooms. There was a door leading to the garage from the kitchen that wasn't locked, and of course the door from the backyard to the garage wasn't locked either. The phone was hanging on the kitchen wall by the garage door. While my sister can't remember the incident (which is weird because she remembers everything), we were scared and trying to figure out what to do. This was around 1970, so we sure didn't have a cell phone. The window in the laundry room was smaller, up higher, and frosted, so we decided to crawl to the laundry room. Once in there we remembered the door from the kitchen to the garage was unlocked.

Somehow, I got up the nerve to crawl to the door as low as I could to reach up and lock the door. We had somehow shut off all the lights while feeling safer in the dark. We went back into the laundry room, locked the door, and discussed what to do next. This had happened so fast and the flashlight-looking light was still coming slowly toward the house. We decided to grab cleaning chemicals, and each of us had something in our hands. I had the bleach. If someone was going to break in we were prepared to douse them with everything we had. We couldn't get to the phone without being seen, and the light continued to be seen by us. We never heard a sound outside, and no one ever tried to break in. We sat there prepared for a fight until my parents came home at least an hour later. They walked in and we walked out of the laundry room. No telling how scared we looked. We told them what happened and as usual were told we all had a big imagination and nothing was ever out there. I can still see the light to this day. I think I was 16 when this happened. My sister would have been 13 and my friend 17 years old.

Then the next year I watched something from my window in the woods behind the house. My bedroom was upstairs and it was a full moon. I went to my window to look at the woods under the moonlight. To my surprise, the woods looked different. It was as if I had been transported back in time and the woods behind the house had become an open field filled with tall grasses. The woods were still there but started one to two houses down from ours. I could see a trail coming out of the woods that continued into the field. While I was trying to wrap my brain around what I was looking [at] without getting too confused, I spotted movement in the woods. The movement came with light, and that light was coming from torches being held by individuals in a group. They were dressed in clothing that someone would have worn at the turn of the century. I felt like they were angry about something and were planning to settle whatever it was that night. I couldn't tell you how many there were in the group, but there were too many as far as I was concerned. They walked with such a sense of urgency and purpose. It was fascinating to watch.

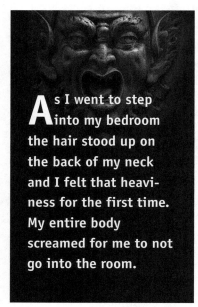

As I went to step into my bedroom the hair stood up on the back of my neck and I felt that heaviness for the first time. My entire body screamed for me to not go into the room.

That was, until I realized the path made a right turn that would take them right into our backyard and straight to our den window. It was then that I decided to run back to what I thought was the safety of my bed and hide under the covers. Yes, at 17 I was hiding under the covers. Many years later I wondered if this was the light the three of us had seen when we were home alone. Then the spring before graduating and my parents moving to Dallas, Texas, I had the final scary incident in the house.

There were other things that occurred, but they were minor. I was walking into my safe haven that I had turned into some semblance of an art studio on the walls. My parents actually let me draw on them with charcoal. That was weird enough as I was never allowed to even put up a poster. As I went to step into my bedroom the hair stood up on the back of my neck and I felt that heaviness for the first time. My entire body screamed for me to not go into the room. I stopped at the doorway, scared, without a clue of what to do or knowledge of what I was feeling. I only knew it wasn't safe to go into or stay in that room. At least that's what my instinct was yelling at me. What was it? Where did it come from, and why was it there?

I had no choice but to go into that room that was suddenly no longer a safe place. I ran in to grab my clothes as fast as I could and ran back out. I think I even held my breath the first time. I told no one what was happening. This went on for about two weeks. I continued to shake and feel something I imagined as pure evil in the room. The good thing was it was only in my room. During the day, I would only go in long enough to grab what I needed and then run out. The difficulty was at night, when I had to go to my room to sleep. I couldn't sleep, and all my senses were on high alert. I was sick to my stomach, scared, wondering what I had done to cause this to happen. I had no doubt in my mind it was supernatural and the intentions weren't good. Each night I stayed in my room only long enough for my parents to come upstairs and go to sleep. Then I would quietly bolt out of my room for the den. It felt safe and I would sleep on the sofa until the sun started coming up. I would always be back in my room before my father got up and sneak back into my bedroom. Eventually, I told my friend about it and we were trying to figure out what to do.

Then the telephone rang one day, and a male friend of mine was on the other end. He went to my school but never once did I see him at school. I can't remember how we met or why we didn't run into each other at school. He asked how I was, if anything was going on, and for my middle name. I told him my middle name was Ilene and asked why. He said that he had been automatic writing my first, middle, and last name at school for a few days. He didn't know why and decided to call. I told him about what was going on in my bedroom but felt odd talking about it with him. I don't think he skipped a beat or blinked his eyes when I told him my crazy and very scary experience. He told me he knew someone he thought could help and said he would call me back. I waited nervously for his return phone call. He called back a few hours later and said everything was taken care of and I would be okay in my room. I went upstairs scared to enter my room, but I went and checked it while he waited on the other end of the phone. I stepped into my room and the heaviness of evil feeling was gone. Once again, my room felt safe. Did I ask what was going on or how he knew who to contact? No! In fact, I never spoke to him again. To this day, I wonder what the heck happened and what was in my room.

To this day, I can put myself back there in a heartbeat. Did it start that one fateful night he and I went to the Valentine dance at his church? I wonder, and I only wonder because of something that scared me a year or two later that involved the pastor of that church. Only I didn't realize it at first. One of my best friends in high school and I were dating two guys who were best friends and roommates. The two guys were going to some type of meeting with the pastor of the church. This church had a prayer tower and is still in operation in Memphis. My roommate's boyfriend would return and tell her that the pastor told him what she had been up to that day. Before that, he had described her to him without ever seeing or meeting her in person. The pastor would tell him where she went during the day and even that she had done something like taking a shower. She and I were afraid he was akin to a Jim Jones and [that] may be the only reason we decided to meet with him one day. I still hadn't put him with the dance and what had happened to me with my room.

I remember I was able to blank out my mind with the snap of a finger back then, yet was still able to stay aware of conversations around me. We prepared to meet with the pastor, but I went with her boyfriend and she went with mine. I don't remember why, but I do remember the feeling I got when we arrived at the Baptist church and I saw the tower. This was the church I was at a couple years earlier for the Valentine dance. We got out of the car and walked under the walkway toward the tower and the pastor met us. When he did, he said, "Hi, Martha." As I began to say hello, I realized he never spoke those words out loud. Poker face full on, I looked at him and said, as if that was normal, hello, but out loud. We shook hands, and I started freaking out inside. I decided to blank my mind because I still didn't know why we were there. My roommate and boyfriend arrived a few minutes later and their greeting was a normal greeting. Up we went into the soundproof tower. It was so quiet I could hear my blood rush and heart beat.

We began to talk, but the pastor did most of the talking. My mind was blank and the pastor kept staring at me off and on. After several minutes, the pastor asked if I was okay. I smiled at him, told him I was great, and continued to keep my mind blocked. I can't tell you why we were there or even what he was talking about other than I felt like he wasn't able to do what he had planned. I was so relieved to walk away from that church and pastor. I know the name of the church and of the pastor and recently found a book he wrote a number of years ago. It will be interesting to see what he has to say in the book. One day I'm sure I'll reconnect with the high school friend who helped me and we can talk about that and the pastor of the church.

(Martha Hazzard Decker is a paranormal researcher and the author of *Paranormal Profiling*.)

Appendix A: Demon Classifications

Archdemon—In the hierarchy of demons, archdemons are at the top. Like archangels, they are large and in charge, the super demons of the infernal world.

Cambion—When a human has sexual intercourse with an incubus or a succubus (see below) the result is this type of demon offspring.

Demoness—A female demon. Can be utterly beautiful or horridly ugly. Interestingly, also the name for a "divine spirit" in Late Latin and Greek.

Djinn/Jinn—A spirits in human or animal form. Related to Genies, they have supernatural influence over people. Arabic shapeshifting demons with incredible powers.

Disembodied Spirit—The chaotic spirits of the dead roaming Earth and causing havoc to the living. Sometimes mistaken for ghosts and apparitions.

Drude—Dream demon that brings nightmares so they can feed upon their victim's fears.

Eidelon—A guilt demon.

Familiar—A witch or sorcerer's animal pet or spirit assistant that can also be a guide or guardian. Usually a domestic animal like a cat.

Goblin/Ghoul—Malformed and monstrous demon often associated with Halloween.

Gorgon—Winged female demon with snakes for hair.

Hag/Old Hag—Hags sit on the chests of sleeping people and make them feel as though they can't breathe. Could be related to succubi, but is usually old and very ugly with terrible breath.

Harpy—Revenge demon. People sometimes pay Harpies to get revenge on someone for them.

Imp—A little devil, small in stature, that creates mischief.

Incubus—Male demon that attempts to have sexual intercourse with sleeping people.

Nightmare Demon—Demon that visits in a sleeper's nightmares and arouses a feeling of intense terror or pending doom, even death.

Poltergeist—Mischievous spirit or demon more modernly associated with paranormal phenomenon than demonology.

Puck—Nature spirit or demon that causes mischief.

Seraph/Seraphim—A serpent demon that later became associated with fallen angels in Egyptian, Babylonian, and Assyrian lore.

Succubus/Subbubi—A female version of the incubus. It seeks out sex with humans. Also associated with wood nymphs.

Trickster—A spirit that, while not necessarily demonic, causes trouble and mischief.

Wrath—A vengeful, angry demon. In Buddhism, wrathful deities are actually associated with determination and the destruction of negativity and ignorance.

Another classification of demons by Michael Psellus in the eleventh century is as follows:

- Demons of air, which cause atmospheric phenomena
- Demons of earth that try to tempt people
- Demons of water that destroy aquatic life and cause shipwrecks
- Demons of the underground, which cause earthquakes and volcanic eruptions
- Demons of night, which avoid daylight and are invisible to people
- Demons of fire, which dwell far from us

APPENDIX B: RANKS OF HELL

In the appendix "Devils and Demons A to Z," there are mentions of various royal titles for the demons and angels in Hell. Below is how these positions are ranked in the demonic hierarchy.

HIERARCHY OF FALLEN ANGELS IN HELL

1. Emperor (Satan)
2. Great Kings
3. Kings
4. Great Princes
5. Princes
6. Great Marquises
7. Marquises
8. Great Dukes
9. Dukes
10. Great Earls
11. Earls
12. Great Presidents
13. Presidents
14. Knights
15. Great Marshals

Appendix C: Devils and Demons A to Z

A

Aamon/Amon (Christian demonology)—Aamon is the grand marquis of Hell. He is considered to be the seventh of the 72 Goetic Demons and one of Astaroth's assistants. Physically, Aamon appears to be a wolf with a serpent's tail, and he can spit fire. A mage may command Aamon to take the form of a man with a raven's head and the teeth of a canine. Aamon can see the past and the future and reconciles controversies between friends and enemies.

Abaddon/Apollyon (Christian demonology)—Abaddon is often referred to as the fallen archangel Muriel. Abaddon is referred to as an adviser and is the lord of the Abyss and the King of the Demons. Abaddon has over 200 legions of demons and is responsible for earthquakes, storms, tsunamis, and tornadoes.

Abezethibou (Testament of Solomon)—Abezethibou is a powerful demon who lived in Amelouth (the first heaven) and fell with Beelzebub. Legend says that when he fell, his fellow angels attempted to catch him but only managed to grasp one wing and it tore off. As he plummeted the remaining wing turned blood red and he now appears as an angel with one red wing. After his fall, he roamed Egypt and was allegedly responsible for causing Pharaoh's heart to harden.

Abraxas (Gnosticism)—Abraxas was deemed a pagan god (and later demon) by the Catholic church. Abraxas is thought to have control over the "365 skies" and "365 virtues." Abraxas is often described as having a head of a lion, along with a dragon's tail and serpents in place of legs.

Abyzou (Jewish mythology)—Abyzou is a female demon that is believed to be responsible for miscarriages and the deaths of babies because she was envious as a result of her own infertility.

Adramelech (Assyrian mythology, Christian demonology)—Adramelech, which means "king of fire," was considered to be a sun god related to Moloch. He is said to appear as a peacock or mule and was a high chancellor of Hell.

Aeshma (Zoroastrianism)—Aeshma is a part of Zoroastrianism, which is an ancient Persian religion founded about 3,500 years ago. He is often considered to be the demon responsible for malice and acts of aggression. He has no physical form but wields a lance and leads an army of demons.

Af (Jewish demonology)—An angel of destruction, a prince of wrath, and ruler over the death of mortals.

Agaliarept (Jewish mythology)—Agaliarept is said to be a demon who is the grand general of Hell and has the uncanny ability to discover all secrets and stirs distrust among men. He is one of two demons directly under Lucifer.

Agrat bat Mahlat (Jewish demonology)—In the Zohaistic Qabalah, Agrat bat Mahlat is described as a succubus demon. She is the queen of the demons and is said to be one of four angels of sacred prostitution. Many refer to her as the manifestation of Lilith.

Ahriman/Angra Mainyu (Zoroastrianism)—Ahriman is considered to be the god of evil and darkness in Persian mythology. He is the force behind greed, anger, envy, and other harmful emotions. He is mostly known for his penchant of bringing chaos, death, and disease into the world. In the Islamic religion, he is identified with Iblis (the devil.)

Aim/Haborym (Christian demonology)—Haborym (a.k.a. Aim) is a fire demon and duke of Hell. He often appears holding a torch and riding a viper. Haborym has three heads—a serpent's, a cat's, and a man's. He sets fire to cities, gives answers regarding private matters, and makes men witty in all ways.

Akop (Philippines mythology)—Akop is an evil entity with no torso who is known to prey upon widowed people. He is believed to attend funerals in order to get close to the grieving widow/widower, and when the spouse is unaware will collect the body fat that seeps out of the decomposing corpse and devours it.

Ala (Slavic mythology)—Ala is a female mythological creature that is considered to be a demon of bad weather. Ala often causes hail, producing thunderclouds in the direction of fields, vineyards, and orchards to destroy crops.

Alastor (Christian demonology)—Alastor is considered to be one of the most famous demons and is popularly known as the evil genius of the household. Alastor was originally a mortal who entices people to commit sins. He is often associated with family feuds.

Alloces/Allocer (Christian demonology)—Alloces is a demon who induces people to commit immoral acts. In addition, he is known to teach arts and mysteries of the sky. He is often portrayed as a knight mounted on an enormous horse.

Amaymon (Christian demonology)—Amaymon is one of the princes of hell and allegedly the only demon who has the power of Asmodai. Amaymon is said to have poisonous breath.

Amdusias (Christian demonology)—Amdusias is the governor of the twenty-nine legions; his true form is a unicorn, but he can appear as a human when summoned. Amdusias can cause trees to bend and incline.

Amon—Fallen angel who is a strong marquis over 40 legions.

Amy—A president in Hell.

Anakim—Offspring of fallen angels and mortal women. Said to be incredibly tall, like the Nephilim.

Anamalech (Assyrian mythology)—Anamalech is an Assyrian goddess who takes the form of a quail and is said to have been worshipped in the town of Sepharvaun.

Andhaka (Hindu mythology)—Andhaka is a malevolent being who is killed by Shiva for trying to abduct Parvati. He is believed to have a thousand heads and two thousand eyes, arms, and feet.

Andras (Christian demonology)—Andras is a very unpleasant demon whose only mission is to hunt and kill men. Andras is a Grand Marquis of Hell, who appears with a winged angel's body and the head of an owl or raven—and riding upon a black wolf. Andras is often seen to be carrying a bright sword. He is considered to be one of the most dangers demons.

Andrealphus (Christian demonology)—Andrealphus is a Grand Marquis of Hell and commander of thirty infernal legions, teacher of geometry, measurements, mathematics, astronomy, and astrology. He first appears as a peacock and then in human form.

Andromalius (Christian demonology)—Andromalius is a fallen angel that appears in the form of a man holding a great serpent in his arms. His duties include returning stolen goods to their owners, revealing thieves, discovering wicked deeds, and finding treasures.

Apollyon—Fallen angel of death; same as Abaddon.

Archon (Gnosticism)—Archon was one of several servants of the "creator god" that stood between the human race and a transcendent God.

Asag (Sumerian demonology)—Asag is known as a hideous demon that causes diseases and plagues. In Sumerian legend, Asag was known to dwell in the human body and cause paralysis.

Asakku (Babylonian mythology)—In Babylonian mythology, Asakku is an evil demon that attacks and kills human beings by means of head fevers.

Asderel—An evil archangel who taught the course of the moon.

Asmodai/Asmodeus (Jewish folklore and Christian demonology)—Asmodai derives from the Avestan language and wis considered to be the king of the demons. He is known as the "angel of death" or "Satan" and appears throughout Jewish folklore and Christian demonology.

Astaroth (Christian demonology)—Astaroth is the Great Duke of Hell, a part of the evil trinity with Beelzebub and Lucifer. He is a male figure named after the Mesopotamian goddess Ishtar and appears as a foul angel sitting upon a dragon and carrying a viper in his right hand.

Azazel / Azaz'el (Jewish demonology)—Within Jewish mythology, Azazel is the chief of the Se'irim, or goat-demons, who haunted the desert and to whom most primitive Semitic tribes offered sacrifices. Azazel is also referenced in the Book of Enoch as the leader of the Watchers who educates humankind on heavenly secrets that ultimately lead humans to sin.

Azibeel—One of the 200 chief fallen angels who engaged in sex with mortal women.

Azi Dahaka/Dahak (Zoroastrianism)—Azi Dahaka was one of the original gods created by Apsu and Tiamet at the beginning of creation. While other deities created, Dahak chose to destroy. He is credited with transforming Hell into a place of flame and terror.

Azrael (Hebrew Angel of Death)—Azrael is often identified as the Angel of Death in the Hebrew Bible. He resides in the Third Heaven and is said to occupy multiple forms. In the Zohar (Kabbalah), Azrael is depicted as a positive entity as he commands the legions of heavenly angels.

Azza—A fallen angel whose name means "the strong"; suspended between Heaven and Earth for having carnal knowledge of mortal women.

B

Baal/Bael (Christian demonology)—Baal is known as the head of the infernal powers. Baal has three heads: a toad's, a man's, and a cat's. He is known to teach the art of invisibility and commands 66 legions.

Babi Ngepet (Indonesian mythology)—Babi Ngepet is an Indonesian boar demon who is believed to have been the manifestation of a person who practiced black magic. Babi Ngepet is responsible for money, jewelry, and gold disappearing from villagers.

Badariel—One of the chief 200 fallen angels.

Bakasura (Hindu mythology)—Bakasura is a demon that lives near the city of Ekachakra and was known as a great devourer of human flesh.

Balam (Christian demonology)—Balam is a prince of Hell who commands 40 legions of demons and is known to appear with three heads: a bull's, a man's, and a ram's. Balam can make men invisible while also providing answers to things past, present, and future.

Balberith (Jewish demonology)—Balberith appears as a soldier riding a red horse, wearing red clothing and a golden crown. Balberith turns any metal into gold and is able to tell a person about their past, present, or future; however, he is known to lie to those he does not like.

Banshee (Irish mythology)—A banshee is a female spirit from Irish mythology who heralds the death of a family member by shrieking or crying. Banshees are often depicted wearing red or green and have long, disheveled hair.

Baraqijal (Christian demonology)—One of the Watchers of the Book of Enoch who teaches astrology.

Barbatos (Christian demonology)—Barbatos is an earl and duke of Hell who rules 30 legions of demons and can speak to animals, divine the future, and lead men to hidden treasure.

Barong (Indonesian mythology)—Barong is a lionlike creature in Indonesian mythology that was the king of the spirits. Barong is often depicted as a lion with a red head that is covered in thick white fur, and he wears ornate, mirrored jewelry.

Bathin/Mathim/Bathym/Marthim (Christian demonology)—Bathin is a fallen angel who appears as a strong man with the tail of a serpent astride a white horse. Bathin can transport people from one place to another in a second.

Beelzebub (Jewish demonology, Christian demonology)—Beelzebub is one of the oldest and most famous demonic figures. He is responsible for spreading disease from the dead to the living and his role is to tempt men's pride. Beelzebub is referenced multiple times in the New Testament and is referred to as the Devil himself. When summoned by sorcerers or witches, he appears in the form of a fly; therefore, he acquired the name "Lord of the Flies."

Behemoth—A male monster of chaos; also called the principal of darkness.

Beleth—An angel in Hell that rules over 85 legions of demons.

Belial (Jewish demonology, Christian demonology)—Belial is regarded as one of Satan's most venerable demons. Belial was reference in the Dead Sea Scrolls as the uncontested ruler of the dark side. Belial was believed to bring wickedness and guilt.

Belphegor (Christian demonology)—Belphegor is one of the seven princes of Hell who is largely credited with seducing people by suggesting plans that will make them rich. Balphegor is connected with the Christian sin of sloth. He is believed to be strongest in the month of April.

Beng (Romanian Gypsy mythology)—Beng is known as the Romanian version of Satan.

Bernael—An angel of darkness and evil.

Bhūta (Sanskrit)—In Buddhist and Hindu mythology, a Bhūta is an evil ghost of a man who died an untimely death (such as an accident or suicide) or had led an immoral or unholy lifestyle. Bhūtas are said to have the ability to take possession of corpses and reanimate them.

Bifrons (Christian demonology)—Bifrons is one of three demons that hold power over the dead. Bifrons is responsible for moving bodies from crypt to crypt and often takes the form of highly educated man who is well versed in astrology, geometry, herbology, mineralogy, and botany.

Boruta (Slavic mythology)—Boruta is a demon in Slavic mythology that dwells within pine trees. He is considered to be a nobleman and was responsible for corrupting nobles.

Botis (Christian demonology)—Botis is a demon within Christian demonology that often appears in the form of a snake; however, he could also take the form of a human with two horns carrying a sword. Botis is a seer and can give answers to things in the past, present, and future.

Buer (Christian demonology)—Buer is a spirit that is described as a Great President of Hell and appears when the Sun is in Sagittarius. Buer is a teacher of natural and moral philosophy and can heal infirmities.

Bukavac (Slavic mythology)—Bukavac is a mythical demonic creature that is believed to appear as a six-legged monster with large horns. The demon lives in lakes and pools and comes out of the water at night to strangle people and animals.

Bune (Christian demonology)—Bune is a mighty Duke of Hell and appears in the form of a dragon with three heads—a dog's, a gryphon's, and a man's. Bune speaks with a high-pitched voice and is said to make men wise and rich.

Bushyasta (Zoroastrianism)—Bushyasta is a Zoroastrian demon that signifies laziness and lethargy.

C

Caim/Canio (Christian demonology)—Caim is a Christian demon that is alleged to provide men with the ability to understand the voices of animals such as dogs and can predict the future. He often appears as a blackbird that quickly transforms into a sword-wielding warrior.

Carnivean—A demon invoked during witch sabbats.

Charon (Greek mythology)—The Boatman of Hell, Charon is best known as a ferryman that carries the souls of the newly dead across the river Styx and Archeron.

Charun (Etruscan mythology)—Charun is a demonic entity that guards the Underworld and serves to escort the dead through its gates.

Chemosh (Moabite mythology)—Chemosh is a Moabite deity whose name means "destroyer."

Chernobog (Slavic mythology)—A chernobog is a demon entity that only appears at night and is known to cause calamity and disaster while bringing misfortune and bad luck to all.

Cimejes/Kimaris/Cimeies (Christian demonology)—Cimejes is the 66th demon of the *Ars Goetia* (a text on conjuring demons) and is often depicted as riding a black horse. The demon possesses the ability to locate hidden or lost treasures and can make a man into a warrior of his own likeness.

Corson (Christian demonology)—Corson is regarded as the demonic king of the West and is one of the four principal kings that have power over King Solomon's 72 demons.

Crocell/Procell (Christian demonology)—Crocell is the 49th spirit of the Goetia that rules over 48 legions of demons. He is able to teach science and math and is often associated with water.

D

Daeva (Zoroastrianism demonology)—Daeva are Zoroastrian demonic entities that are considered to be "false Gods" that promote chaos and disorder.

Dalkiel—Angel of Hell and ruler of Sheol.

Dantalion (Christian demonology)—Dantalion is a great duke of Hell with 36 legions of demons under his command. He appears as a man and often is seen carrying a book in one of his hands.

Dasim—A Muslim angel of discord.

Decarabia (Christian demonology)—Decarabia is a Great Marquis of Hell with 30 legions of demons under his command. His expertise lies in herbs and precious stones, and he often appears as a pentagram star that changes into a man.

Devil (Christian demonology)—The word "devil" refers to Satan in both Christian and Jewish belief systems. He is believed to be the most powerful spirit of evil and is the ruler of Hell.

Diabolus—The devil.

Djinn/Jinn (Islamic demonology)—Djinn is the English word for supernatural creatures in Arabic folklore and Islamic teachings. They could be benevolent, neutral, or evil; however, they are generally regarded as less trustworthy than people, even when benign. Jinn are believed to have been formed from fire.

Drekavac (Slavic mythology)—Drekavac is a mythical creature of Slavic mythology that is believed to possess a horrifying yell and is often seen at night, especially during the 12 days of Christmas.

Drsmiel—An evil angel conjured to separate a husband and wife.

Dzoavits (Native American mythology)—Dzoavits is a spirit ogre hailing from Shoshone Indian mythology and is often associated with cannibalism and volcanism.

E

Eblis/Iblis (Islamic demonology)—Eblis is a fallen angel of Islam that is considered to be the chief of all djinn and is attributed as being the Muslim equivalent of the Devil.

Eisheth (Jewish demonology)—Eisheth is a princess within the Jewish Kabbalah who rules Sathariel and is said to devour the souls of the damned.

Eligos (Christian demonology)—Eligos is a high-ranking demon who is considered to be an expert in warfare and is often see riding on the back of a winged demon horse.

Ertrael—A fallen angel in the Book of Enoch.

Eshmadai—A king of demons in Rabbinic literature.

Euronymus (Greek mythology)—Euronymus is the Greek demon of rotting corpses that dwell in the Underworld. He is said to eat the flesh of the corpses, leaving only their bones.

Ezeqeel—A fallen angel whose name means "strength of God."

F

Flauros—Takes the form of a leopard.

Focalor (Christian demonology)—Focalor is a Great Duke of Hell that appears as man with griffin's wings and has power over the wind and sea.

Foras/Forcas/Forras (Christian demonology)—Foras is a President of Hell that commands 29 legions of demons, teaches logic and ethics, and has the ability to make men invisible.

Forneus (Christian demonology)—Forneus is a Great Marquis of Hell that commands 29 legions of demons, teaches rhetoric and language, and is often depicted as a great sea monster.

Furcas/Forcas (Christian demonology)—Furcas is a Knight of Hell and command 20 legions of demons. He is often associated with the teaching of astronomy, philosophy, rhetoric, logic, chiromancy, and pyromancy. He appears as an older man with white hair and a long bear who rides a horse while carrying a pitchfork.

Furfur/Furtur (Christian demonology)—Furfur is a great Earl of Hell and rules 29 legions of demons. He is a liar who causes love between women and men, teaches secret and divine knowledge, and causes storms, thunder, and lightning.

G

Gaap (Christian demonology)—Gaap is a high President and Prince of Hell in command of 66 legions of demons. The demon commands the element of water. He is known to teach philosophy and liberal science and can make men invisible and insensible.

Gamigin (Christian demonology)—Gamigin is a demon that teaches liberal science and can assume two different forms: the first is a donkey, and the second is of a stout man with a gruff appearance. Interestingly, Gamigin's true human form is of a female.

Glasya-Labolas/Caacrinolaas/Caassimolar/Classyalabolas/Glassia-labolis (Christian demonology)—Glasya-Labolas is a mighty President of Hell who commands 36 legions of demons and appears as a dog with griffin wings. He is known as a teacher of liberal arts and inspires murder, provides invisibility, and predicts the future.

Goap—A president in Hell.

Golab—A spirit of wrath and sedition.

Gorgon (Greek mythology)—Gorgons are snake-haired demons in Greek mythology that had female bodies covered with the scales of vipers. It is said that whoever looked at them would instantly turn to stone.

Gremory/Gomory (Christian demonology)—Gremory is a powerful Duke of Hell who commands 26 legions of demons and appears as a woman with a ducal crown upon his head and rides a camel. Gremory is able to know the past, present, and future.

Grigori (Jewish demonology)—The Grigori (also known as the Watchers) are a mysterious order of 200 fallen angels who mated with mortal women and gave rise to a hybrid race known as the Nephilim, who were described as giants in the Genesis 6:4.

Gualichu (Mapuche mythology)—Gualichu is considered to be an evil spirit or demon that is often compared to the Devil. He is blamed for disease and calamity, as well as everything that is evil.

Gusion/Gusoin/Gusoyn (Christian demonology)—is a Great Duke of Hell that rules over 45 legions of demons and is able to know the past, present, and future. He is often depicted as a baboon.

H

Haagenti (Christian demonology)—Haagenti is the demon lord of alchemy and is believed to have the ability to take the form of anything he wishes.

Halphas/Malthus (Christian demonology)—Halphas is the 38th demon in the Ars Goetia ranked as an earl. He is generally described as a stock dove (a type of bird) that speaks with a hoarse voice and supplies weapons and ammunition.

Hantu Raya (Indonesian and Malaysian mythology)—Hantu Raya is a Malaysian "master" of all ghosts that is considered to be the leader of the underworld. Hantu Raya is believed to be capable of materializing into another human being or animal; the demon is blamed for childbirth deaths; he performs heavy duties for those who summon him.

Harab-Serapel—A leader of the infernal regions and adversary of Elohim.

Haures (Christian demonology)—Haures is the 64th Great Duke of Hell that first appears as a leopard but then often assumes a human form with flaming eyes. He can use fire to destroy enemies and gives true answers to things past, present, and future.

Hecate (Greek mythology)—Hecate is a Greek goddess of the underworld, black magic, and darkness. The queen of witches, she was one of the primary deities that were worshiped in Athenian households as a protective goddess that bestowed wealth and prosperity on the family.

Hosampsich—A leader of fallen angels in the writings of Enoch.

I

Ibwa (Philippines)—Ibwa is a demon from the Phillipines that is alleged to feed on dead bodies.

Ifrit (Islamic mythology)—An ifrit is an Islamic djinn that is noted for strength and intelligence. Ifrits often appear as enormous, winged creatures of smoke that live underground and frequent ruins.

Imamiah—A demon who governs voyages.

Incubus (Christian demonology, Chaldean mythology, Jewish folklore)—Incubus refers to a male demon that often takes on the appearance of a human male that seeks sexual intercourse with women, usually while they are sleeping. According to legend, the incubus was able to manifest in human form by reanimating a human corpse or using human flesh to create a new body.

Inmai (Myanmar demonology)—The Inmai is believed to be the demon that lives in the front portion of a house and causes people to be injured by sharp thorns.

Ipos—Appears as an angel with a lion's head.

J

Jetrel—One of the original 200 fallen angels of Enoch.

Jilaiya (Indian mythology)—Jilaiya is a nocturnal demon found within Indian mythology that flies like a bat in the evening to suck on human blood; in other words, Jilaiya is a variation of a vampire.

K

Kabandha/Kabhanda (Hindu mythology)—Kabandha is a Hindu demonic cyclops that is a fierce cannibal with eight-mile-long arms, one eye on his chest, and a mouth on his belly; however, he lacks legs and a head.

Kali (Hinduism)—Kali is a Hindu goddess associated with empowerment and is known as the destroyer of evil forces.

Kasadya (Jewish demonology)—Kasadya is a demon that is responsible for murder and abortion.

Kazbiel—He who lies to God.

Kokabiel (Jewish demonology)—Kokabiel is a fallen angel that is an angel of the stars who, appropriately, teaches astrology and is said to command an army of 365,000 spirits.

Kroni (Ayyavazhi demonology)—Kroni is a figure within Ayyavazhi mythology that is the ultimate representation of evil and often manifests in various forms. He is often believed to prevent the soul from attaining knowledge of bliss.

Krampus (Germanic-Christian demonology)—In Austro-Bavarian Alpine folklore, Krampus is recognized as a half-goat, half-demon that punishes children that have misbehaved. He is often depicted as being extremely hairy with sharp fangs and the horns and cloven hooves of a goat.

Kunopegos—He appears as a seahorse and sinks ships.

L

Lahash—He interferes with divine will.

Lechies (Slavic mythology)—Lechies are Russian demons that live in the woods and have human bodies from the waist up but with the horns, ears, and beard of a she-goat. From the waist down, they have a goat's body; they are capable of shrinking or growing in size. Lechies lure wanderers back to their caves, where they tickle them almost to death.

Lempo (Finnish mythology)—A lempo is an erratic spirit that is considered to be the god of love and fertility in Finnish mythology.

Leraje/Leraie (Christian demonology)—Leraje is a Great Marquis of Hell who commands 30 legions of demons and causes battles and disputes. He is often depicted as a handsome archer wearing green clothing.

Leviathon—An angel/monster associated with the deep seas.

Leyak (Indonesian mythology)—The Leyak is a Balinese demon that can appear as a human by day, but by night takes the form of a disembodied, menacing head with great fangs and large eyes hovering in the air with the entrails of the body still attached and floating beneath it.

Lilin (Mesopotanian demonology)—The Lilin are hostile night spirits that attack men. "Lilin" is also a Hebrew word for both "succubus" and "incubus."

Lilith (Jewish folklore)—Lilith is a demon goddess that is referred to as the "Dark Maid" in Jewish folklore. She was Adam's first wife and was created at the same time and from the same earth of Adam. Lilith became a succubus that comes to men at night and causes wet dreams.

Lima (Haitian demonology)—Lima is a demon that is worshiped in Haiti and is believed to cause suffering and emotional pain.

Lucifer (Christian demonology)—Lucifer refers to the Devil for some, although other authorities hold that Lucifer and Satan are not the same being. In the case of the former, Lucifer was once an angel that rebelled against God and was cast from Heaven; in the case of the latter, Lucifer is a separate fallen angel.

Lucifuge Rofocale (Christian demonology)—Lucifuge Rofocale is the demon that Lucifer put in charge of Hell's government.

M

Malphas (Christian demonology)—Malphas is a Great Prince of Hell that commands 40 legions of demons and is considered to be second in command after Satan. He is known to build houses and fortresses and destroys the buildings of the enemy.

Marax/Morax/Foraii (Christian demonology)—Marax is a Great President of Hell that commands 30 legions of demons and is known to teach astronomy and liberal science. Marax is often depicted as a man with a bull's head.

Marchosias (Christian demonology)—Marchosias is a Great Marquis of Hell that commands 30 legions of demons and is often depicted as a fire-spewing wolf with gryphon's wings and a serpent's tail. He is a strong fighter and provides true answers to all questions.

Maron—A demon who was once a cherub.

Mastema (Jewish demonology)—Mastema is considered to be an angel that persecutes evil people. He is known to tempt humans to test their faith and is believed to carry out punishments for God.

Mephistopheles (Christian folklore, German folklore)—Mephistopheles is a demon within Germanic folklore that is one of Lucifer's workers who collect the souls of those who are already damned.

Moloch (Christian demonology)—Moloch is a Caananite god that is most often associated with child sacrifice. He is often depicted as a bronze statue that is heated with fire and into which victims are thrown.

Morpheus (Greek mythology)—Morpheus is the god of dreams who has the ability to mimic any human form and appear in dreams.

Murmur (Christian demonology)—Murmur is a Great Duke and Earl of Hell who commands 30 legions of demons and teaches philosophy. He is often depicted as a soldier riding a vulture or griffin and wearing a ducal crown.

N

Naamah (Jewish demonology)—Naamah is a female demon that is believed to cause epilepsy in children. She is described as being an angel of prostitution and the mother of divination.

Naberius (Christian demonology)—Naberius is a Marquess of Hell and commands 19 legions of demons. He is known to make men cunning in the arts and sciences and can restore lost honors and dignities. He often appears as a three-headed dog or raven.

Namtar (Sumerian mythology)—Namtar is responsible for death. He is often depicted with no hands or feet and does not need to eat or drink. Namtar commands 60 diseases and also acts as the messenger to the queen of the Sumerian underworld.

Neqael—An evil archangel in the writings of Enoch.

Ninurta (Sumerian mythology, Akkadian mythology)—Ninurta is the god of war and hunting. He often appears holding a bow and arrow and a sickle sword or a talking mace.

O

Obaddon—Another form of Abaddon. Minister of death.

Obyzouth—She kills newborns and causes still births.

Orcus (Roman mythology; later, Christian demonology)—Orcus is the Roman demon lord of the undead. He often appears as a large human with the head and cloven feet of a demonic ram, the wings of a large bat, and a tail that ends in a stinger. He dwells in a realm called Uligor, which is an entire world filled with the undead.

Ördög (Hungarian mythology)—The Ördög is a sulfurous-smelling, shape-shifting, demonic creature that dwells in the underworld and is thought to look like a black faun with a sharp, pointy tail, and carrying a pitchfork. He collects human souls and makes bets with humans to see if they become corrupted.

Orias/Oriax (Christian demonology)—Orias is a Great Marquis of Hell that commands 30 legions of demons and teaches astrology. He is able to change a man's appearance into any shape.

Orobas (Christian demonology)—Orobas is a High Prince of Hell that commands 20 legions of demons and often appears in the form of a beautiful horse or as a man that speaks about the divine essence. He is able to know the past, present, and future, and can grant favors and help reconcile enemies.

Ose (Christian demonology)—Ose is a Great President of Hell that rules three legions of demons and teaches liberal science. Ose is capable of making a person go insane, or make someone believe they are a king or pope. He is often depicted as a leopard that changes into a man.

P

Paimon (Christian demonology)—Paimon is a King of Hell that governs 200 legions of demons and often appears as a man with a woman's face. He rides a camel and wears a headdress covered in precious gems. He teaches art, philosophy, mysteries, and science.

Pazuzu (Babylonian demonology)—Pazuzu is the king of demons of the wind. His appearance is that of a man with a head of a dog or lion, eagle talons, four wings, and a scorpion tail. He brings famine and plagues of locusts.

Penemuel (Jewish and Christian demonology)—Penemue is an fallen angel in Enochian lore that taught humankind how to read and write.

Peri—Fallen angels of Arabic lore.

Pharzuph—The angel of fornication and lust.

Pithius (Christian demonology)—Pithius is a Prince of Hell who is said to command liar spirits. He appears as a snake or serpent and provides false prophecies.

Pocong (Indonesian mythology)—A pocong is a ghost of a dead person trapped within a shroud. Pocongs have the ability to hop as well as fly.

Pontianak (Indonesian and Malaysian mythology)—The Pontianak is a vampiric female ghost that is the spirit of women who died in pregnancy. Pontianaks usually appear as pale-skinned women with long, black hair, red eyes, and wearing a white dress smeared with blood.

Pruflas (Christian demonology)—Pruflas is a Great Prince and Duke of Hell that commands 26 legions of demons. He is known to cause men to fight, lie, and quarrel. He often appears as a flame outside of the Tower of Babel.

Purah—The fallen angel of forgetfulness and the conjuring of the dead.

Purson—King of the nether regions with 22 legions of demons.

Python—The 2nd of nine archdemons or evil archangels.

Q

Qemuel—A fallen angel who was destroyed by God.

R

Rabdos—A demon who throttles people.

Rahab—An angel of pride whose name means "Violence."

Rakshasa (Hindu demonology)—A rakshasa is a demon that feeds on human flesh. They are shape changers that often appear in the form of humans, dogs, or large birds. Rakshasas have the ability to become invisible, but they cannot enter a home without permission.

Rangda (Hinduism in Indonesia)—Rangda is a terrifying-looking demon. A queen in Balinese mythology, she is responsible for eating children. She is often depicted as an elderly, nude woman with long, unkempt hair, large breasts, and claws.

Raum (Christian demonology)—Raum is a Great Earl of Hell that commands thirty legions of demons and is known to destroy cities and steal treasure from kings. Raum has knowledge of the past, present, and future. He is often depicted as a crow that can adopt human form.

Ravana (Hindu demonology)—Ravana is a multi-headed demon king. His natural form has ten heads and twenty arms, but he can take on any form that he wishes. Ravana is considered to be a scholar, a formidable ruler, and an expert on playing the veena.

Rimmon—A fallen archangel who is an inferior demon.

Rofocale—Controls the world's wealth and treasures.

Ronove (Christian demonology)—Ronove is a Marquis and Great Earl of Hell that commands 20 legions of demons and teaches rhetoric, art, and language. He is often depicted as a monster holding a staff and is described as a taker of old souls.

Rumjal—One of the original 200 fallen angels in Enochian writings.

Rusalka (Slavic mythology)—A rusalka is a female water nymph helps nurture crops.

S

Sabnock (Christian demonology)—Sabnock is a Great Marquis of Hell who commands 50 legions of demons and is responsible for building towers, cities, and castles. He often appears as a soldier with a lion's head who rides a pale horse.

Samael (Jewish demonology)—Samael is a demon within Jewish and Christian demonology that is often referred to as the angel of death and collector of Moses' soul. He commands over two million angels.

Saraknyal—One of the 200 fallen angels who had intercourse with human women.

Satan (Jewish demonology, Christian demonology, Islamic demonology)—Satan is generally regarded as the an abhorrent, evil spirit. He goes by many names such as Lucifer and the Devil. The name Satan means "Adversary" or "Enemy," but he was originally created by God as an angel named Lucifer. Lucifer fell from grace when he led about a third of Heaven's angels in a rebellion against God. Cast into Hell, Lucifer became Satan and his angels are now demons.

Semyaza—A leader of fallen angels and one of the Sons of God.

Seriel—He taught humans the signs of the moon.

Shaftiel—Ruler of hell and lord of the shadow of death.

Shaitan—An Arabic fallen angel.

Shax/Chax (Christian demonology)—Shax is a Great Marquis of Hell who commands over 30 legions of demons on horseback. He is known to steal and lie and is often depicted as a stork that speaks with a hoarse voice.

Shedim (Jewish folklore)—"Shedim" is the Hebrew word for "demons." Descendants of serpents, they possess the feet and claws of a rooster.

Sitri (Christian demonology)—Sitri is a Great Prince of Hell who commands over 60 legions of demons. He is responsible for causing men to fall in love is typically depicted with the face of a leopard and the wings of a griffin.

Solas—He appears as a raven and teaches astronomy.

Sorath—A fallen angel and evil power whose number is 666.

Sthenno (Greek mythology)—Sthenno is the eldest and most vicious of the Gorgon sisters in Greek mythology who often appeared with brass hands, sharp fangs, and hair made of venomous snakes. Sthenno was known to have killed more men than both of her sisters combined.

Stolas/Solas (Christian demonology)—Stolas is a Great Prince of Hell who commands 26 legions of demons. He is a teacher of astronomy and is knowledgable about herbs, plants, and precious stones. He is often depicted as a raven or a crowned owl with long legs.

Suanggi (Indonesian mythology)—Suanggi is a shapeshifting demon who enjoys eating disobedient children that wander outside after dark. While he is able to manifest in any form, he often prefers the form of a chicken.

T

Tannin (Jewish demonology)—Tannin is a demonic sea monster that is often used as a symbol of evil and chaos.

Tartarus—He resides over Hell; his name is often a term for Hell.

Thausael—One of the original fallen angels mentioned by Enoch.

Tmsmael—An evil spirit used in conjuring rites.

Toyol (Indonesian and Malaysian muthology)—A toyal is the ghost of a baby that died before birth.

U

Ukobach (Christian demonology)—Ukobachs are lesser demons that often appear with a flaming or red body, large eyes and ears, and carrying a hot poker. Ukobachs are said to have invented fried foods and fireworks and are responsible for maintaining the boilers of hell.

Usiel—One of the original angels who mated with women to produce giants.

Uzza—His name means "Strength."

V

Valefar/Malaphar/Malephar (Christian demonology)—Valefar is a Duke of Hell who commands ten legions of demons. Depicted as either a lion with a man's head or a monkey's head, he is a demon who tempts people to steal.

Vanth (Etruscan mythology)—Vanth is a female demon who is a guide in the underworld. She is usually shown as carrying a scroll, sword, torch, or key.

Vapula (Christian demonology)—Vapula is a Great Duke of Hell who commands 36 legions of demons in Hell. Depicted as a lion with wings, he teaches philosophy, science, and mechanics.

Vassago (Christian demonology)—Vassago is known as the "Prince of Prophecy" and can also find lost or hidden items. He also has shapeshifting abilities.

Vepar (Christian demonology)—Vepar is a great Duke of Hell who commands 29 legions of demons in Hell. Depicted as a merman, he governs the oceans and can guide ships.

Vine (Christian demonology)—Vine is an Earl and King of Hell who is known to be the trickiest, most deadly demon. Vine has the power to take one's soul without permission and appears as a lion holding a snake and riding a black horse.

W

Wall—A Grand Duke of Hell.

Wendigo (Algonquin mythology)—The wendigo is a cannibalistic evil spirit that appears as a monster with human characteristics. The wendigo is the embodiment of greed, gluttony, and excess.

Wormwood—The "star" that fell from heaven and brings plagues upon the Earth.

X

Xa-Mul (Philippine mythology)—Xa-Mul is a demon that likes to swallow people whole.

Xaphan (Christian demonology)—Xaphan is a fallen angel who plotted to set fire to Heaven before he and Satan's other followers were expelled from Heaven. He has a bellows as an emblem but must fan the flames with his mouth and hands.

Y

Yetzer Hara—An evil spirit that may also be the Hebrew angel of death.

Yurba—The evil genie chief in Mandaean lore.

Z

Zagan (Christian demonology)—Zagan is a Great King and President of Hell who commands over 33 legions of demons. He is known to make men witty and can turn liquids into wine. He is often depicted as a winged bull that can turn into a man.

Zagiel—One of the evil archangels in the Book of Enoch.

Zavabe—One of the 200 angels who fornicated with human women.

Zepar (Christian demonology)—Zepar is a Great Duke of Hell that commands 26 legions of demons. He can cause women to fall in love with men, but he can also make them infertile. Zepar is usually depicted wearing red clothes and armor.

Ziminiar/Zymymar (Christian demonology)—Sometimes called the King of the North, Ziminiar is one of the four principal kings that has power over the demons that were later khave power over the demons that were later constrained by King Solomon.

FURTHER READING

"666 or 616—Which Is the Real Number of the Beast?" *Deleriums Realm*. http://www .deliriumsrealm.com/number-of-beast/. (Accessed June 4, 2017).

"10 Real Demonic Possession Cases and Real Life Exorcisms." *Hell Horror*. http://hellhorror.com/article/9009/10-real-demonic-possession-cases-real-life-exorcisms. Html

"Amityville." *New England Society for Psychic Research*. http://www.warrens.net/Amityville.html. (Accessed June 4, 2017.)

"Amoral Tricksters that Enhance World Mythology and Entertain Cultures." *Ancient Origins*, January 6, 2016. http://ancient-origins.net/myths-legends/amoral-tricksters-enhance-world-mythology-and-entertain-cultures-005108.

Ashley, Leonard R. N. *The Complete Book of Devils and Demons*. New York: Skyhorse Publishing, 2011.

Ashliman, D. L. "The Origin of Underground People." *University of Pittsburgh*. http//pitt.edu/-dash/originunder.html. (Accessed June 5, 2017.)

Blavatsky, Helena. *The Secret Doctrine: The Classic Work, Abridged and Annotated*. New York: Tarcher/Penguin, 2009.

Blumberg, Jess. "A Brief History of the Salem Witch Trials." *Smithsonian.com*, October 23, 2007. http://www.smithsonianmag.com/hisotry/a-brief-hisotry-of-the-salem-witch-trials-175162489.

Boyd, Katie. *Devils and Demonology in the 21st Century*. Atglen, PA: Schiffer Press, 2009.

———. "Demonic Entities vs. Negative Spirits." *BBPC Blog*, February 25, 2009. https://beckahthepsychic.wordpress.com/2009/02/25/demonic-entities-vs-negative-spirits/.

Briggs, Katherine. *An Encyclopedia of Fairies, Hobgoblins, Brownies, Bogies and Other Supernatural Creatures*. New York: Pantheon, 1976.

Brittle, Gerald. *The Demonologist: The Extraordinary Career of Ed and Lorraine Warren*. Graymalkin Media, 2013.

Brown-Worsham, Sasha. "Did the Lutz Family's Practice of Transcendental Meditation Lead to the Amityville Horror?" *Destination America*, July 27, 2016. http://www.destinationamerica.com.

Campbell, Joseph. *Myths to Live By*. London, England: Souvenir Press, 1972.

Carus, Paul. *The History of the Devil*. New York: Radmom House Value Publishing, 1996.

Case, George. *Here's to My Sweet Satan: How the Occult Haunted Music, Movies, and Pop Culture, 1966–1980*. Quill Driver Books, 2016.

Cavendish, Richard. *The Black Arts: A Concise History of Witchcraft, Demonology, Astrology, and Other Mystical Practices Throughout the Ages*. New York: Tarcher/Penguin, 1983.

Chitwood, Ken. "Angels, Demons and Pop Culture." *Ken Chitwood*, February 15, 2015. http:www/kenchitwood.com/blog/2015/2/15/angels-demons-pop-culture.

Collis, Clark. "Little Box of Horrors." *Entertainment Weekly*, August 3, 2012.

Coppens, Philip. "The Cathars: The Struggle For and of a New Church." *Philip Coppens*. http://philipcoppens.com/catharism.html. (Accessed June 4, 2016)

Crabtree, Vexen. "Who Is Satan? The Accuser and Scapegoat." *The Description, Philosophies, and Justification of Satan*. http://www.dpjs.co.uk/satan.html. (Accessed June 5, 2017.)

Crowley, Aleister. *Book of the Law*. New York: Weiser Books, 1987.

———. *Magick*. CreateSpace Independent Publishing, 2014.

Cusamano, Katherine. "10 Supposedly Haunted Museums." *Mental Floss*. http://mentalfloss.com/article/70356/10-supposedly-haunted-musuems. (Accessed June 4, 2017).

David, Rosalie. *Religion and Magic in Ancient Egypt*. New York: Penguin Books, 2002.

Davidson, Gustav. *A Dictionary of Angels Including the Fallen Angels*. New York: The Free Press/Macmillian, 1967.

Dearborn, Leah. "The Devil That You Know: Literature's Evil Archetype." *Lit Reactor*. https://litreactor.com/columns/the-devil-that-you-know-literatures-evil-archeytpe. (Accessed December 2016.)

Deem, Rich. "UFOs and the Existence of Supernatural Demonic Forces." *Evidence for God*, http://www.godandscience.org/doctrine/ufo_existence_of_demons.html. (Accessed June 5, 2017.)

Donovan, Patricia. "Why We Create Monsters." *UB Reporter*, October 27, 2011. http://www.buffalo.edu/ubreporter/archive/2011_10_27/mosnter_culture.html.

Dunne, Carey. "The Changing Face of Satan, From 1500 to Today." *Co.Design*, August 8, 2014. http://www.fastcodesign.com/3034309/the-changing-face-of-satan-artistic-depictions-of-the-devil-1500-t—today.

Eliade, Mircea. "*The Encyclopedia of Religion*. New York, New York: McMillan Publishing, 1987.

"The Exorcisms of Latoya Ammons." *Indianopolis Star*, October 31, 2014.

Foreman, Tom. "Meet American's Top Exorcist: The Inspiration for 'The Rite.'" *CNN*, March 7, 2011. http://religion.blogs.cnn.com/2011/03/07/the-real-exorcist-no-sympathy-for-the-devil/.

Fortune, Dion. *An Introduction to Ritual Magic*. Thoth Publications, 1997.

———. *Psychic Self-Defense: The Classic Instruction Manual for Protecting Yourself against Paranormal Attack*. New York: Weiser Books, 2011.

Frazier, Sir James George. *The Golden Bough*. London, England: Dover Publications, 2002.

Gardiner, Brian. "The Fight to Save America from Satan's Subliminal Rock Messages." *Atlas Obscura*, October 20, 2016. http://www.atlasobscura.com/articles/the-fight-to-save-america-from-satans-subliminal-rock-messages.

Geggel, Laura. "Where Did Satan Come From?" *LiveScience.com*, October 2, 2016. http://www.livescience.com/56341-where-did-satan-come-from.html

Graham, Stacey. *Haunted Stuff: Demonic Dolls, Screaming Skulls and Other Creepy Collectibles*. Woodbury, Minnesota: Llewellyn Books, 2014.

Greer, John Michael. *The New Encyclopedia of the Occult*. Woodbury, MN: Llewellyn Publications, 2003.

Guiley, Rosemary. *The Encyclopedia of Witches, Witchcraft and Wicca*. New York: Checkmark Books, 2008.

———. *The Encyclopedia of Demons and Demonology*. New York. Checkmark Books, 2009.

———. *The Djinn Connection: The Hidden Links between Djinn, Shadow People, ETs, Nephilim, Archons, Reptilians and Other Entities*. New York: Visionary Living, Inc. 2013.

Harari, Yuval Noah. *Sapiens: A Brief History of Humankind*. New York: Harper Collins, 2015.

Harker, John. *Ouija Board Nightmares: Terrifying True Tales*. CreateSpace, 2015.

———. *Demonic Dolls: True Tales of Terrible Toys*. CreateSpace, 2015.

"Haunted Dolls—The Demonic and Spiritual Possession of Inanimate Objects." Altered Dimensions Paranormal, September 9, 2014. http://altereddimensions.net/2014/haunted-dolls-demonic-spiritual-possession-of-inanimate-objects.

Hayes, Lynn. "Lucifer: Satan or Venus?" *BeliefNet*, July 2009. http://www.beliefnet.com/columnists/astrologicalmusings/2009/07/lucifer-satan-or-venus.html/.

Helmuth, Laura. "Witness to an Exorcism: How Pope Francis and the Vatican Deal with the Devil." *Slate*, May 12, 2014.

"History of the Talking Board." *Museum of Talking Boards*. http://www.museumoftalkingboards.com/history.html. (Accessed June 4, 2017.)

Hodge, Bodie. "Who Were the Nephilim?" *Answers in Genesis*, July 9, 2008. http://www.answersingenesis.org/bible-characters/who-were-the-nephilim/.

Hoffer, Peter Charles. *The Devil's Disciples: Makers of the Salem Witchcraft Trials*. Baltimore, MD: Johns Hopkins University Press, 1998.

"The Horrors of the Church and the Holy Inquisition." *The Christian Enterprise*. http//www.bibliotecapleyades.net/Vatican/esp_vatican29.htm. (Accessed December 2016.)

Janisse, Kier-La, and Paul Corupe. *Satanic Panic: Pop-Cultural Paranoia in the 1980s*. Surrey, England: FAB Press, 2016.

Jenkins, Beverly. "10 Most Haunted Objects of All Time." *Oddee*, August 19, 2013. http://www.oddee.com/item_98684.aspx.

Jones, Marie D., and Larry Flaxman. *Viral Mythology: How the Truth of the Ancients Was Encoded and Passed Down through Legend, Art and Architecture*. Pompton Plains, NJ: New Page Books, 2014.

Klinmczak, Natalia. "Lilith: Ancient Demon, Dark Deity or Sex Goddess?" *AncientOrigins*. http://www.ancient-origins.net/myths-legends/lilith-ancient-demon-dark-demon-or-sex-goddess-005908. (Accessed December 2016.)

LaVey, Anton Szandor. *The Satanic Bible*. New York: Avon Books, 1969.

Leonard, Tom. "The Amityville Horror: The Boy Who Lived in the True-Life Haunted House Breaks His 40-year Silence." *The Daily Mail*, March 28, 2013.

Ling, Trevor. "*Buddhism and the Mythology of Evil*. Oxford, England: Oneworld Publications, 1997.

Lopez, Lake. "The Exorcism of Roland Doe." *Lake Lopez*, July 8, 2014. http://www.thescarystory.com/the-exorcism-of-roland-doe.

Mack, Carol K., and Dinah Mack. *A Field Guide to Demons, Fairies, Fallen Angels and Other Subversive Spirits Paperback*. New York: Holt Paperbacks, 1999.

Masello, Robert. *Raising Hell: A Concise History of the Black Arts and Those Who Dared Practice Them*. New York: Perigree Books, 1998.

McRobie, Linda Rodriguez. "The History of Creepy Dolls." *Smithsonian.com*, July 14, 2015. http://www.smithsonianmag.com/history/history-creepy-dolls-180955916/.

———. "The Strange and Mysterious History of the Ouija Board." *Smithsonian.com*, October 27, 2013. http://www.smithsonian.com/history/the-strange-and-mysterious-history-of-the-ouija-board.

Meslow, Scott. "The Real Story behind the Conjuring and Four Other Horror Movies 'Based on a True Story.'" *The Week*, July 24, 2013. http://theweek.com/articles/461862/real-story-behind-conjuring-four-other-horror-movies-based-true-story.

"Mexico's Creepiest Tourist Destination: Island of Dolls." *Web Urbanist*, October 6, 2010. http://weburbanist.com/2010/10/06/mexicos-creepiest-tourist-destination-island-of-the-dolls/.

Milor, John. "Aliens in the Bible." *The Forbidden Knowledge*. http://www.theforbiddenknowledge.com/hardtruth/aliensinbible.htm. (Accessed December 2016.)

Morehead, John W. "Satan and America." *Morehead's Musings*, October 25, 2009. http://johnwmorehead.blogspot.com/2009/10/satan-and-america.html.

Morphy, Rob. "Annabelle: The True Story of a Demonic Doll." *Mysterious Universe*, March 10, 2013. http://mysteriousuniverse.org/2013/3/10/annabelle-the-true-story-of-a-demonic-doll/.

Neiman, Susan. *Evil in Modern Thought: An Alternative History of Philosophy.* Princeton, New Jersey: Princeton University Press, 2002.

Novak, Michael. "Atheism and Evil." *First Things,* July 2008. https://www.firtsthings.com/wen-exclusives/2008/07/atheism-and-evil.

Oppenheimer, Paul. *Evil and the Demonic: A New Theory of Monstrous Behavior.* New York: New York University Press, 1996.

Pagels, Elaine. *The Origin of Satan.* New York: Vintage Books, 1995.

Partridge, Christopher. *Encyclopedia of New Religions.* Oxford, England: Lion Publishing, 2004.

Penman, Danny. "Hitler and the Satanic Cult at the Heart of Nazi Germany." *Free Republic,* January 10, 2009. http://www.freerepublic.com/focus/chat/2164567/posts.

Radford, Benjamin. "Exorcism: Fact and Fiction about Demonic Possession." *Live Science,* March 7, 2013. http://www.livescience.com/27727-exorcism-facts-and-fiction.html.

———. "Voodoo: Facts About Misunderstood Religion." *Live Science,* October 30, 2013. http://www.livescience.com/40803-voodoo-facts.html.

Rahall, Patrick. "Demonic Dolls and Possessed Playthings." *Paranormal Association,* January 13, 2013. http://paranormal-association.com/demonic-dolls-and-possessed-playthings-by-patrick-rahall/.

Redfern, Nick. *Women In Black: The Creepy Companions of the Mysterious M.I.B.* New York: Lisa Hagan Books, 2016.

"Retired Priest: 'Hell' Was Invented by the Church to Control People with Fear." *Church and State,* July 2, 2015. htpp://churchandstate.org.uk/2015/12/retired-priest-hell-was-invented-by-the-church-to-control-people-with-fear.

Richter, Darmon. "11 Hidden Spots to Enter the Underworld." *Atlas Obscura,* October 3, 2016. http//www.atlasobscura.com/articles/11-hidden-spots-to-enter-the-underworld.

Roberts, Chris. "Return of the Devil: Exorcism's Comeback in the Catholic Church." *San Francisco Weekly,* March 9, 2016.

Rudwin, Maximillian. *The Devil in Legend and Literature.* La Salle, IL: Open Court, 1959.

Russell, Jeffrey Burton. *The Devil: Perceptions of Evil from Antiquity to Primitive Christianity.* New York: Meridian Books, 1977.

Sanburn, Josh. "The New Satanism: Less Lucifer, More Politics." *The Nation,* December 10, 2013. http://nation.time.com.2013/12/10/the-new-satanism-less-lucifer-more-politics/.

Shriner, Sherry. "The Difference between Fallen Angels, Demons, Aliens, Jedi, and the Watchers." *Sherry Shriner.* http://www.sherryshriner.com/sheryy/who-is-what.htm. (Accessed June 4, 2017.)

Shumov, Angie. "Demon and Devil Folklore from Around the World." *National Geographic,*. http://channel.nationalgeographic.com/the-story-of-god-with-morgan-freeman/articles/demon-and-devil-folklore-from-around-the-world/. (Accessed June 4, 2017.)

Shurter, David. *Rabbit Hole: A Satanic Ritual Abuse Survivor's Story.* Consider It Creative Publishing, 2013.

"Signs of Demonic Activity." Chesterfield Paranormal Research. http://www.chesterfieldparanormalresearchcom./signs-of-demonic-activity.html. (Accessed December 2016.)

Stenudd, Stefan. "Jungian Archetypes." *Psychoanlysis of Myth.* http://www.stenudd.com/myth/freudjung/jung-archetypes.htm. (Accessed December 216.)

Strochlic, Nina. "Beware: Connecticut's Museum of the Occult May Kill You." *The Daily Beast,* July 3, 2014.

Summers, Ken. "Demons, Curses, and the Truth about Spirit Boards: Is Ouija's Dark Side Just Another Witch Hunt?" *Week in Weird,* April 23, 2015. http://www.week inweird.com/2015/04/23.

Taylor, Troy. *The Devil Came to St. Louis.* Whitechapel Press, 2006.

Veith, Gene Edward. "Angels and Demons Go Pop Culture." *Ligonier Ministries.* http://www.ligonier.org/learn/articles/angels-and-demons-go-pop-culture/. (Accessed June 4, 2017.)

Wagner, Stephen. "Shadow People." *ThoughtCo,* February 14, 2017. http://www.para normal.about.com/od/trueghoststories/a/shadow-people.htm.

Waite, A.E. *The Book of Black Magic.* Newburyport, MA: Weiser Books, 2004.

Walker, Barbara. "How Local Wise Women Who Carried on Ancient Traditions Were Exterminated by Christianity." *Church and State,* September 2008. http://churchandstate.org.uk.2016/09/how-local-wise-women-who-carried-on-ancient-traditions-were-exterminated-by-chritanity/.

Warren, Ed. *In A Dark Place (Ed and Lorraine Warren).* Graymalkin Media, 2014.

Warren, Ed and Lorraine. *Satan's Harvest.* Graymalkin Media, 2014.

Wasman, Olivia B. "Ouija: Origin of Evil and the True History of the Ouija Board." *Time,* October 21, 2016. http://time.com/4529861/ouija-board-history-origin-of-evil.

Weatherly, David. *The Black Eyed Children.* The Leprechaun Press, 2011.

———. *Strange Intruders.* The Leprechaun Press. 2013.

Wilson, Colin. *The Occult: The Ultimate Guide for Those Who Would Walk with the Gods.* London, England: Watkins Publishing, 2015.

Woodbury, Sarah. "Demons of the Ancient World." *Sarah Woodbury,* July 29, 2012. http://www.sarahwoodbury.com/demons-of-the-ancient-world/.

Yeats, W. B., and Gregory Lady. *A Treasure of Irish Myth, Legend and Folklore.* New York: Grammercy Books, 1976.

Zaffis, John. *Shadows of the Dark.* iUniverse, 2004.

Zaffis, John, and Rosemary Ellen Guiley. *Demon Haunted: True Stories from the John Zaffis Vault.* New York: Visionary Living, Inc. 2016.

———. *Haunted by the Things You Love.* Visionary Living, 2014.

INDEX

Note: (ill.) indicates photos and illustrations.

DEMONS, THE DEVIL, AND FALLEN ANGELS

DEMONS, THE DEVIL, AND FALLEN ANGELS